THE

FORESTS AND GARDENS

OF

SOUTH INDIA

THE FORESTS AND GARDENS OF SOUTH INDIA.

BY

HUGH CLEGHORN, M. D., F. L. S.

GYAN

Published by

Gyan Publishing House
5, Ansari Road
Daryaganj, New Delhi-110002
Phone: 011-47034999, 9811692060
E-mail: books@gyanbooks.com

Distribution Network
gyanbooks.com
India, USA, Canada, UK, Australia, France

ISBN: 978-81-212-8312-0 (PB)
First Published, 1861

2nd Impression 2023

Printed at: Gyan Press, Delhi.

THE FORESTS AND GARDENS OF SOUTH INDIA
Author: HUGH CLEGHORN

THE

FORESTS AND GARDENS

OF

SOUTH INDIA.

BY

HUGH CLEGHORN, M.D., F.L.S.,

CONSERVATOR OF FORESTS, MADRAS PRESIDENCY.

LONDON:

W. H. ALLEN & CO., 7 LEADENHALL STREET.

MDCCCLXI.

TO

THE RIGHT HON. LORD HARRIS,

LATE GOVERNOR OF MADRAS,

WHO, DURING HIS ADMINISTRATION,

INSTITUTED THE DEPARTMENT OF FORESTS IN THAT PRESIDENCY,

AND HAS EVER BEEN A ZEALOUS PROMOTER

OF BOTANICAL RESEARCH,

THIS WORK

IS GRATEFULLY AND RESPECTFULLY DEDICATED,

BY

THE AUTHOR.

PREFACE.

It is only of late years that attention has been drawn to the importance of conserving tropical forests. The necessity of organising a system, whereby it would be possible to control the clearing of indigenous forests, did not at first present itself, especially as advancing civilisation and an increasing population apparently indicated an opposite course of procedure. The question when viewed simply in its physical relations, and the propriety of clearing forest lands in order to enlarge the area of food-producing soil, pointed perhaps as much to extensive clearance as to vigilant conservancy. It is a fact, however, that moderate and prudent clearing is quite compatible with the maintenance of a profitable system of superintendence. The matter of complaint was, that throughout the Indian empire large and valuable forest tracts were exposed to the careless rapacity of the native population, and especially unscrupulous contractors and traders, who cut and cleared them without reference to ultimate results, and who did so, moreover, without being in any way under the control or regulation of authority. The results of this wholesale and indiscriminate denudation gradually became apparent, and rendered it imperative that measures should be taken to organise a system of forest administration, which would enable the authorities to economise public property for the public good.

The subject was brought before the attention of the British Association for the Advancement of Science, which met at Edinburgh in 1850; and a committee of their number was appointed to consider the question, and report upon it.* The matter was duly investigated, and the results of the committee's deliberations were laid before the Association at the ensuing meeting held at Ipswich in 1851. In the course of this inquiry, it was ascertained that neither the Government nor the community at large were deriving from the Indian forests those advantages which they were calculated to afford. Not only was there a most wasteful and uncalled-for destruction of useful material, but numerous products—valuable to science, and which might be profitably applied to the interests of social life—lay neglected within the depths of the forests. This report recorded evidence bearing on the state of the forests in Malabar, Canara, Mysore, Travancore, the Tenasserim provinces, the Indian Archipelago, and the wooded tracts which skirt the base of the Himalaya; and it was distinctly ascertained, that in Malabar, Burmah, and Sind, where some supervision had been exercised, considerable improvement was manifest.

The forests in the Tenasserim provinces were brought, at a comparatively early date, under a system of conser-

* The committee consisted of Dr Forbes Royle, King's College, London; Colonel R. Baird Smith, Bengal Engineers; Colonel R. Strachey, Bengal Engineers, and the compiler of this work. The Report was printed in the Proceedings of the British Association for 1851.

vancy. At first, they were thrown open to private enterprise; but the keen competition which ensued among European and native traders led to an indiscriminate felling of the most valuable timber, which threatened speedily to exhaust the forests, and thereby to deprive the State of those supplies which were indispensable to the public service. The unrestrained liberty accorded to any individual to appropriate to himself, under most liberal conditions, the unoccupied forests, contributed, in the first instance, to the prosperity of Moulmein; but a continuance of the same system tended to the extermination of the finest teak, thereby depriving the State, in a large measure, of a principal source of commercial prosperity.

The somewhat chequered history of these provinces, and the difficulties experienced in blending the interests of the State with those of private enterprise on the one hand, and in maintaining a supply of first-class timber without seriously or permanently interfering with the future prospects of the forests on the other, exercised an important influence on the question of forest administration, both in Madras and Bombay. The earliest reports published are those of Dr Wallich, the first of which was dated so far back as 1827, and refers to the Salween Forest, north of Moulmein. The result of his labours may be said to have laid the foundation of a system of conservancy, without which it would soon have become impossible to maintain even the existence of our most valuable Eastern forests. It is true that the rules laid down by him proved to be of too stringent a character to be practicable, and were constructed principally to meet the interests of the State. After having been tested for a period of two years, they were found unsuitable. Since then rules have been formed to regulate and control the present and prospective condition of the forests; but difficulty has all along been experienced in adjusting public and private interests—in giving free scope to individual enterprise, without lowering the character of the timber and permanently diminishing the sources of supply. So much was this the case, that these rules were often a dead letter—they "were violated everywhere: undersized and green timber was commonly felled; the large logs were often sawed up into 'loozars' (short lengths). The felled timbers were in many instances left in the forest, to be burnt during the periodical fires; and no attention was paid to the renewal of the tree." When Dr Brandis was appointed by Lord Dalhousie to the charge of the forests of Pegu, it was intended to pursue a policy of strict conservancy, such as was proposed by Wallich upwards of thirty years before; but, as it was then impossible to adhere to it, it has again been found necessary to relax the stringency of rules which were too severe to be practicable.

In 1805, the Bombay Government, for the first time, laid claim to the indigenous forests of the western coast, and appointed commissioners to fix their boundaries, the Company's right of sovereignty being asserted by a proclamation issued in 1807. From this period up to 1822 a partial and somewhat ill-advised attempt at conservancy was made, but it thoroughly failed in its object; and all the restrictions which had been imposed during its existence were removed. This relaxation, or rather abandonment of law, however, in course of time led to results of a still more disastrous nature, which threatened the speedy and complete destruction of the forests themselves. The attention of Government was again seriously directed to the question; but it was a matter of time and difficulty to establish a system of conservancy which would not infringe upon private rights. The Forest Department was not organised until 1846, under the superintendence of Dr Gibson, who ten years afterwards published a short treatise, in which he gave a historical sketch of the department from its commencement. This handbook and Dr Falconer's "Report on the Teak Forests of the Tenasserim Provinces"* are works of the highest importance, especially to those interested in the preservation of teak forests.

Of all European nations, the English have been most regardless of the value of forests, partly owing to their climate, but chiefly because England has been so highly favoured by vast supplies of coal; and the emigrants to the United States have shown their indifference to this subject by the reckless destruction of forests in that country, of which they now feel the want. It is extremely desirable that correct information on this subject should be promulgated among the revenue officers of India. The publication of such works as those of Meaume and Du Breuil in France, and of Hartig in Germany, show the great importance that has been attached to Forestry in those countries, where the population depends on wood for fuel.

If conservation be needful in temperate climates, how

* Records of Bengal Government, No. ix. 1852.

imperative is it in the tropics, where the supplies of water, and consequently of food and other produce, are in a great measure dependent on the existence of forests, especially in all the elevated parts of that vast country. If the facts which prove the value of preserving forests, and regulating the cutting of timber on certain fixed rules, were generally known, every official in India would cordially cooperate in the work of conservation.

A code of forest regulations for all India is much wanted. If this was drawn up and sanctioned, the rights of Government (which are in some districts in a confused state) would be placed on as equitable and sound a basis as the rights of the people themselves.

The present volume was prepared at the instance of Government, principally for the purpose of furnishing a continuous view of forest conservancy in the Madras Presidency during the four years that the department has been in operation. One of the objects contemplated was to supply a manual to enable the forest assistants to act intelligently, and with good results to the State, in positions of responsibility. The want of such a handbook has been frequently felt, not only in this department, but more or less by all who are practically interested in the natural products of India, and in their employment by different departments of public works.

To the railway engineer, it is hoped that, even in its present form, it will prove of service, enabling him to acquaint himself with the various indigenous timbers, and their adaptation to the requirements of engineering in Southern India. The authorities of the several railway companies have repeatedly adverted to the want of a work such as the present, which could be placed in the hands of their *employés* arriving in the country ignorant of Indian woods, of their appearance, capabilities, and place of growth. Similar statements have been made by the authorities in England; and perhaps to some extent the present volume may supply the information required. The increasing opportunities and encouragement afforded for the development of European capital in India are calculated also to give a practical value to any work which will describe to the merchant or settler his exact relations to the Government, in regard to the forest products of the country.

It ought to be stated, that the greater part of the contents of this volume are on record in the Archives of the Madras Government; but they are not easily accessible. The work lays no claim to literary excellence of any kind. It is simply a compilation of papers, commencing with three Annual Reports, which indicate the progress of the department, and which are followed by a memorandum on *Kumari*,—an injurious practice, which destroys vast quantities of the most valuable timber,—and by other memoranda bearing more or less on the subject of Indian forests. The compilation is not what was originally intended, and what it would have been, if prepared under more favourable circumstances. It has been drawn up during the scanty leisure of a twelvemonth's furlough on sick certificate. The book might have been more acceptable to the general reader had it been less formal in its style, and less fragmentary in its character; but this would probably not have increased its practical utility.

A sketch map is given, indicating, as far as has been ascertained, the position and extent of the forests of Teak, Sàl, and Sandalwood, the most valuable woods growing within the Presidency. The course of the railways, and situation of the chief wood-depôts, are indicated.

A list of the principal works relating to Indian botany, with the most important memoirs on arboriculture, forest management, &c., has been appended, which, though far from complete, may prove useful to the officers of the department, and to botanical inquirers desirous of studying the trees and forest products of India.

The classical etymology has been generally adopted, in accordance with the recent orders of Government; and indeed, this is now employed in all standard works, as in Hooker and Thomson's "Flora Indica," &c. In this matter, also, I have to crave the indulgence of the reader, who will sometimes find the names of places spelt in different ways.

From Walter Elliot, Esq. of Wolflee, N.B., late Member of Council at Madras, I have received much cordial aid in Botanical researches; and to Major Douglas Hamilton, 21st N.I., I am indebted for the representations of forest scenery, which have been lithographed by Mr Macfarlane. Mr D. Paterson, of Madras, has also rendered good service in preparing the work for the press.

EDINBURGH, *August* 1861.

CONTENTS.

DIRECTIONS TO BINDER.

Forest Chart, to face title page.

Plate	I.	„	70
„	II.	„	70
„	III.	„	75
„	IV.	„	107
„	V.	„	108
„	VI.	„	146
„	VII.	„	290
„	VIII.	„	289
„	IX.	„	290
„	X.	„	292
„	XI.	„	292
„	XII.	„	294
„	XIII.	„	296

THE

FORESTS OF SOUTH INDIA.

FIRST ANNUAL REPORT ON FOREST OPERATIONS IN THE MADRAS PRESIDENCY.

From H. Cleghorn, Esq., M.D., Conservator of Forests, to the Secretary to Government, Fort St George.

Mangalore, 1*st May* 1858.

Sir,—1. I have the honour to report, for the information of the Right Honourable the Governor in Council, that during the past year I proceeded on my first tour of inspection, traversed Mysore, and visited the depôts at the mouths of nearly all the rivers on the Malabar coast, examining great part of the Western Ghats, with a view to ascertain the exact state of the government forests, their extent and capabilities. I travelled through the most wooded portions along the chain of ghats, ascending and descending by the following mountain passes, Anisy, Arbyle, Bun, Sampajee, Perambady, Sispára, Tambacherry, Palghat, Sigur, Kunur, from the Bombay frontier down to Ponány. I afterwards went across the Anamalai Hills and round the slopes of the Nilgiri Hills. I also made a circuit of Wainád, and twice visited the Conolly plantations at Nellambur, being altogether eight months absent from the presidency.

2. As I have already submitted my views at length on several topics in accordance with the instructions of government, such as Jackatalla Plantations, Nilgiri Woods, Utakamand Garden, Anamalai Forests, Canara Forests, Striharicotta Jungles, price of timber, memorandum on gutta percha, I shall here confine

myself to a summary of my observations on the forests generally, and of the operations of the forest department during the first year of its existence, mentioning the further measures contemplated when it is in a state of more complete organization.

3. In the beginning of this century, an immense almost unbroken forest covered the Western Ghats, from near the watershed to the most elevated ridges,—left to nature, thinly peopled, abounding in wild animals, and all the higher portions, without exception, covered with timber.* Now the passing traveller, looking down from the higher peaks of Coorg or Malabar, conceives that an inexhaustible forest lies below him; but as he descends the ghats, he finds that the best timber has been cut away, and that the wood-contractor is felling in more remote localities. I refer especially to teak, blackwood, and poon spars, which are every year becoming more scarce in accessible situations. The practice in India has been the converse of that in Europe, where the soft wood is thinned out and the hard wood left. Here the valuable kinds are removed and the scrub left. By one of these authorities (*Buchanan*), the burning of jungles was recommended as a sanatory measure, and to diminish the number of wild animals; but circumstances have much changed. Now the axe of the coffee planter and of the *kumari* cultivator have made extensive and often wanton havoc, devastating a large portion of the area of the primeval forest. The former is encouraged as endeavouring to rescue the soil for legitimate purposes (except when the timber is peculiarly valuable); but the squatter, who clears without leave in one year the land which he abandons the next, is punished and repressed. The waste has been altogether prohibited in Mysore and the Bombay collectorates, and is checked to a great extent in Canara, but has not altogether ceased. The exertions of the collector and sub-collector have, however, been very successful in keeping under the destruction, called *kumari*, caused by vagabond tribes in burning wood, with the view of raising from the ashes a crop of inferior grain.

4. In Canara, the forest rules, framed by Messrs Maltby and

* Dr Hove's Travels, 1786. Dr F. Buchanan's Journey, 1801. Lord Valentia's Travels, 1804.

Hall, and amended by Messrs Fisher and Robinson, are calculated to ensure a regulated and safe expenditure, if the subordinates do their duty, and if the trees be marked by the conservancy establishment. In regard to forest arrangements, I may observe that Canara, though still imperfectly organised, is in advance of every other district. The arrangements for the conservation of the teak and blackwood are so far satisfactory; but there are still difficulties as to the supply of firewood to large towns, and of house-building timber in those parts where there are no auctions.

5. *Wants of Public Departments.*—The requirements of the Indian navy, the Madras and Bombay railways, the public works and telegraph departments, have been unusually heavy, and the partially organised establishment was seriously crippled and curtailed for a time by the removal of officers, overseers, elephants and bullocks, required in the field during this eventful year, so that the pressing indents of various departments have been met with difficulty, and in some cases imperfectly.

6. *Railways.*—The progress of the railway has produced marvellous changes on the face of the country as regards tree vegetation in some districts. I may specify Palghat, the Shevarai Hills, and the North Arcot Hills; in these the old woods have everywhere fallen, to meet the urgent demand for timber; and the pressure continues to exist in the central portions of the line between Vániembady and Palghat: at the two extremities, the supply has been completed. In the Official Road Book, published by Major Scott not many years ago, opposite Waliár, we find this remark, "Dense jungle, beware of elephants;" but in looking from the staging bungalow, the traveller sees several tentative lines of rail, each 200 yards broad, and so extensive a clearing of the neighbouring forest, that no elephant could easily find a cover. The encircling hills, formerly crowned with timber, are now to a considerable degree laid bare. These changes, so far as I can learn, have been the gradual result of unrestricted cutting, but much aggravated, during the last few years, in connection with the enormous demand for railway sleepers, and for the department of public works. In the contracts which have been made for the supply of the Bombay railway, 1½ rupee has

been charged per tree. In some contracts for the supply of the Madras railway, 3 or 4 annas has been the seignorage per sleeper, according to the kind of wood and the facility of transport; and, with the permission of government, I would recommend that at least three annas be invariably paid.

7. In other places, and from other causes, wasteful cutting has been observed to a less injurious extent. Lieutenant Beddome's report on the Pulney Hills, communicated by government to the "Madras Journal of Science" (1857), describes the devastation which has been committed there in the formation of plantain gardens. The green hills have been stripped of their woods, and much of their beauty has departed. The reckless cutting there, however, has been vigorously checked by the collector, under orders from government.

8. *Slovenly felling.*—The axe formerly, in many districts, was laid to the trunk one yard from the ground, while a further waste took place from diffuse hacking over a broad surface. This unnecessary loss of timber has been prohibited by a printed circular, enjoining all contractors, as well as forest employés, to cut within one foot and a half of the ground, otherwise the contractors are not paid.

9. *Wasteful trimming.**—The former plan of cutting logs, by which one-half the timber was wasted, is now obsolete. I have only seen one or two specimens, and I hope that dragholes, as shown in fig. 1, may be altogether dispensed with by an improved applica-

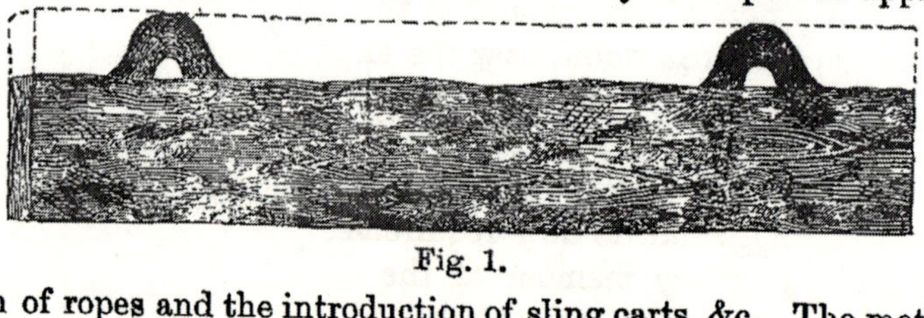

Fig. 1.

tion of ropes and the introduction of sling carts, &c. The method of trimming logs, so that they may fit carts in length and width, is still prevalent in many parts, but is giving way to a better system. The old state of things continues only at a distance

* See Capt. F. C. Cotton in "Madras Journal of Science," N. Ser. vol. ii., p. 94.

from check and control, or where there are peculiarities of tenure and few facilities of communication, as in Wainád.

10. *Proposed system of operations.*—The trees are classified according to size.*

1st class, 6 feet in girth.	3d class, 3 feet and upwards.
2d do. 4½ do.	4th do. under 3 feet.

It is proposed that in every forest to be worked, all first-class trees should be marked, and such a proportion should be cut down as will be naturally replaced by those of the second class. This is clearly a sound principle, and, if carried into practice, will prevent the exhaustion of the forests. It would be obviously impossible to fell and remove one twenty-fourth of the trees of the first class in every district. Therefore, to facilitate the execution of this principle, it is necessary to divide each assistant's range into six divisions, one of which only shall be worked at one time. These divisions should be formed as much as possible in accordance with the geographical features of the district, and the forest operations should be confined to the district having the largest quantity of ripe wood.

11. *Saving of Fragments.*—In my visit to the Anamalai and Wainád forests, I found the larger branches, tops and butts, left on the side of the road, or in the place where the tree was cut, exposed to the heat of the sun and to the annual fires. I desired that all such pieces as would bear the expense of removal should be brought out of the Anamalai and Heggadevincotta forests, and that no wastage be allowed in future. The importance of saving every foot of teak (at a time when Government has been put to great shifts for its own requirements) has been strongly impressed upon every member of the department. I am also anxious that the use of this timber should be disallowed for common purposes, as camp furniture, hospital almirahs, accoutrement boxes, and the like.

12. *Auction Sale of Timber.*—It having been considered desirable that an auction sale of timber unsuited for naval purposes

* The system here suggested was originally proposed by Dr Brandis, Conservator of Forests in Burma.

(tops, bottoms, slabs, and side pieces), should be held at the foot of the Anamalai Hills, Captain Hamilton, the late superintendent was directed to make the arrangements. Great exertions were made by that officer, and when the timber had been collected, every publicity was given regarding the sale. Before the auction took place, Captain Hamilton was removed on account of the paucity of officers with his corps, and the duty devolved on his successor Lieutenant Beddome. The result proved satisfactory; the account rendered shows as follows:—

	Rs.	A.	P.
Amount realized	3391	5	8
Deduct charges	189	6	4
Net profit	3201	15	4

The average price obtained was one rupee per cubic foot. In the forest this year, after the Bombay Marine were supplied, the better logs were selected for the new jail at Salem and the Trichinopoly barracks, while the fragments sold by auction were greedily bought by the general trader, by the railway department for doors and windows, and by a native surgeon for his dispensary building at Pulachi. In like manner wastage has been disallowed in cutting teak for the military buildings at Bangalore.

13. *Teak.*—This invaluable wood has received the special attention of the department, and I may say has occupied two-thirds of my own time during the past year. Along the whole length of the Malabar coast from Goa to Cochin, there is now very little of this wood in a ripe state on Government land below the ghats, and there are only three localities above the ghats where I found teak in abundance and of good size, viz.,—

(1.) The Anamalai Forest in Coimbatore.

(2.) Wainâd and Heggadevankota (partly in dispute between Mysore and Malabar.)

(3.) Gund Plateau, North Canara, near Dandelli.

I shall briefly notice the chief points connected with these forests, which stand in the order of their respective value. The Anamallai forests have been the subject of annual Reports to Government since 1848, when their importance was first declared by Captain F. C. Cotton (Madras Journal of Science 1857), and as Captain Michael's Reports have been published in the Madras Government Records (No. V. 1855), I will only now allude to the recent changes and improvements in management of this forest effected during the past year. After the removal of Captain Hamilton, Lieutenant Beddome, travelling assistant, received charge. He was in the immediate neighbourhood at the time of the vacancy. An additional overseer was sanctioned. The timber slip was repaired by Wuddur contract at an expense of 500 rupees. The bridge at Machenackenpollium, much required for the transport of wood eastward from the Anamalais, has been rebuilt. The road from Colungode has been repaired, and several nallahs bridged to facilitate the cartage to Ponany. The overseer's house was purchased; six sling carts were made up by Mr Ross, railway engineer; a depôt was arranged at bottom of slip, and a site was selected for the overseer's house at Pulachi during the unhealthy months.

I may here mention, that the prospective supply of teak (roughly estimated at the rate of the present requirements) from the forest now rented from the Colóngad Numbady will not apparently exceed 15 years. This is a serious consideration, as it is the only forest from which long planks suitable for a frigate can be procured. I have in view a scheme for consolidating the table-land of the Anamalais, that part belonging to Government as well as that rented from the Colóngad Numbady, into one Government forest, which should be a reserve in perpetuity for the Indian navy, and where planting operations should be systematically carried on. The working establishment of the Anamallai forest has always suffered severely from sickness, and, considering the large number of employés, I recommended to Government the location of a medical officer. Unfortunately, Mr Drew was removed by death before joining, and, as the inspector of jails disapproved of the introduction of convict labour into the forest, from fear of the escape of the prisoners, I have not again asked for the services of a medical officer, more especially as the establishment of a dispensary at Pulachi under Native Surgeon Kanagaroyen will be of much importance to the department; and an adjacent piece of ground has been allotted for the overseers.

14. *Wainád and Heggadevincotta Teak.*—The forests on the borders of Mysore and Malabar are of great value, and stand second in importance. I went through part of these forests in company with Captain Pearse, superintendent of Astagram, which are about forty miles long by thirty broad, and believe that they will supply 2000 cart-loads annually (or, say 40,000 cubic feet of teak) without apparently injuring the resources of the forest. There being no cultivation, and a very scanty population, and the timber consequently not being required for local purposes, I would strongly urge that this should be considered a reserved forest. From the situation and natural slope of the country, the timber must be carried eastward, and will be extremely valuable for military purposes in Bangalore. The new barracks there are being built of teak, and it is probable that this timber will come into use also to meet the increasing demand at Utakamand. It is much to be regretted that no means of transport exists by which the crooks and other naval timber found in this tract can be conveyed to the coast, where they would be extremely valuable. The expense of carriage by the usual route to Mysore and Manantoddy, and down the Peria Ghat to Tellicherry, is altogether prohibitory. The average price of teak at the quarterly auctions held at Mysore has been almost exactly the same as at Anamalai, about one rupee per cubic foot. I have experienced great difficulty in obtaining exact information as to the extent, tenure, revenue, and productions of this forest, on account of its being little frequented, from the fear of wild animals. In no place have I seen such abundant traces of elephants. However, the authorities at Astagram and Coorg, and the commissariat officer at Hoonsoor, all drew my attention to the waste of teak which occurs there, the timber being carted out in large quantities by three roads under the plea of passes from two Devasthánams, the limits of whose Enam land I have no means of ascertaining. A particular survey, well-drawn lines of demarcation between Mysore, Malabar, and Coorg, and an improved system of regulations, are required for placing this forest on a proper footing, and securing an uninterrupted supply of this valuable wood for the future. I think this duty would be best performed by an officer of energy and character, who would work well with the neigh-

bouring authorities, and who would constantly traverse the forests (as was done at Anamalai by Captains Michael and Hamilton), till the system of robbery and spoliation is suppressed. I would also strongly urge the location of a European magistrate in the Wainád, who would enforce the observance of regulations, and see to the management of the roads, ferries, police, revenue, conservancy, &c., in that remote locality.*

15. *Canara Teak.*—This timber generally is of smaller scantling than that of Wainád. It has the advantage of water-carriage to the coast not possessed by the two last, but it has for some years been chiefly obtained for naval purposes from the banks of the Black River, where it emerges from the Supah Hills, and the supply has gradually been sent down from more distant localities, as in Malabar, where the teak is now cut by the Terupad of Nellambur, just under the Nilgiri peak. Above the ghats in the Supah and Sundah talooks there is a very considerable supply of smaller wood suited for the engineer requirements at Belgam, Dharwar, Lingasugur, &c.

16. *The Gund Forest.*—This is the chief remaining reserve in Canara. I saw here several thousand trees on an elevated plateau with precipitous sides. The trees are well grown and ripe, conserved by their inaccessible position, which has been rarely visited by Europeans. The teak here is scarcely intermixed with any other tree (the Billi Nundee† excepted), and grows on slaty rock, in many places having very steep gradients. The early working of this valuable Gund forest is of the first importance, being much threatened with fire; some trees are already scorched at the root, and much dead wood lies in the forest. The question for consideration is, how to get out the wood?—whether by a rocky nullah with at least three small falls, or by making a road twenty-three miles in length. This is a question I cannot venture to answer, but I may mention that the Collector Mr Fisher, and Dr Gibson, I believe, incline to improving the road, whilst Colonel A. F. Cotton and Lieutenant Taylor, Indian Navy,

* The appointments of a magistrate and an assistant-conservator have been made, and the vigorous prosecution of the revenue survey is being carried out.

† *Lagerstrœmia microcarpa* (Wight).

recommend the blasting of the rocks in the nullah. I ordered an experiment to be made of floating twenty logs of junglewood, branded "Gund," at the height of the flood. These were despatched on a given day, but they never reached Sidashegur, having been caught in the rocky turnings of the river. The importance of removing the valuable teak of this forest at an early date is so great, that I would suggest that an engineer officer be deputed to visit and report. Captain G. W. Walker, engineer, shortly expected from England, is one of the few Europeans who have visited this remarkable place, and has, I am told, a knowledge of its requirements. If Government think proper to direct that officer to inspect this locality, Mr Müller would arrange to accompany him. As the Gund plateau is inaccurately delineated in the survey maps, I have the pleasure to forward a rough survey by my industrious assistant, Mr Müller, with the tracing of the roads he suggests for working this forest. I would recommend that it be lithographed, and a hundred copies struck off. When the forest is being worked, I have instructed Mr Müller to be present at the marking and girdling of the trees. I have reason to believe that proper classification and selection of the trees have not hitherto been made in the Government forests. First class trees—*i.e.*, six feet in girth, and those commencing to decay, only, are to be removed at the first cutting.

17. *Teak Plantations.*—I visited the remains of small teak plantations at Honore, Ankola, and Sidashegur, which had been superintended by Colonel Gilbert in 1804. The trees are poor specimens of teak, the soil is laterite, and the exposed situation of the sea-shore is most unsuitable—a worse locality could scarcely have been chosen. The only possible excuse for so grave a blunder is, that the peculiar requirements of the teak tree were not known in those days. Up the Black River at Tarra-Mallapur is a plantation of recent date. The late Mr Poulton commenced this in 1854. There are, I believe, 2000 remaining of 7000 trees put down.

18. *Conolly Plantations.*—The fine and promising plantations on the banks of the Nellambur River, which were commenced about fifteen years ago by the late lamented Mr Conolly, Collector of Malabar, are worthy of a full and separate report, which

will be a historical record of what can be effected by artificial means. These plantations will be an important source of supply in future years. They are under the immediate charge of Chatu Menon, a Nair, who conducted all the preliminary experiments under Mr Conolly's orders, and who has watched the young trees from the day of germination. I propose that two Duffadars should be sent, one to the Anamalais, and one to North Canara, to introduce the Conolly system of plantation into those districts.*

19. *Poon Spars.*†—These are becoming very scarce, and, consequently, are perhaps more valuable than teak. Young trees, especially such as are in accessible places, are most carefully preserved. Strict orders on this subject have been given in Coorg, Mysore, and Canara. In one case which came within my observation, several valuable spars were found in a bridge, the total estimate of which was 250 rupees.‡ This incident will illustrate the importance of officers in the public works and telegraph departments, &c., making themselves acquainted with the description of timber available and suitable for their wants. I may also mention that the superintendent of Coorg has received several tenders for the supply of Poon spars and other timber at the distances of at least three miles from the Sulia River, showing the scarcity of such wood, and the readiness of the Mangalore contractors to carry it several miles to the nearest water carriage.

20. *Blackwood.*§—This valuable wood has risen much in price. Indents were received during the year both from Madras and Bombay gun-carriage manufactories, each for 5000 cubic feet. This tree was formerly given to applicants at three rupees each; but, with the concurrence of the collector of Canara, I have dis-

* Since writing this, I find that the Nair subordinates are unwilling to leave their native place. One has been found ready to proceed to the Anamallais, but no one is willing to proceed to North Canara on any terms; therefore one of the Canara establishment will be detached for instruction to Nellambur.

† *Calophyllum angustifolium.* (Roxb.)

‡ Several instances of the same kind have occurred. Poon spars, although highly prized for shipbuilding, are ill suited for making bridges.

§ *Dalbergia latifolia*, L.

allowed this practice. There is not much blackwood remaining in the Anamalai forest, but there is a considerable quantity in the escheated forest of Chennat Nair, and it is abundant in the Wainád and Coorg. In consequence of its increasing value, I have given instructions for an experimental sowing this year at Nellambur.

21. *Sappan wood.**—This important dyewood has engaged my attention. It appears to grow with great luxuriance in South Malabar, and is cultivated rather extensively by the Moplahs, who plant a number of the seeds at the birth of a daughter. The trees require fourteen or fifteen years to come to maturity, and then become her dowry. I saw more on the banks of the Nellambur River than anywhere else. Why it should be there in particular is not obvious, as Malabar is generally uniform in its character. A better system of cutting and cultivating the sappan is desirable; and the dyewood is damaged, I believe, by being allowed to float in salt water. The quantity raised is not great, but it grows without any care, and, from the facility of water-carriage to Calicut, I think that the district is very favourable for its extension. I sent a packet of seeds to Canara for experimental sowing on the banks of the Black River.

22. *Sandal-wood.*†—This tree has received much attention in Canara, Coimbatore, Salem, and a little in North Arcot. It would appear that its spontaneous growth has increased to a considerable extent; and it seems certain that, with the vigilant supervision of local officers, and slight assistance to nature in clearing the heads of young plants, which are often matted down by strong creepers, an addition might accrue to the revenue of these provinces. From information received from the late Assistant-Surgeon Drew, I was enabled to communicate to the commissioner of Mysore the existence of a large band of smugglers in an unfrequented path near the Carkur Pass, who were captured by the Mysore horse, to the number of seventy-eight, with the sandalwood tied on their backs. This seizure effectually stopped a long-continued system of robbery on the Malabar frontier.

23. *Gutta-percha.*—The "gutta-percha tree of the western coast," so called, has been traced from Coorg to Trevandrum.

* *Cæsalpinia sappan*, L.

† *Santalum album*, L.

All the reliable information procurable has been condensed into a memorandum, and a large sample has been transmitted to England for report as to its suitability for telegraphic and other purposes.*

24. *Catechu.*—The enhanced value of cutt has caused an unusual destruction of the catechu tree (*Acacia catechu*), which was properly restricted by Mr J. D. Robinson to certain places in the North Canara jungles to prevent total destruction.

25. *Kino.*—Two thousand trees of the kino tree (*Pterocarpus marsupium*) were seen along the roads through the Wainád, notched, as delineated in the margin, for the extraction of kino, which is taken to the coast, where it meets with a ready market, and is exported in wooden boxes to Bombay. As the V-shaped incision appeared to be deeper than required, the collector has given instructions for the more careful treatment of the trees. This tree is greatly prized at Dharwar, not for its exudation, but for its timber, which is extensively used in the cotton-gin factory.

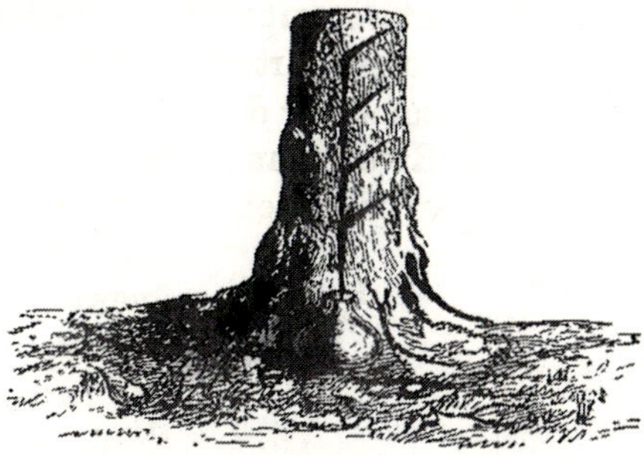

Fig. 2.

26. *Bamboos.*—Immense quantities of fine bamboos are floated down the various rivers of the western coast. It is one of the riches of these provinces. They are ordinarily sixty feet long, and five inches in diameter near the root. These are readily purchased standing at 5 rupees, and small ones at 3½ rupees, per 1000. Millions are annually cut in the forests, and taken away by water in rafts, or by land in hackeries. From their great buoyancy, they are much used for floating heavier woods, as matti (*Terminalia tomentosa*) and biti (*Dalbergia latifolia*); and piles of them are lashed to the sides of the pattimars going to Bombay. The larger ones are selected as out-riggers for ferry-

* The report is not very favourable; the tree is *Bassia elliptica*, Dalzell; "Kew Misc." vol. iii. p. 36; and *Isonandra Cullenii* of Drury's "Useful Plants."

boats, or studding-sail booms for small craft. In addition to the vast export by sea, it is estimated that two lacs are taken eastward from the Supah talook. The Malabar bamboo is much smaller than that of Pegu (*Bambusa gigantea*), which is often eight inches in diameter.

27. *Mode of Floating Timber*.—It is curious to see the clever management of the floaters, who are a distinct class of persons. Rafts are of all sizes, usually longer than broad, and the logs bound together by the stringy bark of various trees, and stout branches passing through the dragholes at right angles to the log. In the centre of the raft a small hut is generally made of thatch, or bamboo laths covered with Palmyra leaves. In this the floaters are sheltered at night. It is not usually considered advisable to float logs when the river is at the fullest, as the raft is apt to go over the bank and be stranded. Numerous logs may be seen high and dry all along the sides, and the following year the flood lifts them. At night, floats are brought to under steep banks in deep water; they are then tied to the trunk of some adjoining tree. Occasionally the banks fall in, and serious accidents occur.

28. *Introduction of Saw Machinery*.—This has been much under consideration. There can be no doubt that it is most desirable to substitute the saw for the axe, especially when the planks are being prepared, economising both time and labour. Great efforts have from time to time been made, with more or less success, to induce sawyers voluntarily to resort to the forests for employment. As to the question of introducing circular saws to the little frequented forests, the measure would be attended with this difficulty, that, when the heavy machinery was conveyed to the forest depôt as the elephant station in the Anamallays, it must either be carried back again at great expense, or left exposed to the mischievous effects of extreme damp, and perhaps to injury from herds of elephants. At present, therefore, it seems more desirable that saw-pits should be for the most part confined to the coast depôts, and that their management be left to private enterprise.

29. *Forges for Charcoal*.—One of the difficult questions connected with forest conservancy, is the making of charcoal for

iron-smelting. The forges in Canara are few, but there are many in Dharwar, Belgam, Bellary, and Mysore; and parties go into Nuggur or North Canara to make charcoal in large quantity. They make a hole 4 feet deep, 8 or 10 feet broad, fill it with wood, and cover it up. Having set fire to it, two-thirds or three-fourths is burnt, one-third or one-fourth remains as charcoal. Not only is there great waste in the making of charcoal, but there is great waste when made, the charcoal being inferior. The blacksmiths insist upon the wood being either of bamboo or jambay (*Inga xylocarpa*), which is without reason, as I saw beautiful charcoal prepared by Mr Lowry at Tuddry of the common woods. Brice and Co. have instructed twenty charcoal-burners, who use these woods, and turn out a superior article. They regulate the furnace by small holes, as do the Porto Novo Iron Company; Dr Forbes also, at the cotton-gin factory in Dharwar. It is difficult to instruct native artisans in this matter, but it is hoped that the example of so many Europeans may be useful.

30. *Executive Engineers, Surveyors, &c.*—These officers, when making traces in the ghats, or visiting secluded forest districts, might render good service to this department by informing the nearest revenue-officer or conservancy employé when they see the firing of the jungles or destruction of timber. I have received, on several occasions, useful information from the chief engineer, who has sent me extracts from the diaries of his officers bearing on the destruction of timber. On the occasion of making a new road, or increasing the breadth of an old one, through a valuable forest (as at Yellapur), it would be desirable that the district engineer should communicate with the forest assistant, so as to give an opportunity of removing the timber, which is often rolled down the side of a ghat, or left to decay where it falls.

31. *Noxious Insects.*—I have called the attention of my assistants to the noxious insects of this country, inasmuch as the depredation of several common Coleoptera (*Xylocopa latipes, &c.*) are most mischievous, rendering the rafters a mere honeycomb. I have had under consideration the importance of immersing the logs of all woods, except teak, in solutions strongly impregnated with mineral salts, according to Boucherie's process.

32. *Provision for the Ryots' wants.*—It is most important that, while strict supervision is enforced in the Government forests, conservancy should not be carried so far as to interfere with the supply of agricultural implements to the *bona fide* ryot, or to obstruct the application of leaves and branches for alkaline material to fertilize his fields. In North Canara, the ryots have their *coomuc*, or enclosed piece of land, available for the use of their fields,—a good arrangement, when allowed to such estates as have been surveyed. I do not recommend this in unsurveyed estates, because it leads to fraudulent abuses. The allowance is two hundred yards above ghat, or one hundred yards below. It is surprising how strictly these coomucs are conserved.

33. *Provision for Mercantile Classes.*—I have already ruled, in cases referred for decision, that the ryot is from old custom entitled to wood for his plough, &c., but that the sowcar, who wishes to make a cradle or a palanquin, or requires wood for house-building, &c., must pay for the material. There are periodical auctions at nine places in Canara, where the sowcars can suit themselves; and an extension of the system, so as to have talook depôts, is under consideration.

34. *Coffee.*—The successful cultivation of the coffee plant is extending remarkably, and applications for grants of forest land pour in upon the revenue authorities. In the Sispara, Perambady, and Sampajee Passes, vast clearings are being made. In the Kunur Ghat, six large plantations may be seen; and there are very large and numerous holdings, above thirty, in the Wainád, which from year to year will increase. The plant has succeeded admirably in Mysore; and there are patches of cultivation in Madura and in North Canara. I may observe, that in granting forest land, it seems to me that while the destruction of forest (teak, ebony, and poon spar excepted) for *bona fide* cultivation may be considered legitimate, yet the preservation of the fringe along the crest of mountain ridges is of special importance in a climatic point of view; and this should never be given over to the axe. As these mountain crests are not suitable for the growth of coffee, the restriction cannot be complained of.

I here beg to annex extract of letter to the collector of Coimbatore, dated 2d October 1857, which contains my views in reply to a reference upon this important matter:—"The higher sholas, clothing the ghats on both sides, are of the utmost importance, and the climate is believed to suffer the greatest detriment from their removal. I would therefore suggest that the high wooded mountain tops overhanging the low country (such as Hoolicul) should be preserved with rigid care; the forest there should not be given over to the axe, lest the supplies of water may be injured. It is the opinion of many persons, in which I concur, that the vast clearings which have taken place have had a share in producing the irregularity of the monsoon, which has of late years been so much complained of in Coimbatore. In order that the course of the rivulets should be overshadowed with trees, I conceive that the hills should be left clothed to the extent of about half of their height from the top, leaving half of the slope and all the valley below for cultivation. This available portion would far exceed in extent the higher ridges, which should be conserved."

It seems to me that the immense tracts of virgin forests in the rich valleys of the Kundahs are eminently suited for coffee cultivation; and the removal of the forest *there* would not be attended with the same disadvantage as on the Eastern Ghats, where the drier climate does not admit of the same effort at speedy reproduction. If it be desirable to lay down a general rule in regard to the limits of elevation within which clearing for coffee cultivation should be allowed, I would specify from about 2500 to 4500 feet, this being, I understand, the extreme range within which coffee planted on a large scale is found to thrive. It is important to give *every facility* for the cultivation of coffee; but it is desirable to limit the clearings of those situations where this peculiar shrub can be grown with advantage. I have observed some clearings, where the ground is so precipitous that it is extremely improbable that the soil can last many years. It may be urged that, in general, people are sufficiently alive to their own interests to select only those sites which are in every way eligible; but, from the inexperience of many who embark in coffee planting, it seems desirable to lay down some rule. I need only point to the vast amount of land cleared and subsequently abandoned, both in this country and Ceylon, either before or after planting.

It is to be regretted that, independently of considerations of climate, coffee cultivation should find a place in those parts of the forest where the timber is of a *superior* description, and which at present Government is put to great shifts to obtain for public purposes. I would therefore add, that in places which are accessible, and which contain very fine timber, it seems desirable that one of the assistants in my department should have an opportunity of removing such timber as is available, or of marking it, with a view to its being taken at a valuation by the occupier, should he desire to do so. I especially allude to teak, black-wood, vengay (*Pterocarpus marsupium*), and kara-marda (*Pentaptera coriacea*).

35. *Tea.*—I think it right to bring to the notice of Government the thriving condition of a tea plantation near Kunur, belonging to Henry Mann, Esq., who has devoted much attention to it, and has spared no expense. This is a very interesting experiment. The best varieties of the shrub were imported from China in 1854, the seeds having been given to Mr Mann by Mr Fortune on his return from the tea-growing districts. There are now about 2000 vigorous plants; and, to ensure success, it seems only necessary to procure a supply of workmen to teach the manipulation and separation of the leaves.

36. *Difficulty of procuring Assistants.*—The removal of Captain Michael to Hydrabad, followed by the withdrawal of Captain D. Hamilton and the death of Assistant-Surgeon Drew, put me in a difficulty for some time. The two first were most zealous and willing assistants, and the last, from his patient habits of inquiry and botanical knowledge, gave promise of peculiar usefulness. The vacancy at Anamalai has been filled by Lieutenant Beddome, an excellent explorer, who has a good knowledge of the vegetable kingdom, and was recommended to Government solely on account of his powers of observation and description. I have issued "General instructions to the forest assistants" in a circular, and try to persuade each to keep a small arranged herbarium of flower and fruit-bearing specimens of all forest trees and their varieties, with notes. By inviting them to do this, I trust some will become at least observers, if not botanists. In India, there is no class of persons who have made it their business to attend

to forestry as a branch of rural economy; and of all those (about two hundred) who applied for employment, there was not one who could be considered an intelligent forester, except Mr M'Ivor, superintendent of the Utakamand Garden; Mr S. Müller, assistant conservator, North Canara, who had been early trained in the Black Forest of Germany; and Corporal Hall, who had been a forester in the Midland Counties of England. Most of the others have to be paid to learn the outlines of their duty; and, generally speaking, those who have been soldiers or artificers are the most teachable, and give least trouble. They have been well disciplined, and obedience comes naturally to them.

37. *Contract.*—Instead of finding a class of persons possessing knowledge of the timber trade, there is only a multitude of rogues ever ready to tender for contracts, to receive advances, and to appropriate them. On the western coast there are a few Moplahs at Calicut, and Prabhus at Mangalore, who possess elephants, the only efficient means of dragging timber. These last take gangs of coolies to the Coorg and Malabar forests, and show considerable energy in forming temporary dams, and floating down poon spars, &c.

38. *Sub-Conservators in Canara.*—The two subordinates I found in North Canara, under Mr Müller (Mr Gilbert and Mr B. Rodrigues), appeared to be much too sedentary in their habits, deputing peons into the jungles when they should have gone themselves, and the like. The former has been removed from the department on account of incapacity; the latter is suspended under an inquiry for receiving bribes.

39. *European Contractors.*—Two contracts have been entered into with Mr Ross, resident railway engineer, Coimbatore, whereby he has been permitted, *first,* to cut sleepers of certain specified woods in the forest near the foot of Anamalai, paying seignorage at the rate of 3 annas per sleeper; and, *second,* to fell 2000 trees in the Waliar jungle, at the rate of 1 rupee 8 annas per tree. Messrs Brice and Co., an enterprising firm, tendered for, and obtained permission to fell 2500 jungle trees within the forests of Ekagolly and Codlugaddi, in the Supah talook, North Canara, for supplying sleepers to the Bombay Railway Company, and agreed to pay 2500 rupees (half in advance), being at the

rate of 1 rupee per tree, and on exportation a further seignorage of 8 annas per tree: also, such quantity of bamboos as they may require to float down the 2500 trees, at the rate of 5 rupees per 1000 bamboos. This contract extends over a period of two years, closing 31st December 1859. In the contracts with Mr Ross and Messrs Brice and Co., strict provisions are made prohibiting the felling of valuable kinds of wood, as teak, blackwood, &c.

40. *Establishment of Depôts on Western Coast.*—I am desirous of having well-arranged depôts at the mouths of the rivers on the western coast, and a classification of timber to suit the various purchasers. European pensioners of reputed integrity will probably be found ready to take charge of these depôts. Contractors have this year been required to separate sound from unsound timber, whilst still in the water. I pointed out at Sidashegur and Hallial some desirable improvements; but the operations were suspended on account of the recent disturbances. At the latter place the depôt occupies an open space, and the large quantity of wood in store is scarcely safe without an enclosure. A small house for the European overseer is also required. The establishment of coast depôts involves an extension of the department not contemplated; but I believe that from the absolute impossibility of finding a trustworthy agency in the interior, this is unavoidable.

41. *Additional Overseers required.*—There are several localities, as Putur in South Canara, Palghat, and the hills west of Vellore, which require the supervision of a qualified overseer. I am now *en route* to explore the capabilities of the first of these places, which formerly yielded much timber. At the second, I believe the salary of an overseer may be more than met from the aggregate receipts of the Waliar Jungle, and the escheated forest of Chennat Nair, at present leased to Mr Tomlinson. At the third, which I visited a fortnight ago, it is of importance that supervision should be exercised over these hills, which the proximity of the railway has tended so much to denude. The demand for firewood has been so much enhanced by the vicinity of the rail, that I have seen root stocks and gnarled stems removed from the hill side, which should have been allowed to remain, in order

to secure a little moisture, and to afford leaves for manuring the adjoining fields. Mr Sullivan, sub-collector, is at all times most ready to assist in checking wasteful cutting, but the appointment of an overseer in his opinion is desirable. The tract of wood must be extensive which will cover the charge of an overseer's salary; and therefore in several instances I have urged the location of two talook peons, as at the top of Palamanair Ghat, and at Devaroydroog in Mysore. The vigilance of two men during twelve months, at a cost of 7 rupees per month, has produced visible results; although the conservancy has not been adequately provided for, yet the jungle already begins to assume a much improved appearance. My attention has been directed to other places, as Ramandroog, the Nalla-malai Hills, the Shevarai Hills, the Nellore Jungles, and various localities in the northern division. I have been in correspondence with the collectors of those districts, but refrain from making any recommendation of establishments to supervise these forests until I have an opportunity of personally inspecting them and judging of their requirements. I hope to visit these localities during the ensuing year. The great difficulty I experience is in finding suitable overseers. The qualifications desired are as follows:—1. Robust health; 2. Rudimentary knowledge of forestry; 3. Acquaintance with accounts; 4. Integrity of character; 5. Knowledge of native languages. In addition to the absolute scarcity of suitable men, the exposure, personal risk, and low salary compared with that sanctioned in the Public Works, have united to deter men from entering the department; whilst the formation of the Police and Revenue Survey Establishments have attracted others whose services might have been available. Out of the large body of Europeans who have this year been sent out to India, I hope to find one or two who have a practical knowledge of woodcraft.

42. *Proposed Depôt of Books and Tools.*—It has been proposed to supply a "Forester's Guide,"* and the more necessary tools, to each overseer on his appointment. The Conservator, as he has leisure and opportunity, spends an hour or two with his overseers to im-

* The excellent work of James Brown, Edinburgh 1860, is perhaps the best manual for the department.—H. C.

prove their minds, and has directed the assistants to teach the overseers, as medical officers are enjoined to train their subordinates. By adopting a system of weekly or occasional examinations, it is to be hoped that a class of foresters superior to the present may be obtained.

43. *System of Correspondence.*—Where overseers are located, or forest operations carried on, orders are given through the assistant-conservator in whose range the overseer is situated; but in any case, when forest management appears to affect the revenue or cultivation of the district, I immediately avail myself of the advice and counsel of the collector; and throughout I have desired to be in the position of his adviser, and not an executive trenching upon his authority.

44. *Manual of Accounts.*—A "Manual of Accounts" for the employés in this department, compiled by J. T. Maclagan, Esq., under instructions of Government, including simple forms of accounts to be used, and printed circulars for the guidance of overseers, &c., was submitted to government on the 6th ultimo. At this early stage of forest correspondence, this manual must necessarily be imperfect; but being clear and concise, I believe that it will be of great use in the preparation of contracts and simplifying accounts.

45. *Proposed Herbarium of Reference.*—Having received from the royal gardens of Kew a valuable set of named Indian plants, being duplicates issued after the publication of the "Flora Indica" of Hooker and Thomson, I intend to arrange these materials in a consultable herbarium at the Presidency. It was indeed upon these conditions that I received the specimens. Such a collection is a great desideratum in the present day, when men of science frequently visit our capital, and we have not a single specimen of the collections of Roxburgh or Wight to show, but can only refer to their description. I shall not ask Government for any pecuniary assistance except to supply paper, the cases, and hereafter perhaps some manual assistance.

46. *Manual of Indian Botany.*—I have the honour to enclose a specimen of the "Manual of Indian Botany," now being prepared in compliance with the wishes of the Honourable Court of Directors. The small amount of time which I can spare from other

avocations, the bodily fatigue and exposure I undergo, and the absence from my library for great part of the year, will necessarily protract the preparation of the work; but the great opportunities I enjoy of collecting materials are eagerly laid hold of, and I trust that the Manual may, when completed, be a useful guide to the botanical riches of the Presidency.

47. *Expenditure.*—The expenditure on account of the department generally has been as follows:—

	Rs.	A.	P.
Salary of the conservator, the assistant in charge of the office at the presidency and the establishment,	17,373	0	7
Salaries of travelling assistants and their establishments,	6,847	10	4
Contingent charges,	3,868	14	4
	28,089	9	3

ORDER OF GOVERNMENT ON THE FOREGOING REPORT.

Extract from the Minutes of Consultation, dated 5th August 1858. No. 1086.

Read the preceding letters* from the Conservator of Forests, *submitting a summary of his forest operations during the past official year* (1st May 1858, No. 337).

1. The first of the papers recorded above contains the report of the Conservator of Forests on his first tour of inspection. His general route is thus described at the outset:—

"I traversed Mysore and visited the (timber) depôts at the mouths of nearly all the rivers on the Malabar Coast, examining great part of the Western Ghats, with a view to ascertain the exact state of the Government forests, their extent and capabilities. I travelled through the most wooded portions, along the crest of the ghats, from the Bombay frontier down to Po-

* The substance of the other letter, relating to the labours of my travelling assistants, is included in the subsequent reports.—H. C.

nany, ascending and descending by the mountain passes. I afterwards went across the Anamalai Hills and round the slopes of the Nilgiris; I also made a circuit of the Wynád, and twice visited the Conolly Plantations at Nellambúr, being altogether eight months absent from the Presidency."

2. The report has been perused by the Government with much interest. It is unnecessary to review the whole in detail; the points which require special notice are particularised below.

3. After noticing the extensive and often wanton havoc and devastation caused by the axe of the coffee planter and the *kumari* cultivator, Dr Cleghorn states that the profuse waste has been altogether prohibited in the Mysore and Bombay collectorates, and is checked to a great extent in Canara, "but has not altogether ceased, though the exertions of the collector and sub-collector have been successful in keeping under the destruction caused by vagabond tribes in burning wood, with a view to raising from the ashes a crop of inferior grain." The Government resolve to communicate paragraph 3 to the collector of Canara, through the Board of Revenue, and that officer will be good enough to furnish a brief report of the result of his exertions for the repression of the system of *kumari* cultivation. The conservancy system in Canara is stated to be in advance of every other district, though still imperfect. A set of forest rules are said to have been framed, which are calculated to ensure a regulated and safe expenditure, provided the subordinates do their duty. The Government will be glad to see a copy of these rules.

4. Par. 5. The requirements of the various departments (Indian Navy, Madras Railway, Bombay Railway, Department P. W., Telegraph Department) have been unusually heavy; and owing to the withdrawal of the employés and matérial of the Forest Department, on account of the mutinies, the latter has scarcely been able to meet the demands made upon it, so that the operations of the past year do not afford a fair criterion of the prospective effectiveness of the Forest Department.

5. Par. 6. Speaking of the marvellous changes in the face of the country as regards tree vegetation, produced by the progress of the railway, it is mentioned that a traveller looking

from the staging bungalow at Wàliàr, sees several "tentative lines of rail, each 200 yards broad." The Government suppose that Dr Cleghorn refers to the first attempts at opening the line through the Palghat gap some two or three years ago, and which Colonel Pears noticed at the time. The question of the payment of seignorage for sleepers, also referred to, will be disposed of elsewhere.

6. Par. 7. The collector of Madura will be called upon, with reference to this paragraph, to state whether he has succeeded in putting an entire stop to the devastation formerly caused on the slopes of the Pulny Hills by the formation of plantain gardens.

7. Pars. 8, 9. The improved methods of felling and trimming which have been introduced are satisfactory, though Dr Cleghorn mentions that, in some places, "peculiarities of tenure" have operated as an obstacle to the introduction of improvement. In what way these peculiarities of tenure operated disadvantageously should have been explained.

8. Pars. 10–12. The proposed system of operations, and the measures taken to economise fragments and pieces of timber unsuited to naval purposes, are approved. The auctions described in par. 13 should be systematically held. At the end of par. 4 mention is made of the difficulties which still exist as to the supply of firewood to the large towns; if a regular supply of timber were ensured to the people by means of these sales, it would go far to prevent clandestine cutting; and judging from the result of the sale of teak held in the Anamalai Forest, they are likely to be a source of no inconsiderable gain, for even the fragments were greedily bought by the general trader, the Railway Department, &c.

9. Par. 13. *Teak.* This invaluable wood, the Conservator states, has received the special attention of the department. There is said to be very little ripe teak on government land below the ghats, along the whole length of the Malabar coast,* and there are only three localities above the ghats where it is found in abundance and of good size, viz.:—

I. The Anamalai Forest.

* Travancore is not alluded to, as not being in the jurisdiction of the Conservancy Department.

II. The Wainád and Heggadevankota Forests; partly, Dr Cleghorn observes, in dispute between Mysore and Malabar.

III. The Gund Plateau in North Canara.

Sundry changes and improvements in the management of the Anamalai Forests which have recently been effected are detailed; and with reference to the further development of the valuable resources of these forests, the Conservator notices that the supply of teak from the forest now rented from the Colangód Numbody (Nambúdri?) will not last more than fifteen years; "which is a serious consideration, as it is the only forest from which long planks suitable for a man-of-war can be procured." Dr Cleghorn has therefore conceived a scheme for consolidating the table-land of the Anamalai range, that belonging to Government as well as that rented, into one Government forest, to be systematically worked, and held in reserve in perpetuity for the Indian navy. It appears probable that the forest now rented is the Janmi property of some Malabar chief, with which it is not likely that he could be induced to part, so that it is not clear how such an arrangement as the one proposed could be carried out, except by means of a money compensation. In the separate communication which the Conservator promises on the subject, full particulars of the renting system should be given, and such peculiarities of forest tenure as may come under Dr Cleghorn's notice.

10. Par. 14. The Wainád forests adjoining Mysore are of great value, and stand second in importance. They are capable, Dr Cleghorn roughly estimates, of supplying 2000 bandy loads, or 40,000 cubic feet of teak annually, without permanently injuring the resources of the forest. But at present no means of carriage exist, by which "crooks" and other timber required for naval purposes can be conveyed to the coast, where they would be extremely valuable. This paragraph will be communicated to the chief engineer, who will (after conferring with Captain Francis, who is, the Government believe, well acquainted with the locality) suggest a remedy, and show what line of communication could be most easily opened to the sea, or to any river navigable from where the timber could be conveyed to it, to its mouth.

In the same paragraph Dr Cleghorn mentions that he has experienced great difficulty in obtaining exact information as to the extent and tenure of these forests. It is not stated whether the required information was sought from the collector of Malabar. The Government are of opinion, that the authoritative determination of these tenures is an important preliminary towards the establishment of any system of conservancy in the forests; and they understand that a report on the subject is now about to be submitted to them by the Board of Revenue with especial reference to Wainád.

11. In the same paragraph of the report, Dr Cleghorn also alludes to a subject (before noticed in the correspondence* respecting the Mysore and Malabar boundary dispute), which demands immediate and careful attention. He states that the authorities at Astagràm and Coorg, and the commissariat officer at Hunsùr, all drew his attention to the terrible waste of teak which occurs in the disputed tract, "the timber being carted out in large quantities by three roads, under the plea of passes from two Devasthànams, the limits of whose Inàm land I have no means of ascertaining."

If these Devasthànams are in the Company's territory, there would be no difficulty in prohibiting all cutting until the Dharmakartà of the pagodas showed title; and if this was deemed good, measures might be taken to prevent rigidly any cutting, except within the limits assigned. But adverting to the scanty means of supervision in these remote regions possessed by Dr Cleghorn, the Government doubt whether it would be found practicable to confine the felling within proper bounds; the better course would be to prohibit any such felling by the pagoda people; and to fix an equivalent in money to the value of the timber, which inquiry may show they have a right to. If the Devasthànams are found to be within the Mysore territory, a communication of the views of Government will be made to Sir Mark Cubbon. The arrangement of the disputed boundary is now before Government. When the difficulty is solved, the Government will be prepared to consider the proposition of the Conservator as to an officer being specially appointed to that tract of country.

* From the Com. of Mysore, 16th January and 16th February 1858; from the Conservator of Forests, 23d January 1858; and from the Sec. Board of Revenue, 1st April 1858. Ex. Min. Con., 3d May 1858, No. 564.

They remark that the timber may be essentially serviceable for the barracks and riding-school at Bangalore, and even for the military buildings at Jackatalla.

12. Par. 19. Dr Cleghorn here states, that a particular survey, and well drawn lines of demarcation between Mysore, Malabar, and Coorg, are, among other desiderata, necessary for securing an uninterrupted supply of teak for the future, and placing the establishment for the conservancy of this forest on a proper footing.

13. As to the suggestion following, that a European magistrate should be permanently located in Wynád, the Government conceive that much benefit would result from such an arrangement. Independently of the fast-increasing European population, which renders the presence of such an authority desirable, the residence of a European officer in regions so inaccessible and so seldom visited as Wynâd, would not only enforce the observance of conservancy regulations, but keep the Government *au fait* as to the real wants and state of this important district: the present casual visits of the collector are quite insufficient to do this. This question is also before the Government for consideration.

14. Pars. 15 and 16. Canara teak is stated generally to be of much smaller scantling than that of Malabar; the chief remaining reserve is a forest on the Gund Plateau, the trees on which, now well grown and ripe, are said to be conserved by their inaccessible position. Dr Cleghorn describes it to be of primary importance, that this forest should be immediately worked, as it is much threatened with fire. There are two ways by which the wood may be got out, either by a rocky water-course with at least three small falls, or by making a road of twenty-three miles. The collector, and Dr Gibson, the Conservator of Forests under the Bombay Government, incline to the latter course; whilst Col. Arthur Cotton,* and Lieut. Taylor, I.N., recommend that the rocks in the water-course should be blasted. Dr Cleghorn submits a map of the forest surveyed by his assistant Mr Müller, in which the roads necessary for the working of the forest are suggested. And he proposes that an engineer officer be deputed to visit the locality, and report on the best mode of getting out the

* Now Sir Arthur Cotton, C.B.

wood; Capt. Walker of the Engineers, shortly expected from England, being one of the few Europeans who have visited the spot, and who has a knowledge of its requirements, might, the Conservator thinks, be directed to make an examination. The Government are fully alive to the importance of this Gund Forest; and as Capt. Taylor of the Indian navy is now surveying the Kala Nuddee near Sidashegur, that officer will be requested to afford the Government any information as to the accessibility of these forests that it may be in his power to give.

15. With reference to Dr Cleghorn's request that 100 copies of the map of the forest now laid before Government should be struck off, it is observed that 200 copies of the report have been asked for; these and a similar number of the maps will be printed and lithographed at once.

16. *Teak Plantations*, p. 17 *seqq*. Colonel Gilbert's plantations, commenced in 1804, are generally failures, owing to the injudicious selection of site too near the sea. The Conolly Plantations, on the other hand, are in a very promising condition; and the Government recognise the very great importance of restoring the ancient and valuable forests of Malabar, and will be glad to receive the report preparing by Dr Cleghorn. The Conservator proposes to depute two of his subordinates to introduce the planting system in vogue there into the Anamalai forests and North Canara.

17. Par. 19. Will be communicated to the D. P. W., with a request that the chief engineer will impress upon his subordinates the necessity of care in selection of timber for Government works. The wood (*Poon spars*) which Dr Cleghorn saw used for the construction of a small bridge, it is most important to preserve for naval purposes.

18. *Sandal Wood.*—The spontaneous growth of the sandal tree has increased, it is stated, to a considerable extent in Mysore, Canara, Coimbatore, Salem, and a little in North Arcot; and the Conservator thinks, that if the supervision of local officers is vigilant, and slight assistance be given to nature in clearing the heads of the young plants, which are often matted down by strong creepers, an addition might accrue to the revenue of these provinces.

19. *Introduction of Saw Machinery.*—Par. 28. The Government concur with the Conservator as to the propriety of deferring the introduction of saw machinery to the little frequented forests. This expensive plant can only be desirable when operations are to be conducted for a length of time on a large scale at the same place. At the depôts, the saw machinery might advantageously be introduced, the timber being conveyed thither entire; meanwhile every endeavour should be made to abolish the use of the axe.

20. Para. 30. Will be communicated to the chief engineer, with a request that he will direct his subordinates to follow the course suggested.

21. Par. 33. The principle here laid down is fair and highly proper, and collectors should give their aid in securing its observance.

22. Par. 34. The Government fully concur in Dr Cleghorn's views, as enunciated in this paragraph; which may be stated in a few words to be, that while it is desirable to give every encouragement to the extension of coffee cultivation, the destruction of timber must be prevented, by restricting grants of coffee land to places where the shrub can be grown with advantage; and, at the same time, the denudation of the higher ridges and slopes of hills, which if allowed may result in a serious diminution of the rain fall, should be absolutely prohibited; while those intending to occupy land containing fine timber, should be compelled to take the land without the timber, or take the latter at a valuation.

The Government are aware that the (late) collector of Coimbatore, Mr Thomas, was fully alive to the importance of the principles laid down; but they desire that the Board of Revenue will communicate to the present acting-collector their wish, that the views expressed in the letter quoted should be adhered to in every way.

23. With reference to par. 35, the Government notice with much interest the successful attempt by a private individual to introduce the tea plant. Dr Cleghorn will be good enough to keep them informed of the progress of an experiment so creditable to Mr Mann.

The Government would be glad to see the general instructions, par. 36, issued by the Conservator, when he next reports progress.

24. Par. 40. The Government will be prepared to take into consideration the establishment of depôts, when the Conservator lays a definite scheme before them.

25. Par. 41. The Conservator here represents the difficulty of procuring suitable overseers; and he shows the causes which combine to prevent qualified persons from entering the department. If, on further experience, these causes are still found to operate detrimentally to the interest of the establishment, it will be Dr Cleghorn's duty to propose a remedy in the shape of a higher scale of remuneration.

26. Par. 44. The "Manual of Accounts" alluded to has already been approved in Ex. Min. Con., 21st May 1858, No. 669, and 200 copies will be struck off for the use of the Conservancy Department, &c.

27. Par. 46. The "Botanical Manual," under preparation, in accordance with the wishes of the Honourable Court of Directors, will doubtless be a most useful production. The Government would wish some uniform system to be adopted in the representation of native terms in the Roman character.

28. The account of the disbursements of the department, in the last paragraph of the report, should have been placed side by side with one of the receipts.

29. The present report, as well as Dr Cleghorn's second letter submitting a detailed account of the tours of his two travelling assistants, will be submitted to the Honourable Court of Directors, with a copy of the foregoing remarks.

T. Pycroft, *Chief Secretary.*

SECOND ANNUAL REPORT, 1858–59.

From H. Cleghorn, Esq., M.D., Conservator of Forests, to the Secretary to Government.

Madras, 31st *December* 1859, *No.* 890.

I have the honour to report, for the information of the Honourable the Governor in Council, that during the official year 1858–59 I proceeded on my second tour of inspection through the Government forests, and visited the Chittari, Yellagiri, and Jawadhi ranges of the Salem district, and afterwards travelled through great part of Canara, north and south [both above and below the ghats], and the principality of Coorg. Subsequently, I had the honour of accompanying Lord Harris over the Shevaroi Hills, and through Malabar and Travancore. After a few weeks' stay at the presidency, I proceeded to the northern division, and visited the mouths of the rivers from Masulipatam to Ganjam. On this occasion I took the opportunity of visiting the Sál forests of Gumsúr.

2. During the year, I have, in accordance with the instructions of Government, submitted my views on several subjects, such as—

Railway requirements in Salem.	Higher ranges of Anamalai.
Do. do. Bellári.	Wynád Boundary.
Utakamand Gardens.	Report on Fuel and Firewood.
Canara Forests.	

3. *Public Departments.*—There has been a constant and heavy pressure upon all the district establishments and local depôts, which has been met with difficulty. The requirements of the Indian navy were not so large as in previous years, but the requisitions of the different railway companies were much greater. The Public Works and Telegraph Departments have continued to press for supplies; and the erection or enlargement of barracks

at Belgam, Bellári, Bangalore, and Jackatalla, have in a special manner taxed our resources.

4. *Military and Naval.*—The requirements of the different arsenals have been numerous and miscellaneous, but, except in the case of the gun-carriage manufactory, not individually very large. The various items mentioned* will give some idea of army and navy demands.

5. *Railways.*—The establishment of railways causes an immense demand for timber, and thus, as I remarked last year, entirely changes the features of the districts through which they pass. Each sleeper measures three cubic feet; and as one mile of single rails requires 1760 sleepers, and these will not, on an average, last above eight years at the most, we have an annual demand of at least 220 sleepers per mile, or 22,000 for every hundred miles. The total length of lines within the presidency, either sanctioned or contemplated, is, I believe, about 1150 miles; so that, if the above estimate as to duration be correct, at least 253,000 sleepers (say 35,000 trees) will be required annually. A portion of these will no doubt be procured from England, Ceylon, Burmah, the Andaman Islands, and Australia; but there will still be a regular and heavy drain on the forests of this presidency. To meet this prospective demand, it seems most desirable that immediate steps should be taken to raise large numbers of hard-wood trees suitable for sleepers, especially as sleepers of indigenous woods may be estimated at one-half the cost of those obtained from England. I have already suggested that railway companies, irrigation companies, sugar-factory proprietors, and others, who consume large quantities of fuel, charcoal, and timber, should plant to some extent for their own use in station compounds, along railway embankments, on the banks of channels, &c.

6. *South-West Line, 400 Miles.*—The supply along the South-West Line has been better managed than at first, when a multitude of contractors appeared who engaged to contract for wood which was not their own. In August 1858 the Salem establishment was sanctioned, and Mr Blenkinsop appointed. The resi-

* Gun-carriages, boats, gun-stocks, scaling-ladders, saddletrees, plugs for Minie-rifle balls, ropes for arsenals, &c.

dent railway engineer reports that the supply of sleepers comes in much faster, and that they are in general of better quality, than those received at first.

7. *Bangalore Branch*, 80 *Miles.*—The country near the line selected for this branch is remarkably wanting in useful timber, which, so far as I can learn, must be supplied in great part from the Denkinacotta táluk of Salem and the Concanhully táluk of Mysore. A special establishment will be required, and this is now engaging my attention. Seasoned teak for the Bangalore workshop can be obtained at a moderate rate from the depôt at Mysore.

8. *North-West Line*, 300 *Miles.*—The first part of this line, which runs through the North Arcot and Kadapa districts, traverses a moderately wooded country, where there is a good deal of excellent timber. I do not anticipate any deficiency of supply in Kadapa and Karnúl; the chief points to be attended to are the opening up of the country with roads on either side of the line, and the selection of people who will not cut wastefully. An establishment to mark suitable trees will probably be required in the Kadapa and Karnúl districts. The Bellári district is absolutely destitute of timber suited for railway requirements, and the price even of firewood is excessive. In anticipation of the railway demands, an establishment has been organised in Mysore, and large quantities of timber have been floated down the Tunga, Bhādra, and Wurda rivers, to a point near where the railway crosses the Túmbhādra. At this spot a depôt has been established. Piles of faggots for making charcoal, and large rafts of bamboos, have also been floated down.

9. *Great-Southern*, 300 *Miles.*—No timber resources are available for that portion of this line which runs from Negapatam to Trichinopoli. It is understood that the directors propose to send sleepers from England for about thirty miles, and it is probable that part of the remainder of the line may be supplied from Ceylon. For the proposed extension to Carúr and Errode, and southwards to Tuticorin, we must look to the forests at the sources of the Ambrawatti and Bhowani rivers, along the banks of the Caveri, and those on the Pulny Hills, especially in the Cambam Valley. Sleepers and fuel can probably be rafted down the abovementioned rivers.

10. *Preserving Timber, Boucherie's Process.*—The process of Boucherie, which impregnates timber with metallic oxides, rendering the softer woods durable under ground, and thus saving much valuable timber, would be of great importance to Indian railways, and should therefore be patronised. A prize medal was awarded for this process at the Great Exhibition of 1851, and a "grande medaille d'honneur" at the Paris Exhibition of 1855.

11. *Telegraph.*—The wire is supported on posts of sawn teakwood, and not on young trees, as formerly. In some places, as near Darwar, "matti" (*Pentaptera coriacea*) is now used, and many of the posts are excellent. In the northern division, the posts are of sâlwood (*Vatica robusta*), from the Gumsúr forests. Two hundred poles of different species of trees indigenous to the Nílgiri Hills were lately supplied by this department for the experimental line from Utakamand to Kunúr.

12. *Auctions.*—I have endeavoured to impress on all in the department, that no wastage of timber (which will bear the cost of removal) can be permitted; and every effort is now being made to turn to account all fragments of sound timber. My assistants have been enjoined to collect all outlying timber, and convey it to the depôts, where it is sold by public auction, a full month's notice of sale being given in all the local as well as the "Fort Saint George Gazette." No auction was held at Anamalai last year, the demand for timber being so great that offers were immediately made for all that could be brought down. Logs, planks, &c., unsuited for public purposes, are being collected at the foot of the ghat for sale by auction. One auction was held at the depôts in Canara during the present year. On the whole, the proceeds were remunerative, and more than covered the expense of dragging the timber out of the jungles, while, the lots being small, the poorer classes were able to suit their wants. Much of the refuse timber which was not required for the Jackatalla barracks, or which would not bear the carriage to Utakamand, is being sold below the ghat at Gúndelpett.

13. *Extension of System*—(1.) *Wainád.*—The great demand for timber in connection with erecting public buildings on the Nílgiris, particularly the Jackatalla barracks and the jail, has called my attention to the extensive forests at the base of these moun-

tains, stretching in a northerly direction towards Coorg, and some parts of which have been the favourite resort of sandalwood robbers and wild beasts. In accordance with my recommendation, Government have sanctioned the appointment of an officer, whose salary is to be defrayed partly by this Government and partly by Mysore.*

(2). *Sigúr.*—This forest has been much exhausted by a succession of unscrupulous contractors, and there is very little teak or blackwood at present fit for felling. It is important that the forest should be allowed to recover, as it is the main source of supply to Utakamand for house-building purposes. I proposed that Captain Morgan should have charge of this in addition to the Múdumalai Forest, with a small establishment costing fifty rupees per mensem. This was sanctioned,† and operations have now commenced. I hope that the sale of sandal and jungle wood will not only cover the expenses, but also yield a profit, while the young teak is coming on for future supply.

(3.) *Nuggur.*—In the Nuggur division of Mysore, also, an establishment has been organised, which promises to be extensively useful for the supply of wood to Bellári and the bare country to the eastward.

14. *Financial results of Conservancy.*—From the returns of my assistants in Canara, Anamalai, and Salem, rendered to the close of the official year, it may be seen that the operations have in these ranges been financially profitable. Large supplies of timber have been furnished to public departments at a time when such was indispensably necessary.

	Receipts.	Expenditure.	Profit.
Anamalai, ...	9,835	33,012	97,318‡
Canara, ...	100,604	34,325	66,279
Salem, ...	7,805	3,048	4,757

15. *Price of Timber.*—The price of wood all over the country

* Ext. Min. Cons., No. 577, Rev. Dep., 28th April 1859, par. 3, and letter of Commissioner of Mysore, 4th April 1859, par. 3.

† Ext. Min. Cons., No. 668, 16th May 1859, Rev. Dep.

‡ To appear in the next account-current, *vide* par. 17.

has been steadily rising for some time, and large timber is obtainable with more difficulty than formerly. In some localities, on the other hand, the price of timber has somewhat decreased, in consequence of the establishment of depôts having broken up the monopoly previously existing in the hands of a few proprietors and contractors.

16. *Canara.*—The forest operations have been more extensive than in any previous year, but chiefly above ghat, and, as predicted in my letter of 7th December 1858 [par. 6], the gross return has not been so large as in the years 1855–56 and 1856–57. Nevertheless, there has been a net profit of 66,000 rupees. The subjoined statement shows the quantity and quality of timber supplied to various public departments during the year :—

DEPARTMENT.	TEAK.		BLACKWOOD.					JUNGLEWOOD.					TOTAL.				
	Logs.	Cands.	Logs.	Cands.	Qrs.	G.	T.	Logs.	Cands.	Qrs.	G.	T.	Logs.	Cands.	Qrs.	G.	T.
Bombay Dockyard, . .	409	904	12	45	2	4	10	...	...	...	...	...	421	950	1	4	...
Hydrabad, Scinde, engineer, .	37	118	...	...	...	...	...	...	...	...	...	...	37	118	2	2	10
Darwar engineer,	187	344	...	...	...	...	...	538	842	...	4	...	725	1186	3	...	5
Belgam do.,	88	146	...	...	...	...	...	375	160	...	3	17	463	306	1	4	17
Lingasugur do.,	103	188	...	...	...	...	...	16	23	...	1	1	119	211	3	3	18
Darwar factory,	...	...	...	...	...	...	...	30	43	3	4	15	30	43	3	4	15
Belgam Barrack,	215	417	7	6	3	1	3	531	907	3	3	11	753	1332	...	2	...
Tuddry workshop, . . .	100	38	...	...	...	...	...	...	...	...	...	...	100	38	2	3	13
Edulji contractor,	9	18	...	...	...	...	...	25	21	2	...	7	34	40	...	...	6
Total, .	1148	2177	19	52	2	...	13	1515	1998	3	...	11	2682	4229	...	1	4

The forest chart, which has been carefully prepared by Mr Müller, shows the position of the teak forests, superior jungles, sandal-wood tracts, poon spar localities, and timber depôts. As this chart is likely to be useful to revenue officers and engineers, I beg to recommend that it be lithographed. The letter of Mr Fisher, collector of Canara (page 49), notices fully the chief points in the forest management for the year. I concur with him in reprobating (par. 13) the admission of the agents of public officers to fell timber in our reserved forests. The deviation was exceptional, and arose from the necessity of meeting large and emergent military demands, especially for the Belgam barracks, which could not be instantly met by the small staff of employés in the Conservancy Department.

(1.) *Gund Forest.*—Some progress has been made in working this valuable forest, and Captain Taylor, Indian Navy, has explored the Black River and taken the levels. He reports favourably as to the quantity of teak, and that although there is a succession of small rapids, amounting to a fall of 120 feet in the river, the timber can be floated down, though not without some difficulty.*

(2.) *Wurdah River.*—Rafts are being floated down the Wurdah and Túmbhadra Rivers to Bellári, to meet the requirements of the north-west line of the Madras Railway.

(3.) *Roads.*—The two lines of road specially recommended by the collector (par. 20) would be of great value to the Forest Department, and enable us to extend our operations into tracts which at present are inaccessible.

(4.) *Wood in Depôt.*—The accompanying table shows the quantity of wood in store in different depôts; the proceeds of the auctions will appear in this year's account:—

Talu.	Name of Depôts.	Teak & Black.					Jungle-wood.					Total.				
		Logs.	Cands.	Qrs.	G.	T.	Logs.	Cands.	Qrs.	G.	T.	Logs.	Cands.	Qrs.	G.	T.
Ankolah.	Sidashegúr,	1112	...	...	...	...	...	...	...	...	...	1112	...	...	...	...
	Gungawally,	2362	...	...	...	...	...	...	...	...	...	2362	...	...	...	...
Sondah.	Sircy, . .	...	...	...	...	...	981	770	3	4	2	891	770	3	4	2
	Malanji, .	...	...	...	...	...	298	292	3	4	10	298	292	3	4	10
	Katur, . .	1356	1498	2	4	15	1873	1812	3	1	4	3229	3311	2	...	19
	Mundagode,	268	224	2	2	12	...	...	...	...	...	268	224	2	2	12
	Kantanally,	...	...	...	...	...	375	549	1	3	5	375	549	1	3	5
Yellapur.	Kolekery,	266	195	...	1	3	1634	1960	1	2	5	1900	2155	1	3	8
	Bagwatti,	60	35	3	4	16	1055	1138	...	2	12	1115	1174	0	2	8
	Hallial,	520	878	3	2	17	368	428	...	...	1	888	1306	3	2	18
	Shivapur,	...	...	...	...	...	1285	2216	2	2	11	1285	2216	2	2	11
Súpah,	Harrigalli,	1411	2198	2	...	12	593	941	3	3	3	2004	3140	1	3	15
		7355	...	...	...	...	8372	...	...	...	...	15727	...	...	...	...

* Captain Taylor's letter to Government in Ext. Min. Cons., No. 677, Rev. Dep., 17th May 1859.

17. *Anamallai.*—Lieútenant Beddome, in his annual report, gives a concise and faithful account of the economy and working of these forests, which is generally satisfactory. The quantity of work done is considerable, but it would have been much greater if a sufficient number of axemen could have been procured; the Palghat labourers, from whom we have hitherto drawn our main supply, find full and remunerative employment at the railway workshops close to their own houses.

(1.) *Extension of Road to Cochin Backwater.*—I hope that ultimately the forest road, which has been gradually extended westwards as our operations have progressed, may be carried on to the Cochin Backwater, forming another avenue of traffic between the rich tâluk of Polachy and the western coast, opening up a very wild country, intermediate between the Palghat Gap and the Aringole Pass. The estimate for the Anamalai Ghat, to supersede the present rude timber slip, has been for some time before Government, and the extension of the road above alluded to is a strong argument in favour of making this ghat.

(2.) *Elephants.*—Mr Beddome has been instructed to pay the *mahouts* what he considers necessary, and the services of a *foujdar* have been procured.

The account-current does not show the actual profit of the year, from the circumstance of the assistant not having entered the receipts of the Bombay timber-agent as cash, in accordance with the order of Government. The sum [107,117 rupees] will of course appear to the credit of Government in next year's account.

It may also be noticed that the great object originally of working these forests was to reduce the price of first-class teak, which was yearly becoming more scarce and difficult to procure; and indeed the Indian navy have latterly procured almost all their frigate scantling from this forest.

18. *Salem District.*—The indiscriminate felling of trees in the Government forests of Salem have been urgently brought to my notice by the collector, coffee-planters, and others. While the demands of the railway company required to be speedily met, I submitted a scheme for the consideration of Government, and suggested that a seignorage of 3 to 4 annas per sleeper, or 1

rupee to 1-8-0 rupee per tree, should be charged; and to carry out this measure, I recommended a temporary establishment for marking trees suited for the railway. This was sanctioned in Ext. Min. of Cons., 9th July 1858, No. 943. As it was desirable to have an assistant immediately in charge of these operations, Mr L. Blenkinsop was appointed* to the Salem range, on a salary of 200 rupees per mensem. I learn from the railway engineer that the selection of trees for sleepers is now more satisfactorily conducted than heretofore, and, as a larger proportion is accepted by the railway, there is less waste of timber. The seignorage derived from this source covers the expense of the establishment, as originally contemplated. The permanent employment of an assistant, overseer, and four peons, was sanctioned by Government.† Looking to the fact that the Salem district is to have the benefit of two, if not three lines of railway, and that the demand for renewing sleepers will certainly be very great, I think that planting operations will eventually be required in this district. During a period of financial difficulty, I did not venture to solicit a grant for this purpose, nor is it yet necessary. The forests on the banks of the Caveri are still unworked, but they are notoriously unhealthy, and little opened by roads. The Shevaroi, Collemalai, Chittari, and Yellagiri forests, have all contributed their quota. The following abstract gives the receipts for railway sleepers compared with cost of the establishment:—

September 1858,	Rs. 18	12	0			
October „ .	328	14	0			
November „ .	127	14	0			Rs.
December „ .	654	6	0	Assistant, .	200 × 9=	1800
January 1859, .	1002	9	0	Overseers, .	60 × 10=	600
February „ .	1152	9	0	Peons, . .		648
March „ .	3261	0	0			
April „ .	1259	7	0		Total Rs.	3048
Total Rs.	7805	7	0			

19. *Ferry-boat.*—Considerable difficulty has been experienced

* Ext. Min. Cons., No. 1137, 13th August 1858, Rev. Dep.

† Ext. Min. Cons., No. 626, 6th May 1859, Rev. Dep.

in obtaining large logs suited for the preparation of jangars or ferry-boats. (*Vide* Sketch). The wood best adapted and most used for this purpose is that of the aynee (*Artocarpus hirsuta*), which, though still existing in considerable abundance along the ghats, has been cut away in all the most accessible localities. The trunks of other trees (*Terminalia sp.* and *Calophyllum angustifolium*) are now hollowed out for making canoes.

Fig. 3.

20. *Teak Plantations.*—(1). *Nellambúr.*—Great attention has been paid to the important work of propagating timber. The thinnings of this plantation [several thousand poles] were advertised for sale, and readily purchased. They were admirably suited for fencing, scaffoldings, roofing second-class houses, and other economic purposes; as also for poles of country carts, yokes, &c. &c. The proceeds during the past year have almost covered the expenses of the plantation, and I believe I can with certainty assure Government of its prospective return being amply sufficient to meet all charges which may be incurred. This plantation was inspected by the late Governor (Lord Harris) in November 1858, and was noticed in his Lordship's minute.* An ornamental wood-

* "On the 19th I visited the Government teak plantations near Nellambúr. I was highly gratified with the inspection of these flourishing woods, which speak most effectually for the sagacity, perseverance, and foresight, of the late Mr Conolly. So far as it is possible to judge at the present early stage of the experiment, complete success has been obtained.

"Specimens are to be seen in different parts of the plantations of trees from one to fourteen years old, all growing most luxuriantly, and with a regularity and straightness which leads me to suppose they will become very valuable timber. The older trees had not, in my opinion, been thinned

man's knife and belt were presented to Chatu Menon, the native sub-conservator, by the collector, under orders of Government. (2.) *Canara.*—Ground has been prepared and plantations commenced on the banks of the Black River, and two young men have been trained at Nellumbúr to carry out the work. (3.) *Nuggur.*—Two teachers of planting have been trained by Chatu Menon, and reported qualified to form a teak plantation.

21. *Australian Plantations.*—These were commenced in 1856 by Captain J. Campbell, and were reported on by me in June 1858,* when I solicited a further grant of 2500 rupees, which Government were pleased to sanction. The increasing European population at Jackatalla and Kunúr renders the preservation and increase of these plantations of essential importance to the barracks now occupied by about 1500 persons. They are now under the charge of Overseer E. Hall. A detailed report on these plantations has been submitted.

22. *Planting at Utakamand.*—Government, in Ext. Min. of Cons., 3d June 1858, were pleased to sanction the disbursement of 2050 rupees for planting out 10,000 Australian trees in the neighbourhood of this station, under the supervision of Mr M'Ivor, who reports "that four thousand plants have been planted in the sholah at Malí Mund; but about one-third of these died from being planted too late in the season. About seven hundred trees have been planted round the Utakamand lake and in the neighbourhood of the station. Six thousand

sufficiently; but I have no doubt this error will be remedied under the able management of Dr Cleghorn.

"There was at first of course considerable outlay, without any return; but the thinnings are already beginning to amount to a considerable sum, and will of themselves shortly repay the expenditure, while the trees left for timber will be almost clear gain.

"I look upon this as a most important matter, and one worthy of being brought to the notice of the Supreme Government, as too great pains cannot be taken for increasing the future supply of timber. The native sub-conservator, Chatu Menon, is stated by Dr Cleghorn to deserve the highest credit for his care of the plantations for fourteen years. He is desirous of receiving some token of the approbation of Government; and I would propose that an ornamental woodman's knife should be given him."

* *Vide* Ext. Min. Cons., 3d June 1858, No. 748, Rev. Rep.

young plants of acacias, cypresses (different sp.), deodars, and willows, have been planted out in clumps along the road to Jackatalla," where shelter is much required.

23. *Distribution of Tree Seeds.*—Many applications have been made with which I have been enabled to comply. The French Government received a considerable quantity of teak and other seeds for experimental introduction into Algeria. Two supplies of sandal-seed were sent to Major Phayre, commissioner of Pegu, for the King of Ava; and at various times seeds of different useful trees have been sent to the Hyderabad territories, and to various stations in the Bombay Presidency.

24. *Arboriculture.*—The masses of the people have until lately been ignorant of the value of trees; but in the vicinity of large towns and along the line of railways they are now alive to the importance of this kind of property. I am full of hope that the ryots will gradually be induced to plant useful trees in their hedgerows and by their wells and water-courses, which, according to the new regulations, will be indisputably their own.

25. *Avenues.*—Much has been done in some districts by the executive engineers in the way of planting avenues, and the trunk-roads are better sheltered by trees than formerly. There are few districts also without a nursery of seedlings, and the canals have in many places been planted. For the most part these avenues are under the charge of the Department Public Works; and, except occasionally supplying seeds, my work is confined to giving advice as to the suitability of particular trees to certain localities.

26. *Reserved Trees.*—The list of trees which, under the native rule, comprised only teak, sandal, and black wood, has been extended to other trees highly valuable for building purposes, which in most districts are—

Jack (*Artocarpus integrifolia*).	Marada (*Pentaptera coriacea*).
Ayni (*Artocarpus hirsuta*).	Cedar (*Cedrela Toona*).
Vengé (*Pterocarpus marsupium*).	Erul (*Inga xylocarpa*).
Palavu (*Mimusops Indica*).	

There are others which require to be conserved in particular districts.

27. *Minor Jungles.*—The shrubby copsewood, which is so useful for fuel, is protected in some degree from wasteful cutting and conflagration. The management of these jungles, however, must always remain with the local authorities, who, in communication with me, promulgated rules according to the necessities of their districts. No circular that could be devised would be generally applicable.

28. *Sandal-wood.*—The preservation of young plants, and the means of ensuring a regular income from this source of revenue, have engaged my attention. The system adopted in Mysore for this purpose appears to be judicious. Colkars are employed to destroy the strong creepers, which tend to choke the young plants springing from seed dropped in hedgerows by birds. It is their duty also to cut annually all ripe trees twenty years old, and no other, and to take care that the billets are properly prepared and sorted, and brought into the sandal godown. The sandal tree grows to perfection in Mysore, and yields a large annual revenue to the State. It also thrives well in some parts of Salem, Coimbatore, and North Canara, in which district it is now under the charge of Mr Müller. I have been in correspondence with the collector of Coimbatore, and have instructed Lieutenant Beddome to visit the táluks (Danaickencotta, Andyur, Collegal, Suttimungalum) in the Coimbatore district, and to supply full and accurate information—(1.) As to the size and abundance of the trees; (2.) As to the method of curing or preparing the wood adapted in the district; (3.) As to the means most likely to improve the quality of the billets, and to secure a regular revenue to the State. Mr New, superintendent of the Lall Bagh Garden, Bangalore, has raised a large number of seedlings in a nursery, and finds the seeds germinate readily if sown within a fortnight after removal from the tree; but they do not bear carriage well to a distance, and few germinate if a month old.

Illicit Traffic in Sandal-wood.—On different occasions, while travelling down the Carúr Ghat, I met parties of Mapillas with fresh cut sandal-wood on their backs. On inquiry, I ascertained that these men barter the wood with the Kúrumbers for salt fish and cocoa-nuts. I addressed the commissioner of Mysore, the collectors of Malabar and Coimbatore, requesting their co-operation in stopping this illegal traffic, and I am happy to say steps have been taken which have nearly put an end to it. Mr Grant suggests that the most effectual way to stop the practice will be to grow the tree in Malabar. This will be tried; but there is reason to doubt whether the aroma, for which it is valued, will be produced in that climate.

29. *Babul Preserves.*—I have suggested that this most useful tree (*Acacia arabica*) should be conserved along the banks of the Túmbhadra, both in the Bellâry district and in the Nuggur division of Mysore. The babul springs up in the alluvial soil on both banks, in similar ground to the shikargahs of Scinde; and if three trees be planted when one is cut, there will be an increased supply of useful material in a few years. The pods and tender twigs form a favourite food of sheep in the hot weather.

30. *Munjit.**—Samples of this dye-root have been sent to Calcutta and England for experimental trial and report. The product is abundant upon the slopes of the Nilgiris; and if it could be prepared for export so as to be packed in small compass, a trade would probably spring up. There appears to be very little difference between the Nilgiri and Punjab article.

31. *Firewood.*—There is no doubt that this necessary of life is more scarce than formerly, and more expensive near all large towns, owing to the greater distance from which it is brought, and the unrestricted license with which it is cut. Zamindars have increased their tax on wood, owing to the great demand for railways and other public works; whilst Government, in a liberal spirit, have left the fuel of a district untaxed, unless special reasons can be shown. Rules for the cutting of Striharicotta and other firewood jungles have been laid down,† and the subject is receiving much attention generally from revenue officers.

32. *Charcoal.*—Native iron-smelters employ fuel from one to three inches in diameter; and, to procure this, they take saplings, or the tops and branches of the largest hardwood trees, allowing the trunks to decay. Large trees are not adapted for fuel for smelting, as the cost of splitting them adds greatly to the ex-

* *Rubia cordifolia*, L.

† Ext. Min. Cons., 4th June 1859, No. 744, Rev. Dep.

pense; and, unless the logs are split, the inner wood is not carbonised. Skilled Europeans prefer branches four to eight inches in diameter, which size they consider most convenient for charcoal burning; if smaller, the wood is liable to be overburnt, and if larger, it is not properly carbonised. In the forests of the Western Ghats, the average price of charcoal, brought several miles to the furnace, is three annas a basket of 50 lbs.

33. *Forest Conflagrations.*—These are of frequent occurrence. The unextinguished fire of a camp of Brinjarris, the sparks from the torches or cheroots of travellers, the spontaneous ignition from friction of bamboos, but much more frequently the wilful burning of grass by the hill tribes (as heather is burnt in Scotland), in order that the ashes of the herbage may nourish the roots of young grass, and thus improve the forage of their cattle—are among the causes of this devastation which extends annually over large tracts. The largest trees skirting the forest suffer more or less from these fires, the saplings are scorched and mutilated, and the smaller seedlings perish. If the same spot is again visited by conflagration in the following year, the largest trees which escaped the first time are often consumed.

34. *Elephants.*—On several occasions my attention has been directed to the unceremonious way in which the *mahouts* of elephants, belonging to *devasthanums*, lop the branches of trees on trunk roads, as if they were entitled to gratuitous forage. This practice should be stopped by the officer in charge of the roads.

35. *Forest Assistants.*—These are four in number. (1.) Lieutenant Beddome succeeded Major D. Hamilton two years ago in the charge of the Anamalai range. His report of the operations in that reserved forest will be found at page 53. He is a botanist of great industry and promise, and has made some important additions to our knowledge of the flora of Southern India. (2.) Mr S. Müller has been in charge of the North Canara forests since the death of Mr Poulton. He is a good Canarese scholar, is well acquainted with his district, and the forests under his charge have been brought into good order. (3.) Mr L. Blenkinsop was appointed to Salem this year, chiefly in connection with urgent railway requirements. It is intended that he should have charge of the sandalwood in the north of the collectorate, and any plant-

ing operations which may be found necessary. (4). Native Surgeon Francis Appávu is in charge of the office at Madras, and, during my absence, countersigns the abstracts and arranges the herbarium. I have also the benefit of the partial services of Captain Morgan, executive engineer, who has the oversight of the Sigúr Jungle, which lies on the road from Utákamand to Múdumalai Forest.

36. *Overseers.*—Two officers of this grade have been appointed during the year—Mr E. Thompson at Putúr, and Mr Curry at Hallial—the former in South, the latter in North Canara. There are several places in which I am anxious to place overseers, as Denkinacotta, Palghat, Pulny, Gumsúr, and Kircumbadi. It is, however, extremely difficult to find men of good character, steady habits, robust health, and some education, who are willing to take appointments involving a lonely residence in unhealthy climates. The risk of fever, the frequent difficulty of obtaining necessaries, and the small amount of salary, deter many persons from joining the department.

37. *Public Gardens.*—The horticultural institutions at Utakamand, Bangalore, and Madras, are respectively superintended by Mr M'Ivor, Mr New, and Mr Brown. These gardens are valuable adjuncts to this department in promoting arboriculture; young trees being supplied to the Road Department, soldiers' gardens, and the public, at low rates. Seeds are also distributed to applicants at cost price.

38. *Manual of South Indian Botany.*—In consequence of extensive travelling and separation from books and specimens, I much regret that little progress has been made in digesting the mass of materials accumulated in my different journeys. I hope to work up these in after years; but at present I can do little more than collect and arrange specimens. Government will, I trust, excuse the delay which has occurred, my time having been so much occupied with investigating trespasses, settling boundary disputes, arranging jungle contracts, and conducting miscellaneous inquiries connected with the vegetable kingdom. The recent publication of Major Drury's "Useful Plants of India," a book which has had a rapid and extensive sale, has, to a great extent, supplied the present want; and the researches of Lieu-

tenant Beddome, alluded to elsewhere, will greatly assist in the preparation of the Manual.

39. *Presidency Office.*—Towards the close of the official year, Mr Maclagan, assistant in charge of the office at Madras, resigned his appointment, having been nominated agent of the Great Southern of India Railway Company. The object contemplated in Mr Maclagan's appointment to the department—viz., the arranging of a system of accounts—having been in a great measure accomplished, I considered that it would now be desirable to have an assistant at the presidency who possessed a knowledge of botany, and who could devote a considerable portion of his time to the herbarium, and answer some of the minor references during my absence. I accordingly recommended the appointment of Francis Appávu, native surgeon, whose assistance I had previously found of great value, when Professor of Botany in the Medical College; and with this recommendation Government were pleased to comply. Mr Spring, my head clerk, has accompanied me in many of my travels, and has made himself generally useful, often at the expense of much personal discomfort. The expenditure has been as follows :—

	Rs.	A.	P.
Salary of the Conservator, the assistant in charge of the office at the presidency and the establishment, ...	17,193	4	7
Salaries of the three assistants and their establishments, ...	18,377	4	2
Contingent charges, ...	5,623	4	4
Rs.,	41,193	13	1

The accounts of the Anamalai and Canara forests for the official year 1858–59 have been forwarded to the Board of Revenue.

After three years' experience I may observe, that it is only by the cordial co-operation of the revenue officers, and those under their orders, that the Forest Department can be successfully carried on; and I therefore strive to keep the collector and sub-collector informed of the nature, scene and extent, of all the forest operations in their districts, with a view to receiving their aid.

In conclusion, I beg to state, that throughout my tour in the provinces, I received every attention and assistance from the local authorities.

From W. Fisher, Esq., Collector of Canara, to H. Cleghorn, Esq., M.D., Conservator of Forests.

Mangalore, *9th July* 1859.

1. I have the honour to submit the following report on the forests of this district, for the year ending 30th April 1859.

2. The account-current shows an expenditure of Rs. 34,325-7-9, and the gross receipts to be Rs. 1,00,604-10-9, leaving 66,729-3-0 rupees as net profit for the year.

3. The principles on which this account is prepared were explained in my report for 1857–58; and, as I need not recur to them here, I shall proceed at once to notice the operations of the year under report, and make such observations on forest management generally as circumstances call for.

4. The transactions of the year may with advantage be divided into *amani* and contract works.

5. In the Supah Forests, 11,880 logs of teak, blackwood, and jungle-wood have been felled, trimmed, and for the most part brought into the depôts, under the superintendence of the Conservancy establishment—the 22,794 candies of timber so secured costing Government about Rs. 1-6-2 per candy.

6. 10,300 teak poles, measuring 2495 candies, from clearings about to be brought under cultivation, are ready for sale, and will be disposed of with other timber after the monsoon.

7. The Wudders employed by Mr Müller have been allowed to export butts and ends of timber lying about the jungle, on payment of R. 1 per candy, and Rs. 139-7-7 have been realised on this account; but the arrangement does not appear to have proved satisfactory, and has, I gather from Mr Müller, been discontinued, in Sonda at any rate.

8. Two thousand trees have been girdled on the banks of the Gangawalli, and some progress seems to have been made in plant-

ing teak; but I learn this from the accounts rather than from Mr Müller's statements.

In the southern táluks, the overseer, Mr Thompson, collected and sent down to Mangalore 189 logs of jungle-wood, the sale proceeds of which more than doubled the expenditure incurred in saving this wood from destruction. Scattered as it was, I am rather surprised that we succeeded so well, and I should have been satisfied by the mere payment of expenses of an operation which necessarily preceded the introduction of a new system. The timber in the forests from which wood can be floated down to Mangalore, is very much scattered; but I am now engaged in arranging contracts, from which I hope to obtain a supply of timber for this market. Four contracts are in the course of completion—two satisfactorily so; the third, however, has in point of fact expired, and some correspondence is now passing between Mr Müller and me regarding it, as Mr Müller does not appear to have put a stop to the contractor's operations, but to have allowed him to proceed with his work, though there is little hope of his ever completing it.

10. Of the execution of the fourth within the period fixed, Mr Müller holds out but small hopes.

11. One new contract has been entered into for the conveyance to the coast of 2000 teak and blackwood trees, girdled in the lower part of the Gund Forest. The rates are Rs. 2-11-11 per candy, no distinction on this occasion having been made between selected and rejected timber.

12. A three years' *vaidah* (permit) has been recommended by Mr Müller on account of the difficulties the contractor will have to overcome in bringing out his timber, which is scattered over a jungle high up the Black River. The trees having been all specially selected and girdled by the Conservancy establishment, it was thought unnecessary in this instance to make the distinction which contracts hitherto entered into have contained, and the contractor will be paid by the candy, and have no share of any sale proceeds.

13. From our depôts, timber has been furnished to the different public departments (Bombay Dockyard, engineers of Hydrabad, Darwar, Belgam, Lingasugúr, Canara, and the Darwar factory);

but so much of it as is still unpaid for, appears in the accounts as at the depôt. Mr Müller has been led, I am sorry to find, into breaking through our forest rules, because otherwise unable to meet the sudden and enormous demands that have been made for timber. I however strongly object to this system of allowing the agents of public officers to fell timber in our jungles.

14. The people so employed are generally the very men whom we have had so much trouble in getting rid of, and who are systematic plunderers.

To return under any circumstances to a system which has cost us so much, not only in timber actually stolen, but in wanton waste, and to re-admit men into the forests who have every temptation to tamper with our establishments, is indeed a false step, and one against which I hope you will steadily set your face.

15. Dr Forbes, I see, continues to obtain his honé-wood (*Pterocarpus marsupium*) at nominal rates, and I think this should be put a stop to. Other public officers pay for the timber they take, and charge for it in their accounts, and Dr Forbes should in my opinion do so likewise. The Bombay Government manufacture and sell cotton gins below cost price, with a view to encouraging their adoption in place of the native instrument; and however praiseworthy or politic this may be, there can be no reason for our breaking through our system, the fairness of which both the Bombay and Madras Governments have admitted, when the only point gained is a reduction in the cost price of the gins at the expense of the Canara Forest revenue.

16. *Sales.*—As the contractors employed failed in delivering their timber in proper time, no coast sales have taken place; and Mr Müller having postponed the Supah and Yellapúr sales, but one of any consequence has come off. The amount realised at this auction in the Sonda tâluk was Rs. 22,465.

17. The only other points which call for comment, are depôts and roads.

18. As regards the former, Mr Müller urges, I think correctly, that depôts above the ghats must from time to time be changed according to the position of the forest being worked, and the means of communication between it and the market. He would not, therefore, go to any expense in protecting them with walls,

&c., where land carriage only is available; and experience shows that protection is unnecessary, no thefts having as yet occurred. Below the ghats, there is great reason to think that properly constructed depôts would save timber, which can at present be occasionally floated away, sunk, or otherwise disposed of, until a sale can be effected.

19. On this subject I have already been in communication with the district engineer, who will take steps, in consultation with Mr Müller, for submitting plans and estimates for your consideration and approval.

20. *Roads.*—In Supah, roads are required* not only to enable the Conservancy establishment to work the forests to advantage, but for every reason, military and political. The subject has been constantly before Government, but hitherto nothing has been done beyond the rejection of the plans and estimates sent in, on account of their extent and magnitude. I would, however, take this opportunity of again urging the propriety of making these táluk roads the subject of special sanction, as one of the best means of restoring peace and safety to the people, and securing the future advancement and prosperity of the táluk.

21. In conclusion, I have to observe, that the establishment seems altogether to be working satisfactorily. Since Mr Müller closed his account of the year's operations, a writer has been found for Mr Curry. Mr Thompson, in addition to the work performed in the Buntwal and Putur táluks, was for a short time employed in looking over the jungles in Barcur and Udipy, in which sandalwood stills are worked. Much of the jungle seems to be of little value, and is well turned to account; but the sandal-oil manufacturers have in some instances, notwithstanding all the precautions I have taken, found their way into tracts of good timber jungle. It is true, perhaps, that at present, at any rate, this jungle is from its position valueless, as it will not pay to work it, but I have taken measures to punish infringement of contracts, and to put a stop to the wasteful proceedings brought to light by Mr Thompson's visit. The amount realised during the year under report, from sandal-wood oil stills, amounts to only

* 1. Hallial to Mallapúr *viâ* Anshì Ghat; 2. Hallial to Tinny *viâ* Jugglepett.

Rs. 75; but the fact is, that, up to June 1858, the proceeds have been entered as motarfa-tax, and those to be realised under the new system have not been collected within the official year.

From Lieut. R. H. Beddome, Assistant Conservator of Forests, to H. Cleghorn, Esq., M.D., Conservator of Forests.

Coimbatore, 1*st May* 1859, *No.* 37.

1. I have the honour to forward the annual accounts of the Anamalai Forests for the official year 1858–59, duly countersigned by the collector of Coimbatore, with reference to E. M. C., 12th November 1857, No. 1153, par. 9.

2. I have experienced much difficulty throughout the season in procuring axemen, as, owing to the great demand for sleepers, many Malabar axemen, who formerly looked to our forest for work, have taken contracts with the railway company. I procured some axemen from Cochin, but I found it difficult to persuade these men to remain long in the forest. From the above cause, I have not been able to cut as much teak for the Bombay dockyard as I could have wished; 275 trees, all of very large size, have been felled in the Colongode Nûmbúdy's territory, and 44 girdled trees have been felled in the Government forest; these were dressed into 1565 pieces, and classed as follows:—

1st class,	131
2d "	137
3d "	281
Rejected,	541
Heads,	345
Butts,	130
Total,	1565

3. I was unable to cut the amount of timber (blackwood) required by the Madras gun-carriage manufactory; but as Colonel Maitland's demands were urgent, I purchased 4000 cubic feet of

it from the Colongode Nûmbûdy. This I succeeded in getting at 40 rupees per 100 kolls, all first-class planks, which, considering the market rate on the Malabar coast is now Rs. 65 per 100 kolls, I consider was purchased at a favourable rate. The cost of this timber forms an item in my annual expenditure, but will be refunded by the gun-carriage manufactory. Late in the season I felled thirty-nine blackwood trees in the Government forest, which yielded 2430 cubic feet, now stored in the forest.

4. The Malsar tribe, inhabiting the foot of the Anamalai Hills, took contracts to supply me with vella naga (*Conocarpus latifolia*) and ven-têk (*Lagerstrœmia microcarpa*), two timbers required by Colonel Maitland for the gun-carriage manufactory. They cut about 2000 cubic feet of the former and 1500 cubic feet of the latter timber. Of this, about 2000 is of the dimensions and quality required by the gun-carriage manufactory, and the remainder can be sold at the annual auction.

5. This tribe have been very useful during last season, as I could not otherwise have procured axemen for this work. The Malsars have hitherto done nothing in the forest but prepare elephant ropes from the "vaca nar" (*Sterculia villosa*), assist in the clearing of brushwood, and repair of roads, &c., for which they are paid daily hire. This season I found them willing to take contracts for the supply of the above timber, though they often would not come up to work in the forest for daily wages. I could not procure the services of any of this tribe for the usual repairs to the forest roads, and was obliged to contract for the same with the Wudders, who are an unsatisfactory tribe to deal with; they will only work by contract, and two-thirds invariably run away when they have received their advances. They also suffer more from fever than the Malsars. I had great difficulty in getting the roads repaired before the carting commenced: hitherto the Malsars have performed this work, but I could not persuade them to give their services this season. They seemed under the impression that they were not allowed to work in the forest even if they wished; and sometimes I had great difficulty in procuring the necessary supply of elephant rope from them.

6. Almost all the girdled trees were felled and trimmed this season, and Rs. 84 were spent in clearing the brushwood round the outlying timber and young saplings, to guard against fire. This amount was expended chiefly in February and March, previous to the periodical fires. No timber was lost by fire this season. I could wish to do more in the way of clearing, trimming, and protecting the young teak saplings in the forest, but the impossibility of procuring labour is an obstacle that I cannot contend against.

7. The timber slip was put into fair repair at the end of November, at the small cost of Rs. 70. These repairs only last for the slipping season, and require to be repeated each year. It is useless attempting any repairs until after the rains, as the slip is then a watercourse, and everything is swept away with heavy rain. The slipping of Bombay planks, however, need not commence until December, and logs and butts are not much damaged by the slip being out of repair.

8. The slipping of planks, &c., has this year been entirely performed by our elephants. The Malsars will never undertake this work; and the Colongode coolies, who undertook part of this work last season, lost so many of their number, and suffered so much from the fever, that they refuse to come this year.

9. I have had great annoyance and difficulty with cart contractors this season; many have left us and gone over to the railway, preferring to take work in and near Palghat to entering the forests. The advances formerly given to these cart contractors were very large. I have lessened these, never in any case giving more than Rs. 10 per cart in advance, and half of this is withheld until the carts are brought up above ghat. I have lost the services of several contractors by so doing, but the measure seemed necessary.

10. Of the planks cut this season, 885 have been carted to Mungara, 105 remain at foot of ghat, and will be carted before the end of the month.

11. I tried this year to procure coolies to float planks down the river to Ponany, thinking that thereby a saving might be made upon the contract system; all the coolies, however, are in the pay of the contractors, who have the monopoly of floating all the

timber that goes down the river. I failed in my attempts, but succeeded in getting the contractors to reduce their rates from 7 to 6 annas per plank.

12. In anticipation of Lord Harris's visit to the forests, a wooden bungalow was erected, at a cost of about seventy rupees. This amount is included in the hutting expenses. The building has proved very useful for the establishment.

13. The Kaders, who were formerly located near Tunacadavú (our forest station), have entirely left our portion of the forest, and have gone over to the Cochin territory. They state their reasons for so doing to be, that the hill produce on our side is exhausted. They pay Mr Kohlhoff, on behalf of the Cochin forests, Rs. 100 per annum for the privilege of collecting cardamoms, ginger, &c.; whereas they paid no seignorage for the hill produce collected in our forests. I regret the loss of their services as guides; but otherwise they were of no use in the forest, refusing to undertake any labour whatever. One of the tribe (Atly) has agreed to reside at Tunacadavú as a guide, receiving an increased salary.

14. There have been great changes in my office establishment during this year. Mr St Martin, head overseer, resigned his appointment. Mr Lennon, second overseer, was then at Madras, and his return to the department was at the time doubtful; so I nominated Mr Smith to the office. He suffered much from fever, and resigned immediately. Mr Lennon was afterwards appointed first overseer, and has given much satisfaction during the last working season. Mr Martin, junior, third overseer, also resigned his appointment about the middle of the working season. I procured a second overseer in Mr Eagles, and I have appointed a native to the office of third overseer. My writers and duffadar have several times been changed, the fever frightening them away; and one writer, who had been two years in the Forest Department, died from jungle fever.

15. The district engineers of Trichinopoly and Salem have indented largely for teak timber this season; the former has paid Rs. 3342 for teak logs, and the latter has received teak to the value of Rs. 2270-12-10. This timber was all supplied from logs cut in former years, and outlying in the forest. These large

demands from public offices precluded the possibility of my holding an auction during the year. I used every effort to meet them, and supplied every log that I was able to cart and slip out of the forest. I hope to hold a public auction in August or September next.

16. I greatly require the services of more elephants, but do not know where to procure them. From the Rs. 10,000 sanctioned by Government for the purchase of elephants, 4945 still remain in hand. I regret to report the death of one of our forest elephants during the past season, and also of two old decoy-elephants lent by the collector's department.

17. The services of a Foujdar to look after the elephants, and to treat them when sick, would be a great addition to the Forest establishment. I have great difficulty in procuring *mahouts* and *under-mahouts*. The pay sanctioned for the former being only five rupees *per mensem*, and for the latter only three rupees, which is less than half the salary generally given on the Malabar coast, I can only procure men of the lowest description, and they are continually running away.

18. The Waliár jungle, close to the Anamalai Hills, has been worked systematically this season by Mr Ross of the Madras Railway Co. Trees only of a certain girth have been cut. He has paid Rs. 3342 seignorage upon sleepers cut from jungle-wood in this forest. Teak and blackwood are strictly preserved.

19. A new platform to the large bridge near Colongode, over which all the timber for the Bombay Dockyard is carted, was made this season, at the cost of Rs. 179-2-9.

20. The account-current does not show the actual profit of the year, as only the sums of money which have been actually paid appear on the credit side; all wood sold and not paid for during the year appears in No. 3 Memorandum. After deducting the sum of Rs. 6,110-12-9 that has been paid for the gun-carriage manufactory, and which is being refunded to us, the expenditure of the year, including the pay of the establishment, amounts to Rs. 22,383-0-2. The amount of timber sold during the year amounts to Rs. 119,701-7-9, which gives a profit for the year of Rs. 97,318-7-7.

21. The following is a comparative statement of teak timber

supplied to the Bombay Government for dockyard purposes in the years 1857–58 and 1858–59, showing the number of planks, quantity, and class, delivered, and the amount realised in each year, the rate being determined by the collector of Malabar from the fair market value :—

For the year 1857–58.								
		Quantity.				Amount.		
No. of planks.	Class.	Kolls.	Barrels.	Visums.	Rate per 100 kolls.	Rs.	A.	P.
715	1st.	49,971	4	2½	80	39,977	1	2
572	2d.	33,503	2	14	70	23,452	4	3
1314	3d.	60,331	10	4	60	36,199	1	9
260	4th.	9,440	4	2	50	4,720	2	9
81	5th.	2,685	2	3	40	1,074	1	2
112	Inferior.	4,841	6	11½	35	1,694	8	8
3057		160,773	6	5		107,117	3	9

For the year 1858–59.									
		Quantity.				Amount.			
No. of planks.	Class.	Kolls.	Barrels.	Visums.	Rate per 100 kolls.	Rs.	A.	P.	Decrease.
748	1st.	56,107	9	3	75	42,080	8	7	Rs. 22,480-12-10.
446	2d.	25,565	10	7	65	16,617	8	6	
743	3d.	33,164	8	10	55	18,240	6	4	
229	4th.	9,345	7	14	45	4,205	6	4	
101	5th.	3,813	11	2	40	1,525	6	2	
157	Inferior.	6,557	7	1	30	1,967	3	0	
2424		134,555	6	5		84,636	6	11	

THIRD REPORT ON FOREST OPERATIONS.

From H. CLEGHORN, Esq., M.D., Conservator of Forests, to the SECRETARY to GOVERNMENT.

FORT ST GEORGE, 31*st August* 1860, *No.* 143.

SIR,—My annual tour commenced on 4th Jan. 1860, by an inspection of the sandal-wood tract in Nuggur, Mysore, and then of the railway operations in the neighbourhood of Shemoga. Afterwards I crossed into North Canara, and observed the general state of the forests in the neighbourhood of Sircy and Yellapur; then I went with Mr Müller to Hallial, and to the Sidh temple on the Belgam frontier, which has been the subject of old standing controversy. We passed down to the plateau of Gúnd, where operations are now commencing, and reached Sidashegur by boat. From this my most distant point I was summoned by Sir C. Trevelyan to meet him at Utakamand, and, *en route* to the Nilgiris, inspected the Nellambur teak plantations. I had the honour of discussing with his Excellency various questions connected with the forest management of the mountain ranges, and visited the Australian plantations, Sigúr and Mudumalai forests, part of Wainâd and Coimbatore. In July, having suffered from the effects of fever, I returned to Madras.

2. *Special Reports despatched during* 1859–60, *and dates of Orders :—*

Mem. on the Introduction of the Cinchona Trees, 30th Aug. 1859, No. 766.	G. O. 10th Sept. 1859, No. 1397.
Kunúr Teak Plantation, 27th Aug. 1859, No. 762.	G. O. 21st Sept. 1859, No. 1272.
Report on the Mudumalai Forest, 8th Aug. 1859, No. 744.	G. O. 24th Sept. 1859, No. 2293.
Report on the Malsar Farm, 15th Oct. 1859, No. 820.	G. O. 4th Nov. 1859, No. 1500.

Suitability of Gali-Paravattam Hill for Coffee, 15th Dec. 1859, No. 874.	G. O. 10th Jan. 1860, No. 73.
Second Report on the Australian Plantation near Wellington, 15th Dec. 1859, No. 877.	G. O. 20th Jan. 1860, No. 101.
The Forests and Fuel of the Nilgiri Hills, 8th Nov. 1859, No. 836.	G. O. 20th March 1860, No. 425.

3. *Pressure on Forests.*—There are many causes at work which are gradually thinning the ranks of our indigenous forests. The first, and by far the most formidable of these, is railway requirements. It is scarcely credible the many thousands of large forest trees which have been felled in the neighbourhood of the various lines of railway within the last few years. Another source of diminution, affecting only scrubby copse and minor forest, is the extension of cultivation consequent upon the reduction of the land-tax and increased facilities of communication. There is every probability that the clearing both of the forest and jungle will go on so long as grain maintains its present tempting price.

4. *Military Requirements.*—The barracks at Wellington are now nearly finished, and there has not been much pressure during the year from the gun-carriage factory or arsenals; the only special references have been with regard to materials for gun-stocks and saddletrees. The palavu-wood (*Mimusops indica*) is in large demand by the Ordnance Department for gun-stocks. Until recently it was not included among the reserved woods, and the tree accordingly was extensively cut for private purposes. Steps, however, have now been taken to prevent this wood being removed; and the collector of Tinnevelly (where the tree chiefly grows) has been requested to inform the subordinate revenue officers in his district that all private cutting of palavu is restricted. The bér tree (*Zizyphus jujuba*) is approved for saddletrees.

5. *H. M. Dockyard.*—A reference was made from the Secretary of State for India, through the Government of Bombay, as to the possibility of supplying a durable timber called *Ayni* or *Angili* (*Artocarpus hirsuta*) for the Royal Navy. The officers

in charge of the forests in Canara, Cochin, Travancore, and the collector of Malabar, were called upon for their opinions as to the size and quantity procurable in their respective districts. The report of the resident of Travancore, and all the papers connected with this subject are recorded in Pro. of Government, No. 806, dated 19th May 1860. Mr F. N. Maltby believes that 10,000 loads per annum for five years might be supplied, at the rate of Rs. 12 to 14 per candy (15⅓ cub. ft.), to the great advantage of the Travancore State. The Admiralty are looking to India for supplies of timber. If the forests of this presidency are called upon to any extent to meet the demands of the Home Government, it is evident that the conservancy of all reserved tracts must be rigorously enforced. There are many temptations to rob the forests of the young trees; and the result is, that mature timber (teak especially) is becoming everywhere more scarce.

6. *Railways.*—The Madras Railway has hitherto used to a very great extent the indigenous woods for sleepers. About thirty kinds of timber* have been tried experimentally, but the experiment has not been attended with satisfactory results—not always because the woods were worthless, but from the timber not having reached a sufficient age, and from its being used in a comparatively green state. Experience has been gained, and better prospects are dawning on the company in this great essential of railway operations. The chief engineer issued a useful

* *Revised Specification List* (1860).

1. Teak (*Tectona grandis*).
2. Sál (*Vatica robusta*).
3. Sissoo (*Dalbergia sissoo*).
4. Pedowk (*Pterocarpus indicus*).
5. Kara mardá (*Terminalia glabra*).
6. Maruthy maram (*Terminalia alata*).
7. Acha maram (*Hardwickia binata*).
8. Véngê maram (*Pterocarpus marsupium*).
9. Cadukai maram (*Terminalia chebula*).
10. Nicani maram (*Conocarpus latifolia*).
11. Sem maram (*Soymida febrifuga*).
12. Karu véngé, or Chila Wungē maram (*Acacia odoratissima*).
13. Perambê maram (*Prosopis spicegera*).
14. Erul maram (*Inga xylocarpa*).
15. Velvéngē maram. (*Vide* 18).
16. Karuvela maram (*Acacia arabica*).
17. Dud Ilupê maram (*Bassia longifolia*).
18. Katvai maram (*Acacia speciosa*).
19. Cumbadri maram.
20. Somida wood. (*Vide* 11.)
21. Arê wood.
22. Angili (*Artocarpus hirsuta*).
23. Chór kalli. (*Vide* 11.)
24. Karungalli (*Acacia sundra*).
25. Nat vadam cottê (*Terminalia catappa*).
26. Vaden Cumé (*Bignonia xylocarpa*).
27. Vella nagá (*Conocarpus latifolia*).
28. Sadachu (*Grewia tiliæfolia*).
29. Mulu véngé (*Briedelia spinosa*).
30. Ané carrar (*Garuga pinnata*).
31. Padri maram (*Bignonia chelonoides*).
32. Púvú maram (*Schleichera trijuga*).
33. Vilagam (*Feronia elephantum*).
34. Ayni. (*Vide* 22.)

circular to the officers of districts regarding the branding of sleepers, of which the following is an extract:—

"At the time of passing the sleepers, they must be branded with a letter showing the kind of wood according to the table annexed. Zinc labels will be prepared, which, being nailed to the sleeper, will remain legible even after its decay. These will not supersede the branding, but be used in addition to it."

Mr Ross, resident engineer at Palghat, is working the Chennat Nair Forest on contract, where there is a large supply of well-grown erúl (14), véngé (8), kara-mardá (5). He conducts the operations with energy and judgment. The work is occasionally inspected by myself, or the assistant in charge of the Anamalai range. Permission has also been given to the same company to obtain timber for the north-west line from the forests of Nuggur in Mysore, which have lately been placed under the care of Dr Oswald. Mr Brice, resident engineer at Bellary, met me at Hurryhur, and we concluded the arrangements with the Mysore Government. The large and extending timber trade on the Tumbhadra is forming a new and interesting feature of the country.

Teak, which is more durable than any description of fir, although prepared with creosote, and the best of all woods for sleepers, is considered by the officials of the company too expensive.

Sál, the next best, is only procurable in any quantity in Orissa. The agent of the Madras Railway has been negotiating with Messrs Binny and Co. for the purpose of procuring it from the district of Ganjam. The pyengadu of Burmah, which Lieut. Williams recommended in his letter to the chief secretary,* as a superior wood, and suitable for railway purposes, is identical with the erúl of Malabar, the jambé of Canara, and is the *Inga xylocarpa* of botanists.

Jarrah or Yarrah (*Eucalyptus rostrata*), a wood from Western Australia, was specially noticed in a despatch from Lord Stanley to this Government (9th Jan. 1859), and furnished to the agents of the railways in this presidency. This pseudo mahogany of

* E. M. C., No. 544, dated 18th Aug. 1859.

the colonists is being largely imported into Scinde and Ceylon; and Mr Acworth intimated to me that he had entered into a contract for 7000 Jarrah sleepers. It is important to watch this experiment, as the result is of the first moment, no wood having hitherto been found to resist white ants (*Termites*), combined with exposure to heat and moisture. A timber trade with Australia would benefit the colony, and supply the Indian market with a substitute for teak, which is yearly becoming more scarce and costly. The first cargo of yarrah has arrived from Swan River. Some species of *Eucalyptus* are considered half hardy in the south of England; and as there are many fine specimens on the Nilgiri Hills, and a few at Bangalore, there is reason to hope that these valuable trees may succeed on our mountain-ranges, and furnish a timber superior to any of the indigenous woods. It has recently been proposed to substitute sleepers of cast-iron for those of wood, and the plan has already been carried out on a large scale; it is thought that iron will in the end be found the most economical material for sleepers.

Trenails and Wedges.—The Indian woods which appear to be best adapted for these purposes are Kara-mardá (*Terminalia glabra*), and Sál (*Vatica robusta*); the former for trenails, the latter for wedges. Sál is a hard wood, possessed of considerable elasticity, and resists the attacks of white ants. These woods should have a second seasoning after they are manufactured, as there is a material shrinking immediately after the piece has been cut out of the log and shaped. The ends of the trenails should be dipped in tar as a precautionary measure.

7. *The Preservation of Timber.*—In an economical point of view, this subject is of the greatest importance. Railway sleepers, which ought to have stood five or six years at least, have been found useless after being laid down not more than one-third of that time; in fact, there are some parts of the Madras line where it was necessary that they should be taken up and replaced before the district itself was completed. The durability of woods is affected by a variety of causes, and their liability to rapid decay may be prevented by certain precautionary measures:—

(1.) *Season of Felling.*—The sapwood is the portion of the tree first liable to undergo fermenting changes; it is to these changes that the decay is traced, and it is therefore of the utmost importance that the tree should be felled at those seasons when it contains the smallest portion of sap; in the case of trees (teak) whose leaves are deciduous, this is indicated by the nakedness of the tree, and in evergreens by the ripening and falling of the fruit. The proportion of heart to sapwood varies* in different trees, according to the age at which they have been felled, and the soil upon which they have grown; for instance, the teak tree in Malabar differs from teak in Anamalai. In mature trees there is no sapwood, and it is one of the main objects of Conservancy that these only should be cut. There is another point in connection with the period of felling which ought to be noticed. It is a wide-spread opinion that trees should be felled during the wane of the moon. This planetary influence is open to doubt, but the opinion prevails wherever there are large forests; the woodcutters of South America act upon it, and the natives of this country believe that the timber is much more likely to decay if cut when the moon is in "crescente."

(2.) *Ringing or Girdling.*—The custom of ringing the tree before felling has been advocated, on the ground that the seasoning is thereby expedited, and also more thoroughly effected. This is doubtful, at least in oil-containing trees (as teak), but the practice appears to be contra-indicated for other reasons; when a tree has been ringed, the woodcutters object to cut it down, on account of its increased hardness; this objection might be waived, were it not for another and more serious one which has been adduced. It is believed to be a fact by some, that trees felled after girdling have the heart-shake increased. It is difficult to explain this if it be actually the case.

(3.) *Splitting.*—It is of the utmost importance that timber, in the process of seasoning, should be protected from heat, and particularly from the hot winds. The external fibres of the wood, being first exposed, contract; and as there is no corresponding shrinking of these fibres in the centre, cracks and splits are the

* As to the varying quality of cedar-wood, see Hooker and Thomson's *Flora Indica*, p. 30.

result. These detract from the value of the wood, as it cannot be applied to purposes for which otherwise it would be available. It is not always possible to obtain suitable shelter for the timber; nor is it at all times desirable that the logs should be under cover—at least they should never be so enclosed that they cannot be exposed to a free current of air. The ends are most liable to split up, and there the cracks are generally radial, but occasionally concentric. The harder the wood, the more likely is it to crack and rapidly extend. The best modes of protection are dipping the extremities of the log or sleeper in *shāni* (cow dung and water), or covering them with grease, mud, petroleum, or matting. The wood oils smeared upon timber also tend to its preservation. The piles of wood should be supported on bricks or stones, and the ground should be strewn with ashes to prevent the growth of grass orfungi.

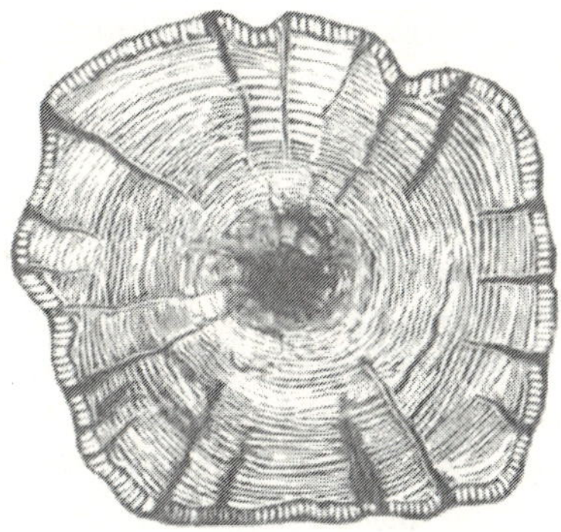

Fig. 4.
Showing Radial and Concentric Splits.

8. *Seasoning of Wood.*—Several methods have been proposed for the treatment of timber after it has been felled. It is of the utmost importance that the sap should be allowed freely to dis-

Fig. 5. Pile of Wood raised on Bricks.

solve out. Some of the modes which have been adopted are incompatible with this, and are therefore so far unsatisfactory. The object of Boucherie's process is to displace the fermentable sap by a fluid less liable to change. His method has been largely practised in France, and there favourably reported on; but subsequent experience shows that its success remains to be proved. Another fact should be mentioned, that this fluid can only be made to penetrate the softer woods, refusing to pass through hard wood, such as fully-formed oak. Reference was made to this process in last year's summary (par. 10). A full account of it is given in the Report of the Permanent Way Company in London, who have adopted this method in the preparation of railway sleepers, using for this purpose a solution of sulphate of copper. Timber, if expected to endure, must be thoroughly dried by exposure to sun and air; this desiccation may be expedited by first immersing the timber in water and then drying it in a current of air. The importance of ventilation cannot be over-estimated; in fact, there are instances where the dry-rot* has assailed beams of wood, and been arrested by allowing a free current of air to act upon it. Instead of immersing the logs in water, the practice is sometimes adopted of burying them in a dunghill. This is simply a modification of the steaming process, by which the nitrogenous matter is dissolved out.

The following modes of preserving timber may also be referred to, viz., Sir William Burnett's process and that of Mr Bethell. The former, which consists in charging the wood with a solution of chloride of zinc, appears, on the whole, to be the best and most practicable. It has been thoroughly tested in Her Majesty's dockyards, and found to withstand not only the effects of moisture, but the inroads of insects and fungi. The fact that insects and dry-rot are in this country the greatest enemies of timber, is all in favour of the chloride of zinc. Mr Bethell uses creosote, with the object of "coagulating the albumen, and preventing putrefactive decomposition." His process has been, and still is, being tested on the railway. It would be premature to

* For details of experiments and summary of this important subject, see Professor Balfour's Memoir, read at the Edinburgh Architectural Institute, April 1857.

give an opinion on this experiment; but expectation is not now so sanguine as it was some time ago. The fact is, the creosoted sleepers have of late been found decayed in the centre, the interior portion scooped out, leaving nothing but a deceptive shell, in some instances not more than half an inch in thickness. Much credit is due to Mr M'Master, resident engineer, Salem, for the careful observations which he has been making for some years, on the sleepers laid down along the districts under his charge. The result of these observations* will be interesting and important. Apart from the tendency of timber to decay from causes existing in itself, and the attacks of fungi, insects, and the like, it is said that another and very important source of destruction is the applying end to end of two kinds of wood, as, for instance, "oak to Malabar teak, or lignum vitæ; the harder of the two will decay at the point of juncture. If this be really true, it is a matter of great importance, and its truth should be established or overthrown by experiment."—*Gard. Chron.*, 30th June 1860). In summing up this subject, it ought distinctly to be borne in mind that no tree ought to be felled except those which have arrived at maturity; unless strict attention be paid to this rule, the most careful seasoning may fail, and premature decay be induced. Another error frequently committed is that of painting *green* wood for stakes, posts, and the like. The almost inevitable result of this is, that the centre is transformed into touchwood. Considerable difficulty is experienced by this department in having always the requisite amount of seasoned wood in store. It is therefore of importance that public departments should forward their indents, so as to allow sufficient time for the proper selection of the tree and due seasoning of the log.

One great advantage of careful seasoning, seldom taken into account, is, the increased facility of carriage both by land and water. Capt. Morgan calculated that the seasoned logs (teak), carried up the Sigûr Ghat to the Wellington barracks, are 25 per cent. lighter after lying two years in depôt below; this would be a material consideration in estimating the cost of the Law-

* Mr M. informs me that "decay of sleepers nearly always commences *under the chairs*; these hold water like a cup, which gradually soaks into the wood."

rence Asylum, or any other large buildings on the Nilgiris. Again, as to floating, the seasoning of the logs is indispensable; two years are required for teak and sál, and three years for blackwood.

9. *Kumari Cultivation.*—The Government have issued (23d May 1860, No. 830) definite orders on the future treatment of kumari cultivation in Canara, which is now prohibited, except in cases where the land has been so cultivated within the last twelve years. It is understood, that under no circumstances are valuable forests to be so treated. It has been shown that the system is injurious to the welfare of the wandering tribes by whom it is practised; for although kumari is itself profitable, the growers are not the gainers, the Soucars on the coast enjoying the larger share of the profits. Moreover, the cultivation is probably prejudicial in a sanitary point of view, and the ease with which a subsistence is obtained has an effect upon the people by no means conducing to enterprise and healthy development in any form. The benefits, such as they are, following this rude system of culture, are only temporary. The crop of the first year brings good returns, and the clearance may be useful to health; but the ground being abandoned after the gathering of the crop, becomes quickly overgrown with dense impenetrable scrub, more injurious to the inhabitants than the forest of lofty trees which had been destroyed. When kumari does not interfere with the growth of valuable timber as in the talúk of Bekul (where it is exhausted), the Government has exercised forbearance, and it has been allowed to continue for the present. The operations of the Malaiális on the Shevarai Hills have in like manner been restricted.

10. *Telegraph Department.*—The demand for telegraph posts is much less than it was formerly. Instead of using teak for the support of the wires, matti (*Pentaptera coriacea*) is employed in those central districts where teak is scarce, and sál in the northern division. So long as the timber was sunk in the ground, the posts were constantly damaged by the ravages of white ants; but now that a metallic socket has been supplied, the wood is safe from their attack. A further precaution is taken to preserve the lower end of the post by running liquid dammer into the metallic sheath, so that the enclosed part of the post is encased with a coating of resin.

11. *Auctions.*—The system of periodical auctions is continued. All sound timber which would otherwise be left to rot or burn is collected and disposed of in this manner. The numerous heavy indents and constant pressure on the forests disposed of most of the wood as soon as it was arranged in the depôts, so that the sales are confined to the second and third classes of timber. It is most important that this system should be continued, as, if we do not enable the people to procure wood by purchase, illicit practices will certainly spring up.

12. *Economical Working.*—In my first report, allusion was made to the system of slovenly felling and wasteful trimming which generally prevailed throughout the country. I am not able to state that these practices have been abandoned by the forest tribes, who are notoriously improvident; but wherever Government is working the forest under the supervision of their own officers, the rules laid down as to felling, squaring, and seasoning are strictly attended to. The introduction of the cross-cut saw in lieu of the rude woodman's axe made by the village blacksmith, is a source of great economy, and the use of

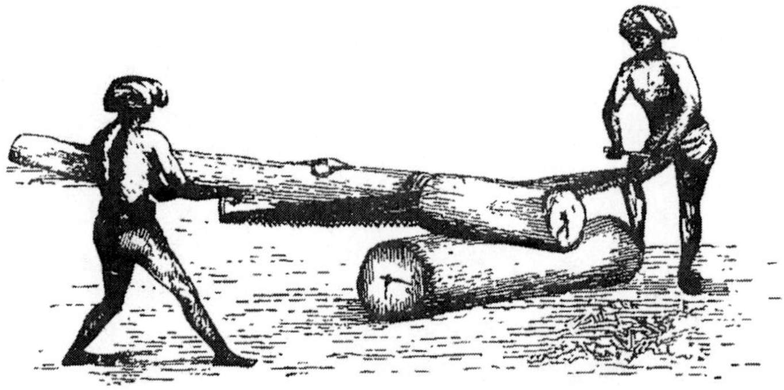

Fig. 6. Natives using the Saw.

this implement is insisted upon wherever practicable. As it is very expensive to bring gangs of trained sawyers from the towns, it is found advisable to instruct the hill tribe (Malsars and Wudders) in this occupation; and by paying ready money for the work done, a great improvement is taking place. Fig. 6 shows the method of using the cross-cut saw, which may be purchased in the shops for about Rs. 8. Planks and sleepers are now prepared for the most part by the saw instead of the axe, and a great saving of material is hereby effected.

The introduction of saw machinery was referred to in my first summary, and the opinion I then expressed, that it should be left to private enterprise, was approved of by Government. Since that time a large steam saw-mill has been in active operation at Wellington, under the superintendence of an engineer, which is indispensable. When the logs are prepared, they are placed upon carts, and carried to the inland depôt or to the rivers, as the case may be. The annexed sketch (plate I.) shows the usual way of loading a country cart with a squared beam of say 18 or 20 cubic feet. The effects of the great destruction of trees are already visible. The extravagant waste of wood in the roofing of native houses is gradually being diminished, at least in our large towns, where the increasing value of timber is distinctly felt. The manufacture of tables or other furniture from a single piece of wood is seldom seen, and materials less valuable than teak are now used for camp chairs and ammunition boxes.

13. *Noxious Insects.*—The injuries sustained by the woods and forests from the attacks of destructive insects can scarcely be estimated. Those which are best known to us as wanton and indiscriminate destroyers are the white ant (*Termites*) and the carpenter-bee (*Xylocopa*). The former attacks the timber, not only during its growth, but after it has been felled; the latter confines its ravages to the dead wood. Much good might be effected if the public servants attached to Government buildings were instructed to destroy this insect whenever it is seen by them. Several species of wood-cutter (*Xylocopa*) tunnel through the beams and posts of our public buildings, which they frequent in numbers. The passages are from 12 to 15 inches long, and more than half an inch in diameter. If the insects are numerous, their ravages are dangerously destructive, and they soon render the beam unsafe for supporting the roof. The accompanying illustration (plate II.) shows the mischief caused by the carpenter-bees in a log* of cadukai (*Terminalia chebula*). The wood appears as if pierced by an auger, and well represents the pe-

* Sixteen carpenter-bees were found in a cubic foot of wood.

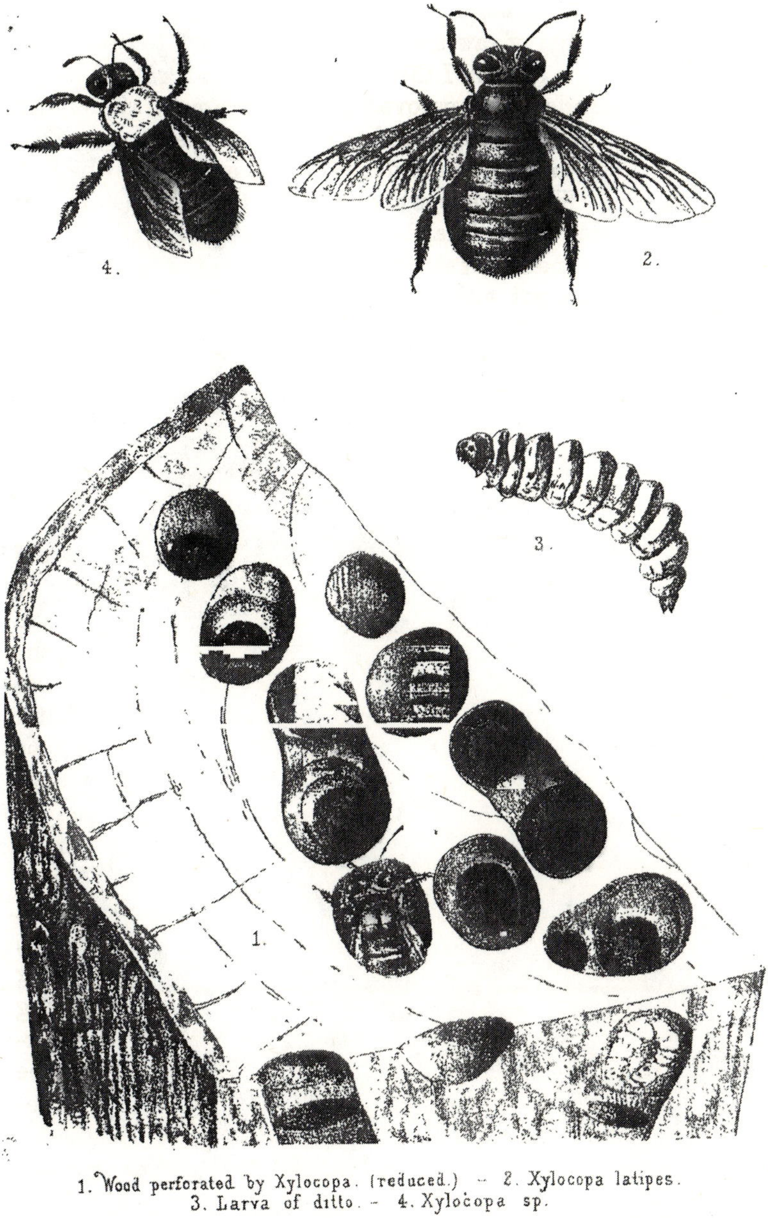

1. Wood perforated by Xylocopa. (reduced.) – 2. Xylocopa latipes.
3. Larva of ditto. – 4. Xylocopa sp.

W. H. McFarlane Lith. Edin.

culiarly injurious nature of their attacks. It would be very useful if officers in charge of buildings directed their attention to the best means of ejecting or destroying these hymenopterous insects.*

White Ants.—Numerous expedients have been suggested to arrest the ravages of white ants, all of which have been only partially successful. Some of these appeared in the Government records, and have been circulated for information.

Capt. Fraser, Bengal Engineers, mixed yellow arsenic (*hurtal*) with the paint, whitewash, and masonry of the King's Magazine, Fort-William, and the building was favourably reported upon after three years. Capt. Man and Capt. M'Pherson painted the joists and planking of several buildings at Singapore with *Gambir composition*;† the result was perfect success, although the buildings had been previously infested with white ants.

Colonel Scott, chief engineer at Bombay, records instances of timber being boiled under pressure in various antiseptic solutions with very satisfactory results;‡ but considerable apparatus is

* Useful information will be found regarding "*Insectes nuisibles*" in the "*Manuel d'Arboriculture,*" par A. Du Breuil. Paris, 1860.

† *Gambir Composition.*—Dissolve 3 pints of gambir in 12 of dammer oil over a slow fire; then stir 1 part of lime, sprinkling it over the top to prevent its coagulating and settling in a mass at the bottom; it must be well and quickly stirred. It should then be taken out of the caldron and ground down like paint on a muller till it is smooth, and afterwards returned to the pot and heated. A little oil should be added to make it tractable, and the composition can then be laid over the material. To be treated with a common brush. Against the *teredo,* I substituted the same proportion of black varnish or tar for dammer oil. I of course omitted the grinding down, which would not answer with tar.

Extract from Milburn's "Oriental Commerce," 1813.—"Gutta gambir is juice extracted from the leaves of a plant of the same name (*Uncaria Gambir*) growing in Sumatra, &c., inspissated by decoction, strained, suffered to cool and harden, and then cut into cakes of different sizes or formed into balls. Chief places of manufacture, Siak, Malacca, and Bittang. It is used by the Malays with the leaves of betel in the same manner as *Cutch* (or *Catechu*) in other parts of India. For this purpose the finest and whitest is selected; the red being stronger tasted and rank, is exported to Batavia and China for the purposes of tanning and dyeing." Gambir is now exported to England to some extent.

‡ Sulphate of copper, arsenious acid, corrosive sublimate.

necessary, and the expense forbids its use except in large public works.

Little or nothing is on record regarding the many insects which prey upon Indian forest trees. The subject is most important; they perhaps effect more injury than all the other sources of decay. The only one who has paid particular attention to this branch of science, and who is able to supply information, is Mr S. N. Ward, C.S. By means of his beautiful figures, I hope to interest the subordinates of the department in this part of practical forestry. If any meet with pieces of timber attacked by wood-boring beetles, I should be glad to receive specimens showing the burrows, especially if they contain the larvæ.

14. *Extension of System.*—I. *Ossur and Denkinakota.*—Steps have been taken towards the appointment of an overseer for the conservancy of the sandal-wood jungles in Ossur and Denkinakota. It was thought desirable to extend the system of conservancy to these forests, it being necessary to provide against the theft of the sandal trees, and to prevent the young plants from being destroyed by strong creepers which grow everywhere around. The progress of the Bangalore Branch Railway, moreover, pointed out the propriety of having a subordinate of this department, to number and register the trees available for sleepers, &c.

II. *Madura.*—In compliance with a recommendation made by His Excellency Sir C. Trevelyan, in par. 33 of his Minute, dated 8th Feb. 1860, an overseer has been appointed to the Madura Forests, to prevent the reckless cutting of timber, and to mark from year to year the trees which arrive at sufficient maturity and are fit to be felled. His attention will be particularly directed at first to the slopes of the Pulny Hills and Cumbum Valley, which are reported to contain valuable timber.

III. *Cuddapah.*—This district has hitherto been inadequately explored and conserved. It has now become necessary that the jungles there be brought under strict surveillance. The railway, which is to run through the whole length of the district, is advancing, and the demand on these forests for sleepers and other timber will soon become pressing. An efficient assistant has been appointed for this duty.

IV. *Karnúl.* The present and prospective operations of the Irrigation Company, as well as other public works, have invested the forests of the Nalla-malai Hills with considerable importance, and the attention of this department has been drawn to them by Government. A brief account of these hills by Capt. J. G. Russell was published in the *Fort S. George Gazette*, p. 1220, Dec. 1852; but it does not convey so favourable an idea of them as the reports of Capt. Rundall* and Lieut. Beckley.† Lieut. Beddome, who is an excellent explorer, has been instructed to visit these forests and arrange measures for the judicious selection of the timber.

In connection with increased attention to the forests of this presidency, I may observe that applications for our rules have been received from Ceylon, Hydrabad, and Nagpore, where forest establishments have been or are about to be organised. The Portuguese conservator in the territories of Goa is in constant co-operation with my assistant Mr Müller.

Financial Results.

Name of Forest.	Receipts by the sale of Timber, &c.			Disbursements, including the cost of Establishment and Contingent Charges.			Balance in favour of Government.		
	Rs.	A.	P.	Rs.	A.	P.	Rs.	A.	P.
Anamalai,..................	2,65,953	1	0	22,484	9	4	2,43,468	7	8
Sigúr,......................	2,593	3	6	2,147	15	3	445	4	3
Salem,.....................	29,482	6	7	4,040	6	6	25,442	0	1
North Canara, ...	2,00,767	13	1	57,664	6	10	1,43,103	6	3
South Canara, ...	8,650	11	7	1,897	11	8	6,752	15	11
Nilgiri Sholas, ...	909	14	0	50	0	6	859	13	6
Total,......	5,08,357	1	9	88,285	2	1	4,20,071	15	8
Deduct General Charges. Pay of the Conservator of Forests, establishment, contingent charges, &c., ...							21,722	12	3
Actual profit,.........							3,98,349	3	5

* Procs. Government, No. 690, 4th April 1860.
† Procs. Government, No. 1188, 18th July 1860.

15. *Financial Results.*—The accounts of the department for the past official year have been forwarded to the Board of Revenue, as directed in par. 37, No. 886, dated 18th Feb. 1860, of the Board's Proceedings, and referred to in the latter part of par. 5 of Procs. Government, No. 1021, 21st June 1860. From the preceding table it may be seen that the operations in the several forests have been financially profitable.

16. *North Canara.*—Mr Müller's report is carefully drawn up. It contains a full statement of the operations in detail, and is creditable to him. The principal portion of it will be found in App. A. Mr Müller enters fully into the effects of introducing the *Amani** system, the benefits of which are not so much seen in increase of revenue as in economy of material. In par. 13 he has given a tabular statement of the receipts and expenditure for seven years, which shows the result of conservancy from the beginning. We have still much difficulty in arranging the contracts for felling and transporting timber on account of Government, but there is less trouble in this respect than formerly. The operations in Gúnd are commenced; and, with the united efforts of Capt. Walker, the district engineer, and Mr Müller, I have no doubt they will be successfully carried out. I may here state, that as regards Government forest on the Malabar coast, it is chiefly from the plateau of Gúnd that we look to meet the prospective demands of Her Majesty's navy. In the adjoining territory of Goa, the cultivators formerly cut down all trees indiscriminately, but of late years a very strict conservancy has been kept up; there is an officer specially appointed to the purpose, who frequently meets Mr Müller on the frontier. I have the great satisfaction of knowing that the collector of this district takes a deep interest in forest management, and co-operates cordially with Mr Müller in the extensive operations now in progress.

17. *South Canara.*—As Canara is now divided, the S. Forests require separate notice. These are under the charge of Mr E. Thompson, overseer, generally stationed at Pútúr, who forwards his reports through the collector, and is in frequent communi-

* Government determining what shall be cut and what shall be sold.

W H M'Farlane, Lith' Edin'

TEAK

TIMBER SLIP.

cation with him. Mr Fraser the collector's report on forest revenue is in App. B. The suggestion made in par. 3, regarding the supply of fuel to sandal stills, met with my entire concurrence, and the system has been altered. These oil merchants now stand on the same footing as the other people. A large contract has been entered into for the supply of Mangalore with wood from Sulia. It will probably be necessary to strengthen Mr Thompson's hands, by granting him a small permanent establishment.

18. *Anamalai Range.*—Lieut. Beddome's report of the working of this fine reserved forest forms App. C. The first point specially calling for remark is the unusually large income, which, as explained in my last year's Report (par. 14), arises from the value of timber sold in 1858–59 being included along with that of 1859–60. It will be observed, that the wood sold to the Bombay Government for naval purposes is much smaller in 1859–60 than in 1858–59. Again, the timber sold to the agents of the Madras and Great Southern of India Railway Cos. is much larger than in previous years. The trees felled comprehended various kinds of the better indigenous trees, as well as teak and blackwood. Owing to the extreme difficulty of obtaining axemen and sawyers, all available hands being engaged at remunerative rates by the Railway Co., there was much less timber felled than usual. The attention of the establishment was directed to the removal of old outlying timber scattered about in the forests. The dragging of this to the* slip by elephants was an important work, and has much reduced the list of "wood unaccounted for." After careful inquiry, the rate of cart hire above ghat has been increased 20 per cent.; this was unavoidable. The Malsar farm was abolished (G. O., 4th Nov. 1859, No. 1500); and the wild denizens of the forest are now under instruction in sawing and carpentry. They are not yet skilled workmen, but they are improving, and their labour is of immense value to us; being indigenous, they enjoy comparative immunity from the diseases incident to casual residents in that trying

* The formation of a ghat in lieu of the rude timber slip (Plate III.) has been entered in the budget, and will greatly facilitate the operations of the department.

climate. The commencement of a teak plantation has been made; the great difficulty is the want of labour, which is much to be regretted, as the soil and climate are peculiarly favourable to the growth of teak: another hindrance is the abundance of wild animals, which occasions the necessity of strongly fencing the nursery. One of the peons has been thoroughly instructed in teak sowing at Nellambúr. It is proposed that the superintendent of this range should visit the neighbouring hills during the non-working season, removing any ripe trees at Pumachi, visiting the Palghat and Waliar jungles, and making arrangements for the periodical cutting of the sandal trees in Collegal.

19. *Sigúr.*—This forest had been held in contract for three years by Hussain Baba, whose lease expired last year (*vide* p. 36), when the forest came under the management of this department, and is now carefully supervised by Capt. Morgan, whose report forms App. D. The sale of jungle timber and sandal-wood has, as predicted, "covered the expenses, and yielded a profit." The young teak trees are growing well; and if the increase of cultivation in this valley does not materially encroach upon the forest, there will be a sufficient supply of moderate scantling for Utakamand in future years. The depôt at Sawyers' village was well stocked when I inspected it a few months ago. As a general rule, we deliver at the depôts; but in this case, the position below ghat is unfavourable for auction sales, which answer better at Utakamand; consequently, the arrangements for transporting the timber fall upon Capt. Morgan.

20. *Mudumalai.*—This forest, rented by Government from the Raja of Nellambúr, is also under the charge of Capt. Morgan; an abstract of the operations forms App. E. During the past year, 37,602 cubic feet in the log have been delivered at Wellington, in addition to a large quantity of wrought timber from Gundelpett workshop, supplied to the barracks. The account-current of the operations passed through the D. P. W., as the expenses have been paid out of the barrack estimates. It is proposed that, during the remainder of the lease (three years), the forest shall be worked by Capt. Morgan on account of Government, and the timber stored at Sawyers' village till required for

the Lawrence Asylum and other* public buildings about to be erected at Utakamand. Periodical sales for the benefit of the community will take place.

21. *Salem.*—A brief report of the operations of this district will be found in App. F.

The proceeds consist of two items—seignorage for sleepers supplied to the Railway Co., amounting to Rs. 23,471-10-0; and seignorage for house-building material taken by wood-merchants at R. 1 per cart load, which realised Rs. 6,010.

The great pressure for railway sleepers is nearly over in this central province, and we have now to consider matured arrangements for the ordinary demands which may be expected. A statement is annexed, showing the number of sleepers delivered during the year in the Salem district, and the trees furnishing them, as far as it has been possible to ascertain them. Considering the difficulty of getting accurate information from native contractors, this return cannot be considered absolutely correct, but it is sufficiently so to enable us to deduce some useful results:—

No.	Native Name.	Botanical Name.	Total.
1	Pillé marda	Terminalia	34,260
2	Maruti	Terminalia alata	26,717
3	Vella naga	Conocarpus latifolia	25,092
4	Véngé	Pterocarpus marsupium	18,960
5	Kar marda	Terminalia glabra	18,502
6	Cadukai	Terminalia chebula	16,132
7	Sadachu	Grewia tiliæfolia	11,138
8	Cumbadri	. . . .	9,405
9	Acha	Hardwickia binata	8,064
10	Eriuvalu	Inga xylocarpa †	7,657
11	Dud ilúpé	Bassia longifolia	7,101
		Carry forward,	183,028

* A church, penitentiary, and soldiers' rest-house have been sanctioned.

† The number of trees furnishing sleepers is not so large as this list indicates: 10 and 27 are *Inga xylocarpa;* 5 and 24 are the same *Terminalia;* 7 seems to be identical with 49; 3 and 21 are *Conocarpus latifolia;* 22 and 39 are *Soymida febrifuga.*

No.	Native Name.	Botanical Name.	Total.
		Brought forward,	183,028
12	Kátvai	Acacia speciosa	7,054
13	Sál	Vatica robusta	6,540
14	Aré	. . . . .	4,860
15	Ané kurrer	Garuga pinnata	4,453
16	Pádrí	Bignonia chelonoides	3,317
17	Karu-véngé	Acacia odoratissima	2,651
18	Pedowk	Pterocarpus Indicus	2,615
19	Ilupé	Bassia	2,463
20	Chella wúngé	Acacia odoratissima	2,411
21	Nicani	Conocarpus latifolia	2,254
22	Sem	Soymida febrifuga	2,215
23	Vel-véngé	Acacia speciosa	2,108
24	Kala marda	Terminalia	1,974
25	Karen-galli	Acacia sundra	1,922
26	Marda	Terminalia	1,851
27	Erúl	Inga xylocarpa	1,856
28	Perumbé	Prosopis spicigera	1,471
29	Nát vaaddam cotté	Terminalia catappa	1,395
30	Puvu	Schleichera trijuga	1,353
31	Karúvalem	Acacia Arabica	1,264
32	Mullu-vengê	Briedelia spinosa	1,212
33	Sissú	Dalbergia sissoo	1,182
34	Valagum	Feronia elephantum	1,108
35	Chórkalli	Chloroxylon Swietenia	675
36	Palai	Mimusops hexandra	669
37	Ték	Tectona grandis	659
38	Nir marda	Terminalia	241
39	Somida	Soymida febrifuga	225
40	Karen-tumbi	Diospyros	203
41	Jallari	Vatica laccifera	116
42	Kurkutta	Zizyphus glabrata	92
43	Yella cadukai	Terminalia	84
44	Athì	. . . . .	80
45	Angili	Artocarpus hirsuta	50
46	Valé	. . . . .	26
47	Miladi	. . . . .	20
48	Coné	Cassia fistula	18
49	Chittacha	(Vide 7)	14
50	Vadur cumé	Bignonia xylocarpa	10
51	Tumbi	Diospyros ebenaster	3
		Total,	245,742

It will be seen, that by far the largest number of sleepers are obtained from trees of the genera *Terminalia* and *Conocarpus*, natural family *Combretaceæ*, remarkable for the height and size of their trunks, and the toughness of their timber; their durability under ground has not been altogether satisfactory, and the Cadukai (*T. chebula*) especially appears to be liable both to the attacks of fungi and of the carpenter-bee, and ought to be excluded from the specification list.

The *Leguminosæ* are next in importance, the trees supplying the wood being *Pterocarpus* (Véngé), *Inga* (Erúl), *Hardwickia* (Acha), and various species of *Acacia*. Well grown timber of these kinds is deservedly prized by the engineers. As the native name frequently applies to a genus rather than to a species, it is very doubtful whether those marked Sál and Pedowk are really the true species, although obtained from trees belonging to the genera *Vatica* and *Pterocarpus*. The railway engineers generally have most confidence in Sál, Ilúpé, Kar-marda, Véngé, Chella wungé; teak being too expensive for general use as sleepers.

22. *Nilgiri Shólas.*—The increasing wants of the hill stations, the requirements of the Wellington barracks, and the assignments to settlers,* have drawn attention to the necessity of conserving the remaining woods on the Nilgiri Hills. The subject is treated of at length in the records noted below. The establishment for supervising the forests on the plateau consists of the following:—

Utakamand, ...	2 Overseers.	7 Peons.
Kunúr, ...	1 "	0 "

These are about to be placed under the charge of an assistant conservator.

The rules approved by Government as applicable to Utakamand are—

(1.) The whole of the shólas, or woods, in the neighbourhood of the station to be absolutely reserved, not only for their beauty, but also from fear of injuring the water springs; their limits to be marked; no private cutters to be allowed inside; old trees to be felled by servants of the department, and brought outside, and to be sold there by public auction. Trees to be planted where required, in vacant spaces.

* G. O., No. 425, 20th March 1860; G. O., No. 1161, 13th July 1860.

(2.) Suitable woods, at a distance from the station, to be selected and marked out in lots of moderate size; and a number of these lots, amply sufficient for a year's supply, to be put up to auction annually. The contractor to be permitted to clear the ground entirely within his lot or lots, with the exception of such trees as may be marked by the Conservancy Department previously to the sale.

(3.) The cleared lots to be planted, as required, by the Conservancy Department.

(4.) No private felling of any kind, or for any person, to be allowed in woods or on land belonging to Government.

23. *Teak.*—Teak scantling of large size is becoming more and more scarce all along the west coast. The fact is, in Malabar, *first-class logs* are not easily procurable. This dearth has led to the employment of other indigenous woods, which previously were in little or no demand. In the railway department, much as teak is valued, it is found to be too expensive* for many

* To show how much the supply has diminished, and the price risen, I give an extract from Milburn's *Oriental Commerce*, 1813, vol. i., p. 328:—

"In the year 1799, 10,000 teak trees were brought down Beypur River. This was the produce of several years; but it was estimated, that from 2000 to 3000 trees may be annually procured.

"Teak timber, of an ordinary quality for ship-building, sells at 9 or 10 rupees a candy, which measures 15¾ English cubical feet; the foot, therefore, costs from 1s. 6d. to 2s. Choice timber sells as high as Rs. 16 a candy, or 1s. 10d. a cubical foot. Bombay is generally supplied with teak plank from this part of the coast. The Company usually contract for what they require, and the resident at Cochin frequently has the contract. The following are the prices at which the Bombay Government was supplied in 1800:—

1st sort,	40 to 50 ft. long.	14 to 16 in. square.	Rs. 14 to 16 per candy.
2d do.	35 to 40 do.	12 to 14 do.	10 to 12 do. do.
3d do.	22 to 35 do.	12 to 14 do.	9 to 10 do. do.
Plank from 1 to 5 borels thick,		. . .	Rs. 30 per 100 guz.

"This was of the first quality, the plank of the usual length, and free from rents. Notwithstanding the coast of Malabar may be considered the storehouse for Bombay, yet the demand for teak timber has so much increased, that within three or four years large quantities have been imported from Rangoon."

purposes to which it was formerly applied; and, as is stated in another part of this summary, par. 8, experiments are now being made with the view of securing suitable and less expensive substitutes. In the building of private houses, the same difficulty is experienced, and builders are having recourse to *Véngé*, *Karmarda*, and the like. Whilst there is a great want of large teak logs, there is no lack of small beams and poles.

24. *Teak Plantations.*—The increasing demand for woods available for Government purposes, renders it of the utmost importance that the various plantations should be carefully watched and conserved, especially now that the Home Government is looking in this direction to supply her dockyards. The largest and most valuable forests are reserved for the purposes of Government; and measures have been adopted not only to prevent inroads upon them with the axe and conflagration, but to watch the growth of the plants, and provide against their being choked by the undergrowth which springs up around them. The most important are the "Conolly Plantations." These young forests have been specially referred to in both of my preceding annual summaries (pp. 10 and 41), and their value to the State will every year become more perceptible. Hitherto they have been a source of expense; but last year the returns for the first time exceeded the expense of their maintenance:—

Expenditure, 1859–60, ...	Rs. 3493-0-6
Income, ...	5165-2-9
	Rs. 1672-2-3

Situated as these plantations are on the banks of the Nellambúr River, the value of the timber is enhanced by the fact that it is so easily transported, while the Malabar forests are so much exhausted. The forest is of such importance, and at such a critical period in its history, that I would recommend that, in the absence of the Conservator, the collector of the district should periodically visit it, and take measures to secure a strict adherence to the regulations laid down regarding it. This course appears to be indicated all the more by the circumstance that the plantation in question was originated by a collector in the district. These forests are situated in the Ernad táluk. Their extent has not as yet been definitely ascertained; it has, indeed, been proximately stated, but it is of the utmost importance that they be carefully surveyed. At present the survey of Wainād is going forward; and as at certain seasons of the year it is, I understand, difficult to proceed with it, on account of sanitary considerations, I would earnestly urge that such intervals be employed for determining exactly their extent, as well as the leases of land set apart for planting puposes. There is one interesting feature of these plantations which ought to be stated. They are now made use of as training schools, where the planting system there followed is taught to subordinates, who are gradually introduced into it. One of these thus taught has been deputed to the Anamalai forests, one to N. Canara, and two to Mysore.

25. *Average Growth of Teak.*—A knowledge of the rate of growth is the basis of all our systems. We are groping in the dark so long as we are without knowledge on this point. The scale which at present guides our operations is:—

10	years' growth,	1 ft.	6 in.	at 6 feet	from ground.
22	do.	3	0	do.	do.
37	do.	4	6	do.	do.
62	do.	6	0	do.	do.
93	do.	7	6	do.	do.

The above figures are taken from a memorandum of Dr Brandis, Conservator of Forests in Pegu, and accords very much with my own observation.

26. *Blackwood.*—Blackwood seedlings have been planted, to the number of several thousands, in N. Canara and the Nuggur district of Mysore. This wood is largely used in the manufacture of furniture at Bombay, &c. The price has been rising for some years, and it is now nearly the same as that of teak.

27. *Australian Plantations.**—The progress of these plantations having been detailed in a separate report (G. O. No. 101, 20th Jan. 1860), I need only state, that Overseer Hall performs his duty efficiently. I have reason to believe, that the object of supplying the Wellington barracks with fuel will be fulfilled. An additional sanction of Rs. 2500 was made by Government

* *Vide ante*, p. 40.

towards an extension* of these plantations. The work is advancing; but meanwhile it would be premature to report further upon it. It is worthy of remark, that the pests of our plantations *below* ghat are, white ants, spotted deer, and wild hogs; whilst *above* devastations are committed, perhaps to a greater extent, by rats, hares, porcupines, grubs, and frost.†

Rats.—The Nilgiri rat (*Mus providens*, W. Elliot), is a serious enemy, working underground, eating across the tap-root, and continuing its devastations after the young plant is safe from frost and hares.

Frost.—The frost, during certain months of the year, is detrimental to the young trees situated in the low lying swampy ground of the hills, but it seldom affects those planted on the slopes. As a general rule, it ceases to act injuriously after the plant has completed the second year. The sign of the young tree being frost-bitten, is a patch or ring of softened and discoloured bark, with fissures, usually an inch or two above ground, and the leaves dropping off.

Hares.—The hares, in the clear moonlight nights, nibble off the leading shoots, returning again and again until the plant's development is seriously checked, giving it a dwarfed and unseemly aspect. After the young trees, however, have attained a height of about two feet above ground, they cease to be a temptation to the hares; but other causes of anxiety and sources of injury now present themselves.

Grubs.—Various kinds of grubs assail the tender plant; some of them entering from below, pierce into the heart-wood, and continue their excavations upwards. Many precautions have been taken to render the plantations secure from these sources of injury, with some degree of advantage. The most successful mode of dealing with rats, is that of depositing phosphorus pills‡ at the entrance of their holes. The formula is furnished in Ure's "Dictionary of

* A consignment of Jarrah seed is expected from Australia.

† The natural enemies of forest trees in Sind are described by Mr N. A. Dalzell in his able Report 1858–9.

‡ "Hog's lard, ground cocoa-nut, and phosphorus, form the most certain bait and poison combined."—(Baker's "Ceylon," p. 109.) Care must be taken in mixing the phosphorus, of which very little suffices.

Arts, Manufactures, and Mines," and is certainly superior to any expedient hitherto adopted to get rid of the nuisance in question.

Overcrowding.—The error of crowding the trees too closely when planted, and subsequently of neglecting to thin them after they have shot up, cannot be too strongly insisted upon. Planting operations elsewhere have suffered, and in certain instances have utterly failed, from the neglect of pruning and thinning;* and trees, which otherwise might have developed into first-class timber, have choked each other—the closeness of growth preventing a free circulation of air and an adequate supply of nutriment to the individual plants.

28. *Distribution of Tree Seeds.*—It is a principle acted on in the department, to send seeds to those quarters where their growth is probable, and their possession would be esteemed an acquisition. This principle is specially regarded in those instances where we have received consignments from distant quarters. The reciprocity of favours operates beneficially, both in a scientific and economic point of view. While this is the case, individuals who thus transmit seeds should use discretion in selecting such species as are likely to prosper in their new habitats. In the course of the year, seeds have been despatched to Scinde, Hongkong, Melbourne, and Sydney.

29. *Avenues.*—(A.) District engineers have generally nurseries for raising shady trees, which have in several places been planted with good effect along the trunk roads. A few weeks ago, the district engineer of Coimbatore sent three selected labourers to be instructed at the Australian plantation, in the planting, pruning, and trimming of trees. Bungalow sepoys ought, I think, to be charged with the care and watering of the trees in the compounds of Dâk bungalows, and the same condition might apply to servants in charge of other public buildings, as choultries, soldiers' rest-houses, &c.

(B.) *Madras.*—It is admitted to be better to grow trees from seedlings than from branches. The former method is slower, and requires more watching and watering, but the trees last much longer and are more symmetrical. It is of the utmost importance that the trees planted be under careful supervision,

* See Dr Falconer's Report on "Teak Plantations in Bengal," in Records of Bengal Government.

otherwise it will be impossible to ensure their healthy development, and the main objects of the avenue, ornament and shelter, will be lost. It is desirable, therefore, that such measures be adopted as will be most likely to secure these objects. Some progress has indeed been made in this direction; the planting of certain portions of the public roads having been placed under skilled superintendence. A few of the principal avenues in Madras, adjacent to the Horticultural Gardens, are under the care of Mr Brown, and the growth of various trees suitable for avenues will be carefully watched by him. At Utakamand, the planting of the highways has had a similar advantageous beginning, the road from Utakamand to Wellington being under the immediate superintendence of Mr W. G. M'Ivor, while the margin of the lake, and the planting of the former station generally, is under the Local Improvement Committee.

(C.) *Districts.*—It is my opinion, after travelling through the greater part of the Presidency, that, as a general rule, the avenues of each district should be placed under the collector. The reasons are, that engineers are tempted to lop and otherwise injure the trees when they are engaged on works in the neighbourhood; and this, in addition to the immediate damage sustained, operates badly upon the natives as an example, and therefore renders conservancy under such circumstances difficult. Besides, the P. W. D. complain that their establishment is insufficient for the permanent management of the avenues; and as it is not desirable to divide responsibility, the plan which most commends itself appears to be the reverting to the former system. The collector also has great influence over the villagers, and has subordinates in every village.

(D.) *Canal Banks.*—The Godavery and Kistna channel banks have been carefully planted by the officers in charge, and this should be carried out along all the ramifications. The Irrigation and Canal Co. are desirous of commencing the same good work, and introducing useful trees at once. The agent of that corporation is now in correspondence with this office, how to conduct the general method of planting, through the medium of the canal officers. The proposal of planting the canal banks is highly to be commended, and the expense will be amply repaid by the increasing value of the timber.

(E.) *Railways*—The Railway Cos. have on several instances applied to the different public gardens for a large number of young trees, so that I presume they intend to plant both along the lines and near to the stations; this measure will tend to the comfort of travellers, and ensure a partial supply of fuel and sleepers.

30. *Firewood.*—The consumption of firewood has always been great, inasmuch as it is essential to cooking, and in particular districts the supply has been described by writers as barely sufficient; but the question of supply is one which is now pressing more urgently on the attention of all the district authorities. In connection with the progress of railways and the undertaking of large public works, the scarcity of fuel is severely felt, and my attention is drawn to it *everywhere*. The *bonâ fide* ryot is understood to have a prescriptive right to the fuel and leaf manure required for his house and field, and an abundant supply of these is obviously beneficial, enabling him to apply the dung of his cattle to fertilize his lands. The large towns are supplied with firewood by persons who purchase annually at auction; the contract for cutting certain portions of the neighbouring jungle, and the apportioning of woodlands, is made with reference to the period when it will reproduce itself. The contractors are allowed to remove, under regulations, the low bushes and less valuable kinds of trees. A list of reserved trees is published in the district gazettes, and hung up at the tahsildar's cutcherry. It is customary to cut the wood into billets of 3 or 4 feet in length, which are split into two or four pieces, according to the diameter, and carried to market, where such billets are retailed and delivered at the door. The price varies exceedingly in different districts and at different seasons; but I may mention that the average has risen about 25 per cent. in most of the large towns within a few years. This is the fuel used for cooking by Europeans and a large proportion of the native population, who also use bratties* made of cow dung. In Bellary and other barren districts, the firewood chiefly consists of branches of thorny

* Bratties, pidacalu, *Tel.*—cow-dung cakes dried in the sun; the dung is frequently mixed with earth and the husk of paddy. This fuel is much used for burning bricks and chunam, also for heating iron tyres of wheels,

bushes, there being almost a total absence of forest trees. In such localities, the cost of conveyance, and the difficulty of procuring wood, is in some cases excessive. Small poles are not to be obtained even for the rafters of huts; the lower fallen leaves of the American aloe come into great use as a substitute for fuel, for which it is not well adapted, containing little combustible matter. The seignorage on firewood varies in different districts;* and the general regulations also differ with reference to the natural supply of fuel, which is more or less abundant all over the country. After watching the effect of the local rules, which are to a certain extent experimental, we will be able, I hope, hereafter, to generalise principles, and to arrange the management of fuel—charcoal and bamboos—upon something like a uniform system. In illustration of what is doing in this respect, I have inserted in App. H. the rules of the Coimbatore district, finally passed by the Board of Revenue, the collector, and myself. An addition has yet to be made in regard to charcoal.

Peat.—On the Nilgiri Hills, turf fuel is now used more than formerly, and it is very desirable that this economical material should be utilized as much as possible, so as to lessen the demand for wood and charcoal. The peat of the Nilgiris is different from that of Europe, as regards the producing plants. Several specimens were lately forwarded to Dr Percy, School of Mines, London, for analysis. The only other sample which has been submitted to chemical examination, so far as I know, was brought from Thibet by Dr Falconer.

31. *Charcoal.*—This subject was alluded to in last year's summary; it is one of great importance, and again demands special notice. There is great necessity for insisting on the strictest

for which purposes it answers well. When thoroughly ignited, the heat given out is intense. It is in general use among natives, being more economical than any other fuel.

* Trichinopoly, 4 ans. per cart load of about 750 pounds.

Coimbatore,	5	do.	do.	do.
Bellary,	4	do.	do.	do.
South Arcot,	4	do.	do.	do.
Utakamand,	8	do.	do.	do. (cut by the department).

economy in the preparation of charcoal; as it is, the native workers have recourse in its manufacture to measures which are at once rude and extravagant.* In various parts of the country there are slight differences in the mode of preparation; but all are faulty and objectionable in an economical point of view. The branches selected for charring are generally those of large, valuable hard-wood trees, which are left to decay. Teak, blackwood, and erul, being always preferred when there is a choice; the charcoal-burners, however, are strictly prohibited from appropriating timber of this description, and are only permitted to use the branches when the trees have been felled for another purpose. Various trees, however, are preferred, depending on the purposes to which the charcoal is to be applied.† Measures have been adopted towards the instruction of some of the hill tribes in the art of economical burning, the principal error being in allowing the process‡ to be performed in the open air instead of in closed kilns. Charcoal is an article of considerable consumption in the towns, especially at Utakamand, and the certainty of a future supply is attended with some anxiety. It has been proposed to levy a seignorage of one anna upon the piled parah, and this seems reasonable.

32. *Bamboos.*—The demand for the bamboo will always be very great. Enormous quantities are brought to the presidency by railway, so that the jungles close to the line are rapidly being exhausted. It seems, therefore, advisable that some measures be taken to regulate the cutting, as has lately been done in the case of fuel. The propriety of this may be perceived by the fact, that while in one district they disappear, in the adjoining collectorate there is frequently a superabundant supply. Throughout Canara, there is a uniform tax of 8 annas per hundred; and I am of opinion, that a similar impost might be made with ad-

* Wall's Report on the Silver and Lead Ores of Karnul, in G. O., No 1040, 27th July 1858.

† Bark charcoal, used by Dhobees. Gunpowder do., small shrubs or herbs, as *Vitex negundo* and *Cajanus Indicus;* also Madar, *Calotropis gigantea*, and *Parkinsonia aculeata*. Charcoal for iron foundries: for this large pieces of hard wood are preferred, as those already mentioned.

‡ Circular, No. 10 in App. explains the proper mode of manufacture.

vantage in other districts, except in certain localities where, for sanitary considerations, the thinning of the jungles should be encouraged. The immersion of bamboos in water, and especially in a solution of sulphate of iron (Anabédi *Tel.*), or in lime-water, is attended with the best results. The sweet sap is thereby extracted, which, if allowed to remain, induces rapid decay. When it is intended to split the bamboos for reepers, this should be done before they are steeped in the metallic bath. The coast merchants prefer bamboos which have been months in the water attached to rafts, these are "*water seasoned*" by being floated to the sea-shore down the Nellambur and Sidashegur rivers. The bamboos are often 18 yards long, and are brought down in immense floats, tied together in bundles of fifty by the root ends, which are turned towards the forepart of the float.*

33. *Fancy Woods.*—The forests of S. India contain a great variety of woods which may properly come under this head; but the markets of Europe are so distant, and the cost of freight is so heavy, that few are exported to England and France, save ebony, rosewood (or blackwood), satinwood, and saudalwood. Occasionally beautiful specimens may be seen, equal to anything ever made up into furniture in England.

Ebony is chiefly obtained from Coorg and Canara (various species of *Diospyros*), and is of a superior description, being jet black in colour. Smaller pieces are procured from Cuddapa, Salem, Nuggur, &c., but there is no steady demand, though it is a peculiarly fine timber for cabinet work, and some of it is well veined for ornament.

Satinwood.—I have seen very fine satinwood at Cotaputty, in the Tengrikota táluk of Salem. I fear that a good deal of the oldest and best was destroyed by the railway contractors; but this locality is evidently suited for the development of the tree, and I hope that it may yield a supply for the gun carriage factory, where the wood is used for naves of wheels. The timber sells at nearly the same price as teak and blackwood, and is employed

* Teak, sál, blackwood, &c., improve by lying in water, or in the soft black mud of an estuary; there is one exception, viz., heddé (Manjé cadambé), *Nauclea cordifolia*, which deteriorates from steeping, and should be carted to its destination.

F 2

by cabinetmakers. It is singular that this tree was not conserved under the native Government, whilst teak, blackwood, and sandalwood were rigidly protected. Here it is proper to observe, that we possess a very limited knowledge of the fancy woods; I believe that several varieties were displayed at the Madras exhibitions, which, if better known in Europe, would be largely employed, as high prices would be given, covering the expense of transport. Their value, doubtless, will yearly increase, as they become better known to foreign timber-merchants.

34. *Dyewood.—Sappan-tree.* Some efforts have been made to extend the growth of this plant, by sowing the seeds on the banks of the Sidashegur river. A packet likewise was forwarded to Scinde for trial on the banks of the Indus. Nearly all the straight pieces are sent to England, and the crooked roots to China, the latter, undoubtedly, produce more dye in proportion.

35. *Cinchona.*—An attempt some time ago made to introduce this invaluable plant into India failed. The Calisaya plants brought by Mr Fortune died on their way from Calcutta to Darjiling. The success of the Dutch in Java has been very encouraging; and if the efforts about to be made in this presidency are attended with similar success, no ordinary benefit will accrue to the country. The great expense of quinine, and the rapid disappearing of cinchona trees in S. America, renders such an experiment of the utmost interest and importance.* The arrangements made by Mr Markham for the transmission of the plants from Peru to this country have been completed, and appear to be judicious. Taking advantage of the experience and success of the Dutch in Java, a careful comparison has been made between the soil and temperature in which the cinchonas have thriven there, and the climate and geological conditions of various parts of the W. Ghats. There are certain important points connected with the growth of this plant, as the rain-fall, of which we are ignorant; but, so far as our knowledge extends, sites have been proposed, so as to correspond as nearly as possible with the soil and climate of the Java plantations. The preparatory steps necessary for the safe transport of Mr Markham's collection from Calicut or Madras to the Nilgiris, have been taken

* Dr Hooker brought this important matter before the Linnean Society.

(G. O., No. 1220, 18th Aug. 1860), and Mr. W. G. M'Ivor selected for preparing sites, and carrying out the preliminary work. The conduct of the Dutch in raising cuttings, and protecting them from the direct rays of the sun, has been noted, and, if necessary, their example will be followed. At present, the experiment is to be confined to Ceylon and the Nilgiris, a few plants being entrusted to Mr Hall at Kunur, and Mr New at Bangalore, who will watch their progress in his conservatory.

36. *Tea.*—Southern India promises well to afford favourable sites for the growth of tea (G. O., No. 1425, 24th August 1860). Numerous experiments have been made, and attended in several instances with marked success, as regards the healthy growth of the plant. In order, however, to complete the experiment, and allow the tea grown in the presidency to occupy its proper place in the market, it is necessary that the art of manufacturing it should be introduced, either direct from China or from Government plantations in the N.W. Provinces. Unless something of this kind be done, tea grown in S. India cannot attain that commercial value which it might probably acquire were it generously taken up. The tea shrub is remarkable for its hardiness; and the cultivation extends over a great breadth of latitude. It prefers a climate where the mean temperature is from 67° to 73°. This valuable plant may be seen at several places on the Nilgiri and Pulny hills, in Coorg, on the hill sanatarium of Nundidroog, on the Shevarai and Bababúden Hills, at Curtallum, and in various parts of Travancore. Although tea plants have been introduced, and are growing at each of these localities, they are not all equally promising; and the place in the market which any of them is to occupy has not yet been ascertained, and cannot be so until the introduction of competent manipulation completes the experiment.*

37. *Coffee.*—Applications for forest land are numerous. The settlers usually select localities in heavy jungle, which are in the immediate neighbourhood of trunk roads; and if the timber appears to be valuable, the collector refers the application to this office for an opinion. It is of the utmost importance that no

* See Sir C. Wood's Despatch, 31st Oct. 1860.

encroachments should take place; boundary lines and trenches ought in every instance to be carefully laid down, so as to avoid subsequent misunderstanding. The Government is establishing rules, which will enable every one clearly to understand the exact limits of his property, and what penalties are incurred if they are trespassed.

38. *Potato.*—It is of great importance that the cultivation of the potato be carefully attended to, and soils best adapted for its healthy and vigorous growth selected. In Bengal, for the last six or seven years, this esculent has been deteriorating; and it was found necessary to apply (Pro. Board of Rev., 7th May 1859) to this presidency for a supply of seed potatoes, the tubers being larger, firmer, and of better flavour on our mountain ranges than in the Sikkim Himalayas. The cultivation is rapidly increasing in Mysore and on the Nilgiris, and the demand for them is not confined to the European, although at first they are not relished by the natives, in a short time the taste is developed, and they are prized, not only because they are palatable and nutritious, but because they are profitable.

39. *Progress of the Department.*—At the close of this Report, it may not be out of place to draw attention to the fact, that since this department was instituted, three years ago, many changes have occurred, and the field of operation has gone beyond the original scheme. In this way difficulties have sprung up which could not have been anticipated, and defects, therefore, can be pointed out which, while matter of regret, are only the natural consequences of circumstances beyond our control. The establishment is now too limited to embrace all the duties which at present devolve upon it. The extent of country to be conserved is out of proportion to the means placed at the disposal of the department for its protection. Originally, it was not contemplated that we should organise a police establishment, as it was understood that the forests would be under the same protection as other public property. The number* of sanctioned peons is quite inadequate, and the forests, consequently, are only partially protected. It was not expected that the police should enter the

* Fifty-three permanent for the whole presidency.

forests, and extend their surveillance to the growing trees; but it seems only reasonable that when the timber has been felled, marked, and taken out of the forests, the Mofussil police should restrain theft, and that they should report any transgression of the forest rules coming within their knowledge, in the same way as they would warn a householder of the insecurity of his premises, or the vicinity of robbers, and so forth. It is only this *general* care that I seek; and if it be not extended to Government timber as to other property, public and private, the necessary result must be a considerable increase to my watching establishments.

40. *Forest Assistants.*—I have reason to be satisfied with the exertions of my assistants. During my absence, Lieut. Beddome has been nominated* to act for me, and Capt. Brine, who conducted the operations in the Paumbem channel, succeeds to the charge of the Anamalai range. In a separate letter, I have recommended that the valuable teak forest on the confines of Wainád should be placed under Capt. Gib; and I hope that this arrangement will take place immediately. The range will extend from the border of Coorg to Gundelpett. One great want of the department is, an additional assistant, who, while learning his duty, could afford useful aid, and afterwards be competent to fill any unexpected vacancy (such as those which have occurred this year). Two hundred rupees staff salary would be sufficient. The advantage of a trained assistant on emergency is self-evident.

41. *Overseers.*—There is still great difficulty in obtaining the services of robust men, possessing all the requisite qualifications indicated in previous reports. If the sanctioned amount allowed for the department had not been expended, I would have recommended the location of overseers at Karnúl, Kotagiri, &c.

42. *Exploring Tours.*—During the past three years, annual tours of about nine months' duration have been made, during which a very large portion of the presidency has been traversed, and all the more important forests have been to some extent explored. Considerable additions have been made to our knowledge of the interesting and important region of the Anamalais and confines of Travancore, by a second exploring tour of Lieut.

* G. O., 17th August 1860.

Beddome, the report of which has already been* published. The sál forests of Gumsúr were visited by me in the early part of last year, and an extract from my diary is contained in App. G. When Mr Beddome has visited the Nalla-malai range in Karnúl, there will remain no extensive tracts of importance wholly unexplored. The further examination of these will be undertaken as circumstances permit.

43. *Selections from the Forest Records.*—The Government have lately sanctioned the reprinting, in a portable form, of a selection from the miscellaneous reports on various subjects connected with the vegetable kingdom, which have been printed in loose sheets during the last few years. For some of these, inquiries are frequently made at this office, and, being scattered through Government records of various years, they are not easily referred to. I hope to pass this compilation through the press during my leave to England.

44. *Public Gardens.*—There has been no change in the superintendence of the three public gardens which, as usual, have formed the subject of separate† reports. That for Utakamand has been recorded in G. O., No. 323, 15th March 1859, and G. O., No. 781, 15th May 1860.

Return of Plants, Seeds, &c., sold at the Government Gardens.

Gardens.	1858-59.					1859-60.						
	Fruit Trees and Shrubs.	Timber Trees.	Shrubs and Flowers.	Parcel of Seeds.	Total.	Fruit Trees and Shrubs.	Timber Trees.	Shrubs and Flowers.	Parcel of Seeds.	Total.	Decrease.	Increase
Madras, . .	71	740	1566	133	2,510	69	821	2781	109	3,780	...	1,270
Bangalore, .	77	9	588	305	979	918	114	519	527	2,078	...	1,099
Utakamand,	287	3350	4376	170	8,183	1336	12,892	2613	170	17,011	...	8,828
Total, . .	435	4099	6530	608	11,672	2323	13,827	5913	806	22,869	...	11,197

* G O., No. 956, 9th June 1860.

† The Annual Report of the Lál Bágh, Bangalore, is forwarded to the Commissioner of Mysore, and that of the Hort. Soc. Gardens, Madras, is published by the committee of management.

The preceding tabular statement is a return of all the plants and packets of seeds sold and distributed during the two last years. The aggregate amount in each institution is considerably increased.

45. *Manual of Indian Botany.*—I know of no book more wanted: there are many inquiries for such a guide amongst the increasing number of Europeans who come out to this country. The characters of the *genera* of plants should be abridged, and the economic uses introduced, of which our knowledge was much increased by the successive Madras exhibitions. The work should be printed in small type,* so as to form a book of easy carriage and convenient reference. I have occupied myself during occasional leisure hours in preparing a manual of this kind, as directed in G. O., No. 767, 10th June 1857. But as the duties devolving upon me increased, the time available for this collateral occupation has unavoidably diminished. I take home the materials, and hope to progress with the work.

46. *Herbarium and Library.*—The department is now so developed as to render it of importance that a herbarium and library for reference be established and attached to the office. Already a nucleus of both of these is in existence, and it only remains that they be fully recognised, and such measures adopted as will render them of real and permanent use to the department. It is believed that, by judicious arrangements, considerable additions might be made from time to time both to the library and herbarium. Important contributions are periodically received from Sir W. Hooker, Director, Royal Gardens, Kew, from Dr Thomson, Calcutta, and regular communication is kept up with other centres of influence. A few purchases would now be advantageous, and I propose seeking permission to make them as occasion arises.

47. *Office Establishment.*—The duties have been carefully performed by native surgeon F. Appávu, who has laboured well to get the accounts into a proper system. The utmost simplicity

* The series of colonial floras, commenced under the auspices of Government, promises to be extremely valuable, and it is hoped will extend to the Indian empire. The *Flora Capensis* and *Flora Hongkongensis* form good models for future operations.

compatible with accuracy is necessary in the financial arrangements, as writers and accountants cannot be persuaded to remain in the forests, and the system existing previous to the formation of the department was very defective.

H. CLEGHORN,
Conservator of Forests.

APPENDIX (A).

NORTH CANARA.

I have the honour to submit my Annual Report, with the accounts enclosed for the official year 1859–60.

2. The collector having furnished the account-current up to 31st Dec. 1859, I have only to submit the accounts for the remaining portion of the official year.

3. For the purpose of bringing the operations of the entire year under one view, I have drawn up another account-current from 1st May 1859 to 30th April 1860. In this all the items belonging to S. Canara, entered before the division of the district, are thrown out.

4. This account shows an income of Rs.200,767, with an expenditure, including the cost of the fixed establishment, of Rs.57,664, thus leaving a profit of Rs.143,103.

5. *Memorandum of Wood unaccounted for.*—This exhibits the logs in store last year, the subsequent supply and disposal with stock on hand. Last year the estimated value of timber in store was Rs.110,771–12–0; while now there is a balance valued at Rs.132,767, exceeding the former by Rs.21,996. This difference is not caused by putting a higher value on the timber, but by having a greater quantity in store.

6. I beg to offer some remarks about forest operations in particular. In doing this, I shall try to compare the works, establishment, and income and expense of previous years with those at present.

7. It has been customary to review forest operations under two heads, viz., *Amani* and Contract works. Strictly speaking, all works are *amani*, or all works are done by contract, which means, every one is paid for cutting, squaring, carting (or floating below ghats) by measurement. The only difference is, that the contracts above ghat (where all timber is carted) are small, lasting for a few months; whereas those below ghat are large, extending over several years, and must therefore be reviewed separately.

8. There has been an increase of work, which necessarily entailed an increase of the establishment. Previous to introducing the system of working the jungles ourselves, and selling the timber at regular depôts by public auction, the establishment had only to mark trees in the jungles, which were sold standing in large lots. After the contractors squared the logs, the establishment had to stamp them, and to look after the contractor's works. This was easy, and much of it was done by peons. Now, trees are cut for Government by contractors. They are first marked, and when the logs are cut and squared, they have to be numbered, measured, and carted to depôts. At the depôts they are sold, delivered, and stamped. For the time being, additional hands are required, called "Temporary Establishment."

9. The following table shows the work of the establishment, leaving the large contracts out of the question :—

Táluks.	No. of Trees cut.	Contents.					Brought to Depôt.					Remaining in Forest.				
		Logs.	Can.	Qr.	G.	T.	Logs.	Can.	Qr.	G.	T.	Logs	Can.	Qr.	G.	T.
Ankóla,	200	452	535	1	3	19	284	284	0	3	13	168	251	1	0	6
Yellapúr,	3696	7,490	10,128	2	3	12	7,087	9,296	1	2	16	403	832	1	0	16
Sundah,	3191	6,433	6,381	2	2	16	63,73	6,293	2	3	9	60	87	3	4	7
	7087	14,375	16,047	3	0	7	13,744	15,874	0	4	18	631	1171	2	0	9

It thus appears that 7087 trees were cut, and 15,874 candies carted to depôts under the superintendence of the establishment. Add to these 1571 logs, containing 1426 candies of old fallen teak and jungle-wood, collected now at the depôts, we have a grand total of 17,300 candies of work begun and finished during the year.

10. By comparing the receipts and expenditure of the last seven years, as per table below, it might be inferred that the system in operation during the last three years does not show much difference, and even what it shows might be said to be in favour of the old system.

Official Year.	Receipts.			Expenditure.			Remarks.
1853–54,	144,235	4	9	50,370	9	0	Under the Old system.
1854–55,	85,014	5	7	37,310	6	8	
1855–56,	150,609	8	0	32,647	8	4	
1856–57,	160,639	6	4	44,490	15	1	
1857–58,	70,656	10	7	22,869	3	2	Under the New system.
1858–59,	100,604	10	9	34,325	7	9	
1859–60,	206,683	7	8	56,959	14	3	

11. This falling off (except for the year under report) is not due to the system, but to our contractors not bringing timber to the coast in 1857 and 1858. Consequently, below the ghats the receipts and expenditure were less; but above, the change of system told immediately. The subjoined table, in which the revenue is divided for the upper and lower táluks will exhibit this :—

Official Year.	Receipts in North Canara.						South Canara.			Total.		
	Upper Táluks.			Lower Táluks.								
1853–54,	29,368	8	9	114,866	12	0	...	...	...	114,235	4	9
1854–55,	12,913	1	7	64,990	6	0	7110	14	0	85,014	5	7
1855–56,	19,050	15	8	129,369	13	4	2188	11	0	150,609	8	0
1856–57,	7,242	10	2	152,016	9	0	1380	3	2	160,639	6	4
1857–58,	13,265	6	2	55,208	7	11	2182	12	6	70,656	10	7
1858–59,	59,756	2	6	35,569	13	4	5278	10	11	100,604	10	9
1859–60,	147,348	7	0	59,335	0	8	...	...	...	206,683	7	8

It appears that the revenue in the upper táluks, previous to introducing the *amani* system, was very small, and that the greater part was derived from the coast sales, &c.

12. The *amani* system above ghat may be said to have been in fair operation during the last three years. The profits of a year's work are always shown in the year following. So we have for the work

Of 1857 the revenue in 1858, . .	Rs. 59,756
Of 1858 the revenue in 1859, . .	147,348
Of 1859 we have stock on hand for about	87,592

The average revenue from the upper forests for the four years from 1853–54 to 1856–57 is little more than Rs. 14,668, while the average of the last three years (excluding the value of stock on hand) is Rs. 73,490, or five times greater.

13. The higher receipts are not the only benefit of the new system; there is also less waste of timber. On looking over the old accounts, it appears that about 20,000 trees annually were sold to contractors. The highest price obtained was R. 1¼, and the lowest only As. 2 per tree. The trees then cut were either small, or if large, only the finest logs were taken, and the rest of the wood was left to burn; now we cut all that is useful, and collect the odds and ends also.

14. As remarked above, the receipts have fallen off in the lower táluks, because the contractors either entirely or partially failed to bring timber in time. What we had was principally defective or small, and therefore the deliveries to the Bombay Dockyard have much fallen off. In former years, from Rs. 60,000 to Rs. 100,000 worth of timber was selected; but during the last two years the value of selected teak did not amount to Rs. 30,000, and this year only to Rs. 10,000.

15. Now as Gúnd is opened up, we shall get large and fine timber in future, and the Bombay Government, instead of going into the market, may obtain their requirements from our depôts

16. The average receipts from the upper and lower forests having been given, I beg to analyse the expenditure in the same manner.

The following table shows, that in the four years previous to the introduction of the *amani* works there was very little expense, while all the heavy items were incurred below ghat. The expenditure bears a fair proportion to the receipts. Above ghat it has been increasing in the same ratio as the receipts. On the coast the expenditure decreased, as also the revenue, caused by the failure of contractors.

Official Year.	Expenditure in North Canara.						South Canara.			Total.		
	Upper Forests.			Lower Forests.								
	Rs.	A.	P.	Rs.	A.	P.	Rs.	A.	P.	Rs.	A.	P.
1853–54,	1,899	4	10	48,471	4	2	...	...	...	50,370	9	0
1854–55,	3,075	6	9	34,017	15	4	217	0	7	37,310	6	8
1855–56,	3,371	2	8	29,276	5	8	...	...	...	32,647	8	4
1856–57,	3,614	15	4	40,875	15	9	...	...	...	44,490	15	1
1857–58,	12,560	4	3	10,000	2	0	208	8	0	22,869	3	2
1858–59,	24,956	14	3	8,305	10	6	900	15	7	34,325	7	9
1859–60,	40,965	0	4	17,974	13	11	...	...	...	56,959	14	3

This table also shows that averages struck over the seven years mislead; but if the comparison be made between the year previous to and that after the jungles were worked by Government, it gives a correct result.

Average expenditure in the upper forests of first four years, Rs.	2,990
Average expenditure of last three years, ...	26.160

In the table of receipts, the average revenue for four years was, ...	Rs. 14,668
Do. expense, do. do. as above,	2,990
Profit,	Rs. 11,678

If the same be calculated for the three years under the new system, the result is:—

Average receipts for last three years, ...	Rs. 73,490
Do. expense do. do. as above, .	26,160
Profit,	Rs. 47,330

—exceeding the former profit by Rs. 35,652 annually. By comparing the work done in the above seven years, it appears that, in those years when business prospered above ghat, the contractors below did not bring timber; and in those years when the contractors worked well, the *amani* system was not introduced.

Assuming, however, that the works above and below the ghats go on satisfactorily, the higher average of the expenditure of both must be taken to arrive at an approximate estimate for future years, thus :—

Average expenditure above ghat, under the *amani* system,	Rs. 26,160
Do. do. below ghat, when contractors have done their work, ...	33,172
Total average, .	Rs. 59,332

On the other hand, the average receipts of those years may safely be taken as below :—

Average receipts on the coast, when contractors brought timber, ...	Rs. 115,310
Do. do. above ghat, under the *amani* system, .	73,490
Total, . . .	Rs. 188,800
Deduct expenditure,	59,332
Average annual profit,	Rs. 129,468

17. *Sandal-wood*, cut and prepared in Bilgy and Súndà táluks, was sold for Rs. 7824-9-1. There is about the same quantity cut and stored at Sircy, which will be prepared into billets during the monsoon, when the establishment has less work. I did not show this in the memorandum of wood unaccounted for, as the quantity now at Sircy is only roughly cut, and can neither be measured nor weighed.

18. *Reckanasta, or stunted Teak and Jungle-wood.*—Last year we had 10,300 pieces, containing 2400 candies; sold for Rs. 3382. This year we have 12,846 pieces, containing 3695 candies, which will be disposed of next season. Jungle places taken for permanent cultivation are chiefly in Yellapúr táluk, where 77 spots (area 1031 acres) have been cleared, at a cost of Rs. 698-10-0. Besides the proceeds of the wood, these places will henceforth yield annually Rs. 1306-12-6 in land revenue.

19. *Seignorage Account.*—This shows an income of Rs. 4700-10-2, chiefly collected from villagers at 8 As. per tree. In táluks where there is no establishment, extra hands are required for this, and seignorage *Gúmastahs* on Rs. 5, are appointed for the fair season.

Inland, the *Patells* superintend the cutting according to the permits, and get a fee of 1 anna* for each tree marked.

20. *Bamboos* pay a seignorage of As. 8 per 100 throughout. There are three items in the account-current. Taking the first only, viz. bamboos to villagers, it is shown that they have paid Rs. 868-7-0 for an article which was formerly free. This amount is collected from the villagers on the frontier, or from persons living in towns, as ryots, who live in the jungles, do not pay for bamboos used in building their huts.

21. *Firewood Account.*—If compared with previous years, this shows a decrease of income. It is, however, only apparently so. Above ghat, we received nothing at all. The Darwar forests were thrown open (of which the *Desais* or *Inamdars*, who had some forests on their *inams*, chiefly availed themselves), and so no one required this article from us. The Darwar forests being now closed again, it is likely that next season there will be calls for firewood.

22. *Billet-cutting* from the kanagalu† trees was stopped last year, but 6284 defective jungle trees, of 43 kinds, in six jungles, were marked and sold by auction in six lots. In the aggregate, Rs. 1715 were realised. The purchasers were permitted to cut the wood in any shape they pleased, but have to pay, besides the jungle *darkhast*, As. 2 additional for every candy of wood used for building purposes, and As. 12 for every ton of firewood. Two years were granted for the work. There are now cut 5928 pieces, containing 2706¾ candies, and 124,000 billets of firewood, the produce of 5191 trees. The result is :—

5191 trees cost, ...	Rs. 1406	11	0
2706¾ candies at As. 2, . . .	338	5	0
124,000 billets of firewood, about 372 tons,	279	0	0
	Rs. 2024	0	0, or As. 6¼ per tree.

The benefit consists not only in getting a small value for wood

* This experiment was agreed upon by the collector, sub-collector, and myself, which Mr J. D. Robinson has reported as working well.

† *Dillenia pentagyna.* This tree is in great request by the Bombay merchants, from the wood splitting easily.

formerly thought useless, but in saving the good trees, especially the kanagalu, now nearly extirpated. The result is a profit, but also an additional work for the establishment.

23. I have marked 5000 defective jungle trees for next season; but the present lot is somewhat better, containing some good trees. They will be disposed of in the same manner as before.

24. *Contracts and Contractors.*—The present state of the works of each contractor is as follows:—

(1.) *Messrs Brice and Co.'s* contract for 2500 jungle trees for railway sleepers ended 31st Dec. 1859. The forest work was finished within the prescribed time, but the sleepers have not yet been exported. The seignorage due has been paid.

(2.) *Pondshenwi*, for conveying 3747 teak trees from the Sunksal jungles to Gungawalli, had two years for the work, ending 31st March last. Of 6217 logs delivered to contractors, he brought 3065 within the stipulated time. The balance (3151 logs) remain to be brought. Considering the large number of logs to be conveyed from the ghats to the coast in two seasons, and the otherwise satisfactory working of the contract, I recommended an extension of time till Feb. 1861, before which the logs can be easily brought down, being now collected near the river ready for floating.

(3.) *Vishwanatha.*—Contractor for conveying 2000 jungle trees from Sulagiri to Sedashigur. Two years of the three granted for the work have passed without a single log arriving at the depôt. In my last report, I stated that this work was in a backward state. This is now more obvious, and the prospect of the contract being fulfilled is much diminished. However, the contractor assures me that he will not fail to bring the whole next season.

(4.) *Mr Pinto*, contractor for 2000 teak and blackwood trees fromthe lower parts of Gúnd, has his work in an advanced state. He has now collected 2102 logs, of which 502 have arrived at Sedashigur.

(5.) *Venktesha Prabhu's* contract for Shivapur teak has been annulled, and the remaining logs in the forest (2268) have been given to a new contractor, Mr Pinto. Two years, ending 31st March 1862, are granted for the completion of the work.

The terms of Venktesha Prabhu's contract were :—

For selected, .	Rs. 2-6-7 per candy.—	For rejected,	As. 2-7
Mr Pinto's terms are,	2-5-9 do.	Do. .	2-8
Decrease, . . .	0-0-10 Pie.	Increase, .	0-1 Pie.

From this it would appear that the present terms are lower. Considering, however, that 775 logs were in the Kalanadi, and about 400 are nearly brought down to the foot of the Shivapur Ghat, on which the new contractor will have less expense, the terms are in reality higher. The above 775 logs have arrived at the depôt.

25. *Teak Planting* has been stopped from want of funds; 7000 seedlings were raised last year. The expense was rather high, considering the small number of seedlings; however, the same number now will, I hope, not cost half of what they came to last year.

The planter Abreo* has returned from Nellambúr plantation. Want of funds precluded me from spending money in preparing ground for seedlings. The time has now passed, and the work on a larger scale is necessarily deferred to next year.

26. *The present Establishment* numbers fifty-one persons, exclusive of those in my office, and are classed as under :—

Establishment.	Overseers and Subs.	Mutsadis and Gúmastahs.	Peons.	Total.
Fixed or sanctioned,	3	10	16	39
Temporary, .	0	0	12	12
Total......	3	10	28	51

Temporary hands are not included, as they are required for a few months only; whereas the above are engaged throughout the year. The statement of wood unaccounted for shows, that about 48,000 candies of timber were taken from the depôts during the year. Besides, there have been at least 20,000 logs numbered, measured, and stamped, including stunted teak, defective jungle-

* Having been fully instructed at the Conolly plantation, I trust that he will introduce the system successfully and economically.—H. C.

wood, and fragments which cannot be exhibited in the memorandum. We have now eleven depôts in four tâluks; considering that one peon is required to watch the timber, eleven men are thus employed. On the coast (Sedashigur and Gungawalli), one man at each place is scarcely enough, as there, during the night, continual attempts are made to steal teak, which is easily floated off to outlying pattimars. From this it is obvious, that the establishment is small compared with the work. Sickness has reduced the effective strength of the forest establishment. During the year, sometimes nearly half were laid up with fever, and one man died of it. The same was the case with workmen; several died of cholera at Kulgi, and those who were unaffected ran away. Of 190 coolies at Kaneri, 35 were sick for a long period. I am thankful to state, that my health has been very good during the whole year.

S. Müller,
Assist. Conservator of Forests.

Sedashigur, 24*th May* 1860.

Note.—This report conveys some idea of the extensive operations in N. Canara, which, from *three* visits of inspection, I can testify require great physical exertions and incessant vigilance. Allowance must be made for Mr Müller's difficulty of writing in a foreign language.—H. C.

APPENDIX (B.)

SOUTH CANARA.

The annual report on forest revenue being now due, I have the honour to forward an account-current, showing the transactions of the S. Canara collectorate during the past official year 1859–60.

The forest revenue in this district is a mere trifle as compared with that of N. Canara; and no remarks are necessary on the items comprising it for the year under review, save that for sandalwood stills. The increase in this item over the revenue of last year, is due to the whole rent being credited to forest revenue, instead of as before to Mótarfa. I think the present mode of supplying the workers of these stills with firewood is a mistaken one. Instead of assigning to each still a certain area of forest, I would make them purchase their firewood at the same rate as other parties do. They are nearly all Mangalore merchants, who make the oil for export to Bombay; and I do not think they are entitled to any special privileges in the way of firewood. Any additional cost in the preparation of oil, by putting the supply of firewood required in its manufacture on a proper footing, will fall on the consumers, who are well* able to pay the charge, as the article is a luxury, not a necessary.

Mr Thompson, the overseer, has addressed me on the subject of renting out to contractors the privilege of cutting in the Government jungles, and transporting by water from Bantwal, firewood for use in Mangalore. I think this is a most advisable proceeding,† and I shall endeavour to get contracts, as the town is now mostly dependent for this necessary on Bekal. A supply from Bantwal will lower the present market price, which is high.

I beg to forward a receipt, to show that the whole of the revenue borne by the account-current has been duly credited to Government in the year under report.

J. FRASER, *Collector*.

MANGALORE, 14*th June* 1860.

APPENDIX (C.)

ANAMALAI RANGE.

I have the honour to forward the annual accounts of the Anamalai Forest for the official year 1859–60, countersigned by the collector of Coimbatore, according to E. M. C., 12th Nov. 1857, No. 1153, par. 9.

* The collector's suggestion was at once adopted.—H. C.

† A contract has been given, the trees being first marked in the Sulia Jungle by Mr Thompson.—H. C.

Cleghorn's Forests of S. India

W. H. M'Farlane Lith' Edin'

I. FORESTS.

2. The two first items on the credit side are for timber sold in 1858 and 1859 to the Bombay Dockyard. The next item, viz. Rs. 52,657-1-0 is for the teak planks cut last season, and which I handed over to the dockyard agent last February. In addition to this, the sum of Rs. 15,033-0-7 has been realised during the year by the sale of timber at public auction, and by private sales to the P. Works and Railway Departments. These sums added together give the amount of Rs. 67,690-1-7 as the receipts of the year, whilst the expenditure has been Rs. 12,592-12-9 exclusive of the pay of the establishment, which amounts to Rs. 9891-12-7 making in all an expenditure of Rs. 22,484-9-4

3. Owing to the impossibility of procuring many axemen in the past season, very little timber has been felled; this, however, has been advantageous in one way; it enabled me to employ the elephants in getting out much of the old timber lying about the forests. The sum of Rs. 15,001-0-11, above alluded to, has chiefly been realised by the sale of logs, heads, and butts, that have long been outlying in the forest. In addition, an enormous amount of seasoned logs have been brought to the head of the timber slip, and to the various depôts at the sides of the cart road, including all the large logs that were outlying between the cart road and the bungalow station of Tunacadavú.

4. Regarding the items on the expenditure side of the account, I have to mention that the rate of cart hire above ghat this season has been increased from Rs. 2 to Rs. 2-8-0 per plank; the particulars of all these items have been reported from time to time in my monthly reports, and I have nothing further to add respecting them. The Malsars have commenced sawing in the forest this season; they are as yet rough at the work and irregular in their attendance. I hope, however, to induce some of them to become permanent sawyers. They are, as you are aware, a wild, unmanageable race; and when they have earned a few rupees, they generally refuse all work until they have spent them.

5. A peon has been trained to planting at Nellambúr, and I hope to commence the formation of a small teak plantation immediately. The want of labour will be my chief difficulty.

6. Memorandum No. 2 has been carefully prepared as regards

the timber remaining in the forests; there is not much now outlying in the jungles. 129 logs and heads are all that we could find in the dry season after the fires had bared the forest; these have all been stamped, numbered, and brought to account in this memorandum.

Comparative Statement of Teak Timber supplied to Bombay Government for Dockyard purposes, in the years 1858–59 *and* 1859–60, *showing the quantity and class delivered, and the amount realised in each year, the rates being determined by the Collector of Malabar from the market valuation.*

For the year 1858–59.									For the year 1859–60.									
No. of Planks.	Class.	Quantity.			Rate per 100 Kolls.	Amount.			No. of Planks.	Class.	Quantity.			Rate per 100 Kolls.	Amount.			Decrease.
		Kolls.	B.	V.		Rs.	A.	P.			Kolls.	B.	V.		Rs.	A.	P.	
748	1st	56,107	9	3	75	42,080	8	7	311	1st	22,301	9	6	100	22,301	12	6	31,979–5–11 Rupees.
446	2d	25,565	10	7	65	16,617	8	6	226	2d	13,069	8	6	90	11,762	11	7	
743	3d	33,164	8	10	55	18,240	6	4	305	3d	13,713	11	14	80	10,971	3	0	
229	4th	9,345	7	14	45	4,205	6	4	81	4th	3,115	1	1	75	2,336	5	0	
101	5th	3,813	11	2	40	1,525	6	2	23	5th	750	3	2	70	525	2	11	
157	Infer.	6,557	7	1	30	1,967	3	0	242	Infer.	11,899	8	6	40	4,759	14	0	
2424		134,555	6	5		84,636	6	11	1188		64,849	6	3		52,657	1	0	

R. H. BEDDOME, Lieut.,
Asst. Conservator of Forests.

COIMBATORE, 1st *May* 1860.

Note on paragraph 5.—It is worthy of remark that teak-planting seems now to be forced upon us; the demand is increasing, while the supply is diminishing. For instance, the Dutch governor Van Rheede records of the *Tectona grandis*, in the *Hortus Malabaricus*, 1690, "*Ingens arbor usque ad Calicolam.*" In the present day, nothing but scrubby stumpshoots are to be seen within three stages of Calicut, indeed till we reach Mombat, and these are the reproduction of a former growth, natural to the country, and which will, with care, again become of importance.—H. C.

D Hamilton, del^t TEAK PENTAPTERA BAMBOO

THE ASS^T CONSERVATOR

APPENDIX (D).

SIGUR FOREST.

In May 1859, a sanction of Rs. 50 per month was granted by Government for the conservation and working of Sigûr Forest. (G. O., No. 668). With this sum, amounting to Rs. 450 (in nine months), and the sale of timber and sandal-wood, the following results have been obtained. Rs. 1000 have been remitted to the accountant-general, Rs. 100–10–11 is the balance of cash in hand, and the timber on the ground may be valued at Rs. 4000. With so small a sum as Rs. 50 to commence with, it was some time before any wood could be collected. By an early sale of sandal wood, the means for working the forest on a larger scale were obtained; and next year, if wood be carted to Ūtakamand, I have no doubt but that a sale of Rs. 10,000 worth might be effected.

Carriage of Timber.—At present, the great drawback is the carriage of the timber. Parties who purchase timber from the depôt at Masnikovil find themselves without the means of conveying it away; consequently, the number of purchasers is very limited; the sales of teak and vénge for eight months only realizing Rs. 457–1–6.

Timber Felling.—The operations in the forest have been chiefly confined to the felling of ripe teak trees and vênge.* The trees are felled in November, December, and January, when the tree is wintering; during the rising of the sap in March, April, May, and June, the *kurumbars*† square the felled trees. During the remaining five months, the men are employed in felling the trees after the fall of the moon, when the sap descends, and when the sap is ascending, they square the felled logs. By this order the timber seasons well and readily. There are but fifteen kurumbars and five pairs of buffaloes working in the forest at present. If the sale of timber be increased, I propose to enlarge the establishment.

Steam Saw-Mill.—The works at Wellington Barracks being nearly finished, I strongly recommend that the steam saw-mill

* *Pterocarpus marsupium*, L.

† A wild forest tribe.

now working there be removed *to Utakamand and made over to the Mudumalai and Sigúr Forests. The great drawback to the sale of timber on the Nilgiris is the want of sawyers. If the timber were sawn in Utakamand, the P. W. D. there could be readily supplied, and the surplus sawn timber disposed of by auction.

Sandal Wood.—The sandal wood cutting is proceeding regularly. A large number of the trees cut are decayed and fetch little in the market; if these trees had been cut in their prime, much loss would have been avoided. I propose a regular cutting of all trees which have made heart-wood and show signs of decay in their tops. The value of the sandal-wood is decreased some twenty or thirty per cent. by heart-shake. The stealing of sandal-wood† by Mapilas is now suppressed; the vigilant measures pursued in Malabar and Mysore have contributed to this end.

W. R. MORGAN, Captain,
In charge of Sigúr Forest.

UTAKAMAND, 30*th April* 1860.

APPENDIX (E).

MUDUMALAI FOREST.

Supply of Wood.—During the past year, the supply of wood delivered at Wellington has amounted to 41,079 cubic feet; this contrasts favourably with the former year, when the supply was only 13,279 cubic feet, owing to my having been removed from the forest and another officer placed in charge. In addition, 6244¾ cubic feet of wrought timber from Gundalpet workshop were delivered at Wellington. If this wrought timber had not been required, the delivery from the forest would have amounted to nearly 60,000 cubic feet, the carriage having been diverted to Gundalpet workshop.

Roads.—The forest roads have been much improved from

* The removal of the steam-saw-mill, as suggested, may hereafter be advisable, but the services of an engineer would be indispensable.—H. C.

† The suppression of the illicit trade in sandal-wood is highly satisfactory.—H. C.

Tippúkadú to Karúr Hill. A road has been made 13 miles long, with branch roads to Goganalla, Nardi, and other parallel valleys; in all, 21 miles in length. The road near the Karkhana passes over the bund of a tank with two *calingulas* bridged. The formation of this tank was of great benefit, securing a supply of good water in the hot weather to the people and cattle of the establishment. The bund makes a good road where formerly an impassable swamp existed, which cut off all communication with the best parts of the forest.

Kurumbars.—The number of kurumbars has increased. When I commenced felling in the forest, there were eight men; there are now 110 men steadily at work.

Sawyers.—Fever and death have terribly thinned the sawyers. There are now five sets; there should be at least ten; consequently there are many logs which cannot possibly be moved until they are sawn.

Elephants.—The elephants now working in the forest are five in number. We had six, but one died in August, owing to the severity of the monsoon; and the others were so affected by the weather that it became necessary to send them to Gundalpet for a time.

Buffaloes.—I have increased the number of buffaloes to 25 pairs, and by feeding them on grain in the hot weather, they are in good condition. The buffaloes are only available for small logs; the sides of the hills, where the teak is felled, are very steep, and any log over 16 cubic feet requires elephant power.

Timber Carts.—I have now in the forest ten large carts, capable of carrying beams of 30 cubic feet slung under the axle; these sling carts have been found very useful. There are also 24 small carts for working in the forest, with 20 pairs of bullocks and 20 drivers. Our carts are employed in bringing beams from the out-stations to the Karkhana and to the main road near Tippúkadú, where depôts are formed. In the monsoon weather, when the forest roads are impassable, contractors' carts carry the timber from the depôt at Tippúkadú to Utakamand. I have found it very advantageous to employ the forest bullocks, these people being apt to overlook the important matter of feeding cattle entrusted to their care.

Coolies.—The general rise in wages, the increase of coffee cultivation in Mysore, and the great demand for labour on the Nilgiri Hills, have rendered it difficult to procure hands for the forest; however, as the main roads have been finished, and little labour being required to keep them in order, this disadvantage has not been much felt.

Mode of Felling the Trees.—During the past year, a large amount of timber has been felled, attention being paid to the seasons. In December, January, and February, when the sap is at rest, the kurumbars are employed in felling. In March, April, May, and June, when the sap is rising, the kurumbars square the felled trees, and during the remaining five months they fell and square, felling after the full of the moon when the sap is descending, and squaring the other half of the month, when the sap is ascending. By preserving the above order, the timber seasons more readily and better.

Provision Store.—The former provision store-house being thatched, was exposed to danger of fire; moreover, in the monsoon season, grain was apt to be damaged. I have therefore built a new store-house with a ventilated flat roof; this secures us from all danger of fire and loss by damage of grain.

In conclusion, I have the honour to remark, that three years of the forest lease are still to run; and the most profitable course* to pursue, is to get the most we can out of the forest in that period. If a large depôt be formed at Masnicovil, and only small quantities of timber be carted up to Utakamand, the means of transport now in use to Uty might be employed in carrying to Masnicovil, and in three years a supply might be obtained sufficient for public buildings for some years to come—a supply which might fairly be estimated at 200,000 cubic feet of seasoned timber.

W. R. MORGAN,
In charge of Mudumalai Forest.

UTAKAMAND, 30*th April* 1860.

* The energetic working of this forest is clearly advisable, and has been ordered in G. O., 16th July 1860, No. 1521, par. 4. It should be worked on behalf of Government upon the same system as the N. Canara and Anamalai Forests.—H. C.

APPENDIX (F).

SALEM FORESTS.

I have the honour to submit, for the information of Government, the following brief report of operations in the forests of Salem for the year 1859–60.

2. On several occasions I visited the Kotapati jungles with the officers of the Railway Co., for the purpose of supplying sleepers to the Madras line from Tripatore to Salem.

3. I believe there are now few contractors under engagement to the Railway Co.; and as these men were not cutting quick enough to meet the immense demand, the company was obliged to purchase sleepers from persons who would supply them even with four or five at a time, and consequently I was overwhelmed with applications from petty contractors, so that the peons were not able to mark trees with sufficient rapidity, and I had no alternative but to allow these men to cut in the jungles with little control* over them.

4. At first (1858), the amount of rejected sleepers was above 15 per cent., but latterly the woodcutters got into the way of cutting those trees only that are fit for sleepers. On looking over the statements, I find the average rate of rejected sleepers now is 5 per cent.†

5. The trees marked by the forest peons were all approved by the officers of the Railway Co.; these were mostly véngé, acha, kalli, kadukai, karu-véngé, karúngalli, and vel-véngé (p. 77).

6. The method of cutting is still without judgment, and great waste of timber is the consequence. A tree is marked by a forest peon, registered as containing four sleepers, and given over to the woodcutter who fells the tree, and may perhaps adze it into one sleeper. As the woodcutter pays nothing to Government for the timber, he cares little whether the tree will cut into one or

* *i.e.*, Comparatively.—H. C.

† The diminished ratio of rejected sleepers, from 20 per cent. to 5 per cent., is satisfactory.—H. C.

four sleepers, and has not the requisite skill to quarter the log. The only method I can see of preventing this wastage of timber is, that Government should gradually take the whole control of working the forests under the *Amani* system.

7. Beside the supply of sleepers, there is a considerable amount of timber cut for building purposes, and an increasing demand for export. I have granted 300 licenses for permission to cut 6470 cart loads of timber in the forests of Salem, for the year 1859–60. A seignorage fee of R. 1 is paid for each cart load of wood; this amount is collected at the different police stations under the management of the collector, and has been entered in the books as land revenue, without a separate column. I have no hesitation in stating that a much larger amount might be realized, if the holders of the licenses were made to abide by the terms laid down in the license.

8. I recommend a strict limitation of the practice of *Púnakad** cultivation by Malialais in these jungles, and an entire prohibition in the virgin forests which remain. This rude system has increased of late years to such an extent on the Shervarai Hills that the topes are denuded of timber. I also remarked the same destruction prevailing in the Javadi Hills, and have addressed the collector on the subject. Mr Fane, when acting collector, issued a prohibitory proclamation; and it is very desirable that leave should in every case be obtained from the revenue authorities, as in Canara.

9. Overseer Yarde reports having marked 2803 sandal-wood† trees on the Javadi Hills, varying from 3 to 14 feet in length and 10 to 30 inches in girth. About 15,000 young plants have been counted and registered. I am now proceeding to these hills for the purpose of ascertaining whether any of the sandal-wood trees are full grown, and fit to be cut into billets.

L. Blenkinsop,
Asst. Conservator of Forests.

* The restraining of *Púnakad* (i. e. *Kumari*) is important, it should be under the same restrictions as in Canara. Orders to this effect have appeared in the Salem Gazette.

† The discovery of so many sandal-wood trees in a new locality is interesting, and may be a source of revenue hereafter; the quality of the wood has yet to be ascertained.—H. C.

APPENDIX (G).

NORTHERN CIRCARS.

Extract from Conservator's Diary.

Eskapilly.—On 31st Jan. 1859 I took advantage of the departure of Her Majesty's steamer, Dalhousie, to visit the N. Circars. On the following day, the vessel touched at Eskapilly in Nellore, to take in treasure. The shore is barren of wood; palmyrahs are seen among the sand hills; but, except the extensive salt-pans, there is nothing of any interest.

On 2d Feb. I landed at Masulipatam, which used to be considered a bleak station, but it has been much improved since the year 1838. There are now avenues of *Casuarina muricata, Pongamia glabra, Inga dulcis,* and *Dalbergia Sissóo.* The trees have not yet grown large, but they afford shade and shelter, and relieve the former dreary aspect of the station; the best of the sissoos have a bole of 15 or 16 feet high, with one foot diameter.

My attention was directed to a Mangrove* belt on the edge of the backwater, which was formerly barren waste. In the year 1839, two cart loads of seeds of species of *Rhizophora* (Uppa ponna), *Avicennia tomentosa* (Mada chettú), and *Sonneratia acida,* had been procured by Mr Rohde (at that time Judge), at a cost of 25 rupees; the seeds were dropped into the mud of the estuary by convicts. The belt sprung up quickly, and has been annually cut, yielding a trivial revenue as firewood and for feeding cattle. It is also useful in preventing the channel from being clogged with drift-sand. In the canal basin, I saw a dozen firewood boats which had come in during the night from the Godavari, and concealed below the heaped up billets I recognised house beams of Yépi (*Hardwickia binata*), and Siriman (*Conocarpus latifolia*).

Vizagapatam, 6th—This is a picturesque station, but the red soil does not seem suited for tree culture; and the only places

* This affords a main supply of fuel to the station, and is conserved under the orders of the collector.

where I found fine trees were the gardens of Goda Surya Prakasa Rao and Narayan Rao; there were mangoes, sapodillas, oranges, and *Lagerströmia Reginæ*. The cashew thrives well at Waltair. On my return, a few weeks later, I inspected, at the suggestion of Mr T. Knox, C. S., an interesting private garden, formed at Ankapilly, by the late Goda Surya Prakasa Rao. This interested me exceedingly, and I addressed the Agri-Horticultural Society on the subject, thinking the matter deserving of special notice. A silver medal and certificate were awarded to the family. The size of a few exotic trees, as mahogany, cayaputi, and other *Myrtaceæ*, particularly attracted notice, showing the richness of the soil and the comparative humidity of the climate under the shelter of the Vindyan* Hills. The greater part of the collectorate is Zamindari. I have nothing to remark, save that I hope enlightened proprietors will take up the subject of planting on river banks as a speculation, which will probably prove profitable, as the present demand for timber is sure to continue.

Bimlipatam.—In proceeding along the beach, I found the sand binders *Spinifex squarrosus* and *Ipomœa pes capræ* (goat's-foot creeper), with the addition of *Phœnix acaulis* (the stemless date), not found further south. The large sugar factory at Chittavalsa receives its supply of firewood from a great distance, and experiences considerable difficulty in obtaining sufficient quantity.

Chicacole.—The Belgam walnut (*Aleurites triloba*) thrives well, several hundred trees have been planted along the road by the district engineer. The Dividivi (*Cæsalpinia coriaria*) is in great use among the chucklers (tanners), and fruits freely. My attention was directed to a wood called "*Damonu*" or "*Karkana*," light and elastic, this comes nearer than any other indigenous wood I have seen to lancewood or hickory. It is said to be *Grewia tiliæfolia* or *G. elastica*, it is procurable in the bazaars (8 inches broad), and is used for houseposts, gig shafts, dooly poles, spear handles, and fishing rods. Many hundred poles could be obtained from the Parla Kimadi jungles, and seem eminently suited for purposes where strength, lightness, and elasticity are

* Under G. O. 73, 10th Jan. 1860, two Wardian cases, containing coffee plants, were forwarded from the Bangalore Garden to the new sanitarium on the Galiparvatam behind Vizagapatam.

required. The bark should be allowed to remain, the poles steeped in water, and then rubbed with oil. Topes of mango and tamarind are to be seen at Chicacole, Masulipatam, Berhampur, and Russelconda; they would be of great use to the travellers along the northern road about Harripur, and in the neighbourhood of Tikali. The scrubby jungle begins at Kasibuga, and extends beyond Itchapur; but it is evident that the sea-face of the mountains in this district does not produce any tree vegetation which can be denominated timber. I met in a Dâk bungalow, Mr Clarkson, an intelligent officer of the Trigonometrical Survey, who corroborated this statement, and pointed out on the map the position of the tracts of sál forest; I found his information very correct.

Berhampur.—On the 12th February I reached Berhampur, and had a conference with the collector, Mr G. S. Forbes, as to the sál forests of Gumsúr. It will be remembered that his predecessor, Mr W. Knox,* "urged the propriety of some measure being adopted for the due economy and preservation of the forest timber of this district."

It may be well to mention the attempts hitherto made to turn these forests to account. In 1851 Mr G. Williams entered upon a contract to supply railway sleepers; this was the first effort made to work the sál forests of the N. Circars. The wood was found to be superior, but the contract failed. The correspondence was published in the Madras Railway Records of 1852.

The late Overseer Harton felled and despatched sál-wood from Cuttack to Madras, on account of the gun-carriage factory, and Overseer Weldon† is now employed upon this duty in the Sumbulpúr mahals. With these exceptions, I believe that no systematic operations have been attempted. The following extract from a minute of the late commissioner of Cuttack will explain one source of failure:—"There is much difficulty in getting timber of the dimensions required by the gun-carriage factory. The largest trees near to the river have been removed, and the rajahs do not evince a willingness to cut those in the more

* E. M. C., 27th March 1858, par. 4, R. D.

† Subsequently to my visit Mr Weldon was recalled, on account of various difficulties he met with in fulfilling the duties entrusted to him.

distant forests, and require much persuasion to induce them to ffford the requisite aid, without which no timbers of the desired dimensions can be procured. Again, the labour of the coolies employed by the rajahs to remove the timber is compulsory and unremunerated. On the other hand, if they be employed by the agent, the rajah or his servant exacts a portion of their hire. They are therefore not overwilling to lend a helping hand."*

The only printed record of the Gumsúr forests is a list of the trees, with remarks on their uses (Balfour's *Cyclopædia of India*, p. 1910), carefully compiled by Lieut. Macdonald, giving much useful information; the botanical names, chiefly extracted from Sutton's Uriah Dictionary, are somewhat antiquated, and occasionally erroneous. I took this list with me, and have corrected the names of such trees as were observed in my short excursion.

Sál.—The sál tree of Hindustan extends in a nearly unbroken belt of forest along the Terai, from the Ganges at Hurdwar to the Brahma-putra (*Falconer*). It is abundant also on the banks of the Indrawati (*Beddome*). It belongs to the genus *Vatica* of Linn. (*Shorea*, Rox.), (Sala, *Sans.;* Soringhi, *Ur.;* Gugillam, *Tel.*); and is indigenous to the mountainous parts of the Vizagapatam and Ganjam collectorates. It is a smaller tree in Golconda and Kimadi than in Gumsúr; I have not seen any specimens south of the Godaveri. There was some doubt as to the botanical identity of the Gumsúr tree; but I was able to determine this point when in Calcutta three years ago, by comparing specimens received from the Honourable Walter Elliot, then commissioner of the N. Circars (who drew my attention to the subject), with the sub-Himalayan specimens at the botanical garden, Calcutta; and again, by bringing down twigs this year, I find them accord precisely with Roxburgh's plant.

It may be well to notice the singular aptitude of the seed of this tree for speedy germination in connection with prospective measures of conservancy. "The seed has the utmost susceptibility of germination, with a vitality so limited in duration, that it will not survive many days unplanted. The sál seed ripens at

* Records of Bengal Government, No. iii. of 1851. Settlement of Cuttack, Minute by A. I. M. Mills, Commissioner, par. 70.

the commencement of the rains, and after the first shower falls *actually sprouting* from the tree. I have frequently seen in the forests near Hardwar, the radicle of the germ protruded (that is growing) while the fruit was still attached to the parent tree. In consequence, young plants come up in the utmost profusion, and very often so thick as to choke each other; they form patches of forest, which are literally impenetrable till the woodsman removes them as "*Bullees*" or "*Kurrees.*" In this manner the forests are maintained wherever a tree remains standing to perpetuate the stock." (Falconer's "Report," p. 30.) The most important and accessible of the sál forests are in the taluk of Gumsúr and in the Zamindari of Bodogoda, both of which are traversed by rivers which admit of rafting timber to the coast during the freshes, which, however, are of short duration. The names of the principal jungles in Gumsúr are Kukuloba, Galleri, Jagatnáth-prasad, &c. It would not be of use to particularise all the mutas or estates. The sketch map,* prepared by Capt. Phillips, 5th N. I., indicates the route I followed, the area occupied by sál forests, with the roads and water communication between the forests and the coast. The sál is the most useful as well as the most abundant tree in these forests, which are therefore distinctively called sál forests. It was coming into foliage at the time of my visit, and I had opportunities of observing its mode of growth which never occurred to me before.

The tree grows remarkably tall and straight. In open places, it yields a thick trunk, throws out branches, and becomes umbrageous; young and old are cut down without distinction, from the five years old sapling to the full grown tree; and this has been proceeding for a lengthened period without any conservancy rules. Thousands of young trees are removed to form posts for native houses and telegraph poles; others of a larger size are useful for public works and officers' houses, and if sawn longitudinally, they give excellent half round sleepers. With this heavy drain upon the forests, young plants spring up in the greatest profusion, and often so thick as to choke each other. The woodsmen remove the promising poles; and provided that a

* Spare copies are procurable at the office of the Forest Department.

few trees remain as standards per acre, to perpetuate the stock, so remarkable is the germinating power of the seed, there is no fear of exterminating the forest. I measured the straight stump shoots of two years' growth, and found them 12 feet high and 3 inches in diameter at the base. Large patches of sál forest are cleared annually for the purpose of cultivation, and this is usually effected by fire. I came upon several places where some hundreds of fine straight charred poles were standing.

The Kúnds do not, however, destroy fruit-trees indiscriminately. They are careful to preserve the mango and the date, the wood-apple and the *Rottlera tinctoria*, the bastard sago and the Bassia; the two last, as already stated, yield intoxicating liquors. In Gumsúr and the other Government tracts of forests, no taxes are levied as by the adjoining Zamindars,* and no revenue whatever is derived from them.

Throughout the inland part of Gumsúr there is far more timber than is required for local consumption; but there is no doubt that, with the exception of the hill tracts, the jungles are rapidly diminishing from Government lands on the level country and up to the foot of the ghats, partly owing to increased cultivation, and partly to meet the demand for timber at Aska, Berhampur, Russelconda, &c. In the days of the rajahs, the felling of timber was systematically discouraged, so as to render the country less accessible to a military force. At present there is no system of forest conservancy, but orders have been issued by the collector, forbidding the indiscriminate destruction of trees. I may also state that I explained fully and particularly to the principal wood-merchants and to the Aska fire-wood contractors, that low cutting of trees and reservation of the finer kinds was of the utmost importance to the Government and to the people themselves. They promised to follow my instructions. The probability of the appointment of a Government

* Such as As. 2 on a new cart, R. 1 on a new boat, R. 1 As. 8 on a mast, As. ½ on a cart load of firewood, As. 2 on a bandy of bamboos, 2½ on a cart load of planks, and other small sums on wood taken for ploughshares, sugar-mills, oil-presses, &c. The Zamindars also collect money on honey, dammer, arrow-root, and other jungle products, which are sold separately or collectively to a jungle renter.

overseer was intimated to them, and that his salary would be met by a small tax. Certain trees are always carefully preserved: they are chiefly—1. Mango; 2. Date; 3. Wood-apple, koeto; 4. *Bauhinia*, bovada; 5. *Rottlera tinctoria*, Sùndosagúnda; 6. *Caryota urens*, solopo; 7. *Bassia latifolia*, mohollo. The two last are reserved, on account of the intoxicating liquors they yield, which are in great request. From what I witnessed, it is to be feared the Kúnds are becoming a dissipated people.

Ganjam.—There is an abundant supply of wood for burning in this district. In some parts it has been much reduced, as in the Beredy Zamindari, where all the large trees have been consumed in boiling salt, the usual mode of manufacture by solar evaporation not being practised there. Again, in the Gumsúr táluk, on the banks of both rivers leading to Aska, great clearances have been made, often preceding cultivation, but sometimes occasioning the destruction of fine sál timber.

As this district requires opening up, and there is a great abundance of wood, all that seems necessary is to reserve the sál and a few other superior woods, confining the firewood cutting to the woods of less value. Instructions to this effect were fully given in my presence to the contractors who tender for the supply of the Aska factory. The road from Russelconda has been cleared up to Durgaprasad, near the foot of the Kalingia Ghat. The Kúnds come down once a week to the market at Belligunza, bringing oil-seed, wheat, turmeric, and a little cotton; they return the following day. Capt. Harrington is building a large choultry (rest-house) for them. It is intended to continue this road to Sambalpur, where it joins the high road to Nagpore. The trace traverses much of the sál forest, avoiding the river, and keeping to the high ground, where the trees are not so well grown. Side tracks would be required in various directions, but these would be easily made. It may be well to mention, that there is a good road from Ganjam to Russelconda (*viâ* Berhampur), in which the streams are all bridged, and carts have recourse to the forest from Russelconda, and even Ichapur, a distance of 76 miles. It was a most interesting sight to see 80 children of the state (*Sirkar ki Bucha*), as they call themselves,—rescued Merias,—engaged in making a road, calculated to develop the resources of the country, and to civilise the Kúnds. The wage of these Merias was Rs. 4, and boys Rs. 3 *per mensem.* I put the following questions to the headman of a Meria village, who was the first man rescued from death.

1*st Question.*—Are there any persons who would prepare and float rafts to Ganjam? Constant employment would probably be given. *Answer.*—Yes, my people would readily prepare rafts of sál on the river bank, but we do not wish to leave our fields (*i.e.*, floaters must be engaged).

2*d Question.*—What would be the cost of cutting a log 5 ft. in circumference and 15 ft. long? *Answer.*—Such a log would be cut and squared for As. 4, and dragged to the river for As. 2 more.

The general result of my tour of inspection may be summed up thus:—

The sál forests of Gumsúr are the most valuable tract of wood on the eastern coast, and the only one I have seen which would repay European superintendence; still, it scarcely ranks in value with a second-class forest of the western coast. Perhaps there are parts of Rajamandri and Masulipatam which may hereafter contain teak of more value than the sál of Kimadi and Gumsúr; but at present there is nothing left on Government land save seedlings of comparatively small girth, the Godaveri river banks having been cleared, and the best wood exhausted. In consequence of the unhealthy climate of Gumsúr, and the difficulties which would be experienced by European or Eurasian overseers, I think the work of felling and preparing rafts should be organized at Ganjam. The operations in the sál forests of Gumsúr would be divisible into three distinct stages—

1. Felling and transport of logs to river bank.
2. Floating the rafts to depôt (Ganjam).
3. Shipping timber to Madras.

In addition to those operations, the forest assistant or overseer should be charged with the necessary measures for conserving the young trees.

The first operation should be carried out by natives,—Kúnds, Merias, or Urias, with a Conocopoly, and perhaps a *Gúmastah;* the latter might probably be obtained at the rate of Rs. 12 or

Rs. 15 *per mensem*. The second would be arranged by floaters, procurable in the towns of Russelconda and Surada, or Ganjam. The third must be left to coast traders. The depôt should be at Ganjam, where there is a salt agent and subordinate of the D. P. W. The rafts would come down early in the monsoon (July or August), and the timber remain in store till the close of the rains, when ships arrive. A sufficient quantity to meet the demand of the season should be sent by the first freshes, as cartage is expensive. The timber should be put under cover, as sál suffers much injury from exposure, splitting and warping. When there is a sufficiency of timber, an advertisement might be inserted in the Fort St George Gazette, intimating that a ship might obtain freight.

NOTE.—The sanctioned amount allowed for the fixed establishment of the Forest Department being all but expended, I am unable to propose any definite arrangement at present. I feel certain that it would pay well to have overseers for Gumsúr, Karnúl, Kótagiri, and Salem.

APPENDIX (H).

RULES FOR THE PRESERVATION OF JUNGLES IN THE DISTRICT OF COIMBATORE.

1. No timber exceeding 12 inches in diameter, nor any of the trees specified in par. 8, are henceforth to be felled in any of the jungles the property of Government.

2. The villagers may cut fuel and firewood for domestic purposes in low jungles and brushwood, without taxation, as hitherto, but *not for sale*.

3. Charcoal-burners may only cut in such places as may be assigned to them, and are *not* to cut the trees noted in par. 8, whether in those places or elsewhere.

4. The land to be assigned for cutting fuel, &c., shall, in all

practicable cases, be selected near the inhabited villages, so that the clearings may prove an advantage to the residents.

5. The people may likewise cut wood required for the erection of their dwelling-houses, but this privilege will be restricted to *boná fide* ryots : the wood to be so felled must not be more than 3 feet in circumference at two feet from the ground, nor be one of the kinds noted in par. 8. In all cases, 30 standard trees must be left on every acre of ground.

6. Wood required for agricultural implements will be allowed to be taken untaxed by all ryots; and in the same manner bamboos also may be cut for the actual and *boná fide* erection of their houses, *not for sale.*

7. No fruit tree shall be cut down or injured. In the same manner, all trees likely to become timber, as well as saplings of every kind, should be preserved.

8. The names of the trees and shrubs to be always reserved for the value of the wood, or of their products, are mentioned below:—

I.—*Trees reserved for the value of their timber.*

1. Sandal.	7. Palmyra.	13. Kadam.*
2. Red Saunders.	8. Jack.	14. Babul.
3. Ebony.	9. Acha maram.	15. Sirissa.†
4. Satinwood.	10. Marda.	16. Catechu.
5. Teak.	11. Common Terminalia.	
6. Blackwood.	12. Glabrous Terminalia.	

II.—*Trees or shrubs reserved for the value of their products.*

1. Custard apple.	5. Ilupé.	9. Sikai-maram.‖
2. Guava.	6. Cashew-nut.	10. Pinné.¶
3. Soap-nut.	7. Tetancotay.**	11. Tamarind.
4. Capila-rung.‡	8. Surul Chaki.§	

9. On fuel, firewood, and bamboos, cut for sale, a fee will be levied as follows:—1 man's load, 2 maunds, 3 pice; 1 bullock, 8 maunds, 1 anna; 1 cart, 40 maunds, 5 annas; and the amount so collected will form a fund to be laid out in new plantations, or in the preservation and improvement of the existing ones.

* *Nauclea cadamba.* † *Acacia speciosa.* ‡ *Rottlera tinctoria.*
§ *Ventilago Maderaspatana.* ‖ *Acacia concinna.* ¶ *Calophyllum inophyllum.*
** *Strychnos potatorum.*

10. A fee of A. 1 will be levied on every basket of charcoal made in Government woods.

11. The village officers are authorised to collect the fee at the rates above set forth, and remit the same to the táluk treasury, like other collections of revenue. Any extra collection, misappropriation of the funds, &c., will render them liable to the penalties provided for in Reg. 9 of 1822.

12. Every case of evading payment of the fee, and of the unauthorised cutting of wood, will be considered as a fraud, and dealt with accordingly.

13. The preservation of the Government jungles, topes, fruit, and timber trees from destruction, devolves upon the village officers, who will be held responsible for any breach of these rules; where the forests are extensive, and cannot be conveniently and efficiently overlooked by them, they will be aided by the táluk establishment.

14. These rules are applicable to all the táluks, exclusive of the Nilgiri Hills.

CORRESPONDENCE REGARDING KUMARI CULTIVATION.*

Extract Letter to Government.

7th December 1858.

IN E. M. C., 28th Feb. 1857, No. 217, R. D., I was directed to write a full report upon this wasteful system. I have paid much attention to the subject, and after consultation with Revenue officers, coffee planters, &c., I annex the opinions of Mr T. L. Blane, collector of Canara; Mr G. S. Forbes, sub-collector of Canara; Mr Thomas Cannan, coffee planter, and Mr T. Beaumont of Beypur, which serve to illustrate the general views of the collectors of revenue, coffee-planters, and the energetic agent of the Beypur Iron-Works.

It is not possible, nor is it desirable, to suppress the kumari cultivation altogether, as the growth of the various millets is necessary to the aliment of certain classes of people; but I think it most important that it should be *greatly limited*, as suggested by Mr Blane, and *not permitted* on the banks of navigable rivers, on the sea-shore, close to trunk roads, or in any locality where superior timber exists. The revenue arising from the tax of R. 1 per acre is trivial compared with the value of the wood lost to the state, and it is well known, that in the unfrequented valleys of the ghats much kumari takes place without the knowledge of the Revenue officers, European or native.

In every case, I think an application for a specified amount of kumari land should be made; and when kumari takes place without sanction, the cultivator should be severely fined. In

* This rude system of culture, described at p. 131, prevails under various names in different eastern countries. *Kumari* in Mysore and Canara, *Ponnam* in Malabar, *Punakad* in Salem, *Chena* in Ceylon. Much information relating to it will be found in Buchanan's "Journey through Mysore," &c., *passim*, and in Tennant's "Ceylon," vol. ii. p. 473.

this way the destruction of virgin forests has been brought under both in Mysore and in the Mahratta country. I do not here allude to the private lands of Malabar, with which I have nothing to do.

H. CLEGHORN.

(A.) T. L. BLANE, Esq., Collector of Canara, to BOARD of REVENUE.

31*st August* 1847.

" The practice of kumari cultivation is one of so wasteful and improvident a nature, that it appears to me it ought not to be tolerated except in a very wild and unpeopled country, and the time seems to have arrived, when it would be most advisable to place it under considerable check and regulation, if not entirely to prohibit it. This latter course, I must observe, the authorities in Mysore have only within this last year thought it necessary to adopt. It was never permitted under the Rajah's government, and can only be said, therefore, to have been in operation for twelve or fifteen years at most; yet so rapidly has it increased, that the superintendent of the Nuggur division, with whom I have had much conversation on the subject, has determined on putting a stop to it, with a view to the preservation of the woods which still remain."

" I am not disposed at present to recommend its entire prohibition; but I think it would be well to do so in all places accessible to the seaports whence timber and firewood could be brought down, and to place it under regulation in every other part of the district. The revenue paid upon this destructive kind of cultivation is very trifling; and if the wood were preserved in accessible spots, the duty upon the export of timber and firewood would, under proper regulation, exceed it tenfold. I have particularly noticed the destruction which has taken place of forest on the hills immediately above the fine port of the Tadri, where it would have been very valuable, from its vicinity to the coast. The forests which have been here felled and burned, and the magnificent trees which have been left to rot on the ground, would have supplied the market at Bombay with firewood for years. The same fact has been noticed by Mr Forbes, my head assistant.

"I have referred above to the manner in which the practice of kumari cultivation has increased of late years. It was formerly confined entirely to the race of wild and uncivilized people who dwelt habitually in the jungles; but others have since taken it up, and many of the ryots from the plains, and others who have come from the Mysore and Mahratta country, have adopted it as a means of livelihood. There is little doubt also that the prohibition of this practice in the Mysore country will drive a great many of those who have carried on their operations in the forests of that country into Canara, and the destruction will thus be carried on more rapidly than ever, until the woods are finally exhausted. Independent of these considerations, it is not a pursuit which it is at all desirable to encourage the people newly to engage in. It has no doubt some attraction for those who are impatient of control, and are fond of a wild roving life; but it leads to unsettled habits, and takes many away from the regular cultivation of a fixed spot."

(B.) Mr G. S. Forbes, Sub-Collector of Canara.

"The third source of consumption I have to mention arises from the cultivation of kumari, which, as you are aware, is carried on upon tracts where the trees have been previously felled and burnt. The value of timber thus destroyed by one man, calculating it by the number of logs it might have yielded, is at least twenty times as great as the value of the crop of rági obtained in the two years that cultivation is continued; and the amount of duty which the trees would have yielded, if exported as firewood, bears the same proportion to the paltry sum paid to Government for the clearing. To abolish this species of cultivation would deprive a great number of persons of their accustomed means of support, and I have only therefore to suggest that the cultivation of kumari be forbidden in all localities where trees for timber or firewood are likely to be felled; such localities may be determined by the means of carriage which exist. On hills and on tracts distant from the lines of water-carriage, the timber consumed could not be turned to any other account (it being always understood that no teak or sissoo, &c., should be touched). The above remarks apply chiefly to the forests situated below ghats, and which extend several miles from the hills towards the sea, and from the Goa boundary to the river Tadri, which bounds the Ankola táluk."

(C.) Mr Thomas Cannan, Coffee-Planter.

"With regard to kumari cultivation, the Government, in my opinion, is the great loser, there being very seldom more than one crop of rági taken from any one patch, which, if cultivated with coffee, would have yielded something every year for half a century, in the way of rent or tax. In an old kumari the jungle trees grow up again, but they are of kinds unfit for building purposes; and in this respect, settlers in the country are put to expense and inconvenience, as well as the Government in their building operations, and coffee-planters generally find their planting operations brought to a very unsatisfactory and abrupt termination by a kumari, on which I have never been able to get coffee to grow yet. In Nuggur, where kumari cultivation was prohibited, stringent regulations with regard to the cutting of timber were issued at the same time. Every person requiring wood was obliged to apply before felling it; the cultivator had not to pay for it, but the non-cultivator had, and I am of opinion that these measures have operated pretty well. The more I think of kumari, the more surprised I feel that it has been tolerated for such a length of time. It is carried on by a set of savages, in every sense of the word, who would be much more profitably employed on public works or on coffee plantations."

(D.) Mr A. Poulton, Government Timber-Agent.

16*th October* 1852.

"I have also observed that the restrictions on kumari are producing a good effect on the cultivation of rice, as considerable portions of new cultivation have taken place, more particularly about the village of Hansu and Ulvi, which were only a short time since entirely dependent on the kumari, but have now a considerable extent of rice lands under cultivation."

(E.) Mr J. BEAUMONT, Manager of the Beypur Iron-Works.

11*th November* 1858.

"I venture to invite your attention to the wanton sacrifice of tracts of forest, by a practice prevailing to a large extent in Malabar. I allude to the cutting of maiden forest by the Malai-karen and native landowners for the purposes of cultivation. The grains usually planted are paddy,* sháma,† and tomara. For the two last, Government receive no tax. For the first (paddy), which is principally sown, it is true that the sircar receives the usual nigady; but, for the following reasons, this affords to the country an inadequate return for the destruction of forests, which in later years would prove of immense value. The tract of land denuded of forest, from the want of irrigation, *can only be cultivated profitably once in five, or sometimes in twenty, years.* Thus does the country receive but one year's tax, out of say nine, upon ground so cleared. It will, upon the other hand, readily be perceived, that these wholesale depredators, being unable to cultivate the same land except during one year, will remove to another locality where maiden jungle stands, and there resume the work of devastation. It is unnecessary for me to enumerate, to one so well acquainted with the district, the numberless tracts of magnificent forest which, during my short residence in Malabar, I have seen swept from existence, by the process now undermentioned; but I cannot refrain, whilst an opportunity offers, of recording my decided opinion, that unless Government take some step (and the remedy is easy) to check this system of wanton destruction, in a very few years the chief portion of these magnificent forests will present little but a barren waste, studded with the stumps of the finest trees which can adorn or fertilize the district in which they stand."

* *Oryza sativa.* † *Panicum miliare.*

Extract from the Minutes of Consultation.

30th March 1859.

" In pars. 16 to 18 (p. 126), the Conservator responds to the call made upon him in E. M. C., 28th Feb. 1857, to report fully on the "kumari" system of cultivation. Dr Cleghorn has consulted various persons whose opinions on the subject may be considered to bear weight, and has come to the conclusion that it is neither possible nor desirable to suppress kumari cultivation altogether; but that it should be carried on under stringent regulations; the chief of them being, that a previous application for a specified extent should be made in every case, and that any unauthorised operations should be punished by severe fine; and that it should be wholly prohibited and stopped in the neighbourhood of trunk roads, navigable rivers, or the sea-shore, as well as in all localities where there is valuable timber.

" These views appear to the Governor in Council to be judicious and practical; but before issuing final orders on the subject, he resolves to refer the question for the consideration of the Board of Revenue, who have had the question of kumari under their consideration at various times within the last few years. Whatever rules may be established, the active co-operation of the Revenue Department will be necessary in order to enforce them.

" J. D. Bourdillon,
" *Secretary to Government.*"

Extract Proceedings Board of Revenue, 16th April 1859.
No. 1350.

" 3. As the term Kumari is peculiar to the Canara district, it is necessary in the first place to explain what it is.

" 4. *Kumari described.*—The name given to cultivation which takes place on forest clearings. A hill side is always selected, on the slopes of which a space is cleared at the end of the year. The wood is left to dry till the following March or April, and then burned. In most localities the seed is sown in the ashes on the fall of the first rains, without the soil being touched by implement of any kind, but in the táluk of Bekul the land is ploughed.* The only further operations are weeding and fencing. The crop is gathered towards the end of the year, and the produce is stated to be at least double that which could be obtained under the ordinary modes of cultivation (par. 10). A small crop is taken off the ground in the second year, and sometimes in the third, after which the spot is deserted until the jungle is sufficiently high to tempt the kumari cutter to renew the process. In the south, where land is more scarce compared with the population, the same land is cultivated with kumari once in 12, 10, or 7 years; but in N. Canara, the virgin forest, or old kumari not cultivated within the memory of man, are generally often selected.

"5. In some parts of Bekal (par. 13), which is the most southerly of the táluks of Canara, kumari cutting forms part of the business of the ordinary ryots, and as many as 25,746, or one-sixth of the population, are supposed to be engaged in it; but to the north of that táluk (par. 15), it is carried on by the jungle tribes of Malai Kaders and Mahratais to the number of 59,500.

"6. In Fasli 1266, the area under kumari cultivation throughout the whole district was 17,084 acres, of which 8556 acres were Sarkar kumari, that is, kumari carried on in forests not claimed by the owners of estates, and 8528 acres, of which 5983 acres were within the limits of the Bekal táluk, were attached to wargs or holdings of proprietors.

"7. The question of whether it is expedient to allow this species of cultivation, first came under discussion in reference to the report of Dr Gibson to the Government of Bombay, which was referred to Mr Blane, collector of Canara, for his observations. In accounting for a growing scarcity of timber, Mr Blane noticed, among the most influential causes, the increase in the kumari cultivation, which bid fair, he then considered, to destroy the whole of the large virgin forests within a short time. He expressed his opinion that it should either be placed under considerable check and regulation, or entirely prohibited, as had been done in Mysore (par. 14). Mr Blair, a former collector, he

* From Collector, 30th August; in Con., 13th October 1858, par. 4.

stated, had in 1843 issued a proclamation, directing that five valuable kinds of timber, viz., teak, pún, blackwood, jack, and sandal, should be preserved *in the Government forests;* but this, Mr Blane states, had practically no effect, inasmuch as the timber-merchants continued to fell the timber wherever they found it, on the plea that they cut it from private jungles, and had obtained the permission of the owners to do so. To defeat this subterfuge, Mr Blane had directed that when jungle is claimed as private property, the right must be established before timber is cut. The clearance of the jungle, so injurious in many respects, had been attended with one great advantage. According to all reports, it had diminished the prevalence of fever. 'On this account principally, he confined his recommendation to the confirmation of his prohibition of the felling of the five superior kinds of timber, and to the preservation of the jungle in spots near the rivers on the sea coast, where, from its position, the timber would be easily made available, and the inferior kinds of wood might be allowed, under proper regulation, to be cut as firewood for export.'"

"8. On this report being laid before Government, they, agreeably to the recommendation of the Board, authorised the collector of Canara to restrict the cultivation of Kumari to 'such places and to such an extent as might, in his opinion, be expedient for the preservation of the forest and the general welfare of the province.' He was also instructed to assert the right of Government to all forest lands to which a title cannot be clearly established by private individuals."*

"43. The Kumari in Bekal has been shown to be peculiar. It is chiefly Wargadar Kumari, and the extent of land for which the shist is paid is specified in the pattah, and the wargadar enjoys twelve times as much, on the supposition that he will go over the whole once in twelve years, though he now cultivates it more quickly.

"Since the discussion has commenced, cultivation within three miles of the coast, and three of the banks of the river, has been prohibited; a rule which Mr Fisher thinks operates with harshness in a country which is everywhere intersected by rivers.

* E. M. C. of G., 3d Dec.; in Con., 16th Dec. 1847, No. 3226, par. 3.

"44. The Board see no reason to alter the system, except that as the táluk does not contain any valuable timber, they would recommend that the prohibition against cutting within certain distances of rivers and the sea may be withdrawn by the collector at discretion.

"45. In the other táluks of S. Canara, Mr Fisher would allow one acre of Kumari for every ½ rupee of shist paid, the Bekal system being introduced, and the people confined to certain plots, portions of which they must cut periodically if they cut at all. Of this suggestion the Board approve.

"46. In the Payenghat táluks of N. Canara, the collector proposes to allow each wargadar an acre per annum for every rupee of shist paid, but he would exclude from their possession 'tracts producing the more valuable kinds of timber, and such positions on the banks of our numerous rivers as would, under proper care, produce valuable plantations of timber suited to ship-building and domestic purposes,' and would settle all claims made on these 'by exchange of ground, or such other means as may hereafter be decided upon.' Of this proposition, also, the Board approve.

"47. In Supah and Yellapur, in the balaghat of North Canara, which contain the most valuable timber, Mr Fisher would continue the present system of remitting the Kumari shist and prohibiting the cultivation, "except in such portions and to such an extent as the Revenue officers may determine," where he would allow it on the Bekal system. The Board approve.

"(A true extract.)

"J. D. SIM, *Secretary.*

"To J. D. BOURDILLON, Esq.,
"*Secretary to Government, R. D.*"

Order of Madras Government.

1st June 1859, *No.* 737.

1. Before passing a final order on this paper, the Governor in Council resolves to transmit a copy to the Conservator of Forests,

for his opinion as to the sufficiency, as regards the Conservancy Department, of the means proposed by the Board (in pars. 43 to 47) for checking the practice of Kumari cultivation.

2. The chief mischief of this practice is found in its destruction of timber; but the Governor in Council wishes to have Dr Cleghorn's opinion whether, in the existing state of the forests of Canara, it is important to stop it on that account, in localities where valuable timber such as teak and blackwood is not met with. In Bekal táluk it is stated (par. 44) that there is no valuable timber; but in Supah and Yellapur, which contain a large quantity, it might be expedient to make the prohibition even more absolute than the Board advise (par. 47).

3. Par. 43. With regard to considerations apart from the Conservancy, the Governor in Council is not prepared fully to adopt the reasons advanced against the prohibition of the practice. It is urged that this sort of tillage affords a livelihood to wild races who can only gradually be brought to regular habits of agricultural industry. The Government have strong doubts whether the way to teach industrious habits to such classes is thus to tolerate and even encourage the continuance of contrary habits. It appears, too, that there must be something very profitable or otherwise very attractive in Kumari cultivation, as a very large number of ordinary ryots appear to be engaged in it—nearly 26,000 in the single táluk of Bekal (par. 5).

4. Again it is stated* that the grain thus obtained is necessary to the subsistence of the population. It may be granted that the grain is necessary, but it does not follow that this mode of raising it should be so; and the Governor in Council wishes for Dr Cleghorn's opinion whether it would not be better that land required for cultivation should be permanently cleared and cultivated.

Lastly, the Government will be glad of Dr Cleghorn's opinion whether Kumari cultivation has diminished the prevalence of fever, as stated in the 42d par. In appears to Government that it embraces opposing influences in that regard—some adverse to the production of malaria, others favourable to it; while permanent clearings appear of more unmixed advantage.

* Also in par. 17 of Conservator's Report, Dec. 7th, 1858, No. 492.

5. In Mysore, it is stated, Kumari has been wholly prohibited; and it has been very nearly so also in the forests of the Bombay territory.* It is matter for consideration in the opinion of Government whether it may not properly be so in Canara also.

6. Dr Cleghorn will also be requested to inform Government whether the kind of cultivation in Malabar called *Punam* resembles Kumari in respect to the temporary and successive clearing and abandonment of land, or whether the land is there cultivated more permanently. If the latter is the case, it would seem to afford an additional argument for putting a stop to Kumari.

J. D. Bourdillon,
Secretary to Government.

From Conservator of Forests to Secretary to Government.

17th August 1859, *No.* 755.

1. I have the honour to acknowledge receipt of the Pros. of Government, 1st June 1859, No. 737, enclosing Ex. Pros. Board of Rev., No. 1350, 16th April 1859, and calling for an opinion as to the sufficiency of the means proposed by the Board for checking the practice of Kumari cultivation. I would have replied sooner, but have just received an interesting letter from

* The following are the rules in Belgam:—"1*st*, Kumari cultivation is absolutely prohibited, except within 2 koss of the ridge of the ghats in the Bidi táluk, and within 1 kos of the ridge in the Padshapur táluk.

"2*d*, Within the said limits, *i.e.* within 2 koss of the ridge of the ghats in the former, and 1 kos in the latter district, no timber trees, whether large or small, are to be cut down for clearing Kumaris, and no ground within the said limits is to be cleared for Kumari without the written permission of the district officers."

In Dharwar collectorate it is stated to have been stopped entirely. See letter from Captain Anderson to the Military Board, Bombay, February 6th, 1855, among the papers received with letter from Bombay of 9th April 1855, No. 1462.

Capt. W. C. Anderson, Supt. Rev. Survey, S. Mahratta country, an Ext. from which, along with Mr Grant's description of the Punam cultivation in Malabar, are forwarded as enclosures to this communication.

2. In addition to climatic considerations, the chief evils of this rude system of culture are the destruction of valuable timber, at present urgently required for ship-building and railways, and the rendering of land unfit for coffee (see Mr Cannan's letter, p. 129) cultivation. Where trees do not attain a great size, laterite being near the surface, or where the timber cannot be removed to a road or river from physical obstructions, or where there is extensive bamboo jungle, there is not the same objection to this cultivation; the clearing of bamboos is useful, and the Kumari yields a supply of millet grain to the hill tribes.

3. In the course of my tours, I have constantly an eye to the extent of Kumari cultivation, and it is a matter of satisfaction to me to find that owing to the practice being disallowed, it has ceased in Mysore, has also greatly diminished in the Southern Mahratta country, and is rapidly decreasing in Canara. The system is objectionable for the reasons above given, and I think every effort should be made to do away with it as far as possible, although motives of policy may perhaps require that this consummation be gradually brought about. This I would leave in the hands of the collectors, with the proviso, that no virgin forest or forest of old standing be broken up, but that Kumari be henceforth confined to land which has been within twelve years devoted to that purpose.

4. *South Canara.—Bekal.*—In Bekal táluk there is not *now* any valuable timber. Kumari cultivation has always prevailed there to a great extent; and from its adjoining Malabar, where Kumari is unlimited, it would be difficult to restrict it more than is suggested by the collector. The prohibition not to cut within nine miles of the coast and three of the banks of a river is wise, but there are exceptional tracts; and the granting of these should be left to the discretion of the collector. I may observe that it is more important to reserve on the banks of a river than on the sea shore, where trees do not thrive, and are chiefly valuable for firewood.

5. *Sulia.*—In Sulia, there is much young teak and blackwood coming on under the supervision of Mr Thompson, forest overseer, who resides at Putúr, and any application for Kumari land in the neighbourhood might be submitted to him for previous report.

6. *North Canara.*—In N. Canara (Supah and Yellapur), where there is much most valuable timber, and the conservancy of which is financially profitable, I would be more careful. I would disallow all Kumari without previous sanction. The sub-collectors at Sirci and at Honore, if not able personally to examine the spot, could refer the question to Mr Müller, assistant conservator at Sedashegur, or to the forest overseer at Halliál: permission being granted in each case by the European Revenue authorities. Great supplies of timber have been made to public departments from these two táluks, and the railway pressure is now heavy upon them. We cannot afford to give up any of the fine forests for Kumari. There are here and there pieces of inferior jungle, where Kumari might probably be allowed without much mischief, but the spot should always be first inspected.

7. *Permanent Cultivation preferable.*—With reference to par. 4 of the Pro. of Government under reply, there cannot be a doubt that it would be better if cultivation was confined to lands *permanently cleared*, and there is every reason to believe that the millets would be produced abundantly in the rich soil of the ghats, particularly if the plots were enriched by cattle and leaf manure. Perhaps some of the land now used for Kumari culture would not bear a series of millet crops; but in all probability a judicious rotation would obviate the necessity of change of a locality. When the cultivation is confined to one kind of cereal, the land is impoverished, and nothing would answer so well above ghat, after cereals, as potatoes.

8. *Result in Mysore.*—It was partly at my suggestion, in 1846, that the Kumari culture was prohibited in Mysore, and the superintendents of Coorg, Nagar and Astagram, under the Commissioner, have all assured me that the system works well; and I may remark, that the same amount of timber would not have been available for railway purposes, had it not been for this precaution.

9. *Result in Belgam.*—The result of the rules in Belgam (noted at foot of the Pros. of Government, p. 136), will be found clearly given in Captain Anderson's letter, and appears to be very satisfactory.

10. *Sanitary considerations.*—In regard to the result of Kumari cultivation in a sanitary point of view, I can affirm, from personal observation and consultation with my professional brethren, that "permanent clearings are of unmixed advantage;" the dense thorny scrub which succeeds a deserted Kumari is decidedly more injurious to health than lofty forest open below, and harbours destructive animals to a greater extent.

11. *Punam of Malabar.*—The enclosure B. of Mr Grant shows that the Punam culture of Malabar is identical with the Kumari of Canara; the soil, however, of that district is generally richer, and the results more profitable. The lands of Malabar being private property, I have never interfered. I may refer to Mr Beaumont's letter* showing the effect of excessive Kumari on the operations of the Iron Company; and I may add, that I hope, with Mr Grant, that the enhanced price of timber will lead the Jenmakars to stop Punam cultivation in many jungles.

12. *Punakad of Salem.*—This is an erratic system of rude cultivation, carried on by the Malaiális, a hill tribe inhabiting the Shevarai and Chittéri Hills of Salem collectorate. Mr Fane, C.S.,† lately directed the attention of the Revenue Board to the injurious effect of this upon the future prospects of coffee planting.

13. *Value of a Kumari.*—In conversing with different Revenue officers, I have heard many opinions as to the profit realized by Kumari cultivation. In a minute by Lord Harris, late Governor of Madras, dated 9th March 1857, in E. M. C., No. 235, Rev. Dep., par. 171, it was computed, on the authority of Mr J. D. Robinson, at Rs. 3 per acre, which seems to be rather low. I accordingly instructed Mr Müller to ascertain the actual gains as nearly as possible. He reports as follows:—

* Ex. Min. of Cons., 30th March 1859, No. 425.

† Pro. of Board of Revenue, 7th July 1859, No. 2663. I understand that the same matter has attracted much attention in the Coffee districts of Ceylon.

"I beg to submit a statement of what I ascertained from the Kumari people on the spot :—

		Rs.	a.	p.
Expenditure.—	Assessment per 1½ acre,	1	8	0
	Two men cutting for ten days,	3	0	0
	Ragi seed, nine seers,	0	4	0
	Clearing grass for one month, one man,	4	0	0
	Watching three months, at Rs. 2 per mensem,	6	0	0
	Gathering crop,	4	0	0
		Rs. 18	12	0
Receipts.—	Ragi, 28 mudas at R. 1,	28	0	0
	Profit,	Rs. 9	4	0"

But as the Kumari cultivators, who seldom break ground singly, employ their wives and children for all except felling, which they do themselves, the actual expenditure is reduced to the assessment, and that, in secluded valleys, is very often evaded. It is generally believed that one half of the profit goes to the coast saukár, who gives an advance. The Kumari cultivators live in wretched temporary huts and make a very poor livelihood, offering a great contrast to the substantial homestead of the Canara ryot, who is generally well housed, and lives in considerable comfort.

The system of the hill cultivators is nearly the same in different countries. The Irulars and Kurumbars on the Nilgiris, the Maláiális on the Shevarais, the Karens in Burmah, the Punam cultivators in Malabar, the Kumari Mahrattais in Canara, all endeavour to obtain a precarious subsistence by scattering grain after burning the jungle, and thus avoid the toil of careful cultivation.

In a thinly peopled country like Burmah, there is little objection; but in the limited plateau of Yerkâd, where the best land is almost all taken up for coffee plantation or fruit-gardens, and in the balaghat táluks of North Canara, where the remaining timber is much enhanced in value, and not more than sufficient for present demands, there are strong objections to this wasteful and barbarous system. I think that in Government forests, before clearances are made, permission should first be obtained from the Revenue authorities in communication with this department, the locality and extent of the clearance being defined.

(A.) Extract of a Letter from Captain W. C. Anderson, Supt. Revenue Survey, Mahratta Country, 26th July 1859.

"I do not think Kumari is absolutely necessary to the people except near the ghats—say within eight or ten miles at farthest, where the fall of rain is so heavy as to interdict ordinary dry crop cultivation on the same land for several successive years. Where permitted, you will find the people resort to it very extensively, more so than to any other description of cultivation, for several reasons. It requires no stock or agricultural capital. It requires less labour than any other description of cultivation: a month in May or June, in felling, burning, and sowing, and a fortnight for reaping, after the rains, affords a subsistence, such as it is."

(B.) From P. Grant, Esq., Collector of Malabar, 5th July 1859.

"1. I beg to inform you that Punam and Kumari cultivation are the same.

"2. Punam cultivation is carried on extensively along the slopes on the W. Ghats, and on many of the other lower ranges of hills; but as they are mostly private property, I do not think that anything can be done by Government to put a stop to it.

"3. Once a jungle has been felled and burned, and the land cropped, a period of eight or twelve years is allowed to elapse ere another crop is taken off the same land.

"4. The Punam crop is generally a heavy one, and remunerative to the grower. Say a piece of land yields 100 parahs of paddy, 40 go towards the expenses of cultivation, leaving 60, of which the Government share, at the rate of 25 per cent., is 12 parahs; the balance, 48 parahs, goes to the grower.

"5. When the crop is supposed to be ready to be cut, the Government officials proceed to estimate it as it stands on the ground; considering the localities in which it is grown, their distance from bazaars, &c., it is natural to conclude that the ryot has many circumstances in his favour.

"6. In accessible parts of the country, the rising value of timber is likely to lead the Jenmis to put a stop to Punam cultivation in many jungles."

Statement exhibiting the Extent of Punam Cultivation and the Revenue thereon during the last Five Faslis (Years).

Fasli.	Acre.	Revenue.			Remarks.
		R.	A.	P.	
1263, . .	18,285	11,226	5	9	
1264, . .	22,097	14,134	1	6	
1265, . .	22,296	14,566	11	4	
1266, . .	25,161	16,178	10	7	Average per acre is 0–10–2.
1267, .	25,947	16,574	5	9	
Total, .	114,486	72,680	2	11	
Average, .	22,897	14,536	0	7	

P. Grant, *Collector.*

Extract Order on the foregoing Papers.

23d May 1860, *No.* 830.

"1. In this paper Dr Cleghorn replies to the reference made to him in the order of the 1st June 1859, No. 737, on the subject of Kumari cultivation in Canara, and the proper measures to be taking for checking it. The practice referred to is that of felling and burning the timber and jungle on portions of forest, cultivating the ground for a single year or two years, and then leaving it, to repeat the same process on another spot. It is of course very destructive to timber. It prevails in the jungles of the western coast, but not to its former extent; in Mysore, and in Belgam and Dharwar, it has been almost put an end to; in Canara, also, much has been done during the last ten years to check it, but it is still largely practised; in Malabar, where the forests are private property, there has yet been no interference with it on the part of Government."

"14. Dr Cleghorn gives his opinion, as requested by Government, respecting the several pleas urged in defence of Kumari. It is pleaded that Kumari is necessary to the subsistence of certain tribes; Dr Cleghorn was asked whether permanent clearing and cultivation would not be better for them. He replies decidedly in the affirmative (par. 7); and he describes (par. 13) the degraded condition of the Kumari cutters, who are kept abjectly poor by the coast saukárs and others, who enjoy the greater part of the fruits of their labour. Again, it is urged in defence of Kumari that it diminishes malaria and fever. But here also Dr Cleghorn's opinion is adverse. He declares in very decided terms (par. 10), that while permanent clearings are of unmixed good, the dense thorny scrub which succeeds Kumari cultivation is decidedly more injurious to health than lofty forest open below. In other words, that instead of promoting the healthiness of a locality, Kumari has the opposite effect.

"15. In the order of Government of June 1st, 1859 (No. 737, par. 3), the idea is thrown out that Kumari must be profitable, in order to attract so many persons. It appears from Dr Cleghorn's letter that this is really the case. In par. 13 he gives the details of the cost and returns of one and a half acre of Kumari, as ascertained from the cultivators themselves by Mr Müller, assist. conservator; and there could not be a better source of information on the subject. From this it appears that the value of the crop is Rs. 28, or Rs. 18 an acre. The deductions for clearing and cultivating would indeed reduce this to about Rs. 6 an acre, if really paid out; but in point of fact the cultivator and his family do all the work, so that the only actual expense is the assessment, which in N. Canara is R. 1 an acre, and in S. Canara R. ½"

"19. With regard to Sarkár Kumari, it seems to be a great evil even as respects the interests of the cultivators themselves. It appears certainly to retard the improvement of the forest races, and tends to keep them in their present degraded condition. It has been already noticed, that in Mysore the practice of Kumari cutting has been entirely abolished; and that in the jungle districts of Bombay it has been so very nearly. The Government now prohibit Sarkār Kumari, or Kumari cultivation in Government forests, without previous permission. This permission should be given sparingly, and never for spots in the timber forests.

"20. It only remains, lastly, to direct, that the collections on account of abolished Wargadār Kumari held in deposit be now brought to account.

"J. D. BOURDILLON,
"*Secretary to Government.*

"To the Conservator of Forests."

NOTE.—The documents relating to this system of upland cultivation are very voluminous; but I have endeavoured to select from them every important statement bearing on the subject. The opinion of Sir J. E. Tennent, as given in his great work on Ceylon, vol. ii. p. 463, is worthy of perusal. I would only remark that the "chena cultivation" of Ceylon there described is more careful and varied than the Kumari practised in Mysore and Canara. "Chena" lasts two years, and includes the culture of chillies, yams, sweet potatoes, cotton, hemp, &c. H. C.

FIREWOOD.

MEMORANDUM ON THE STRIHARIKOTA JUNGLE.

The banks of Cochrane's Canal are clothed with saline plants (*Salsola*, *Salicornia*, and *Suæda*), which, with their succulent cylindric leaves, may be seen in great abundance wherever the salt water or marsh extends : their ashes afford soda by incineration. The canal is lined by rows of young trees (*Casuarina muricata*, *Melia azadirach*, and *Pongamia glabra*), and there is a hedge of *Parkinsonia aculeata* on both sides, thriving as well as can be expected in an exposed situation and on a sterile soil. These valuable improvements have been effected since I last travelled by this canal in 1851. The Palmyra palm (*Borassus flabelliformis*) grows spontaneously in vast abundance along the narrow strip of land between Pulicat Lake and the sea. Other trees begin to appear at some distance beyond Coromandel (properly *Kára-mannil*), where the tract of jungle under consideration increases in breadth; but the trees are nowhere of large size, and there is no part which can be designated forest, the general appearance being that of a dense, scrubby jungle. The length of this belt is under forty miles, varying in width from half a mile to eight miles; but it has not been accurately surveyed, and is not so broad as usually represented, or the area has diminished in extent. The fine loose sand blown by the

Fig. 7.

wind along the flats has a tendency to collect round every obstacle, even a blade of grass; and a succession of mounds are formed along the coast, generally of the shape and appearance shown in Fig. 7. The subsoil is indurated clay; and at the edge, where there is a considerable depth of loose sand, the Caldera bush (*Pandanus odoratissimus*) grows in abundance, and fringes the line of sandhills. There are some lower portions in which the waters of the monsoon have collected, and given to the sand an admixture of mould, which so far fertilizes the soil that millets may be cultivated. I only saw one or two small patches of paddy (*Oryza sativa*). The prospect of converting this waste tract into cultivated land is very distant, and, for reasons submitted, I think it should be allowed to remain a jungle tract bearing underwood for fuel and beams for housebuilding, and thereby of extensive and important use to the community.

A large town like Madras requires much fuel for daily consumption; the sources of supply cannot be exclusively confined to mountainous or unculturable land. Difficulty is now experienced in supplying the market with timber and firewood, and the scarcity of fuel has long induced the poorer inhabitants to resort to Striharikota, where, in addition to stunted trees, underground roots and stems, running along the loose sand, are pulled up with ease; and according to the statement of the Military Board, at least one half of the fires in Madras are fed from this source. The simple method of carrying the fuel from the jungle to the cargo boats is shown in the accompanying sketch (Plate 6). However convenient this supply of firewood is to the Madras traders as well as the poor residents, the destruction of the shrubs, roots, &c., will become hereafter a serious inconvenience to the public and a source of detriment to the canal, as the isthmus may revert to its desert state, the dry and loose sand be drifted into the canal, and overspread the adjacent country. If an opposite system be pursued, and the growth of trees and shrubs encouraged, the belt of wood will protect the soil from sweeping winds and afford fodder for cattle. It appears to me, therefore, that while conserving Striharikota, it would be important also to commence the systematic planting and reclaiming of the sandy flats or downs which lie along the coast between the canal and the sea. There is no apparent obstacle to this being effected. What has been done by nature at Striharikota indicates the pro-

W H M' Farlane Lith' Edin'

NATIVES CARRYING FUEL.

cess by which similar waste tracts may be made productive. An undulating surface must first be formed, and then a few clumps of bushes may be laid down; this is the beginning of a jungle. When a belt of trees or bushes is once established in such a situation, it should be kept undisturbed as long as it will serve the purpose of protecting the trees within, though it may be of no other value. I remember Pulicat fifteen years ago, when the old Dutch station was almost without a tree; but now there are avenues and ornamental shrubs round the fort and on both sides of the backwater.

The kind of trees suitable for planting admits of some doubt, and may perhaps be learned from some of the residents at Ennore and Coromandel. The *Casuarina* thrives well, and furnishes a useful wood, which, however, does not answer for fuel, as it does not split easily, and yields little wood when pollarded. Besides, it would be better to plant quick-growing woods.

There are numerous and excellent works on planting, such as Loudon's "Arboretum Britannicum;" Brown's "Forester," 1861; Pontey's "Forest Pruner;" Monteath's "Forester's Guide;" Mathew on "Arboriculture;" and all the operations connected with it, as the growth of trees for timber, for scenic effect, &c.; but I know of no work in England, or even in Germany (where the forests are under an organised system of management), affording information on the statistics of wood fuel. I am not aware of any statistical records, although such are not wanting with regard to peat and coal, which constitute the principal fuel of Great Britain, where the raising of trees for firewood does not constitute any part of forestry. As to the area necessary to produce a continual supply of firewood for 700,000 people, we have no available data for the basis of calculation; and as to the number of years necessary for the reproduction of the jungle, it seems to me that although seven years is found to be a sufficient period of rest on the western coast, it is too short for the renewal of hard wood on the eastern coast. The best kinds of wood to rear for fuel are the quickest growers of the country, such as the firs in Scotland, the poplar and willow in England, the beech in Germany, and the various species of *cassia*, *ficus*, &c. in India, which grow rapidly, and sow or extend themselves. As a general rule, indigenous trees will answer better than exotics (Utakamand is an exception); for the native hill trees are much slower in growth than the naturalised Australians. All that is wanted is conservancy, so as to prevent tracts being quite cleared, to hinder persons from injuring the roots, and to arrange for the renewal of trees cut down. One part of this scheme would be to leave a certain number of standard trees per acre, say thirty or forty for *shade* and for *seed*, instead of shaving off everything to the root, by which means both the medicinal products as well as the larger fuel will gradually but certainly disappear. If the foregoing suggestions meet with the approval of Government, the measures to be adopted for increasing and extending the growth of tree plantations are next to be considered, and I offer the following remarks upon the subject:—

1. The superintendents of both the N. and S. Canals, the overseers and employés of the D. P. W., who have already commenced planting along the banks of these canals, might set a good example by extending their plantations. The successive rows of trees will be better and better protected, and each stronger than the preceding until they attain the full height. They would, I imagine, be of great value in preserving the bank as well as the water in the canal, whilst the loppings and prunings would probably repay the cost of planting. A considerable revenue has been derived from the culture of trees on the banks and cuttings of the great Ganges Canal. (Col. R. Baird Smith's Report.) Moreover, the embankments would be rendered beautiful and interesting.

2. The collector might also encourage heads of villages to take an interest in planting topes, by holding out the promise of a reduction of land-rent whenever he is shown so many hundred trees in a flourishing state. The remission should depend solely upon the ryots carefully watering (if necessary) and keeping up their topes or avenues. This course has been adopted in Mysore and in some parts of Bengal with considerable success.

3. Of course the officials of the D. P. W. could only be expected to plant close to the canal, and the ryots in the immediate neighbourhood of their villages. Many failures in the plants put down must be expected the first year; but the result, with

perseverance, would be a large supply of wood near Madras, with water carriage to bring it to market.

4. At the close of the present lease it will be well to consider whether it be advisable to continue the system of renting out an eighth portion of the forest *to be cut down to the ground.* If the trees were headed down to 6 or 8 feet, and allowed to produce lateral shoots, these would become very numerous and produce a greater supply of branches to be sold in bundles for firewood.

5. I do not think it would be profitable to plant these lands (as a Government scheme with a fixed establishment) for the exclusive purpose of raising firewood; but a resident cultivator holding a lease of these waste lands rent free for a certain number of years, and planting Palmyra palms for shelter close together, so as to encourage the growth of coppice within, would receive a fair return for his labour, and little or no professional skill would be required.

H. Cleghorn,
Conservator of Forests.

MEMORANDUM.

FUEL AND FIREWOOD JUNGLES.

1. The supervision of the minor jungles was not contemplated three years ago in the original scheme of the department; nor, so far as I am aware, have they been taken into systematic consideration in Bombay or Pegu. These jungles hitherto have been either unprotected by any rules whatever, or left to the management of the local authorities.

2. Regulations exist for the management of the Sind preserves, which supply fuel to the Indus Flotilla; and I understand that the civil authorities at Simla have been obliged to enact stringent regulations for the regular and economical supply of that station.

3. In almost every district of this presidency there have been references in regard to firewood and bamboos, which are subject

to various rules in the different collectorates. and the question is frequently asked by private individuals, "What is the best kind of tree to grow for firewood?" There can be no doubt that, in the neighbourhood of large towns, along the lines of railway, in the vicinity of iron foundries, sugar factories, engineers' workshops, &c., this necessary of life is more scarce and expensive than formerly, owing to the greater distance from which it is brought, and the unrestricted license with which it is cut.

4. The marvellous changes which are taking place will probably render new regulations necessary for the continuance of the supply. The consumption of fuel is very great near some of the works alluded to. It is not far from the truth, that four sugar factories (Astagram, Aska, Chittavalsa, and Rajamandri) burn from 10 to 20,000 tons each in the working season; and the railway demand for sleepers requires 20,000 tons for every fifty miles under construction, besides other factories and great works hastening the clearance of the jungles.

5. One thing seems evident, that in future incorporated bodies must plant quick-growing trees* for their own use, and begin early, so that no time may be lost, and the trees be coming on whilst the preliminary operations are in progress. It would be well if such companies take up so many acres of land at each station where they have a European officer.

6. So great has been the demand for wood and fuel in the vicinity of the railways, that zamindars have raised the Kuti kanam or stump-money, and have levied a tax on every cart of firewood, seldom less than As. 2, and very often As. 4. On the other hand, the Board of Revenue, Pro. 19th June 1858, No. 2131, recommend a liberal policy, laying down "the principle of leaving the fuel of the inhabitants of a district untaxed," unless the collector can show special reasons for the restriction; and more recently the Government abolished the jungle rents in several districts (petty items of Pullari). The natural effect is, that the consumption of fuel is greater in Government jungles than it has ever been. I cannot but think that the Government

* *Acacia arabica.* *Acacia speciosa.* *Cassia javanica.*
,, *leucophlea.* *Cassia florida.* *Inga dulcis.*

have done wisely in abolishing the variety of small taxes usually levied by native proprietors on jungle products; planks, plough-shares, fuel, oil-grasses, gums, honey, resin, arrowroot, having all different imposts levied upon them, giving opportunities for extortion and obstruction of trade.

7. It must however be observed, that the abolition of these jungle rents and petty imposts tends to the extirpation of many drugs and dyes, and to the diminished supply of fuel, which is maintained by the levy of a small seignorage.

8. The products* which require the destruction of the tree should be reserved in any agreements made with contractors to prevent extermination. Those which yield articles of produce† taken without injury to the tree, as tamarind pods, soapnuts, guavas, custard apples, &c. &c., may be rented separately, and with less fear of exhaustion.

9. The subject of firewood is surrounded with many difficulties; the European merchant, the cultivator of the soil, and the sepoy, are all deeply interested in a cheap supply of this necessary of life, essential to the poorer classes; and the consideration of the question requires much attention, and very careful proceedings.

10. The circumstances of particular districts vary so much in regard to indigenous supply and local demand, that it appears to me impossible to lay down rules which admit of general application.

11. The forests of Malabar and Canara still abound in fuel, whilst the jungles of the E. Coast are generally small and stunted, except the mangrove belts of the Godavari and Kistna deltas, and the woods of the moist climate of Orissa, where there is a more rapid growth of luxuriant vegetation. Here clearing is advantageous to the increase of cultivation and the easy access of troops. In other parts of the Presidency there are vast tracts of scrubby jungle in excess of local demands, but these are generally at a distance from roads.

* Satin-wood, Sandal-wood, Red-wood, bark of *Acacia leucophlea* (used in distilleries), Catechu.

† Gums and gum-resins, as kino, gamboge, dammer, &c.; also alliaku leaves (*Memecylon tinctorium*), kapila-rang, sika-kai (*Acacia concinna*), &c.

12. To illustrate the varying circumstances of different districts, let us take Madras, Mangalore, and Utakamand. The rules which experience has suggested for any one of these are unsuitable to the other two.

13. In Madras, according to the published records of the late Military Board,* the consumption of firewood and charcoal was estimated in 1852 at 98,652½ tons per annum. This has increased much as railway operations have advanced, while the source of supply has diminished. The spontaneous reproduction of neighbouring jungle being inadequate for the purpose, the deficit has been made up from a distance by increased facilities of communication.

14. In Mangalore, the capital of a wooded district, the price is high, owing to *external* demand. At the auctions, the lots are greedily bought by country traders for Bombay, Karáchi, &c., and the sale of firewood in Canara thereby yields a very considerable revenue.

15. In Utakamand, the ripe trees of the indigenous sholas are sold by auction, fetching a small return (Rs. 20 or 30 per shola). As the influx of settlers increases, the original tree vegetation will disappear entirely, prohibitory rules will be futile, and then proprietors will plant according to their own requirements, and a few probably for profit. The experimental plantations of Government show that this may be done successfully.

16. The consumption of firewood for cooking and artificial temperature is much greater in the hill stations than in the Carnatic; indeed, the consumption may be expected to increase in the ratio of the altitude.

17. I have been asked to lay down conditions of management for the firewood jungles of Striharikota and the sholas of Utakamand. It is necessary that they should be very simple, or they will be inoperative. The native lessees are ignorant and unscrupulous; and unless the conditions be made penal under the new police, all forest rules will be violated with impunity.

18. To furnish rules for the economical conservation of the Striharikota and other small jungles is a difficult matter; but.

* Report of the Military Board to Government, 26th April 1853, p. 98.

my former Memor. (p. 145) tended to prove, that the system of renting and sub-renting lately commenced had been highly prejudicial to the jungles, and oppressive to the people. I had reason to mark that it was so in Striharikota; and I have no doubt that the same system is attended with the same results in Nellore and Guntur, and other districts, from which supplies of firewood are conveyed to Madras. The renters assume great pretensions, and, if not watched, levy cess on the villagers in the neighbourhood, and on the boats plying in the creeks.

19. The least objectionable course, in my opinion, would be to throw the privilege of cutting, and the duty of maintaining, the jungles on those who can perform both at least cost, and are most interested in their preservation, viz. the villagers. No tax should be levied from them but upon the cargo, as I believe was the system formerly.

20. It is generally admitted, that the nearer the tax is placed to the consumer, and the further from the producer, the better.

21. As to the introduction of a system of preservation and progressive improvement, to undertake this in sterile tracts on behalf of Government, by paid agents, is hopeless. The salary of a moderately-skilled overseer and peons would exceed the proceeds; the villagers alone can be looked to as the instruments in this matter. They have felt the inconvenience of a foreign renter, and will look on the permission as a boon, whilst a threat of returning to the rent will make them anxious to deserve the continuance of the privilege.

22. The next question is the mode of preservation and improvement, so as to keep up the largest supply on the ground. I think the best arrangement is, to reserve thirty standard trees to the acre, preferring such as are valuable for fruit, leaves, gums, or medicine. Whenever salt water tidal creeks occur, with muddy banks, seeds of the mangrove tribe, common to such localities, should be sown.

23. The villagers will probably do this if properly encouraged: the Palmyrah (*Borassus flabelliformis*) has increased very much by their means: the babul (*Acacia Arabica*) and punga (*Pongamia glabra*) grow and germinate freely, and cattle do not touch them. They will undertake the sowing of these with the dirisana

(*Acacia speciosa*), if a word of encouragement is given by the collector, his assistants, or other Europeans.

24. I may mention that, in particular districts, the names of certain civilians are long remembered in connection with the planting of topes and trees. For instance:—Mr Orr, Salem; Messrs Sullivan and Thomas, Coimbatore; Mr Robertson, Bellary; and Mr Rohde, Guntur.

25. On granting permission to cut, I would enjoin the planting of trees round the boundaries of village cultivation, and the sowing of trees after each year's felling. The soapnut and tamarind trees are by far the most valuable, and are often grown with profit by ryots.

26. Finally, I would urge the reserve of the jungles to the villagers without direct taxation, but under conditions:—viz., the cutting each portion once in eight years only, the preservation of thirty standard trees to the acre, including all valuable fruit, dye, or drug-bearing trees.

27. For the Striharikota or other small jungles near the seashore, the following simple rules might be observed; and the valuable trees enumerated (see p. 124) should be reserved in all districts:—(1.) Avenue trees not to be cut. (2.) Trees cherished by villagers not to be cut. (3.) Thirty standard trees to the acre to be preserved. (4.) The stem not to be cut lower than two feet from the ground, the highest point to which the driftsand will probably reach. (5.) A fringe next to the sandy beach to be left untouched. Great care should be taken not to lay bare spots of more than one hundred yards width; and the clearances should be made parallel to the sea-shore, or the part from which the sand drifts in, and an uninterrupted belt of jungle should be left all round.

28. These remarks do not apply to uninhabited forests, where there is useful timber, and where there are no local rights to be considered, but to frequented tracts of inferior jungle or brushwood, where there is a constant pressure for fuel.

29. *Taxing of Timber.*—In the Government forests of the W. Coast, whilst ryots retain their privileges, the mercantile classes are referred to the depôts, and supply themselves at the periodical auctions, and occasionally obtain by permit a specified number of

trees marked by the Conservancy Dept. at a fixed rate, varying from As. 8 to R. 1-8-0 per tree for house-building.

30. In Salem lately, with the concurrence of the collector, and in accordance with the Bombay rules, R. 1 per cart was charged, at the outlet of the Kotapati and other valleys, for wood exported for building purposes. I found, on inquiry at Vaniambadi and Vellore, that the average value of such cart-loads of timber is Rs. 5 to 6; the charge, therefore, seems reasonable, and is readily paid. I consider that a similar charge will be necessary for the protection of all Government forests along the line of the railways, more especially as zamindars have increased their imposts on all wood from their forests.

31. *Palmyrahs.*—In regard to these, I am of opinion that their preservation and increase should remain in connection with the Abkari department.

32. The Palmyrah grows well on all the barren ground of the coast at present unproductive. The sandy soil is congenial to it. The seeds buried in drifting sand often take root, and make their way to the surface. This palm also grows well in the stiff black mould near the backwaters, where the seed should be planted eight inches deep, when the soil is moist.

33. *Bamboos.*—Bamboos for exportation are allowed to be cut below ghat at a charge of Rs. 5 per 1000 for all sizes; and those granted above ghat (independent of those taken for exportation) are divided into four classes, according to size.

34. Bamboos are valuable according to their position (vicinity of large towns); sometimes they are of no value, and it would not be just to fix a common rate. In Gumsúr and Kimadi, it has been considered desirable to get rid of the bamboo jungles. In Salem and N. Arcot they are rapidly becoming scarce within ten miles of the railway, and the question of subsequent management has been under the consideration of the collectors and myself. Bamboos are exported largely from the Shevarai Hills to Trichinopoly and Madura, and the trade is said to be lucrative.

35. In conclusion, it will be seen that vast changes take place in a few years, and that it is impossible to lay down absolute rules for general application. The subject of fuel requires close attention, both as regards household requirements, climatic

changes and mercantile considerations; and in remodelling the rules of any particular district, the full concurrence of the collector should be obtained, and due respect be paid to private interests.

H. CLEGHORN,
Conservator of Forests.

MADRAS, 5*th April* 1859.

Extract Order on the foregoing Report.

4*th June* 1859, *No.* 744.

In the Memorandum, the Conservator of Forests replies to four separate references made to him by Government on various subjects. In pars. 18 and 19, Dr Cleghorn speaks of the Striharikota firewood jungle in Chingleput. He thinks that the plan of renting lately adopted has acted injuriously. The abuses noticed should be stopped, and the Board of Revenue will give their attention to the subject. Future rents should stipulate that trees should be cut down only to within two feet of the ground, as suggested. In pars. 22 to 27, Dr C. treats of the best manner of preserving light firewood jungles; and the Board will use the means at their command to make known the measures there detailed, and give them effect. The suggestions for the preservation of the Striharikota jungle, and others similarly situated, should be carefully attended to.

With these few remarks, the Government resolve to transmit Dr Cleghorn's report to the Board of Revenue. As population increases and cultivation extends, the subject of maintaining the supply of firewood becomes very important. In more advanced countries, it is recognised as one of the modes of employing capital for profit, to maintain plantations for the purpose. India has not yet reached that state; but the time is approaching when a commencement of that system will be necessary in the neighbourhood of large towns and of extensive factories. The terms on which land may be had for planting are so liberal as to offer no obstacle; but planting for this purpose is novel in this country, and there is the usual backwardness to make a beginning. The Board and the various collectors may be able to aid in removing this feeling by inducing men of more than usual intelligence and enlightenment to take the lead. This is particularly desirable in the neighbourhood of Madras. It will be well also to draw the attention of the proprietors of the factories named to Dr Cleghorn's remarks and suggestions in par. 4.

The chief engineer will also be requested to acquaint Government with what has been done in the way of planting along the N. and S. Canals, and with what effect. This important subject should be everywhere attended to.

J. D. BOURDILLON,
Secretary to Government.

FIREWOOD.

TRICHINOPOLY AND SOUTH ARCOT DISTRICTS.

Government, on the 9th June 1860, authorised the levy of a payment of As. 4 per cartload of about 750 pounds for the privilege of cutting firewood in the Government jungles in the district of Trichinopoly. This rate is to be paid by the East India Iron and Steel Company, and other parties, not belonging to the village communities. The order is also to apply to the Government jungles in South Arcot, where the Company's lease has expired.

FIREWOOD OF NILGIRI HILLS.

Letter to Secretary to Government, R. D.

Utakamand, 8*th Nov*. 1859, *No*. 836.

I have had the honour of receiving Procs. of Government, Rev. Dep., 26th Sept., No. 1300, referring for report a letter (15th Sept.) of the collector of Coimbatore, regarding the "urgent necessity" of conserving the forests and fuel of the Nilgiri Hills.

2. The subject has engaged my attention for a long period; but it is attended with great practical difficulties. There can be no doubt that the forests in the vicinity of the hill stations have greatly suffered of late years; but private planting, at least at Utakamand, is largely on the increase. I have no doubt that, in the course of the next ten years, the wants of the community, so far as fuel is concerned, will be in great measure supplied from private plantations. The great object in the meantime is to prevent the Government woods being destroyed.

3. The conservation of these is necessary to preserve the water-springs, for shelter, &c.; and I may here add, that so long as persons can cut *ad libitum* in Government forests without payment, the most powerful incentive to private planting is lost.

4. It is difficult to say exactly what the requirements of the Utakamand community may be. There are at present 7420 houses (European, 273; native, 7147),* and I suppose about 4000 fires are daily burning during great part of the year. For six or seven years past the main supply has been brought from the westward; and on the side of the road to Pykara, about twenty sholas (large and small) have been very much thinned out.

* "The population consists of—Europeans, 2500; natives, 34,500; East Indians, 500. Every European house has three or four fires daily."—E. B. Thomas, *Collector*.

5. At Wellington, the consumption of fuel supplied by contract, from Government forests of course, is about 5000 lbs. daily; and this is exclusive of what the engineer department requires.

6. At Kúnúr and Kótagiri the demand is smaller.

7. In addition, much timber is required for building and other similar purposes: the whole of this necessarily comes from Government forests.

8. With so great a demand, conservancy is extremely difficult. The establishment at our disposal comprises only a single forester and six peons, and is obviously insufficient. *

9. I would now propose that, in communication with the collector, I should at once mark all such forests as should be wholly reserved for Government or public purposes. These would be marked in the station maps, and public notification be given of their reservation. When it became necessary to fell trees for thinning or other reasons, this should be done by this department, and under my orders.

10. During my visits to the hills, I would inspect these reserved tracts, and give the necessary instructions. The sales of wood would be by public auction, and the proceeds would be credited to Government. I propose this measure, because experience has shown the impossibility of preserving a forest, if woodcutters and cattle are allowed to enter it.

11. This being done, the question arises, How the other woods are to be dealt with? Many of the residents keep woodcutters on monthly pay. These men go and cut timber wherever they can; and if they would be satisfied with old and decayed trees, I should not complain, but, unfortunately, they generally select small trees, as being more easily felled, and, I am told, not unfrequently ring and fire good timber to ensure a future supply for their own use. The wants of other residents are supplied by private traders, who in like manner appropriate Government timber.

12. Two methods of action have suggested themselves to me :—

* *Present Establishment.*—Forester, Rs. 35; 6 peons at Rs. 5 = Rs. 30; Total, Rs. 65.

(1.) That the tracts which are not reserved for Government purposes, as above proposed, should be periodically rented out by public auction to the highest bidder (as at Striharikota); the timber to be cut close to the ground, and removed within a stated period upon pain of forfeiture. After being thus cleared, the tract to be replanted by my department with fast growing Australian trees, which need little care or trouble. The auction proceeds would admit of this being done, and would, I think, leave a surplus to meet the general charges of conservancy, and admit of further planting. The only objection to this plan is, that it would overthrow the present custom of persons employing wood-cutters. The result of the system would doubtless be, that the renters would establish depôts for the sale of timber and fuel.

(2.) Another plan suggested is, that woodcutters should be required to take out a licence from my office, paying Rs. 12 per annum for a daily cooly load, and Rs. 48 per annum for a cart-load. This charge would in reality fall upon their employers, and would add little to the price of fuel. The licensed cutters would be provided with a ticket for production when required by my subordinates. The cost of wood is now Rs. $2\frac{1}{2}$ or Rs. 3 per cart load, and As. 3 per man's load, so that these charges are light.

13. I prefer the first plan, as the simplest and most effectual. It would of course be my care to let a number of lots amply sufficient for the requirements of the community, without trenching on the supplies of future years, and to arrange the lots so as to preclude a monopoly,—an object which could always be attained by throwing fresh lots into the market.

14. With the funds thus procured, I expect to be able to entertain one, if not two additional European foresters. The expense thus incurred will be Rs. 35 for one forester, with six peons at Rs. 5 = Rs. 30; and for two foresters, with three peons each, Rs. 35 + 65 = 100.* Without additional aid of this kind it is hopeless to attempt efficient conservancy.

15. I further propose to notify to the collector, from time to

* *Proposed Establishment.*—2 foresters, Rs. 70; 6 peons, Rs. 30 = Rs. 100.

time, such forests, shólas, &c., as I think should *not* be felled. I would suggest that these should be marked on the station-maps as *reserved*, and some distinguishing mark should be placed round them for general information,—a measure which would cost little.

16. Any person cutting timber in such tracts should, according to circumstances, be prosecuted *at once* in a suit for trespass and damage, or treated as a case of petty theft of Government property, to be dealt with by the magistrate. Unless such proceedings are checked by speedy punishment, as a matter of course they will recur and render my exertions futile.

17. Similar means should be adopted to check Kurumbar clearings, charcoal burning, &c., which at present are unrestricted, except that, by order of the collector, they must not take place within three miles of the top of the Kúnúr Ghat.

18. I have above stated (par. 5), that the demand for fuel at Wellington is about 5000 lbs. daily. This is supplied on contract made without any reference to the collector, or to me, and the contractors cut in Government forests without seeking permission. The Badagas, again, take under contracts, as reported by the tahsíldár. The Rallia and all the jungles near Kúnúr have thus suffered much. I would propose that I should first be consulted as to the place where so large a quantity may be cut; and that this right of cutting, in authorised places only, should be let to the highest bidder. I should in such cases select proper places, and restrain the contractor from cutting trees below a certain size, and trees of value for timber or fruit, as teak, blackwood, &c.

19. When large quantities of fuel are required for public purposes, as for instance the new jail being erected at Utakamand, every effort should be made to economise the supply available. With this view, I have arranged with Mr Rohde, that the fuel for brick-burning shall be obtained by felling trees overhanging the trace of the proposed road to Karkúr, which sooner or later, I presume, is sure to be widened. In like manner, much wood may be available for the Wellington Barracks, when the new ghat is opened out from Kúnúr to the railway station.

20. I would also very strongly recommend economy in the use

of fuel, by employing improved kitchen ranges, and substituting peat in part for wood. The regulation allowance of fuel, I believe, is 3 lbs. per man. I understand that an improved range has been lately invented by a Capt. Grant in England, whereby a very large saving is effected. Dr Duff, at Madras, has also produced a range which greatly economises fuel; and I would urge the employment of either of these at the barracks instead of the common open range now used. I would also make it a condition of the bakery and other contracts, where much fuel is used, that these inexpensive ranges should be used by the contractors. It is obviously unwise to continue the present ranges, which consume so much fuel, when we are pressed for wood, and are in other ways trying to economise it. These remarks apply more to the mainguard, hospital, and barracks, than to the "married quarters," where the open range probably has greater advantages.

21. As the price of wood will, to a certain extent, be increased by the alterations proposed, the residents will necessarily have recourse to the use of peat,* which was strongly advocated by Lord Harris in his "Minute on the Nilgiri Hills." I would recommend the early adoption of measures tending to the economical employment of this indigenous fuel.

H. CLEGHORN.

Extract Order on the foregoing Letter.

20th March 1860, *No.* 425.

7. When recently at Utakamand, the Hon. the President (Sir C. Trevelyan) gave careful attention to this subject, and discussed it fully with the conservator, as well as with numerous resi-

* Peat in large quantity exists, and may be purchased at a reasonable rate; and if a proportion of this was used in houses with the wood, the expenditure of the latter would be much lessened, and the total cost to the consumer considerably reduced. Turf fuel is now cut and stacked in several places close to the station, and is to be had at the rate of Rs. 2 or 2½ per cart-load. It burns well and makes a cheerful fire, especially when mixed with wood.

dents of the hills. He was thoroughly convinced of the urgent necessity of conservancy, on the one hand to preserve the beautiful shólas which now form the ornament of the hill stations, and of Utakamand in particular; and on the other, to secure Government property from waste and spoliation, and to perpetuate the supply of firewood. After much discussion, the following measures were agreed to as the best to be adopted in the case of Utakamand—they agree generally with those proposed by Dr Cleghorn :—

The reserved woods at Utakamand.—1. The whole of the shólas, or woods, in the neighbourhood of the station to be absolutely reserved, not only for their beauty, but also from fear of injuring the water springs; their limits to be marked; no private cutters to be allowed inside; old trees to be felled by servants of the department, and brought outside, and to be sold there by public auction. Trees to be planted where required, in vacant spaces.

2. Suitable woods, at a distance from the station, to be selected and marked out in lots of moderate size; and a number of these lots, amply sufficient for a year's supply, to be put up to auction annually. The contractor to be permitted to clear the ground entirely within his lot or lots, with the exception of such trees as may be marked by the Conservancy Department previous to the sale.

3. The cleared lots to be planted, as required, by the Conservancy Department.

4. No private felling of any kind, or for any person, to be allowed in woods, or on land belonging to Government.

These measures are now approved by the Governor in Council; and the conservator will adopt the necessary means to carry them into effect, with no more delay than is necessary to prevent a failure of the supply of fuel during the transition, and to secure existing rights.

J. D. BOURDILLON,
Secretary to Government.

REPORT ON THE MUDUMALAI FOREST.*

1. The Mudumalai forest is in the district of Malabar, lying between the Sigúr Forest in Coimbatore and Gundalpet in Mysore, and includes (*fide* Capt. Morgan) "an area of about 200 square miles. The extreme length is 24 miles, the average breadth 8 miles." It is rented by Government from the Tirupad of Nelambur for the supply of teak to the Wellington barracks. The lease was entered into in 1857, with the concurrence of Mr Robinson, then acting collector of Malabar, and was for a term of five years, of which 3½ are still to run. The annual rent is Rs. 2300.

2. *General Character.*—The general character of the forest is good, containing a large quantity of Teak (*Tectona grandis*), Blackwood (*Dalbergia latifolia*), Ventek (*Lagerströmia microcarpa*), Marda (*Terminalia glabra*), Véngé (*Pterocarpus marsupium*. There are some grassy knolls covered with good pasture, the largest teak trees are in the valley of Gogahala and on the banks of the Moyàr river. The trees are considerably more lofty than those in Sigúr, and the jungle generally much resembles that on the north and eastern frontier of Wainád.

3. *Boundaries.*—East, Tipakadu; north-west, Nellikota; south, Sigúr.

4. *Detail of Forest Operations.*—The wood-cutters are Kurumbars, inhabiting the forest; the sawyers come from Mysore; the dragging of the logs to the forest track is performed partly by elephants,—of which eight belong to the commissariat and six to

* This is the only notice of this forest on record. It was called for by Government in connection with the supply of timber to the Wellington barracks.

the forest stock, paid out of barrack estimates,—and partly by buffaloes purchased for the purpose.

5. The carriage from the forest to the barracks is performed by two sets of contractors, chiefly Mahomedans, one set carrying only as far as Utakamand, and the second from Utakamand to Wellington. The reason that the whole work is not performed by one set of contractors is, that the bullocks would then be two days above ghat, which the owners say proves injurious to the cattle from the low country, giving rise to bronchial affections.

6. *Charge for felling.*—The logs are cut and squared by Kurumbars, at the rate of A. 1 per cubic foot, which is a fair wage, and corresponds with the charge in many parts of western Mysore.

7. *Sawing.*—The rate is 40 running feet per rupee, when the log does not exceed one foot in the square; when the cut exceeds 13 inches in depth, the rate is 20 feet per rupee. The Mysore rate is 45 square feet per rupee,—the average here is 30, which, considering the unhealthy climate and distance from their home, is not excessive. There is little sawing done now, except dividing large logs, which are otherwise unmanageable for carts.

8. *Carriage.*—When the weather is favourable, the commissariat bullocks are employed in conveying logs from the western extremity of the forest to the eastern limit, viz., the high road at Tipakadu, a distance of 18 miles, from which the wood is conveyed by contract carts to Utakamand.

9. *Measurement.*—The logs are measured at Mudumalai by the manager or his assistant, and payment is made accordingly. Every axeman (Kurumbar) receives his due partly in money, but chiefly in grain (by preference, and I may say of necessity), at the market rate, and a settlement takes place weekly; the average earnings of an axeman is Rs. 5 per mensem, but an industrious man easily earns Rs. 8.

10. The measurement in the forest is of the actual cubic contents of each log,—a difference, however, occurs in the accounts of remeasurement at Wellington; which (from the explanation given to me) arises from taking the measurement to which the log would square to in its whole length, the former I need hardly remark is the usual mode. A further difference arises from the officers at the barracks measuring within the draghole, which is

in accordance with the general custom. This explains the difference of measurement noted in par. 5 of G. O., 4th July 1859, No. 1637.

11. *Fragments.*—There is a large quantity of slabs, cracked planks, tops, butts, &c., which, though not suitable for the barracks, are saleable in the Utakamand market and elsewhere. Those at the karkhana might be disposed of at a fixed rate (say As. 10 to 12 according to quality) by the manager, to any person who sends for them; those at the Gundalpet workshop might suit the engineer of the Bangalore Railway, and I have addressed Mr Beattie on the subject. Any remaining fragments, after the completion of the barracks, might be sold by auction. The probable receipts from the sale may be put down at Rs. 5000.

12. *Carriage cost.*—The distance from Tipakadu to Utakamand is 23 miles, and is paid for at As. 5 per cub. ft. The distance from Utakamand to Wellington is 10 miles, and the timber is carried by a distinct set of contractors, or by bullocks belonging to the barracks, the rate is equal to As. 3 per cub. ft., making As. 8 in all from the forest to the barracks.

13.—*Logs in forest.*—During the four days I traversed the forest I saw and counted 1030 logs, averaging 15 cub. ft., equal to 18,000 cub. ft. In addition, Capt. Morgan informed me that there were in other parts, which I had not time to visit, and at the Gundalpet workshop which I inspected, 11,000 feet, making a total of 30,000 feet of seasoned teak.* It will thus be seen that there is no dearth of good wood, but the chief difficulty of supply is the steepness of the Sigúr ghat, and the heaviness of the roads during the monsoon months.

14. *Establishment.*—The establishment is employed temporarily; the monthly cost at this date is Rs. 542 (including the salary of the Supt.); this is Rs. 20 less than the sum stated in Col. Lawford's letter, 26th May 1859. Mr De Monte is in charge of the workshop, all the other employés are natives. Several valuable lives have been lost from the unhealthiness of the forest. I found several cartmen and bullock-drivers suffering from fever and its consequences, enlarged spleen and general

* 25,000 Mudumalai; 5000 Mysore.

debility, and insisted strongly upon their being supplied with thick cumblies and sleeping on high cots.

15. *Elephants.*—There are at present 14 elephants at work in these forests. Eight belonging to the commissariat having dragged to the road the greater part of the logs, will be transferred in the course of this month to Anamalai, where they are much required.

16. *Bullocks.*—Of 50 pairs of bullocks received two months ago from Hunsur, 47 pairs are at work, one bullock was killed by a tiger, two died on the ghat, and in two months six untrained animals were lost in the jungle.

17. *Karkhana.*—The whole of the buildings are mud edifices. These are Capt. Morgan's hut, the office, bullock-shed, and sawpits, all roofed in with bamboo mats. I think it might be worth while to build a small brick granary for the remainder of the lease; the loss and injury to the food supplies (rice, ràgi, grain, chillies, cocoa-nuts, &c.) during the monsoon is considerable, and the risk of fire in the dry weather is great.

18. *Tank.*—A small tank, constructed by Capt. Morgan, is of great use to the department; there are now ten feet of water in it, and in the hot weather this gives the sole supply for the elephants and establishment.

19. *Roads.*—The forest is divided into two parts by a long narrow swamp, in which the elephants often stuck fast, and over which they could not drag the heavy logs. By damming one end of this, the tank beforementioned has been formed, and this band now forms a communication for carts, &c.

20. A fair cart road has been constructed from the karkhana to Nardi, a distance of 10 miles, and a second road to Kâkanâla, distance of 7 miles. The road from the karkhana to Tipakadu (8 miles) has been opened and improved, another road to the Gogohala valley has been commenced, and will soon be completed.

21. The working of this rented forest has not hitherto fallen under my supervision, but, in accordance with the order of Government, I beg to offer the following suggestions:—

(1.) That the management continue as at present under the charge of Capt. Morgan, executive engineer, who shall reserve the best timber for the Wellington barracks and other Government purposes. This officer is well qualified for the work, and, after many attacks of fever, is in a measure acclimatised.

(2.) That to assist in defraying the working expenses, the inferior logs and fragments be sold as opportunities offer.

(3.) That in anticipation of the continued demand for teak on the Nilgiris for Government purposes even after the barracks are finished, a new ghat be kept in view. At present, the carriage up to Utakamand adds 50 per cent. to the value of the wood below. Indeed, additional carriage is not available, none but practised bullocks come up the ghat.

(4.) There being no public officer so much interested in the state of the ghat and road from the Mysore boundary to Wellington, and no one who sees so much of the traffic and its requirements, I venture to suggest that this line of road be placed under Capt. Morgan, and this would give him full employment.

(5.) In order to lighten the carriage as much as possible, I would advise that, after the elephants have dragged the logs to the depôt below, the end pieces with the dragholes be sawn off. This seems a trivial matter, but when many hundred logs are being carried, the removal of 8 or 10 inches (useless) would be of some importance. There is much old wood lying on the side of the ghat, belonging to Edalji and Husain Bava, the former contractors of the Sigúr forests. As this tends to cause confusion, and to facilitate pilfering, I warned these timber merchants that they must remove to one place whatever they could prove to be their property in course of a fortnight.

(6.) In reference to the method of keeping the accounts, Capt. Farewell, special executive engineer, informs me that he has instructed Capt. Morgan to adhere strictly to the rules of the D. P. W.

(7.) If any other large public building is likely to be erected on the hills, requiring much timber, early intimation should be given, as the collecting of sawyers and kurumbars is a matter of difficulty, and attended with considerable expense.

H. Cleghorn, M.D.,
Conservator of Forests.

(B.) *Extract Letter on the same subject to the Executive Engineer, Wellington Barracks.*

Utakamand, 27th July 1859.

There are four forests from which you can receive the required timber for the Wellington works, viz.:—1. Anamalai; 2. Sigúr; 3. Mudumalai; 4. Mysore.

Anamalai.—(1.) The Anamalai timber was tried, and found to be superior, but very expensive, the carriage up the Kúnúr ghat being most difficult, even for logs of moderate size (as 20 cubic feet): besides this, the long scantling is peculiarly suited for ship-building, and the short pieces being in great demand for the railway, gun-carriage manufactory, &c., it seems undesirable to have recourse to this source of supply for barrack buildings.

Sigúr.—(2.) The late contractor at Sigúr (*Husain Bava*) has a considerable supply of wood in his yard at Utakamand, and a large quantity at his depôt below ghat: the wood is good, but generally of short lengths, averaging 12 feet, which does not suit your purposes; the cost is ¾ rupee per cubic foot below, and R. 1 As. 4, above ghat, in sawn logs. There can be no objection to a selection of such rafters, &c., as are found to suit the required measurements.

Mudumalai.—(3.) I have visited Mudumalai Forest to enable me to report on the system of management, in accordance with the order of Government, 4th July 1859, No. 1637. The size of the logs there is greater than at Sigúr, averaging 16 or 18 feet; and I think if Col. Lawford had the same opportunities of judging as I have had when traversing the forests, he would not have condemned the timber. The quality generally appears to be excellent; the quantity in seasoned logs is not far from 25,000 feet; of this I saw 18,000 feet, which had been dragged to the side of the forest road.

Mysore.—(4.) There are quarterly auctions held in the town of Mysore, and about 1000 logs are available in the Heggadévinkóta Forest; the rate of the last sale of teak was R. 1 per c. f.

Two hundred selected logs have been sent to the Gundalpét workshop, and this seems to be a good arrangement.

Conclusion.—I have thus reviewed the different sources of supply, and would only remark in conclusion, that there is no lack of good timber; the great difficulty in supplying it to the Wellington barracks, is from the steepness of the ghat, and the state of the roads during the wet season. It seems indispensably necessary to have an officer of experience and energy to superintend the Sigúr and Mudumalai Forests; the supervision of these with the Gundalpét workshop occupies Capt. Morgan fully. I have borne testimony to his peculiar fitness for this office, and I think that his removal at present would occasion much difficulty.

NOTE.—The remarks made in the preceding page regarding the Anamalai and other Forests are introduced in anticipation of the wants of the growing settlement of Utakamand. Apart altogether from the possibility of the seat of Government being transferred to the Nilgiri Hills, other important movements are either progressing or contemplated; and, indeed, it has recently been found necessary to appoint a special assistant to take charge of this important range, whilst another officer superintends the Wynad and Hegadévinkóta Forests.

PLANTATION OF AUSTRALIAN TREES, NILGIRI HILLS.

Much has been written on the subject of planting the Nilgiri Hills, chiefly by the gentlemen named below,* who have successively recommended the establishment of tree plantations. It is scarcely necessary to dwell upon the advantages to be derived from promoting this desirable measure; but they may be briefly stated:—1. Plantations create and improve the soil, and secure the permanency of the springs; 2. Plantations shelter from the violent winds and modify the climate; 3. They furnish material for house-building, furniture, &c.; 4. They furnish fuel, fencing materials, &c.; 5. They are ornamental.

Private individuals are planting largely near their dwelling-houses, through the instrumentality of the well-furnished arboretum existing at the Govt. Gardens; but the experiment recommended in the first instance, and superintended in its progress by Capt. Campbell, is the only attempt at forest planting in the Nilgiri Hills on a considerable scale on the part of Government. Having in my first visit been pleased with the general arrangements and the healthy appearance of the young trees, I requested Capt. Campbell to favour me with a summary of the progress of his operations, specifying, 1. The establishment employed; 2. The method of procedure and number of trees planted; 3. The sum of money received and expended; 4. The prospects of the plantations, and his own wishes in regard to its future management. The annexed memo., 10th August 1857, furnishes these details.

* Honourable J. Sullivan, "Agri-Hort. Socy.'s Proceedings;" Capt. Allardyce, Dr Wight, and Capt. Ouchterlony, in "Madras Journal of Literature and Science;" E. B. Thomas, Esq., Capt. J. Campbell, and Mr W. G. M'Ivor, "Official Reports."

"*Memorandum* of the Condition and Prospects of the new new forest of Kónagati, near Wellington, Nilgiris, commenced March 1856, under sanction of E. M. C., 7th February 1856.

"1. *Site and Physical Features.*—The valley selected for experiment, partly on account of its vicinity to works under my charge, extends in an easterly direction from the saddle of Billi Kumbi (where the public road from Kúnúr to Kótagiri, distant 3½ miles from Wellington, bounds it for a few yards) till it joins the great "Kóta-shóla," from which the Public Works have, during the last five years, drawn 15,000 tons of wood. The valley, which attains a mean elevation of 6400 feet, is well sheltered by high ranges of hills from the dry, cutting northerly winds and the sweeping easterly blasts, and is intersected by a small stream of water which reveals a variety of soils from rich black mould to a thin red oxide of iron, mixed with siliceous masses resembling laterite, all reposing on a stiff felspathic clay, in which very faint traces of lime may occasionally be detected.

"2. *Establishment.*—No regular establishment has been kept up; working parties, European or native, chiefly the latter, as they could be spared from other duties, have received orders direct from myself, the funds at my disposal not admitting the entertainment of a qualified overseer. During the last six months, however, I derived much assistance from Corporal Hall,* H.M.'s 84th Foot (whose services have been partially available). He has some acquaintance with forestry, and is a steady, zealous workman, in whom I place confidence.

"3. *Number of Trees Planted and Method of Procedure.*—At intervals of 4 feet on four acres of grass land, 14,400 seedlings of *Acacia robusta* were planted out this year, the ground being previously well trenched at a cost of Rs. 90 per acre. 3300 running yards of ditch, 4 feet deep and 7 feet wide at top, have been dug, and 1200 yards of paling put up. The trees are planted in long lines of mathematical accuracy, so that one cannot be cut without detection. No manure has been used; close planting and trenching have produced vigorous plants from seedlings

* "Placed under orders of Conservator of Forests, M. of C., 6th Jan. 1858."

raised on the most exposed situations, now averaging 3 feet in height and one inch round the collar. In the Kóta-shóla success has been attained on easier terms; we have there 36,000 hard-woods, comprising *Halay*, *Kalangu*, *Backani*, *Halluni*, *Narsippi*, *Nakalu*, and other varieties, pitted on 11 acres of clearing bared by the wood-cutting parties; yet in both instances the young trees are, of their age, the largest and healthiest I remember to have seen (even in America), unstimulated by manure, which I have always found produces soft heart and sometimes premature decay.

"4. *Money Received and Expended.*—Of the Rs. 7500 placed by Government at my disposal, I have spent Rs. 5640–10–10 as follows:—

	Rs.	A.	P.
To trenching 6 acres at Rs. 90, . . .	540	0	0
... 3300 yards ditching, fencing, and on water-courses,	618	5	0
... 15,000 seedlings at Rs. 7 per 100, . .	1050	0	0
... Seeds and nursery beds, ...	371	8	6
... Baskets, ...	212	1	11
... Purchase of land, . . .	700	0	0
... Forester's house, ...	100	0	0
... Rifle for shooting wild animals, . . .	80	0	0
... Ventilating paths, ...	8	2	0
... 36,000 hardwoods, including the necessary watering, nurseries, and fencing, ...	1780	9	5
	5460	10	10
Leaving unexpended balance, .	2029	5	2
Total, ...	7500	0	0

"5. *Proposed Management.*—The prospects of the plantation are such, that if, owing to the present financial pressure, Government should not feel disposed to make a further grant of money before May 1858, I can manage to carry on fencing, pitting, nursery beds, &c. on a reduced, but still safe and efficient scale, for the next 9 months, when I expect to have one lac of young trees ready to set out. By that time funds will probably be available.

JOHN CAMPBELL,
Capt. 7th L. Cavy."

10*th August* 1857.

Remarks on the foregoing Memorandum.

Site.—The plantation is situated, as observed, 3 miles from Wellington, close to the road from Kúnúr to Kōtagiri, and near the site selected for the proposed European Jail. The valley is well chosen, being sheltered from the prevailing winds and watered by a stream. The soil is generally good, and the slopes enjoy a variety of aspects well suited for experimental planting.

Price of Land.—Rs. 700 was paid to the Badaga villagers after negotiating with the collector of the district. The extent of land is 600 acres.

Area Planted.—When I visited the hills, six acres were planted, fenced with wooden paling, and protected by a hedge of *Cæsalpinia sepiaria*, the Mysore thorn. This was required, the wild animals being destructive. The plantation has since been extended to eight acres.

System pursued.—The seeds are sown in 4-feet beds, and in dry weather are watered once in three or four days from a small channel cut for the purpose. Long rows of *Acacia robusta* were coming above ground, four rows in each 4-feet bed, so that the rows were 1 foot apart. This tree is considered the best suited for the rapid production of firewood. The quick succession of suckers which it throws up led to its exclusion from the Horticultural Garden ; but this renders it valuable for the prospective supply of fuel. Several suckers are thrown out from each tree, which form much wood if all have room to grow. In addition to these nursery beds, there were some thousands of seedlings in baskets under cover. Altogether, 100,000 seedlings have been prepared in anticipation of the next rains. There were also many young *Kalangu*, an indigenous Cedrelaceous tree, the timber of which is prized by the Badagas. There were other trees in small number, as *Cedrus deodara* and *Pinus longifolia:* the *Acacia robusta melanoxylon*, and *lophantha*, however, form the bulk of the plantation.

Planting out.—The seedlings were afterwards planted in pasture land, covered with coarse grass and tangled bracken (*Glei-*

chenia Hermanni). There is no scarcity of such land on the Nilgiris. At first, Capt. Campbell trenched 14 inches deep, and put in 11,000 young Acacias 4 feet apart. Of these, a large proportion were looking well. In the course of the experiment he ascertained that the expense of trenching is unnecessary. He now makes holes 1 foot square by contract, and has engaged a gang of Badagas to prepare them at the rate of 150 holes per rupee; 24 holes are made by each cooly per diem. The distance between the trees has been increased from 3 to 6 feet, but varies according to situation. The arrangement is everywhere *quincunx;* and where other trees are mixed with the Acacia, the alternation of hard and soft wood (as shown in the diagram, Brown's "Forester," p. 442) is adopted.

The *Acacia lophantha* thrives in every soil, and answers well as a nurse to guard slow-growing wood. (*Bot. Reg.* v. t. 361.)

It may be of use to direct attention to careless management in transplanting seedlings, which causes serious injury both in public and private plantations. Observing some stunted plants in the Australian plantation, surrounded by vigorous young trees, I pulled up the nearest to ascertain the cause, which became at once apparent. The cooly employed in transplanting had pressed down the tap-root with his feet, producing the contorted appearance seen in fig. 8; the double twist interfered with the circulation of the sap, and the plant drooped in consequence.

Fig. 8.

This disregard to the requirements of the tap-root is not applicable to one part of the country, or to one set of plantations: there is a general carelessness in this matter, and the evil results are visible even in the coffee gardens of experienced planters. To prevent the occurrence of this mischief, Capt. Campbell places trees intended for transplantation in wicker baskets supplied by contract; through the sides of these the roots readily penetrate; and when the time for transplanting has arrived, the half-decayed baskets are potted in the holes which have been prepared. This answers well.*

In working the great Kóta-shóla for the requirements of the barracks, Capt. Campbell has attended to conservancy rules and economical management. He has planted the cleared portions with thousands of young trees, of sorts most esteemed by the Badagas, species of *Cleyera*, *Gordonia*, *Ilex*, &c. He has pruned the stumps, and made ventilating paths through the densely wooded portions. Hitherto, when a glade has been doomed to the axe, it has speedily disappeared; but in this case, when the demand for fuel was urgent, there has been simultaneously an organised system to promote reproduction. A broad outer fringe has been left to protect from high winds and to keep out herds of cattle; the timber has been removed by well laid out cross roads fenced throughout; a necessary measure, as the depredations of cattle and wild animals of various kinds are very injurious to the welfare of young plantations. The roads are sufficiently broad to allow two laden carts to pass one another easily. In several rocky turns of the road, a few Himalayan Deodars and other trees have been planted in an ornamental manner.

2. *Planting in the vicinity of Utakamand.*—In E. M. C., No. 989, 26*th Sept.* 1857, *R. D.*, a sum of Rs. 2500 was placed at the disposal of the collector, Mr Thomas, for planting trees in and about Utakamand. Mr T. states, 13th July 1857, that he has planted about 8000 Australian trees, different species (*Acacia* and *Eucalyptus*), at a cost of Rs. 400, and re-sown the old denuded forests to a certain extent. To prevent the destruction of the young trees by cattle, he finds it best to employ a watcher on Rs. 4 or 5 a month, as a ditch or fence, to be really effective, and to protect a plantation of several acres, would entail large expenditure, and would be unsuited to his operations. So far as I could judge in my visit to the Nilgiris, the watchman was inefficient, and many young trees had been eaten down by hares, or broken by cattle and deer roaming about. A hut is an essential

* The employment of moss for this purpose has been adopted by Mr W. G. M'Ivor. It has the advantage of economising space in carriage and soil in planting.

addition, and Mr M'Ivor considers that wire-fencing* is absolutely required. Mr Thomas's labours have not been confined to a single locality; but, though apparently desultory in character, when compared with Capt. Campbell's system of planting, they have been in their way highly useful. He has earnestly and unceasingly exercised a personal supervision of the woods round Utakamand when he visited the Nilgiris, and has manifested a warm interest in the progress of this department, as evinced by the establishment of his private garden at Barliár, which has been productive of much good in disseminating fruit and other trees. I do not hesitate to affirm that, but for his continual exertions, the neighbourhood of Utakamand would have been denuded of its remaining beautiful shólas long since.

3. *Preservation of the Nilgiri Forests.*—For the maintenance of the Nilgiri Shólas (glades), it is hopeless to expect conservancy by rules altogether prohibitory. Much timber runs to waste, and this, when decayed and fallen, is now sold; the wood-cutter's axe is necessarily in demand previous to its removal. The greater part of the wood brought into Utakamand is fetched by Badagas, and is cut within 2 to 7 miles of the limits of the cantonment. The right to remove *dead* trees necessarily induces an interest in destroying them. The present establishment, consisting of a forester and 6 peons, for the conservancy of the Nilgiri Shólas, seems susceptible of improvement. One or more foresters are required; but the peons, unless instructed and carefully selected men, are comparatively useless. They have no authority, but assume much. The duty of forester may be easily performed by one man, provided the rules are such as to limit the authorised operations of the wood-cutters to certain localities, as has been the custom: but a better course appears to be, to portion out the sholas; to conserve only a certain number of the finest growing trees to the acre, or by estimate to the shólas; to limit the period of cutting say to one year in ten for each shóla, and to plant afterwards young quick growing-trees in and around each shóla. The forester would, by personal inspection, ascertain that no cutting, was going on out of the authorised limits. All power to cut

* The only objection to wire-fencing is expense and carriage.

dead wood would be withheld, and the shólas would be let under proper restrictions, which the forester would see enforced. Previous to the letting of the shólas, all reserved timber should be marked.

It might be a good plan, in the first instance, to try the experiment of a man marking or scotching all the decayed moss-covered trees in a shóla, and then selling them by auction; this would get rid of much old and useless wood, and give room for the young saplings to grow. This arrangement might supply all timber needed for seven years. The woods might then be worked, as in England, with a reserve of 10 large or 40 smaller trees per acre, with the fringe outside, which is of great importance; certain shólas being set apart for each year, and no axe on any pretence allowed in the rest. The annual influx of residents, tradesmen, and coffee planters, and the increasing demand for firewood, has produced a marked and most prejudicial effect on the indigenous woods of the Nilgiris.

Peat Bogs.—Turf might be more extensively used as a substitute for wood than at present. I have examined the Tallichéri bog, which is regularly worked by Capt. Campbell. This turf is an excellent fuel, and I advocate its use by the military as well as in private houses. With a little admixture of wood it answers every purpose, and it is most desirable to encourage the consumption of this material. I am aware that Capts. Francis and Campbell have used it for brick and lime burning, and I would urge its employment (in lieu of wood) to the utmost extent in all Public Works. The price per ton is less than that of wood. The chief impediment to the working of the bogs on the western part of the hills is, the small number of sunny days to dry the turf thoroughly. But this does not apply to the eastward; and the objection to the use of peat which I have heard, viz., that the dust created is injurious to furniture, has been exaggerated. Several Europeans work the peat bogs, which are not burdened with any tax; but the profits being smaller than those obtainable in other vocations, the trade is not briskly followed up.* (P. 162.)

* It has been affirmed that peat has never been found in the Tropics. This is incorrect, although it is true as stated (p. 87), that the only peat

Suggested Improvements.—I may allude to the importance of planting near the cantonment of Wellington, at present unprotected from the prevailing strong winds, which blow over the bare hills without any screen. I have solicited the opinion of the medical officers stationed on the hills as to the prospective value of planting generally. This measure might be gradually accomplished at little expense, as there will always be amongst the soldiers several gardeners, so that tree planting may be well and economically carried out. The concurrent testimony of three medical officers is appended. The thriving young plantations around several residences show what may be effected in that locality. The new road from Wellington to Utakamand is almost without a tree throughout its entire length (12 miles). Much of the ghat is scarped out of rock, and the slope, at many points, is too bare and precipitous for planting, but in the angles and sheltered corners, clumps of trees might be advantageously laid down, which would, in some measure, diminish the force of the wind. Again, on the road from Avalanche to Sispára, there is a long stretch of bleak and treeless country, in which every year a number of Malabar coolies perish benumbed with cold: (additional rest-houses have been ordered for their protection). It has occurred to me that a belt of the Australian Acacias might be useful in sheltering travellers, the seed being sown in quantity and run in with the plough; in this way a tolerable barrier might be raised against the wind, which, for great part of the year, blows fresh, and sometimes so strong that men can hardly stand.

Ornamental Planting.—Ornament may seem to be a secondary condition, still it would not be altogether out of place in the vicinity of Utakamand, where, with a little attention in planting and laying

obtained from India which has been subjected to analysis was a specimen from Thibet. Large tracts, however, of valuable peat bogs occur in the valleys of the Koonda Mountains. As to the character of this peat, its composition has not yet been determined by analysis, but this will speedily be ascertained. The general appearance of the bogs considerably resembles those which occur in Britain; and although the botanical species which compose them are not identical, the same genera are often present in both—such as, *Scirpus, Carex, Parnassia, Utricularia;* others being absent, as *Erica, Eriophora,* &c.; the *Spagnum* prevailing very extensively in the upland marshes of the East as well as in Europe.

out the ground, great effect might be produced with little trouble, and with a fair prospect of ultimate profit. Much might be done in this way, where the advantages of climate are so great, and a Government arboretum already exists. Taking this view, I consulted Mr M'Ivor, and visited with him several localities in the immediate vicinity, which seemed particularly eligible for ornamental planting. I also called upon him for an estimate of the expense of planting 10,000 trees, which is annexed, for the favourable consideration of Government. I formerly ventured to suggest (Memo., 6th August 1857), that Mr M'Ivor having now served the Government for ten years without increase of salary, might reasonably be allowed an addition so as to raise his allowances from Rs.125 to 200 per mensem, *on the express condition that he devotes his whole time unreservedly to Government service.* I would respectfully renew this suggestion. In addition to his regular garden duties, Mr M'Ivor may be required to conduct the experimental planting of 10,000 trees, in accordance with his estimate, and to supervise the renovation of shólas within five miles of Utakamand.

Dr J. Maitland writes—"I have the honour to acknowledge the receipt of your letter, and proceed to give my opinion on the subject of tree planting on the Nilgiri Hills, with reference to health, price of firewood, &c. The subject I consider to be one of great importance, both in a sanitary and economic point of view.

"(1.) With reference to its bearing on health. Let us take, for example, Wellington. That station may be said to be entirely destitute of trees. Having had frequent opportunities of observation during the last three years, I am strongly impressed with the opinion that the larger proportion of disease at Wellington than at the neighbouring station at Kúnúr, is due, in a great measure, to this circumstance, viz., the want of wood; as, in all other respects, height, temperature, exposure, &c., there is scarcely any appreciable difference between the two places. I think, therefore, that, by planting trees judiciously, great benefit would be derived, not only from the shelter they would afford, but from the good effects produced by a moderate quantity of vegetation in purifying the atmosphere. These remarks, of course, apply with equal force to every inhabited portion of the hills, where there is a scarcity of wood. I think, moreover, that, by carrying out the project still further, and planting largely on the vast uncultivated tracts which exist all over the Nilgiris, the climate might in time become so far modified that the extremes of temperature would not be so excessive, or the variations so sudden, thereby rendering the hills more suitable as a sanitarium for invalids.

"(2.) Considering the question as it affects the supply of wood for domestic purposes. There is no doubt, that if the demand for firewood and small timber for building native houses continues, even at the present rate, and without making any allowance for the greatly increased consumption to be expected by any addition to the troops stationed on the Nilgiris, or to the population generally, the supply must soon become exhausted, especially as there is an immense amount of waste yearly, from the reckless destruction of wood by the hill tribes in their periodical burnings of the dry grass. To provide for this immense and steadily increasing consumption of wood, there is no resource but to plant trees to a large extent on the hills, as the difficulty and expense of procuring wood from the low country put that source of supply entirely out of the question."

The next opinion expressed on this subject is by Dr G. Mackay, who writes—"The subject of planting on the Nilgiri Hills is one of paramount importance.

"In the stations of Utakamand, Kúnúr, and Kotagiri, improvements in that way must, I presume, be chiefly carried out by private individuals, landowners, and tenants; but with reference to the cantonment of Wellington, it seems to be a matter worthy of your best consideration. By judicious planting I feel sure that the health and comfort of the troops stationed there would be greatly benefited, while the appearance of the station would be vastly improved.

"Belts of trees planted along some of the ghats and roads leading from the low country, would be a great protection, particularly to the natives bringing provisions, &c., to the hills, many of whom at present perish on the journey, and others come into hospital, in a hopeless state, from the effects of exposure.

"In a climate where the temperature is so variable, and moisture so prevalent as on the Nilgiri Hills, an abundant supply of firewood or other fuel becomes an absolute necessity for the preservation of health, among all classes, both Europeans and natives.

"I need hardly remark that the providing of fuel is a matter which cannot be left till the urgent demand arises, but should be anticipated by every possible means. When the barracks at Wellington are fully occupied by troops, and the European population on the hills generally increases, which there seems every prospect of, the demand for fuel will be proportionably increased; and I can fancy no greater hardship that could arise, or anything more likely to affect the health of all classes, than a scarcity of so necessary an article as good fuel."

The testimony of Dr W. Aitken is as follows:—"Much may be done by planting judiciously within moderate limits, not only to meet any prospective increase in the demand for firewood, but also to produce timber fit for various useful purposes. I am disposed to think that some measures for the extended cultivation of trees are urgently called for, as well as for the preservation of those portions of the natural forests which still remain; as it appears doubtful if the latter will long be able to afford a supply sufficient for even the present demand for firewood, except at the expense of their indiscriminate destruction in the vicinity of the Stations; an event which might easily be obviated by the adoption of suitable precautions. The means which I should suggest as most likely to meet all the requirements in the least objectionable manner, is the planting in every direction of open clusters of trees, which would interfere little, if at all, with cultivation around and beneath them, and also of comparatively open rows on ground unsuited to other kinds of cultivation."

EXTRACT ORDER ON NILGIRI PLANTATIONS, 3d June 1858. No. 748.

1. After enumerating the advantages which ensue generally from planting, and observing that Capt. Campbell's attempt is the only instance on the Nilgiri Hills of forest planting on a considerable scale on the part of Government, Dr Cleghorn proceeds to remark upon a Memo. on the subject by Capt. Campbell, which he submits with his Report, in which the site and altitude of the plantation, the establishment, and mode of working, are described, the receipts and disbursements are shown up to August 1857, and suggestions are offered for conducting operations in future.

2. Dr Cleghorn next notices the efforts made by Mr E. B. Thomas, Collector of Coimbatore, to promote the growth of timber in and about Utakamand. That officer has planted about 8000 Australian trees of different species at a cost of Rs.400; and the old denuded forests have been re-sown to a certain extent. A watchman, on Rs.5 a month, has been employed to protect the young trees, but Dr Cleghorn found him inefficient, and Mr M'Ivor, the Superintendent of the Government gardens, considers wire-fencing to be absolutely required as a protection. Mr Thomas is, besides, reported to have earnestly and unceasingly exercised a personal supervision of the woods round Utakamand, and the Conservator of Forests "does not hesitate to affirm that, but for his continued exertions, the neighbourhood of Utakamand would have been long since denuded of its beautiful woods."

3. Dr Cleghorn further goes on to discuss the prejudicial effect on the indigenous woods of the Nilgiris, arising from the enormously increased demand for firewood on the hills, and he shows the necessity for encouraging, as much as possible, the consumption of turf or peat, for fuel, in private houses, in the barracks, and in the Department Public Works.

4. And lastly, Dr Cleghorn advocates the formation of plantations round the barracks at Wellington, of an avenue or belt of

trees (where practicable) along the Utakamand to Wellington, and Avalanche to Sispara roads, and the planting of 10,000 trees in the vicinity of Utakamand for ornamental purposes at a cost of Rs. 1350.

5. The Government attach the greatest importance to the preservation of the woods on the Nilgiris, and resolve to communicate a transcript of Dr Cleghorn's suggestions relative to improvements in the system of conservancy to the Collector of Coimbatore, who will, in communication with the Conservator, frame a set of rules based on those suggestions, and submit them to the Government for approval. The proviso respecting the non-removal of dead timber seems highly necessary. When the wants of the Forest Conservancy Department on the hills in the way of an establishment have been fully considered, the Government will be prepared to make the necessary application to the Government of India for the entertainment of the additional servants required. In reporting further on the subject, the present system of licensing or renting the woods should be accurately detailed, and a table of receipts and disbursements drawn up, showing the items from which income is drawn, and the chief heads of expenditure.

6. The Government readily sanction the small sum of Rs. 1350, requested by Dr Cleghorn for the ornamental planting of 10,000 trees in the neighbourhood of Utakamand, under the superintendence of Mr M'Ivor, under the conviction that the outlay is trifling in comparison with the advantages to be derived from the proposed plantation, even in an economical point of view, and that it is highly desirable that an example of successful planting should be placed before the residents on the hills in each of the chief places of resort, as an encouragement to others to engage in an enterprise which, while it will be generally beneficial, will also be individually remunerative. * * * * *

W. H. BAYLEY,
Secretary to Government.

Additional Remarks on their Progress.

KUNUR, 15*th December* 1859, *No.* 877.

I have the honour, in continuation of my letter, 10th April 1858, in E. M. C., 3d June 1858, R. D., to submit a further report on the Government plantation of Australian trees, in the neighbourhood of Wellington, originated by Capt. Campbell.

2. *Object.*—The object of this plantation is to meet the very extensive requirements of the large cantonment at that place.

3. *Site.*—The site originally selected comprised about 600 acres, ranging from three to four miles from Wellington, in an easterly direction. Last year, in communication with the acting collector, Mr Cherry, and at the suggestion of Capt. Campbell, the more distant portion was exchanged with the Badagars for a larger extent, running from the lower extremity of the original site towards Wellington. The land thus gained is of finer quality, is situated between two good roads to Kunur and Wellington, and brings the lower extremity of the plantation within a mile of the latter cantonment. The advantages which will thus be gained in saving carriage and obtaining manure renders this a very valuable acquisition.

4. *Area planted.*—In my report quoted in par. 1, the area planted was given at about 8 acres, in April 1858. Since then, above 90 acres have been planted, and the total number of trees may now be set down at 2 lacs, ranging from three years to two months old. About 8000 more will be put out in the course of this month, which closes the regular planting season.

5. *Nurseries.*—The nursery beds, three in number, are in good order, and contain an ample supply for the probable requirements of next season.

6. *System pursued.*—The only alterations in the system pursued are, that the trees are planted at 6 feet, instead of (as originally) 3 or 4 feet apart, and that watering has been dispensed with. The greater space now allowed for the trees has proved manifestly advantageous; and though, from not watering the plants, we lose a few here and there, the saving of expense more than compensates for this, as care is taken to plant only during the

rains. It has hitherto been usual to dig holes 1½ feet square for each plant, at a charge of R. 1 for every 150 holes. I am now trying whether the seeds may not be sown profitably in furrows a few inches deep. If this plan succeeds, there will be a considerable saving of labour and expense in this preliminary operation.

7. *Establishment.*—The plantation continued under the general superintendence of Capt. Campbell, who originated and gratuitously managed it, until his departure in May last; and the charge has since devolved upon Corporal Hall, who lives on the plantation, and has had almost from the beginning the executive management of it, and, I am happy to add from personal observation, has performed his duties with the utmost zeal, efficiency, and fidelity. The Badagar maistry has also given great satisfaction. The rest of the establishment consists of coolies, paid only for the days on which they actually attend, the rates being As. 3 for men and As. 2 for boys, *per diem.* These rates are somewhat higher than those formerly given, owing to the greater demand for labour at present. The average charges *per mensem* are about Rs. 125, exclusive of Corporal Hall's allowances.

8. *General Expenditure.*—At the date of my report, quoted in par. 1, I had a balance of Rs. 2039-5-2, and Rs. 2500 were sanctioned in the E. M. C., 3d June 1858, par. 5, making a total of Rs. 4539-5-2 for which I have now to account. The charges up to the 31st October have been Rs. 5259-8-6, consisting of the following items:—

Remained, . .	Rs. 2039 5 2		
Government grant, . .	2500 0 0		
By fines, sale of seedlings, &c.	420 7 2		
			Rs. 4959 12
Paid Corporal Hall for 6 months up to 31st October, 1859, . .		Rs. 240 0 0	
,, Establishment up to 31st October, 1859, .	Rs. 2407 9 4	4051 6 8	
,, Trenching, &c. do.	1643 13 4		
,, For seeds, tools, baskets, &c. .		968 1 10	
			5259 8 6
Deduct amount received, . .			4959 12 4
Balance, .			Rs. 299 12 2

It will be seen from the above, that the whole of the sum placed at my disposal is exhausted, and a further sum of Rs. 299-12-2 expended; the excess I have met from other funds as a temporary arrangement. I have now the honour to request, that a further grant of Rs. 2500 may be sanctioned at the early convenience of Government. The total expenditure from the commencement (March 1856) up to 31st October, has been Rs. 10,071-15-2, for which Government possesses about two lacs of trees, which have thus cost less than one Anna per plant.

9. *General Condition of Plantation.*—The plantation is, on the whole, in a very promising condition; and I think that some return may be expected from thinnings in two years. The importance of the plantation may be gathered from the simple fact, that Government now pay Rs. 700 monthly to a contractor for the supply of firewood to the troops in Wellington. This payment, it must be remembered, is exclusive of the requirements of the Public Works Department, and of the officers of the regiment. The wants of the cantonment and those connected with it are so great, that the natural forests will soon be insufficient to meet them.

10. I take this opportunity of requesting the sanction of Government to place Corporal Hall, whose great merits I have above mentioned, on my establishment as an overseer. If my request is complied with, I shall employ him partly in conserving the forests in this direction, a duty which he can well perform without prejudice to the plantation. I have no one to the eastward of Utakamand to aid in conservancy; and my knowledge of Corporal Hall enables me to make this proposition with full confidence that he will perform these duties efficiently, and that the arrangement, whilst a just recognition of his services, will also be to the advantage of the state.

Order on the Preceding Papers.

20th January 1860, *No.* 101.

1. In this letter Dr Cleghorn relates the progress made in these plantations since the date of his last report of the 10th April 1858, noticed in the order of Government, No. 748, 3d June 1858.

2. The site originally selected comprised about 600 acres, lying east of Wellington, at a distance of from three to four miles. During 1858, arrangements were made with the Badagars for exchanging the more distant portion of this for a larger extent of land, which has the advantages of being of better quality, nearer Wellington, and between good roads.

3. Up to date of last report the area planted was 8 acres; since that time above 90 acres have been planted, and there are now two lacs of trees from three years to two months old. Eight thousand more were ready for putting out; and the nursery beds, of which there are three, contain an ample supply for next season. Some alterations have been made in the mode of planting, &c., by which a considerable saving, it is hoped, will be effected.

4. Since Capt. Campbell's departure in May last the charge has devolved upon Corporal Hall, on whose "zeal, efficiency, and fidelity" Dr Cleghorn lays particular stress.

5. The average charges per mensem are about Rs. 125, exclusive of Corporal Hall's allowances. The expenditure from April 1858 to 31st October 1859 amounted to Rs. 5259-8-6; the funds in hand to meet this were Rs. 4959-12-4, leaving a deficiency of Rs. 299-12-2. The total expenditure from the commencement in March 1856 up to 31st October 1859 has been Rs. 10,071-15-2.

6. There has not been as yet, apparently, any cutting or thinning. The Conservator mentions (par. 9) that some return may be expected from thinning in two years.

7. The Government desire to express their gratification at the steady progress apparently made, and sanction the grant of Rs. 2500, as requested in par. 8 of Dr Cleghorn's letter.

C. G. MASTER,
Deputy Secretary to Government.

NOTE.—In order that these plantations receive a fair trial on the mountain ranges of S. India, every facility for the periodical transmission of seeds from Australia ought to be afforded, and care taken that such transmissions are regular. The Horticultural Society having had their attention drawn to Australian plants, laid particular stress on the importance of steady supplies of seeds.

H. C.

MEMORANDUM ON GODAVARI TIMBER.

Mr G. A. Smith, collector of Rajamandri, reported, 18th August 1838, on the timber of his district (*vide* "Papers on Teak Forests of India" p. 187), in Records of the Bengal Government, No. IX.

1. The great depôt for the Gódávarí teak is Kòringa, where many vessels are built; yet even there it is found more profitable to plank vessels chiefly with teak brought from the opposite coast of Pegu. Either from want of means of transport, or the force of habit, the wood-cutters about the Godávari cut short almost every log to a length of 18 or 20 feet, and cut away one-half of the thickness of the finest logs, leaving three projecting pieces (as represented in fig. 1, p. 4), which are pierced for staples, for convenience in lashing either the yokes of the buffaloes for conveying them from the forest, or in rafts on the water. The Palmers of Hyderabad at one time farmed teak forests, and sent down some very fine timber; but the speculation was given up, as their agent at Nellapallé was unable to obtain the prices. Government might perhaps prevent the waste noted by charging an excessive duty on all timber so hacked. It is strange that this waste is only in the teak timber, and not in woods of an inferior description.

2. In 1850, Captain Fenwick proceeded on an expedition to investigate and report upon the forests in the valley of Sávitri (Sebbery), and the country between it and the Indrawati. The result was not very favourable; no large teak was said to have been found, and forests of salwood, of various dimensions, were almost all that Captain Fenwick reported.

3. In 1856, Mr Tuke was sent to explore the Sávitri river.

He penetrated to a forest about 130 miles distant from its mouth. He mentions, that he had no doubt that there were 800 good (teak) trees in the neighbourhood of Kannírirâda. He specifies, that he met with trees measuring 11 and even 15 feet in circumference, and from 30 to 45 feet in length, proving that the teak grows to its full size in that country. Mr Tuke wrote, "much teak may be found in the Suncham Tàluk, growing in patches," He was informed that "the Dorapallé and Gollapallé Parganas were most abundant in teak wood." The Rissaldár, in charge of the Raja's horse there, informed him that large teak is abundant all along the banks, and in the neighbourhood of the Indrawati, but that it has never been cut, owing to the obstructions in the river, which prevented its being brought down.

Mr R. Watson, the agent of Livingston, Withers, & Co. of Liverpool, who "lately returned by river from Chànda, informed me (1859), that in the district of Chànda, territories of Nàgpur, principally in the Zamindari of Ahèri, belonging to the late Bhujanga Rào, and now in possession of his widow, Lakshmi Bhài, extensive forests of teak and other useful woods exist, the use of which is at present obstructed by a loan to a native merchant of Hyderabad, Hari Dàs & Co." These forests are wastefully managed, under-sized trees being felled, and the logs generally rudely converted. Many fine trees still remain, which, "from their immense size, are unmanageable" without special appliances; and it seems desirable that the attention of Government be directed to this matter, as these logs are of a number and scantling which, with the extended operations now in progress for opening the river traffic, would apparently afford an abundant supply of valuable timber for the various requirements of the eastern ports, railway companies, &c. From Aherí all the way south to the commencement of the Ellana Zamindari, there is fine teak; logs 30 feet long, and 4 feet in diameter, are procurable.

Mahadeopuram, on the right bank of the Godavarí, is the great depôt for Secunderabad; large rafts come down from Aherí by the Varada and Indrawati rivers. The timber is carried to Secunderabad on carts for building purposes, 18 feet long by 1 cubic foot square.

Bija Sal or Vengê (*Pterocarpus marsupium*) attains an enormous size, and is used for godowns, &c., at Chànda.

5. Lieutenant R. H. Beddome, Asst. Conservator of Forests, prepared an accurate and useful list of the timber trees (with native names), which he met with in the Hyderabad portion of the Gódávarí forests. This catalogue is printed in the "Jury Reports of the Madras Exhibition, 1857" (p. 46), but detailed information regarding the teak forests in the valley of the Godavari is still wanting.

H. Cleghorn.

Note.—Subsequent to the visit of Sir C. Trevelyan to the Godavari and to the publication of this Memorandum, which was drawn up immediately after, few additional facts have been ascertained on this subject. Capt. Stoddard, however, in a letter to Government, dated October 24, 1859, states, that "there is an abundance of the very finest teak growing between the Severi and Indrawati rivers, which might, by European enterprise, be brought down to the Severi," which he considers quite navigable for boats drawing from 5 to 6 feet from June to November.

H. C.

AVENUES.

EXTRACT LETTER to Major BIRDWOOD, Deputy Chief-Engineer.

MADRAS, *9th December* 1859.

SIR,—I had the honour of receiving your letter of 16th August last, No. 3900, forwarding for my opinion a letter from Mr Fraser regarding avenue trees on the Nilgiris and in the Coimbatore district.

1. As regards the general question, I shall be happy at all times to afford your department every assistance and advice, but I cannot undertake the charge of avenues generally, for I have a much smaller establishment at my disposal for this purpose than district engineers possess, and my time is fully occupied with my own duties.

2. If, as I gather from Mr Fraser's letter, the D. P. W. cannot efficiently manage the avenues of Coimbatore, the natural course, I think, is to replace them under the collector, who has subordinates in every village quite competent to manage them. There is, in fact, nothing difficult in managing them ; all that is requisite is ordinary care and frequent attention ; and as neither your department nor mine have the requisite number of subordinates to do the work, the best plan will be to retransfer it to the collector, who has. In fact, Mr Fraser does himself propose what in effect amounts to this—viz., that the village authorities should be made to look after these trees ; but he requests that they should act in this respect under my superintendence. This last suggestion is in my view objectionable, because, in the first place, I cannot superintend them ; and in the second, because it never

answers to place officers under several authorities. The village officials have masters enough already; and to place them for such a comparatively subordinate and occasional duty under either your orders or mine, would be a mistake. Such a system would lead to collision and endless correspondence. The simplest plan is to leave the business to the collector, with whom both your department and mine would cordially co-operate. In particular localities, your department alone might do the work; for instance, channel banks, tank bunds, and trunk roads, could probably be supervised by your establishment; but for general avenues along miles of cross roads, the collector seems to me the proper officer at present.

3. So long as the avenues are under your department, I think the collector should have the power noted in Mr Fraser's letter. Your overseers and maistries are often pressed for fuel, as he says, and thus they have sometimes a temptation to fell or prune excessively for fuel and other such purposes rather than for the good of the trees. It is necessary, therefore, that there should be a check on them; and as I cannot exercise it, it must devolve on the collector. In my view, the best and simplest plan is that given above for such districts as Coimbatore.

I will now notice the propositions in Mr Fraser's letter:—

(1.) Nurseries are absolutely necessary; but I cannot form them everywhere. The best plan would be to select suitable sites, and place them under the nearest competent officer resident there, whether in the Revenue, D. P. W., or Forest Department. The trees might be supplied on the requisition of the officer in charge of the avenues, &c.

(2.) Plantations might be formed where the requirements of Government are sufficiently large and steady to warrant them; but I would strictly limit them to the wants of Government. The growth of firewood for the community should be left entirely to private enterprise. When, either from scarcity of natural jungles or other causes, the price of timber rises sufficiently to render private plantations duly remunerative, capital will probably be readily vested in them. The interference of Government would be impolitic, and will only postpone the time when the people will grow wood for themselves as they now do grain. Even restricted as above proposed, it may be doubted whether it would not be better in the long run for Government to trust to supplies from private enterprise than to plant on its own account; but each case must be considered on its own merits with a tendency against, rather than for Government interposition. In particular and special cases, as at Wellington (firewood), and at Nellambur (teak), Government plantations will be formed; but I should deprecate such a step, which is much more costly than conservancy of reserved tracts.

(3.) The reservation, &c., of jungles are very important subjects, and are now engaging my attention. In the selection of these I am desirous of taking counsel with the collector and engineer of the district.

4. Avenue trees are of immense consequence to the trunk roads of the country, and in some districts, they are nearly as essential to the convenience of travellers as a smooth surface. It has been proved, I think, that carts travel further in a shady road than in an exposed tract.

5. Those who have seen the beautiful avenues of the dupada maram (*Vateria indica*),* the jak (*Artocarpus integrifolia*), and *Lagerströmia regina* in Canara and Malabar, sál in Gúmsur, and those of the tamarind, banyan, and mango in Salem and Mysore, cannot fail to appreciate their value and importance.

6. In the favoured climate of Mysore, the system has been to reduce the rent to ryots or patéls planting avenues. Rows of useful trees yielding fruit—mango, tamarind, and jamún—are kept up and watered by ryots on waste land till they are in a flourishing state; they are then counted, and the ryots receive so much land rent free, or reduced, for so many hundred trees, according to a scale.

7. Seeds and seedlings are procurable nearly at cost price from the public gardens at Madras, Bangalore, and Utakamand. District engineers may confidently expect the best counsel and advice from myself and assistants; but the executive management and

* This tree forms beautiful avenues in Nagar, Malabar, and Canara, the foliage is dense, and the blossom very fragrant. It was a favourite with the ancient Rajahs, and there are magnificent old trees near Bednore, &c.

responsibility should, I think, remain as at present, or with the collector.

8. I have conferred or corresponded on the subject of avenue trees with not a few of the engineers, and am always happy to supply young trees for avenues, channel banks, &c., as far as my limited means will allow, if due notice is given, so that they may be ready in baskets for delivery at the proper season.

H. CLEGHORN,
Conservator of Forests.

MADRAS AVENUES.

LETTER TO GOVERNMENT.

MADRAS, *7th August* 1860.

1. In obedience to the G. O., 4th June 1860, No. 923, R. D., I called upon Mr Brown to prepare an estimate of the cost of restoring the avenue between Marmalong Bridge and Madras, which, amounting to Rs.750, is herewith submitted.

2. I inspected the Mount Road with Mr Brown. One thousand trees will be required; and the Commissioner of Police, Colonel Boulderson, has offered to instruct the Inspector of Ranges to see the trees watered daily. For this purpose, two or three water-barrels will be required. The cost of bullocks and drivers he estimates at about Rs.35 per mensem.

3. The first auction of thinnings at the Róshan Bágh took place on the 6th ult., and Rs.558 were realized. There are still many old trees to be removed, and much under-clearing is required. Mr Brown is progressing with this work, and further auctions will take place.

4. I would recommend that the avenues in Madras generally should, as opportunities offer, be recruited with tamarind trees. These grow slowly, and need care for five years; but they are extremely handsome, lasting, and the fruit sells well. The plan, in order to meet present and future requirements, should be to plant tamarind trees alternately with banyans and others of quick growth, the latter form the temporary avenue, and are removed as the tamarinds, the permanent avenue, grow up.

5. There is a nursery of ornamental avenue trees at the Horticultural Gardens, containing a number of species, which might be introduced here and there with advantage, especially near the gardens, where Mr Brown could watch their growth. Those entered below seem to be particularly adapted for avenues in Madras.

(1.) *Ficus Tsiela*, Jóvi or Pedda Jóvi, *Tel.* A large and very handsome tree, generally planted by the road sides for the sake of its shade; and as it does not send down roots from the branches, it is preferable to *Ficus Indica* (Banyan tree), and *F. Benjamina*, the pendulous roots of which are often dangerous impediments on a road.

(2.) *Guatteria longifolia*, Mast tree. Deodaru, *Tam.* Asóka chettu, *Tel.* A highly ornamental erect tree, which should be planted in avenues more than it is at present. Some fine trees may be seen at Triplicane and Pondicherry.

(3.) *Tamarindus Indica*, Tamarind tree. Pulia-maram, *Tam.* Chinta chettu, *Tel.* Tinturi, Amli, *Hind.* This tree is one of the largest in India, with an umbrageous head, and yields hard wood.

(4.) *Casuarina muricata.* Casuarina tree or Tinian pine. This tree, grown close, forms pretty avenues, suited for narrow roads near the sea, as at Ennore and Pulicat.

6. When I conferred with the Commissioner of Police, it appeared advisable to us both that the whole of the avenues in Madras should be placed under a system of skilled superintendence. Considering, however, that there are nearly 200 miles of roads planted with trees in Madras and the suburbs, it is impossible that Mr Brown, who is under engagement to the committee of the Agri-Horticultural Society, could undertake all this duty. He might look after the roads which are adjacent to the sphere of his labours. H. CLEGHORN.

Order on the foregoing Letter.

August 18, 1860.

1. The Government sanction the estimate, amounting to Rs.750, for restoring the avenue between Marmalong Bridge and Madras. The work will be carried on at once out of the proceeds of the sale of thinnings at the Róshan Bágh.

2. Adverting to par. 2 of Dr Cleghorn's letter, the Government are of opinion that the watering and general care of the trees belong to the Municipal Commissioners, where the road is within their district. They accordingly resolve to request the Commissioners to state if they are willing to pay for the same.

J. D. BOURDILLON,
Secretary to Government.

INSTRUCTIONS FOR PLANTING TREES, WITH A LIST OF THOSE BEST SUITED FOR AVENUES ALONG PUBLIC ROADS.*

So little attention has been paid to the planting of trees along the roads, that healthy or well-shaped ones are seldom seen; and to remedy this defect, the following instructions are drawn up:—It is usual to plant large branches of the portia (*Thespesia populnea*) and banyan (*Ficus Indica*) trees in such a slovenly manner, that there is little probability of the trees thriving or being ornamental. The portia and banyan branches selected should be straight, neatly trimmed, of an uniform size, and planted perpendicularly (not obliquely as is generally the case). A fence of bamboos is required to protect them from cattle. Prickly pear (*Opuntia Dillenii*) is unsightly, and should not be tied on the trees. The branches of the babul (*Acacia Arabica*), and other thorny plants, make good fences, and are cheaper than bamboos. After the cuttings begin to throw out young shoots, they should be carefully pruned, two or three of the strongest near the top being selected as leading shoots, to form the future tree The young trees require water regularly in hot and dry weather, care being taken that they are not loosened at the roots, which cause the trees to lean to one side. To raise young trees from seed is a slower process, but it is the best and most natural method. The trees are more regular in their growth, and last twice as long as cuttings. Portia trees, grown from large branches, are usually decayed in the centre, and the branches are

* The above instructions contain the experience of Mr R. Brown, Superintendent of the Agri-Horticultural Society's Garden.—H. C.

apt to be broken off in high winds. It would be more profitable to raise all trees from seed, as a tree grown from a branch tends to fall into a state of decay after a few years, and is useless for timber. The natural habit of the banyan makes it an exception to this rule. The whole of the *Ficus* tribe grow well from branches, and they are not so apt to decay as other trees. The planting of seedlings requires more care and attention than cuttings. A pit should be made three feet square, and filled with good soil, mixed with rotten dung. The plants require to be fenced and watered regularly, and the earth should be dug and kept clear of weeds. In forming avenues, the trees should be planted 30 feet apart; and when there is space, a double row should be planted; it looks well, and forms a shady arch for pedestrians. Good maistry gardeners should be employed, each having the oversight of three miles of road, until the trees are independent of water. It would be the duty of these men to keep the avenues complete.

Fig. 9.*

* Trees are much exposed to injuries which disfigure their appearance, or retard their growth, and not unfrequently destroy the plants altogether. To prevent these accidents, it is customary to surround the stem with branches of some spiny plants. Those most easily procured in S. India are *Acacia arabica* and *leucophlea*, which are widely diffused: they are often placed without care, overtopping and choking the young tree.

LIST OF AVENUE TREES.

1. *Ficus Indica.* Banyan tree. Ala-maram, *Tam.* Marri, *Tel.* Bur, But, *Beng.*
   The banyan is the largest, and probably the most shady, of all avenue trees.

2. *Ficus religiosa.* Poplar-leaved fig-tree. Arasa-maram, *Tam.* Rávi, Rági, *Tel.* Pipul, *Hind.* Ashwuth, *Beng.*
   A large and handsome tree, of common occurrence near pagodas, houses, and other buildings.

3. *Ficus Tsiela.* Jóvi or Pedda Jóvi, *Tel.*
   A large and handsome tree, generally planted by road sides for shade; not sending down roots from the branches, is preferable to either *Ficus Indica* (banyan tree), or *F. Benjamina*, the pendulous roots of which are dangerous impediments on a road.

4. *Ficus nitida.* Chinese banyan tree.
   A handsome tree. Native of China.

5. *Guatteria longifolia.* Mast tree. Deodaru, *Tam.* Asóka chettu, *Tel.*
   A highly ornamental tree, which might be planted in avenues more than at present.

6. *Tamarindus Indica.* Tamarind tree. Pulia-maram, *Tam.* Chinta chettu, *Tel.* Tinturi, Amli, *Hind.*
   This tree is one of the largest in India, with an umbrageous head.

7. *Casuarina muricata.* Casuarina tree or Tinian pine.
   This tree forms pretty avenues, especially in narrow roads.

8. *Casuarina equisitifolia.*
   A tree similar to the above.

9. *Bignonia suberosa.* Indian cork tree.
   A good tree for planting in avenues. The flowers are pure white and very fragrant.

Fig. 9, from *Du Breuil, cours d'Arboriculture,* illustrates the manner in which avenue-trees are protected in the Boulevards of Paris. In France, the branches of *Prunus spinosa* are usually employed for this purpose.

10. *Parkia biglandulosa.*

This large and elegant tree was introduced into India from Africa. It is one of the best trees for avenues, but requires care and regular watering.

11. *Poinciana Regia.* Royal Poinciana tree. Flamboyante.

This tree does not attain a great size; but it is very showy, and should be planted in mixed avenues.

12. *Adenanthera pavonina.* Red-wood tree.

A large and handsome tree, and is well suited for avenues.

13. *Azadirachta Indica.* Neem tree. Vépa-maram, *Tam.* Nim, *Beng.*

A good avenue tree, but the foliage is deciduous.

14. *Sterculia fœtida.* Fœtid sterculia. Pínáta or Pínári-maram, *Tam.* Gurapa bádam chettu, *Tel.* Junglí badam, *Beng.*

This is a large tree, only objectionable from the fœtor of the flowers, and the falling of the leaves.

15. *Bombax Malabaricum.* Red cotton tree. Mullu Elavu-maram, *Tam.* Búraga chettu, *Tel.* Rukta simul, *Hind.*

This tree attains a great size, leaves deciduous.

16. *Thespesia populnea.* Portia tree. Púrsa or Púvarasa, *Tam.* Gangarávi, *Tel.* Poresh, *Beng.*

This is the principal tree in the Madras avenues, and is valuable from its easy growth, and from the large amount of annual cuttings. It prefers the sea air and saline soil.

17. *Acacia speciosa.* Kátuvági, *Tam.* Dirisana, *Tel.* Sirissa, *Beng.*

A large and handsome tree, of rapid growth.

15. The above are the best avenue trees in Madras. There are many others suitable for the same purpose, where mere ornament is the object in view. Some of the palm tribe may be occasionally used.

R. Brown, *Supt.*

HEDGES.

These are susceptible of great improvement. There is a universal prevalence of spiny shrubs and prickly bushes throughout India. They are a continual source of annoyance to the bare-footed pilgrim, and a frequent cause of admission into hospital. The absence of proper fences all over the country is one of the chief impediments to the progress of agriculture. It is only in the neighbourhood of large towns, around upland villages, in military cantonments, or near the dwellings of European residents, that we find any serviceable enclosures. This does not arise from any want of material; in this respect, indeed, the Flora is peculiarly rich; and in dealing with this our difficulty lies in selection for particular localities. The strong close hedges which are occasionally met with around more valuable crops, such as betel-vine and sugar-cane, show what can be done, and prove satisfactorily that this department of agriculture is susceptible of very considerable improvement. The losses sustained by the ryot from the inroads of cattle and wild animals, and other causes, due to the absence of these fences, is enormous.

In confirmation of the foregoing views as to the deficiency of fences, and the consequent injury to agricultural produce, we may quote a single extract from Dr Buchanan's Report on the District of Purneah—(*Montgomery Martin's History*, vol. iii., p. 279):—" I nowhere saw round the same field a hedge and a good ditch; nor did I ever see a hedge that was a good fence. The want of fences is a great evil, and the cattle commit uncommon depredations. A large proportion of them belong to the pure castes, who in this district enjoy high privileges, and are uncommonly insolent to the vulgar. Their cattle trespass with much impunity, and the poor of course retaliate, as far as they dare by stealth, so that the community is a great sufferer. The people who tend the cattle seem to be sent rather with a view to prevent them from straying, than to keep them from destroying the crops; at least, I saw many instances of most culpable neglect." It is remarked, in "Colebrooke's Husbandry of Bengal," that "the old laws of the Hindus gave redress for the trespasses of cattle in enclosed fields, but not in unfenced lands, unless the transgressions were wilful on the part of the herdsman, or of the owner. Unfortunately these laws seem to be now obsolete."

Again, in reference to the Experimental Cotton Farm at Gorakpúr, Mr Reade, then collector, affirmed, that "the pest of this place is countless cattle, whose pertinacity and agility in overcoming fences is proportionate to their cupidity of Mr Blount's cotton plants."—*House of Commons Return.—Indian Cotton Cultivation.*

These remarks were written regarding two districts of the Bengal Presidency; but they are so descriptive of parts of S. India, that they have been introduced here. We have witnessed serious depredations from sacred buffaloes, which, owned by no master (though attached to particular temples), pasture where they may, unchecked in their trespasses, till they attain the age for sacrifice.

Indigenous to S. India, we have of *Acacia** and *Mimosa* (about 30 species):—*Zizyphus* (4 sp.), *Carissa* (several sp.), besides *Toddalia aculeata* (Pers) and *Pterolobium lacerans* (R.Br.), *Azima tetracantha* (Lam.), *Scutia Indica*, (L.), and a host of other armed plants, more or less widely diffused: these often grow interlaced in thickets, or surround the clumps of jungle like a fringe, presenting a *chevaux de frise*, which is almost impassable, especially when a dense tangled underwood has followed a forest conflagration. With such abundant materials at hand, it is somewhat remarkable that advantage has not been taken of this provision of nature. The few hedges observed by travellers

* One of the most remarkable is, *Acacia latronum* (W.), common in the barren tracts, armed with large stipulary thorns, united at the base. Linnæus designated it, "*Frutex horridissimus, ramosissimus;*" it is well entitled to this distinction. It is known amongst Europeans as the "*Robber Thorn,*" from relieving the cotton bullocks of their load as they pass through the jungle.

generally consist of *Opuntia Dillenii* (Haw.), *Agave Americana* (L.), *Euphorbia tirucalli* (L.), and *E. antiquorum* (L.) It is a curious fact, that the two first of these are not indigenous, but have been introduced from America, and the third was probably imported from Africa. Here and there we see other plants employed for the purpose, as *Jatropha curcas* and *Adhatoda vasica,* which being thin-growing and unarmed shrubs, can scarcely be said to make a fence.

This important subject has engaged the attention of the Government, as well as of railway and irrigation companies. It is consequently one of increasing interest, affecting not only the appearance of the country and private interests, but the expenditure of public bodies, and of the country at large.

Extracts of correspondence bearing on this subject are annexed.

Letter to Government.

MADRAS, 19*th September* 1856.

I have the honour to acknowledge receipt of E. M. C., 18th July 1856, No. 1211, regarding the planting of trees and hedges along the irrigation channels of this presidency. The subject is of great importance, and there is no part of rural economy more neglected in this country. It is one to which, some years ago, I devoted much time and attention,* and, as a full consideration of the various points involved would occupy considerable space, I cannot do better than place my MSS. at the disposal of Government, and limit myself at present to a few general and practical remarks.

The selection of trees and hedge plants for anything approaching to extensive planting must depend on the soil and other peculiarities of each locality. It is impossible for me at Madras to predicate what will answer in every district, but the local officers may safely be guided by observing what trees, &c., naturally succeed best within their ranges. The *Casuarina* at Madras is a valuable tree; but it would be absurd to plant it extensively in the red soil at Bellary. The *Inga dulcis* forms a neat and

* *Vide* Ann. Nat. Hist., Oct. 1850.

becoming fence for gardens of private residences, but would be too expensive for a ryot's holding, or a channel bank, and, I believe, on this account, has been considered unsuitable for hedging the Madras Railway.

First, as regards trees, the object is to obtain shade, and to preserve moisture, whilst we seek to secure some return for the expense of planting, &c. I would therefore give the preference to fruit, over timber trees in most situations; for the former, as the mango, tamarind, and soapnut, may be early rented to advantage, while the latter yield little or no return until they have attained maturity; and then they must be felled, and the process of planting again gone through. I would name the trees noted below* for selection according to locality: by no means, however, intending that no other fruit trees should be planted, or that timber trees should be wholly forbidden.

The planting of the following exotics might be tried in particular localities likely to suit them. They are all much esteemed in the countries whence they are derived. American Sumach (*Cæsalpinia coriaria*, L.), introduced from St Domingo. The pods of this valuable tree contain about 50 per cent of tannin (Drury), and small plantations exist at Bangalore, Guntur, Hunsúr, Masulipatam, &c. The tree grows well in most of these situations.

(*Hæmatoxylon Campechianum*, L.) Logwood. This is said to be an excellent plant for fences, and is much used in Jamaica. It prefers a dry soil near the sea, and therefore would probably succeed along the Coromandel coast. Amongst timber trees, if these should be wanted, I conceive the following to be the best—(jak, sál sissú, tún, tamarind, and teak), all furnishing wood of great value for economic purposes; and here, I may observe, that a circular order was issued to the Public Works Department, No. 744, 1855, which contains some appropriate remarks on this subject.

* Wherever they will grow, those marked † having the preference—viz., † Tamarind, † Mango, Jak, Bassia, Eugenia (*Jamun*), † Soapnut, Nim, † Coconut, † Calophyllum, Pongamia, In sandy tracts where more valuable trees will not grow, the following, (Casuarina, Date, Palmyra, Cashew, and Babúl) may be used.

For hedges, I think the various species of Aloe wherever they thrive, will form the most economical fence, they are almost impenetrable, require little or no care to keep the fence in order, and the leaves yield fibrous material. These plants are cultivated from suckers which take root readily, and would probably answer well in the Kistna District (under reference.)

In some places, the Bamboo may be planted in contiguous clumps at the foot of embankments. The uses of the Bamboo are very numerous, and a fence is easily formed by bending down a few of the shoots of each clump and interlacing them. "Bamboo fences are peculiarly well adapted to pasture land, the cattle browsing on the young shoots, keeping down the growth, so that very little care is required to keep them within bounds." In other localities, the Coconut, and where it will not grow, the Palmyra and Date may be planted *close* together, as I believe, is done in Tanjore and Rajamandri; the trees form a living wall through which cattle cannot pass. The *Inga dulcis* (Kurakapulli), I fear, will be too expensive to keep in order; when trimmed and pruned it forms a hedge superior to any other in India; and, indeed, is not excelled by the English Hawthorn, which it much resembles.

The *Parkinsonia aculeata*, *Cœsalpinia sepiaria* (Mysore thorn), *C. sappan* (Sappan tree), *C. coriaria* (American sumach), and *Capparis sepiaria*, may all be used; but, I think, the Inga should have the preference, and the Aloe be resorted to where those mentioned do not succeed. The use of the prickly pear (*Opuntia Dillenii*), I strongly deprecate, although impenetrable and inexpensive, it conveys an idea of sterility, and is rapidly becoming a nuisance in this country. (See *Ann. Nat. Hist.*, *Oct.* 1850.)

I have thus briefly indicated the trees and hedge plants which seem to be most likely to suit the object which Government has in view. In the north-west provinces, the loppings and prunings of the canal plantations pay well; and if Government are prepared to keep up the necessary establishments, I have no doubt that a similar system would pay here, although trees do not generally attain the same size in Southern India, and the markets for timber of this description are not of the same extent.

Reference is now made, 1*st*, to the plants adapted for ordinary hedges; and, 2*d*, to those more suited for inner garden fences, or for ornamental purposes. Of these hedge plants some are already in use, and there are others which appear equally well fitted for fences.

Inga Dulcis (*Willd.*), Sweet Inga.

W. and A., pr. i. p. 268; Grah. Cat. Bom. pl. p. 56; Voigt. Hort. Calc., p. 259; Wight. Icon. i. t. 198; *Mimosa dulcis*, Roxb. Cor., pl. i. t. 99; Fl. Ind. ii. p. 556; *Pithecolobium dulce*, Benth. in Lond. Jour. of Botany, ii. p. 423, &c.; Kuraka pulli, *Tel.*

A large and handsome tree with drooping branches, armed with straight stipulary thorns. The introduction of this plant to Asiatic countries has only lately been traced. Roxburgh was of opinion that it was a native of the Eastern islands, from whence it was brought to the Calcutta garden; but in Blanco's Flora of the Phillipine Islands, we find that it had been imported thither from Mexico. It is now frequently met with, particularly towards the coast. This plant, like its congeners, is easily raised from seeds. The hedge, when clipped once in two months, forms a neat and serviceable enclosure, a beautiful example of which may be seen round the Horticultural Garden, Madras. In fact, it is now the favourite hedge of S. India, where there is a proximity to the sea, and not undue moisture.

Bambusa Arundinacea (*Willd.*), Common Bamboo.

Roxb. Cor., pl. 1, t. 79; Fl. Ind. ii. p. 191; Grah. Cat. Bom., pl. p. 239; Voigt. Hort. Calc., p. 719; *Arundo Bambos*, L. (partly); Bansh., *Beng.*

The well-known tribe of arborescent grasses, called Bambuseæ, constitutes one of the most beautiful features of tropical vegetation, and is expressive of buoyant lightness and flexible slenderness. In fact, the cheerful elegance and feathery appearance of the bamboo are proverbial. The true bamboos are only found in Asia; the Guadua is the arborescent grass of South America; there are several species of Bambusa, well adapted for hedges, elsewhere described. Of these, *B. spinosa*, from the number and strength of its branches and spines, is said to form the most impenetrable jungle in India. *B. nana*, introduced from China into the Botanic Garden, Calcutta, makes beautiful close hedges. *Roxb.*

The Bambuseæ require a humid climate, and do not thrive in dry or sandy soil, hence we seldom meet with flowering plants in the Carnatic; but they are abundant beside the water courses of the Western Ghats, and in all parts to which the influence of the S.W. monsoon extends.

The bamboo is extensively used as a fence for gardens and fields in Coorg, the S. Mahratta country and Guzerat, where it delights in the rich soil along the edge of the mountain streams. It forms a dense and graceful underwood; but unless its luxuriance is checked, it spreads into clumps, and has a tendency to harbour vermin. The young thick shoots should be watched and carefully removed, and the lateral branches only allowed to remain. It has been introduced into Jamaica; and Macfadyen, in an excellent account of the hedge plants of that island, already quoted, states that "Bamboo fences are peculiarly adapted to pasture-land, the cattle browsing on the young shoots keeping down their growth, so that little additional care is required" (*Hook. Bot. Misc.*, iii. p. 83). Thunberg mentions, that the sugar plantations in Java are fenced with bamboo (*Travels*, vol. ii. p. 312).

The town of Bednore (literally Bideruru or Bamboo-place), was defended in Hyder's time by a deep trench filled with bamboos, which formed an additional means of defence, and hence the name of the town (*Buch. Jour.*, iii. p. 261). When we visited the place in 1856, we found the trench still remaining with many bamboos growing in it.

Buchanan also mentions, that Mr Place, then collector of Chingleput, caused each village to be surrounded by a hedge of bamboo; but few of these remain; indeed, they are scarce and dear in the Carnatic. It would be tedious to enumerate the great variety of economic purposes to which the bamboo is applied; but its use is so extensive, that it might be introduced with advantage under the bunds of tanks, or wherever a moist spot is obtainable.

The inflorescence only occurs in rich, moist situations, and in these the thorns are sometimes absent. In times of scarcity, the seeds of the bamboo, mixed with honey, are eaten like rice by the poorer classes of natives (*Buch. Jour.*, ii., p. 341); and in Orissa (Stirling in *Asiat. Res.*, vol. xv. p. 205.

The bamboo is easily propagated by means of suckers, which strike root in moist soils. An interesting notice on the rapid growth of the bamboo, by Mr R. Scott, is published in the *Trans. Bot. Soc. Edin.*, vol. iv. p. 25, 1849.

Cæsalpinia sepiaria (*Roxb.*), Mysore thorn.

Roxb. Fl. Ind., 2, p. 360; W. and A. pr. p. 282; Wight Icon., t. 37; Grah. Cat. Bom., pl. p. 61; Voigt. Hort. Calc., p. 244; Roxb. in E. I. C., tab. 1240. Hyder ka jar, *Hind.* Chillur, *Duk.*

This plant possesses a historical interest, Hyder Ally having directed it to be planted as a means of defence around his strongholds. In the territories of Mysore, the mud fortifications which surrounded all the villages in the days of plunder and rapine are rapidly disappearing; but hedges of this plant (with *Pterolobium lacerans*) still remain to attest Hyder's skill in the art of defence. *C. sepiaria* is indigenous in Mysore; but is now generally diffused over our Indian possessions, and known as the Mysore Thorn. It is employed as a fence in the Baghyat lands of the Dekkan, and possesses the twofold advantage of beauty and durability.

Immediately the shoot appears above ground, it separates into numerous lateral branches, which are strongly armed with recurved prickles. In the cold season, the yellow racemes of flowers which spring from the higher branches form a striking and beautiful object. For general use as an enclosure, it is one of the best plants with which we are acquainted; it is easily raised from seed, and grows vigorously both above and below the Ghats. (*vide* p. 174.) The hedge requires little care beyond occasionally trimming the side branches, and perhaps the introduction of a few dead stakes at intervals to steady and strengthen it.

CÆSALPINIA SAPPAN (*L.*), Sappan tree.

W. and A. pr. 1, p. 281; Grah. Cat. Bom. pl. p. 60; Voigt, Hort. Calc. p. 244; Roxb. Cor. pl. 1, t. 16; Rheede Hort. Mal. 6, t. 2. Patangha, *Cing.*; Chapenga-mara, *Can.*; Bukum, *Beng.*; Sapanhout, *Dutch*; Pao de Sapan, *Port.*; Sowa or Sobok, *Japan.*

A large scandent shrub or small tree, armed, indigenous in Ceylon, Malabar, and the Tenasserim provinces, where it is found in isolated patches near the sea. In habit, this tree resembles the *Hæmatoxylon campechianum* (logwood), which is cultivated in Jamaica as a hedge plant, and said by Macfadyen to make excellent fences. Sappan has been planted in the garden fences of the Dekkan and W. Mysore, chiefly for the sake of the wood, which, after ten or twelve years, becomes valuable for its red dye,* and has long been an article of trade. "Red wood" (Mad. Top. Rep. 1, p. 495, and Jour. Ind. Arch.) It is easily reared from seeds; but when introduced into a dry climate, it requires watering during the hot season.

AGAVE AMERICANA (*L.*), Great American Aloe.

A. vivipara, Buch. Jour. i. p. 36; *A. Cantala*, Roxb. Fl. Ind. ii. p. 167; Grah. Cat. Bom. pl. p. 222. *Fourcroya Cantala*, Voigt. Hort. Calc. p. 597. *Aloe Americana*, Rumph. 5, t. 94. *Bilati ananas*, *i.e.*, English pine-apple. Kantala, *Sans.*; Seubbära, *Arab.*

The Agaveæ are all natives of tropical America. This stately aloe-looking species was early taken eastward, and is now dispersed along the coasts of Africa and the shores of Southern Europe. The American Agave has also been imported from Holland to the Cape of Good Hope. (Thunberg's *Travels*, i. 283.) It is now so long established in many parts of India, as to form a striking feature in its scenery, and, as has been remarked, "stands isolated in the midst of dreary solitude, and imparts to the tropical landscape a peculiarly melancholy character."

* The process of dyeing cotton cloth, by dipping it in a decoction of chapenga wood with a little alum, is given by Buch. (*Jour.* i. 224).

This plant is so well known and generally diffused as scarcely to need description. Till lately, the flowering was considered to be of rare occurrence; this has been disproved. When inflorescence takes place, the cylindrical stem shoots forth with amazing rapidity and vigour from amidst a whorl of succulent, spinous-pointed leaves, by which its base is entirely surrounded. The plants which produce these stems are comparatively rare, and this circumstance perhaps enhances the effect produced by their magnificent panicle, which in some instances rises to the height of 15 feet, and is without a parallel in the vegetable kingdom.

The agave, like the prickly pear, thrives best in dry sandy soil; but is capable of enduring a great variety of climate, and has blossomed on the coast of Devon. The agave is propagated by means of suckers, which are found under the leaves of the old plants. When the seed-vessels are ripe, the seeds drop to the ground in a germinating state, and thus also young plants are obtained. It may be added, they are in great demand. If, in the first instance, the plants be placed at regular distances, and care taken to preserve the fibrous roots from moisture by a ditch, an elegant and serviceable enclosure is formed.

The agave is said to harbour vermin, particularly snakes and Bandicoot rats; but, by keeping the lower leaves free and clean, this may be obviated.

The economic uses of the agave are various. The leaves and stem are employed in roofing; the decayed leaves are also used as fuel when firewood is scarce; the terminal spines serve instead of pins and nails; and an excellent cordage (Pita flax) is formed by separating the long fibres of the larger leaves by maceration, and beating them on a stone to get rid of the parenchyma. Specimens of this cordage, made at the Monegar Choultry, Madras, were sent to the Exhibition of 1851, by Dr Hunter.

Capparis sepiaria (*L.*), Hedge caper.

W. and A., pr. i. p. 26; Grah. Cat. Bot. pl. p. 9; Voigt. Hort. Calc. p. 75.

The genus Capparis comprises a large number of fruticose

plants, many of them climbers with spinous stipules. One species, the Common Caper (*Capparis spinosa*), is found in S. Europe; the others abound in the tropics. They are attractive from the great beauty of their polyandrous blossoms, and in some cases from their fragrance.

C. sepiaria is a thick ramous shrub, from 4 to 6 feet in height, and armed with strong, sharp recurved thorns. The flowers are white interminal umbles; the berries black, about the size of a pea. It is common in the uncultivated parts of the Carnatic and Table-land, where, with another species (*C. incanescens*), it forms a low impervious jungle. We observed fine hedges of the *C. sepiaria* around villages in Mysore, and consider it one of the best indigenous hedge plants with which we are acquainted. Buchanan, referring to it in his Herb. Cat., says, "*Habitat ubique in Indiæ dumetis solo aridiore.*" It is easily grown from seeds, or by means of cuttings, and only requires occasional trimming. There are several other species of this genus worthy of trial as fences, though they may not be equal to *C. sepiaria*, being less compact. Of these, *C. horrida* and *Roxburghii* are common in Mysore, and are handsome climbers. We have also met with *C. aphylla*, and sought for its berries, which make an agreeable pickle. It is found in the barren land of the Dekkan and Scinde.

I. PLANTS ADAPTED FOR FIELD ENCLOSURES.

* Opuntia Dillenii, *Haw.*
* Agave americana, *L.*
* Euphorbia Tirucalli, *L.*
  antiquorum, *L.*
  nivulia, *Buch.*
Cæsalpinia sepiaria, *Rox.*
  Sappan, *L.*
Pterolobium lacerans, *R. Br.*
Guilandina Bonduc, *L.*
* Parkinsonia aculeata, *L.*
Poinciana pulcherrima, *L.*
Mimosa rubicaulis, *Lam.*
* Inga dulcis, *Willd.*
Acacia arabica, *Willd.*
  concinna, *D. C.*
Vachellia Farnesiana, *W. & A.*
Hemicyclia sepiaria, *W. & A.*
Epicarpurus orientalis, *Blume.*
* Jatropha Curcas, *L.*
Pisonea aculeata, *Rox.*
Capparis sepiaria, *L.*
  aphylla, *Rox.*
Scutia indica, *Brong.*
Azima tetracantha, *Lam.*
Gmelina asiatica, *L.*
Balsamodendron Berryi, *Arn.*
Toddalea aculeata, *Pers.*
Bambusa arundinacea, *Willd.*
  spinosa, *Rox.*
  nana, *Rox.*
Dendrocalamus tulda, *Nees.*
Pandanus odoratissimus, *L.*

II. ORNAMENTAL PLANTS FORMING INNER FENCES.

* Lawsonia inermis, *L.*
Lonicera ligustrina, *Wall.*
* Citrus Limetta, *Riss.*
Morus Indica, *L.*
* Punica granatum, *L.*
* Hibiscus rosa sinensis, *L.*
Adhatoda vasica, *Nees.*
  Betonica, *Nees.*
* Graptophyllum hortense, *Nees.*
Gendarussa vulgaris, *Nees.*
* Gardenia florida, *L.*
* Allamanda cathartica, *L.*

III. PLANTS USED FOR EDGING GARDEN WALKS.

Pedilanthus tithymaloides, *Poit.*
* Vinca rosea, *Willd.*
* Heliotropium curassavicum, *L.*
Rosa indica, *L.*
* Rosa semperflorens, *Curtis.*
* Rosmarinus officinalis, *L.*

* Introduced.

MADRAS EXHIBITION—1855.

CLASS IV. SECTION VI.

*Timber and Ornamental Woods.**

SUB-JURY.—Lieut.-Col. G. Balfour, C.B.—*Chairman;* Lieut.-Col. T. T. Pears, C.B.; J. D. Sim, Esq.; H. Cleghorn, Esq., M.D.—*Reporter.*

ASSOCIATES.—John Rohde, Esq.; Lieut. French; Mr Deschamps; Mr G. Williams.

The importance of this section of the Exhibition can scarcely be overrated in a country like this; for it must be remembered that the value of wood and timber here is not to be measured by the estimation in which they are held in temperate climates. Here, they are not only applied to those economic uses with which we are all familiar, but they also furnish fuel to all classes, supplying the place of that valuable mineral coal, which has not yet been found in any quantity within the limits of the Presidency. Besides this, the influence of trees on climate is very considerable, tending as they do to prevent the too rapid withdrawal of moisture from the soil—a point of great importance in a country where the heat of the sun is intense—and the supply of water is dependent only upon periodical falls of rain.

The value of timber would be best shown by the vast extent to which it is employed in the various purposes of life. It is impossible to ascertain the amount used in this country; but the quantity of firewood alone imported by sea into Madras during five years, is given below; that for 1849–50 being estimated by the military board to be equal to 12,000 tons.

* The list of woods furnished in this Report is alphabetically arranged according to the botanical names; in 1850, Dr Wight prepared a similar list alphabetically arranged also, but according to Tamil nomenclature; it is of great value, and is referred to here.

Years.	Billets.	Value Rs.
1845–46,	6,361,816	32,536
1846–47,	4,277,013	22,746
1847–48,	5,678,794	31,974
1848–49,	10,475,590	58,026
1849–50,	9,851,050	66,101

The above is exclusive of imports by Cochrane's Canal, and the trunk roads, which the military board estimated at upwards of 85,000 tons per annum.

The trade reports of this presidency show that the exports of the following five woods alone amounted in value to Rs. 384,000 in 1854, viz.—

	Cwt.	Value Rs.
Sandalwood,	11,684	137,944
Redwood,	47,431	59,570
Sappanwood,	5,248	15,350
Ebonywood,		4,859
Teak,		216,368

These returns are all the jury have at command; but they may mention that the imports of timber into Great Britain alone in 1850 amounted to ten millions of cubic feet. From these facts may be deduced the great importance of endeavouring to ascertain, 1*st*, which is the best kind of timber for each particular purpose; and, 2*d*, whence the supply can be obtained with the greatest certainty and economy.

The number of individual contributors in this division is, as might be expected, small; but the specimens sent are numerous, and include many objects of great value and interest. It is evidently impossible for the jury in their report to remark in detail on each specimen which has come under their consideration. They have therefore referred to the lists of the different collections published in the general catalogue, and for facility of reference they have drawn up a classified list of 155 woods, containing, in a condensed form, all the information within their reach. To this, therefore, the jury solicit the attention of those who, either for practical purposes, or as a branch of scientific inquiry, feel an interest in this important subject. The jury limit themselves to a few general observations on each collection, to a statement of the grounds on which they have adjudged the awards recommended by them, and to a brief notice of those points to which, in the ensuing exhibition, the particular attention of contributors should be invited.

Travancore.—The collection of woods, forwarded by the committee of Travancore, is the most numerous (158 specimens) and best selected, and for these reasons the jury consider it deserving of a 1st class medal. Among the many interesting specimens which this collection includes, the jury would draw attention to one of a tree, considered to be of the cedar family, and named, though doubtfully, *Cedrela toona.* The specimen is of considerable size; the outer wood is whitish in colour and of little use; but the internal portion, forming about two-thirds of the entire trunk, is close-grained, hard, of a rich dark red, and takes a high polish. The tree is stated to be abundant twenty-five miles north-east of Trevandrum, and to yield planks from two to three feet in diameter, and the jury are informed, by competent practical advisers, that it promises to be a good substitute for mahogany.

2. *Mr A. T. Jaffray.**—The collection which ranks next, in the opinion of the jury, is one contributed by Mr A. T. Jaffray, Sup. of Hort. Garden, Madras. The specimens, 88 in number (with one or two exceptions), were obtained from the gardens under his management, as a necessary consequence; they are of small size and chiefly of sapwood; but this defect is counterbalanced by their careful botanical nomenclature, a point in which the other collections are unfortunately deficient. A few of the large timber trees, for the same reason, have no representative in this miniature collection, which is, however, rich in many new and interesting introduced woods, such as "lignum vitæ, mahogany, logwood, &c." The specimens are well prepared, showing the horizontal as well as vertical section of each tree, the bark being in all cases retained. The jury recommend the award of a 2d class medal to Mr Jaffray; and they would submit that his collection, or one prepared in the same manner, of full grown trees would be valuable to the Government, as an index to the specimens in its possession, which show only the timber without any guide to the external appearance and character of each tree.

3. The *Tinnevelly* collection is numerous, containing 63 speci-

* This collection is lodged in the Government Museum, Madras.

mens, in the form of "truncheons." The native names are carefully given. From the short period allowed for preparation, the specimens are necessarily unseasoned, and many of them are sapwood: but the collection deserves honourable mention, and gives a good idea of the resources of the southern portion of the Peninsula.

The *Mysore* territory, which forms the central portion of S. India, and occupies a generally high level, is well represented in the collections of Capt. Miller, Asst. Comy. General, of Capt. Gustard, Supt. of Coorg, of Apothecary Xavier, and of Dr Cleghorn.

4. *Captain Miller's* contribution contains 67 specimens, in the shape of truncheons, with the Canarese and botanical names attached, though the accuracy of the latter is in some cases doubtful; for this collection the jury award honourable mention.

5. The *Coorg* collection is numerically small, considering the vast forests in that territory. They are, however, excellent samples, in regard to size and preparation, being cut from sound heartwood, and well adapted for testing the working qualities of each tree.

6. *Mr Xavier's* contribution contains 56 specimens, accompanied with an account of the general uses and local distribution of each tree, altogether reflecting great credit on that exhibitor; its deficiencies being obviously attributable to his limited resources, and the jury award honourable mention.

7. *Dr Cleghorn's* * collection was made about eight years ago. It consists of small thin slabs, of 43 different kinds of woods, carefully selected from trees of full growth. From the size of the specimens, the utility of the woods for building, and other such purposes, cannot of course be tested; but the collection is of value, from its showing well the grain of the different woods, and their adaptation for cabinet purposes. The jury would specially remark the *Michelia Rheedii*, Sumpagi-mara, which yields a pretty olive-coloured mottled wood, close-grained, without being heavy, and well suited for cabinetmaking.

8. *Mr Rohde.* The jury are indebted to Mr Rohde for six specimens of wood, the highly ornamental character of which is

* Deposited in the office of the Conservator of Forests, Madras.

well displayed to many, probably for the first time. They are turned into cylinders, which form seems well suited for displaying the character of the wood, and its suitability for cabinet purposes. The jury would point to the tamarind and margosa trees, which abound in every part of the country, and, by Mr Rhode's skilful treatment, are shown to be suited for the most ornamental as well as the commonest purposes.

9. *Hyderabad.* The jury next notice the collection received from Hyderabad, from which some knowledge may be gained of the resources of the territories of His Highness the Nizam. The specimens are in a rough state, and obtained generally from trees of mature growth. The collection contains several woods of great promise, now probably used only for firewood, and shows the need of a careful and systematic inquiry into the resources of this large track of country. The jury have only to refer to the fact, that timber is now imported from Rangoon for the building of churches and barracks at Secunderabad. M. Deschamps, who favoured the jury with his council, produced a specimen of an unknown wood, procured from the Dekkan, and eminently suited, from its great beauty, to the purposes of the cabinetmaker.

10. The jury have before them a few specimens from Rajamandry, Nellore, and Masulipatam. They can scarcely be termed collections, but are interesting and useful, and deserve mention here. The jury are aware that little time was allowed to the local committees for the collection of specimens, and even that little was not exclusively available for any one of the important subjects which the exhibition embraces. The jury regret that they are compelled to pass, almost without remark, a large collection from Ganjam. It has evidently been collected with much labour; but as the specimens consist chiefly of sapwood, and moreover sustained injury in transit, the jury are unable to form a judgment of its value. The tract of country which this collection embraces is known to be rich in woods; and as the province has a long sea-coast, with facilities of water-carriage from the interior, the expense of transit would probably not be such as to throw its resources out of the market. The jury here had the advantage of referring to the valuable collection of woods, made many years ago, by the late Col. Frith, and now exhibited

by the Military Board. A duplicate of this collection is lodged in the United Service Museum, London; and a list of the specimens is given in the Jury Reports of the London Exhibition of 1851. The jury would submit, with reference to this well-known collection, that as many of the specimens are of sapwood, it does not in all cases furnish a fair criterion whereby to test and identify subsequent collections. The jury would, in conclusion, briefly notice some single specimens of peculiar merit.

The first is a very large plank, contributed by Capt. Cunningham of the Mysore Commission, obtained from *Michelia Champaca* (Sumpagi). The extraordinary dimensions (length 11½ feet, breadth 4½ feet, thickness 3 inches) which the tree assumes, though rarely, and the ornamental character of the wood, are well shown in this specimen, which may with justice be declared *unique*. The jury, considering the rarity of such a specimen, together with the expense and difficulty of the preparation and transmission, beg to recommend that a 2d class medal be awarded to Capt. Cunningham. The second specimen referred to is a large and well-seasoned plank of Moulmein teak, contributed by H. W. Porteous, Esq. (dimensions, 10½ feet in length, 3¾ feet in breadth, 1½ inch thick), to whom the jury feel indebted for one of the finest individual specimens contributed to the collection. It must not be supposed that timber of such dimensions as the two above mentioned is often procurable; but the specimens are valuable, as showing what magnitude these trees can attain under favourable circumstances.

Another specimen which the jury would notice is a slab of kyabuka wood, imported from Singapore, and exhibited by J. Sanderson, Esq. A small portion is polished, and shows well the highly ornamental appearance of the timber in its marking. The specimen exhibits the very knotty character and curly fibres of the wood, from which pieces of even a foot square, free from flaws, can rarely be obtained. The botanical name of the tree is believed to be "*Pterospermum Indicum*." The jury remark also two specimens of a rare wood, marked "Sassafras," from Mergui. The wood is fragrant, and contains an essential oil of value in medicine (*Sassafras officinalis*).

Another fragrant wood, the "aguil," contributed by M. Nursing

Rao of Shemoga, also deserves mention. The jury understand that the wood is sold by weight, and is prized next to sandal-wood by natives. There is reason to believe that this is the *Aquilaria agallocha*, the lign aloes of Scripture. The habitat of the tree has not been ascertained, although it is supposed to have been brought from the Malayan peninsula. The jury recommend a 2d class medal.

The jury have looked in vain for any wood likely to answer the purposes of English or Turkish box, the most generally useful in Europe of all the hard woods. It is more than probable that its equal for many, if not all the purposes to which it is applied, is to be found among the less known shrubs or small trees of our jungles; and it appears to the jury worthy of consideration, whether a medal or prize should not be specially offered to any one who shall exhibit and prove, to the satisfaction of competent persons, the like properties in any abundant Indian tree. To prevent misapprehension, it may be desirable to state, that uniformity of structure and considerable toughness, hardness, and retention of any sharp angles to which it may be cut (whether on the end, or on the side), are essential properties; colour, except for certain purposes, is of little consequence.

The jury must not omit to acknowledge the valuable aid cheerfully accorded to them by Mr Rohde, Lieut. French, Messrs Deschamps and Williams, in all matters requiring special practical knowledge and experience. They have also availed themselves of the very useful treatise on "Turning and Mechanical Manipulation," by Mr Holtzapfell of Long Acre, with botanical notes by Dr Royle; and "Observations on the Forest Trees of S. India," by Dr R. Wight, with practical notes by Mr Rohde: these are the most reliable works for reference on this most important subject.* The jury regard the subject of the woods of India as in all respects so highly important, that they venture to make a few suggestions regarding the collection, &c., of specimens, in the hope that the deficiencies of the present exhibition may be remedied, and the labour and expense which many of the contributors have incurred may not again be neutralized by the

* Consult also "Wallich's Catalogue of Indian Woods" in *Trans. Roy. Soc. of Arts*, vol. xlviii. pp. 439–479.

want of some particular information, or the neglect of some little precaution.

The jury have endeavoured to make the most of the materials at their command, and have spared no pains to obtain the most authentic information within their reach upon a subject confessedly difficult; but a comparison of their report with the numerical lists of specimens will show how large a number of the samples are of little practical value, from the causes above noticed. They briefly mention the points to which contributors should pay special attention:—

NOMENCLATURE.

Most of the woods in general use have a variety of names, and much confusion arises from this circumstance. There is first the *local* name, varying often in the same district. This should always be given in the native character, whether Tamil, Telugu, Hindustani, &c. Many woods have also a *commercial* name, by which they are known in the market, as "Trincomallee" wood, "Coromandel" wood, &c. These names are sometimes derived from the place of export; but often it is impossible to trace their derivation. If this name is known, it should also be given, as it is very desirable to identify some valuable woods known in Europe only by their commercial name. Lastly, there is the *botanical* name, the sure determination of which is a matter of the first importance; for if this be known, the tree can be identified with certainty all over the world. It is very necessary, therefore, that the means of determining this should be furnished with each specimen. A small shoot, bearing flowers, fruit, and full-grown leaves, either together or separately, pressed flat and dried, so as to be fixed on a sheet of paper, is such a specimen as is required; and if it comprehends all these parts, is a representation of the largest tree in the forest, and gives a sufficient idea of the plant to the botanist to enable him to find its place in the *Systema Vegetabilium*. The fruit and seeds sometimes will not bear compression; in that case they should be sent separately. Succulent fruits are best preserved in a strong solution of salt. It is important to observe how the specimens should be marked. Paper labels are unsafe, writing on cadjan leaves is less liable to be defaced, but the woods should in addition to a label be cut or branded with a number. The botanical specimens should be securely sewn up, or pasted in a paper envelope, with a corresponding number.

SIZE OF THE SPECIMENS, ETC.

For a complete collection, there should be several of each wood from various localities. 1*st*, A horizontal section of the tree, with the bark complete, and about 3 inches thick. 2*d*, A plank about 3 inches thick, and about 3 feet long, cut from the log about half way between the pith and heart, the bark, sapwood, &c., being retained. 3*d*, Two or three bars, about 2 feet 6 inches long, 2¼ inches square, cut from the sound wood. 4*th*, A turned cylinder of hard or ornamental woods, 1 foot long and 3 inches in diameter. The use of the above specimens is obvious; the 1st shows the character of the entire timber, having sufficient to illustrate this; the 2d shows the value of the wood for carpentry, &c.; the 3d enables trials to be made of the strength of the wood, its power of supporting weight, its deflection, &c.; the 4th shows its ornamental nature and suitability for turnery. These specimens should be planed smooth at each extremity, but neither varnished nor polished.

But the value of wood depends much on its age. The young tree possesses strength and elasticity in the greater degree; when mature, *i.e.* when it would shortly cease to increase in diameter as it increases in age, it acquires its maximum of stiffness and durability; in its aged state, it will also best suit the purposes of the cabinetmaker. The grain of the wood depends also greatly on the nature of the soil, being generally straight and open in a tree growing rapidly on a rich, and the reverse in a poor soil. In some cases, specimens of the root of the same tree in different stages of growth would be very serviceable, as affording wood of great resisting power for furniture; thus the root of a healthy oak is preferred for spokes of wheels, while veneers from the root of an aged specimen often bear a high value for cabinet purposes. The objects for which the wood seems adapted must be a guide to the collector in the choice of these forms. The jury need scarcely remark, that specimens in the above forms are not required of all woods, but only of new, little known, or valuable species. It would be a waste of time, labour, and expense to have specimens in these forms sent from every district of the Tamarind, the Mango, or other such trees of common occurrence everywhere; but new species, or those little known or little used, should be thus sent, and then all that is required can, once for all, be ascertained with certainty and precision.*

GENERAL INFORMATION.

I. The uses to which the several parts of the tree is applied, and those for which experienced natives consider it especially adapted.

II. Its distribution in the district; the localities where the best is procurable, with the nature of the subsoil; the distance from the nearest seaport or town of any size; whether water carriage is available.

III. The extent of supply; whether this is increasing by self-sown seedlings or fresh plantations, &c., or decreasing; the average size in height and circumference of the mature tree; its character, whether straight or crooked; the average length, &c., of the logs or planks; the time required for seasoning, and the amount of seasoned timber generally procurable.

IV. The age at which the tree reaches maturity, *i.e.* when increasing age brings no further increase of diameter. This is a point of great importance, though hitherto quite neglected in this country, for on it depends the relative value of trees for planting. Thus, supposing there are two species of trees, of equal value as regards timber, &c., but one attains maturity in 25, while the other requires 35 years, it is obvious that the first is much the more valuable of the two, its money value being realized 10 years sooner. The jury would remark, that in every case the information given should be precise. If any doubt attaches to any point, let that be fairly stated; for it is undeniable that much of the confusion now existing owes its origin to doubtful information being given without any indication of its real value, and being too readily assumed to be an ascertained fact; whereas,

* For additional remarks on these points consult directions issued by the Smithsonian Institution, and introdnced at the close of the Jury Reports.

had the doubt been mentioned, inquiry might have been made, and the error, if it were one, detected at the outset. In all cases, therefore, writers ought to state whence the information has been obtained, and how far it can be depended upon. Every effort should at the same time be made to test the intelligence given by one individual by inquiries from others, &c.

The jury trust that their remarks will not deter parties from sending good specimens merely because all the information above required cannot be furnished. Their intention in giving these hints will be misunderstood, if such is the case; for these remarks owe their origin to the fact, that above 200 specimens, collected with much labour, time, and expense, are practically useless, to the disappointment equally of the disinterested contributors and the public.

CLASSIFIED LIST OF WOODS, NATIVE, OR GROWN IN THE MADRAS PRESIDENCY.

1. *Acacia arabica.* Babul, *Eng.* Babula, *Hind.* Kar-vaila, *Tam.* Nalla tumma kara, *Tel.*—This hard tough wood is extensively used, but cannot be obtained of large size, and is generally crooked. It is used for ploughshares, naves of wheels, &c., and generally for all purposes for which a bent hard wood is required. It makes excellent tent pegs. The tree is found in every district, and is worthy of cultivation on account of its gum, timber, and its pods, which are a favourite food of sheep and goats. It is of rapid growth, and requires no water, flourishing in dry arid plains, and especially in black cotton soil, where other trees are rarely met with. The bark is extensively used for tanning, and gives a reddish tinge to the leather. (Wight, No. 19.)

2. *Acacia catechu.* Kheir, *Hind.* Wodahalle, *Tam.*—The wood of this tree is less hard and durable than that of the other *Acacias.* The tree is small, and occurs more frequently in the Dekkan than in the Carnatic. The watery extract (*kut*) is largely manufactured. (Wight, No. 124; Coimbatore, Travancore, Canara.)

* See Dr Gibson on Babul preserves in "Trans. A. H. Soc., Bombay," p. III. 1852.

3. *Acacia leucophlœa.* Vel-vaila, *Tam.* Tella tumma, *Tel.* Kikar, *Hind.*—A good dark-coloured wood, but generally small. The specific name is given from the whitish colour of the bark, which is used in distilling arrack. This Acacia is easily distinguished by its panicled globular inflorescence and stipulary thorns. (Wight, No. 115; Tinnevelly.)

4. *Acacia odoratissima.* Karu-vengé, *Tam.*—A strong and heavy wood, of rapid growth, attaining considerable size, and well suited for naves and fellows of wheels. The tree is abundant, and grows in almost any soil. The grain is ornamental, but rather open. (Wight, No. 1889; Coimbatore, Travancore, Palghat, Palamkota, Bellary.)

5. *Acacia speciosa.* Dirasana, *Tel.* Vel-vengé, *Tam.*—A very serviceable timber, easily procured at Madras. This is the *A. sirissa*, which is extensively planted along the Ganges Canal. The tree is of large size and rapid growth; the wood of light colour, durable, and very hard. (Wight, No. 116; Coimbatore, Guntur, Hyderabad.)

6. *Acacia sundra.* Karangali, *Tam.*—A very hard, heavy, and durable wood, used for posts and rice pestles. The tree is rather large and abundant, but the wood is not generally to be obtained in the market in planks of any size. At Guntur, Mr Rohde states that posts 5 feet long are procurable at Rs. 12 per 100. These are well suited for fencing, though the non-elastic nature of the wood is unfavourable to the holding of nails driven into it. The natives regard it as the most durable wood for posts in house-building. (Wight, No. 13; Coimbatore, Travancore, Palghat, Hyderabad.)

7. *Adansonia digitata.* Baobab tree. Papara pulia-maram, *Tam.*—A tree of immense girth, introduced from Africa, but now found all over the Presidency; the leaves are eaten, and the fruit is used as a float, but the wood is useless, being light, open, and perishable. (Hort. Garden, 1.)

8. *Adenanthera pavonina.* Wood hard, durable, red, yielding dye, not procurable generally in any quantity.—The tree is of handsome appearance. (Hort. Garden, 2.)

* *Acacia stipulata* yields a close-grained timber. This was not exhibited, nor were any of the Australian species, introduced to the Nilgiris.

9. *Agati grandiflora.* Agathi, *Tam.* Avisi or Agisi, *Tel.*—A very common tree of rapid growth, cultivated for the sake of its flowers and pods, both of which are eaten by the natives. Wood quite worthless. (Hort. Garden, No. 77.)

10. *Ailanthus excelsa.* Peddu-manu, *Tel.* Peru-maram, *Tam.*—A large tree, resembling the ash in general appearance, wood light and white, used formaking sword handles, &c. (Wight, No. 71; Travancore.)

11. *Alangium decapetalum.* Alangi-maram, *Tam.* Anisaruli-maram, *Can.* Akola, *Hind.*—The wood is said by Roxburgh to be "beautiful," and Wight found it to sustain a weight of 310 lbs., but he had never seen a ten *inch* plank. The jury have no means of verifying thesestatements, onlyone specimen having been forwarded to them. (Wight, No. 3; Coimbatore, Mysore.)

12. *Anacardium occidentale.* Cashewnut tree. Caju. *Hind.* Jidi mamidi, *Tel.*—A small handsome tree, a native of the W. Indies, yields a large quantity of transparent gum, which, with the nuts, is an article of trade; wood made into chests.

13. *Anona muricata,* Sour sop.—A fruit tree; wood inferior. (Hort. Garden, 61.)

14. *Anona reticulata,* Bullock's Heart, Rama Sita-maram, *Tam.*—A fruit tree. (*Idem*, Hort. Garden, 62.)

15. *Aquilaria Agallocha.* Eagle wood or Aloes wood. Agallochum of the ancients. Agar, *Hind.*—Contains a fragrant resinous substance. The specimen from Shemoga is green and old (the two others are yellow, and appear to have been obtained from a different tree). The jury desire information regarding this odoriferous wood, which is sold by weight, and is reported to have been brought from the Malayan peninsula. (Wight, No. 2; Travancore, Tinnevelly, Shemoga.)—See p. 218.

16. *Areca Catechu.* Betel-nut palm, Supari *Hind.* Camugu, *Tam.*—A palm of remarkably perpendicular growth, attaining a height of 60 or 80 feet, with a tuft of feathery leaves at the extreme top; the trunk is only a few inches in diameter; the structure of the wood is like that of palms in general, and is often used in turnery for small objects. The nut is used by the natives with the betel leaf. It is hard and peculiarly streaked, and is also used in turnery for small ornamental work. The wood is

employed in Travancore for spear-handles and bows, for which it is well suited, being very elastic. (Travancore.)

17. *Artocarpus hirsuta.* Angeli-maram, *Tam.*—A large tree used on the Malabar coast, for making canoes, &c., the trunk being hollowed out. Rheede figures the tree (*Hort. Mal.* 3, t. 32), and praises the timber.* It is confined to the W. Coast. (Wight No. 4; Travancore, Malliatur, Mysore, Coorg. Cleghorn; Mysore.)

18. *Artocarpus incisa.* Bread-fruit tree.—A tree of slow growth, not uncommon in gardens about Madras, and thrives well on the Malabar Coast. (Hort. Garden, 15.)

19. *Artocarpus integrifolia.* Jak-tree, Pila, *Tam.* Panasa, *Tel.* Alasegana-mara, *Can.*—Excellent timber, at first yellow, changing to brown, much used for furniture in Ceylon, somewhat resembling mahogany in colour and appearance, but does not bear great alternations of dryness and moisture; suitable for house carpentry in general. The tree grows rapidly, is suited for avenues, and the fruit is prized. (Wight, No. 64; Mysore, Bangalore, Tinnevelly, Palghat, Travancore, Coorg, Rajahmandri, Hort. Garden, 14; Penang, Canara. Cleghorn; Mysore.)

20. *Atalantia monophylla.* Catyalu micha-maram, *Tam.*—A small tree, wood close grained, hard, and heavy. It is pale yellow, and, if procurable of sufficient size, would be very valuable for cabinet purposes. (Wight, No. 28; Hort. Garden, 47.)

21. *Averhoa Bilimbi.* Bilimbi-maram, *Tam.*—A small fruit tree, of little value as timber. (Hort. Garden, 10.)

22. *Averhoa Carambola.* Tamarta-maram, *Tam.*—A small fruit tree, of little value as timber. (Hort. Garden, 11.)

23. *Azadirachta Indica.* Nim tree, Vépa-maram, *Tam.* Vepa-manu, *Tel.*—Hard, heavy wood; when old, difficult to work, but *beautifully* mottled, as in Mr Rohde's specimen. The seed affords a valuable bitter oil. The tree is found everywhere, attaining a large size in some localities, deserving of attention for ornamental work. (Wight, No. 108; Coimbatore, Palamkota, Mysore, Bangalore, Travancore, Guntur, Palghat, Masulipatam.)

24. *Bassia longifolia.* Mohwa. *Hind.* Elupa-maram, *Tam.* Ippa manu, *Tel.*—Good wood for trenails; it is comparatively

* This wood has been the subject of correspondence with H. M. Dockyard authorities, an abstract of which follows; see Index.

free from the attacks of the *Teredo navalis;* it is procurable among the logs brought down the Godavari. It is valued for all purposes, in situations where it is not exposed to air, as planking of ships below the water line, frames on which well walls are built, &c. (*J. R.*) Nearly equal to teak, but smaller. Much used for construction of carts at Coimbatore; and in Malabar, where it attains a large size, it is used for spars. (*R. W.*) A valuable fatty oil is obtained from the seed. (Wight, No. 24; Mysore, Bangalore, Palamkota, Travancore. (Cleghorn, No. 20.)

25. *Bauhinia Richardiana.* Introduced from Madagascar. Of this wood we have no knowledge, the trees in the country being still young. (Hort. Garden, 58.)

26. *Bauhinia tomentosa.* Kat atti, *Tam.*—A tree of small size, the wood dark brown, and hard—not much in use. Bark used as cordage. Several of the Bauhinias yield dark-coloured, heavy, and durable timber. (Wight, No. 9; Hort. Garden, 59.)

27. *Bauhinia variegata.* Irkumbalitha-mara, *Can.*—A beautiful tree with variegated flowers, wood of little use. (Mysore, 34.)

28. *Berrya Ammonilla.* Trincomallee wood, *Eng.* Tircanamalai-maram, *Tam.*—Introduced from Ceylon, the wood is annually imported from Trincomallee, by which appellation it is known in the market. It is highly esteemed for its lightness and strength, is straight grained; slightly pliant, tough, and little affected by the atmosphere; employed in the construction of the Massula boats of Madras (*Wight*). Used for spokes of wheels, helves, handles, planes, frames, poles, and shafts of carriages; it is inferior to Sal for spokes, and to the Babul for some other purposes, but it is comparatively light, and easily worked (*Rohde*). The market is still dependent on importation from Ceylon. (Hort. Garden, 12; Ceylon.)

29. *Bignonia suberosa.*—A very handsome tree, with fragrant flowers and spongy bark, which is a very inferior kind of cork. (Hort. Garden 82.)

30. *Blighia sapida.* The Aki tree.—A native of Guinea, fruit the size of a pear. Wood light and useless. (Hort. Garden, 38.)

31. *Borassus flabelliformis.* Palmyra. Panna-maram, *Tam.* Táti chettu, *Tel.*—This tree is very abundant, especially in sandy tracts near the sea. It is used chiefly for rafters, joists,

and laths; when of good age, the timber is very valuable for this purpose; the trunk is split into 4 for rafters, into 8 for laths; these are dressed with an adze. Jaffna Palmyras are famous, and were largely imported in former times. From the structure of the fibres, it splits easily in the direction of its length, but supports a greater cross strain than any other wood: iron nails, however, rust rapidly in it. The fruit and the fusiform roots of the young trees (in the N. Circars) are used as an article of food by the poorer classes. The leaves are used for thatching and coarse fibre. Jaggery and toddy are extracted from the tree, the former is extensively used in the manufacture of sugar in Vizianagram and Rajah mandr. Very neat baskets of Palmyra leaf are exhibited from Tinnevelly. (Wight, No. 69; Hort. Garden, 73; Travancore, Masulipatam.)

32. *Briedelia spinosa.* Mullu vengé, *Tam.*—Wood not known in Madras; the tree is not uncommon, and attains a considerable size in the hill jungles. (Wight, No. 46; Travancore.)

33. *Butea frondosa.* Palas, *Sans.* Dhak, *Hind.* Porasam, *Tam.* Thorus-mara, *Can.* Moduga chettu, *Tel.*—A common tree thriving well in many parts of the country; flower deep red, used as a dye. The field of Plassey took its name from this tree. (Wight, No. 82; Coimbatore; Hort. Gardens, 67; Bangalore, 62; Palghat, 35.)

34. *Cæsalpinia coriaria,* the Divi-divi.—The tree was introduced from seed supplied by Dr Wallich, about 20 years ago; the pods are collected with care, being valuable for tanning purposes.* (Hort. Gardens, 26.)

35. *Cæsalpinia sappan.* The Sappan tree. Patangé, *Hind.* Tsiapangam, Vatangi, *Tam.*—Used for dyeing; cultivated in Palghat, for the purpose of dyeing the straw used in mat-making (*Wight*); from its high price for this purpose, not used for carpentry. (Wight, No. 104; Coimbatore, Travancore, Tanjore, Kadapa, Goa.)

36. *Calophyllum inophyllum.* Alexandrian Laurel, *Eng.* Pinne-maram, *Tam.* Wuma-mara, *Can.* Ponna chettu, *Tel.*—A beautiful tree with an appropriate name, very common; a good

* For particulars of profitable culture see *Jour. Agr. Hort. Soc. Ind.*, vols. iv. and v.

lamp oil obtained from the seeds; wood coarse grained, strong, durable, and ornamental. The tree is worthy of attention, as it grows well in sandy tracts close to the sea, where few others thrive. (Wight, No. 73; Bangalore, Travancore, Palamkota, Coorg, Hyderabad.)

37. *Careya arborea.* Budadanedi, *Tel.* Khumbi, *Can.*—Wood useless; the bark serves as cordage, and is used as slow match for guns in N. Circars. (Wight, No. 65; Hort. Garden, 23; Coimbatore.)

38. *Careya sphœrica.*—Wood useless; the bark serves as cordage, and is used as slow match for guns in N. Circars. (Hort. Garden, 22.)

39. *Caryota urens.* Bastard Sago Palm. Utali pana, *Tam.* Bhyni, *Can.*—A very ornamental palm, furnishes an inferior kind of sago and also toddy. Is extensively used under the name of Napiera in Ceylon, for rafters, which are exceedingly hard and durable. (Travancore, 325.)

40. *Casuarina equisitifolia.*—This tree was introduced about 50 years ago, and is now well established, growing freely, and ripening seed in great abundance. In general appearance, it much resembles the larch fir; it grows in 10 years to the height of about 30 feet. It generally grows very straight, and where the main shoot is broken or lopped off, throws out secondary shoots readily, and these are usually straight and erect. It thrives best in sandy tracts along the sea-shore, and it would be desirable to plant it largely on the sand-hills north and south of Madras, where some numbers have already been grown. The wood is reddish in colour; in density and appearance it somewhat resembles Trincomallee (*Berrya Ammonilla*). It bears a great strain, is well adapted for posts, and is said to bear submersion in water very well. The bark contains tannin, and a brown dye has been extracted from it by M. Jules L'Epine of Pondicherry. On the whole, this tree deserves extensive cultivation on the sandy tracts, where it grows so readily. (Hort. Gard., 13.)

41. *Cathartocarpus fistula.* Konné-maram, *Tam.* Relli, *Tel.* —A tree of great beauty when in flower, but generally too small and crooked to yield valuable timber; wood close-grained, and used for tomtoms, &c. In the Malabar forests, it attains suffi-

cient size for spars of native vessels (*Wight*). The bark is one of the best for tanning. (Wight, No. 31; Coimbatore; Hort. Gard. 27; Guntur.)

42. *Cathartocarpus Roxburghii.*—A highly ornamental tree, in form much resembling the weeping ash. It is at present only found in gardens; but the wood is hard, and handsomely marked, and may hereafter prove a valuable addition to the timbers of India. (Hort. Gard. 28.)

43. *Cedrela Toona.* Tun-maram, *Tam.* Tuna, *Hind.* Tundu, *Can.*—A valuable tree, of large size; wood reddish-coloured, used all over India in cabinetmaking; scarcely inferior to mahogany, but lighter, and not so close in the grain. Often sold in Madras under the general name of "Chittagong wood." It is the most valuable of the woods known by that commercial name. It is very deserving of careful inquiry as to locality, supply, &c., with a view to being brought into more extensive use in this Presidency. The specimen sent by General Cullen shows the grain and polish remarkably well. It is, however, of a brighter colour, and apparently a denser quality, than any met with in the market, inducing a doubt as to its being of the same species. Found in the Mysore and Salem jungles in large quantities; also along the crest of the ghats from Travancore to Goa. (Wight, Nos. 103, 126; Travancore.)

44. *Chickrassia tabularis.* Aglé-maram, *Tam.*—Wood extensively used in cabinetmaking, also coming under the denomination of "Chittagong wood," being imported from that province; but it is abundant in the mountainous parts of the peninsula. It makes beautiful and light furniture, but is apt to warp during the season of hot land-winds. The wood is well known, and easily procured. (Wight, No. 2; Travancore, Mysore.)

45. *Chloroxylon Swietenia.* Satinwood tree. Kodawa pursh, *Tam.* Billu chettu, *Tel.*—This tree grows abundantly in the mountainous districts of the Presidency, but seldom attains a large size; occasionally planks of 10 to 15 inches in breadth may be procured. The wood is very close-grained, hard, and durable, of a light orange colour; takes a fine polish, and is suited for all kinds of ornamental purposes, but is somewhat apt to split. For picture-frames, it is nearly equal to American maple. In some

instances it is beautifully feathered. The timber bears submersion well. There is this peculiarity: satinwood loses its beauty by age, unless protected by a coat of fine varnish. (Wight, No. 34; Rajamandri, Coimbatore, Mysore.)

46. *Cicca disticha.* Aranelli, *Tam.* Harfaruri, *Hind.*—A small tree bearing a round acid fruit, the country gooseberry; wood inferior. (Hort. Gard. 31.)

47. *Citrus aurantium.* Orange tree. Kolinji-maram, *Tam.* Kichili, *Tel.*—The well-known orange tree; wood hard, but not available of any size, or in any quantity. (Hort Gard. 65.)

48. *Cluytia collina.* Wodugu-maram, *Tam.* Vodisa, *Tel.*—A small tree; wood red-coloured, exceedingly hard and durable; but little is known of it. (Wight, No. 123; Palghat.)

49. *Cocos nucifera.* Coco-nut tree. Tenna-maram, *Tam.* Naril, *Hind.* Tenkaya-chettu, *Tel.* Tingena, *Can.*—This tree thrives well on the sea coast. Its uses and produce are well known. The wood is occasionally used for rafters, for which purpose it is inferior to the palmyra. In Ceylon, however, and on the W. Coast, hard and durable rafters are procurable. The Cochin fibres were sent in a large box of this wood, the planks of which are prettily striped, and of remarkable size. (Hort. Gard. 74; Travancore, Mysore, 15; Penang, 1.)

50. *Cordia latifolia.*—Wood very inferior, and of small size. (Hort. Gard. 51.)

51. *Cyathea arborea.* Tree fern.—The section of this tree fern displays well the structure of an Acrogenous stem, hollow in the centre, marked on the outside by the scars of the fallen leaves, and showing the elongation of the axis by the junction of the petioles. Wood quite worthless as timber. (Hort. Gard. 87.)

52. *Dalbergia latifolia.* Blackwood. Erupottu, *Tam.* Irugudu chettu, *Tel.* Biti, *Can.*—A magnificent tree, from which the well-known Malabar blackwood is obtained; planks 4 feet broad are often procurable, after all the external white wood has been removed: it is heavy and close-grained, admitting of fine polish, very much used for furniture. One of the most valuable woods of this Presidency. Mr Ouchterlony exhibits his prize coffee in a large box of fine blackwood from his Nilgiri estate. (Wight, No. 25, Travancore; Coorg, Palghat, Cannanore, Nilgiris.)

53. *Dalbergia sissoides.* Blackwood. Biti-maram, *Mal.*—This is a smaller tree than *D. latifolia*, but more common in the forests; both yield a black wood, in Madras indiscriminately called "Rosewood." The wood contains much oil, which unfits it for receiving paint. (Wight, No. 21; Travancore, Palghat, Canara.)

54. *Dalbergia sissoo.* Sissu, *Tel.*—Introduced from Bengal at the recommendation of Dr Wallich; grows to a large size; has been planted on the banks of the Tumbhadra, and is thriving wonderfully. It is growing extensively in the cantonment of Masulipatam as an avenue tree, and has been planted in some places on the banks of the Kistna Anicut. There are few trees which so much deserve attention, considering its rapid growth, its beauty, and its usefulness. Wood hard, strong, tenacious, and compact; whilst its great durability combines to render it one of the most valuable timbers known. The tree grows rapidly, is propagated and reared with facility, and it early attains a good working condition of timber. It is used in Bengal for gun carriages. (Hort. Gard. 39; Bengal.)

55. *Dillenia pentagyna.* Kanagalu, *Can.*—A stately forest tree, common on the face of the W. ghats. The wood is said to be exceedingly strong and durable, even when buried under ground. This wood splits easily, and hence is much prized by firewood contractors. (Wight, No. 74; Coimbatore, Travancore.)

56. *Diospyros cordifolia.* Vuckana-maram, *Tam.*—A hard heavy wood, coloured dark-brown. It is difficult to work. (Wight, No. 121; Travancore, Tinnevelly.)

57. *Diospyros ebenaster.* Acha-maram, *Tam.*—Ebony of very superior quality is procurable in the W. districts, as well as the N. Circars. Mr Rohde has received 16-inch planks, of a fine uniform black. Ebony is much affected by the weather, on which account European cabinetmakers seldom use it except in veneer. To prevent splitting, it should be well covered.

The tree bearing the name "Acha" at Madras is *Hardwickia binata.* (Wight, No. 1; Travancore, Coorg.)

58. *Diospyros mabola* (often called "Mangosteen," under which name it is cultivated in gardens at Vizagapatam).

59. *Diospyros melanoxylon.* Ebony. Tumbi-maram, *Tam.*—

The species of Diospyros have this peculiarity, that the black heart wood is surrounded by white sapwood. There are several fine specimens of the genus, but the jury are unable to determine the species, or verify the names. The subject is important, and merits careful elucidation. (Hort. Gard. 88; Wight, No. 102; Coimbatore, Kadapa (Col. Pears), Hyderabad.)

60. *Ehretia lævis.*—Wood of very small size. The wood seems good; but the only specimen is from the Hort. Society's Garden, and a safe judgment cannot be formed upon it.

61. *Elate sylvestris.* Wild date. Ejata, *Can.*—Has the general characteristics of the family, but is inferior to the Palmyra, Coco-nut, &c. (Mysore 43.)

62. *Emblica officinalis.* Emblic myrabolan. Aoula, *Hind.* Nelli-maram, *Tam.* Nelli-mara, *Can.* Usirika, *Tel.*—A fruit-tree, the wood of which appears to be of service for making boxes, &c. (Travancore, 280; Mysore, 24–36; Palamkotta, 264.)

63. *Embryopteris glutinifera.* Kusharata-mara, *Tam.* Tumiki, *Tel.*—A middling-sized tree; the wood is of indifferent quality. The viscid juice of the fruit is used for paying boats, and strengthening fishing-nets and lines. (Bangalore.)

64. *Eriodendron anfractuosum.* White cotton tree. Elavu-maram, *Tam.*—A soft almost worthless wood, used for toys, floats, and such purposes. (Wight, No. 23; Travancore.)

65. *Erythrina Indica.* Indian coral tree. Murku-maram, *Tam.* Badida chettu, *Tel.*—This is the "Muchie" wood of Madras; soft, and only used for toys, light-boxes, trays, &c. The varnished toys from the Northern Circars are made of this wood. (Wight, No. 48; Travancore.)

66. *Euphorbia tirucalli.* Milk hedge. Kalli, *Tam.*—Wood light-coloured. The root of old shrubs is understood to be well adapted for gun stocks, but plants of sufficient age are seldom met with. (Wight, No. 27; Humsagar.)

67. *Euphoria Litchi.*—A fruit-tree introduced from China. The Litchi attains a height of 25 to 30 feet, but does not ripen its fruit at Madras. In Orissa and Bengal it succeeds. (Hort. Gard. 18.)

68. *Eurya longifolia.*• (Hort. Gard. 86.)

69. *Feronia elephantum.* Wood apple. Kait, *Hind.* Vela-maram, *Tam.* Bilwar-mara, *Can.* Velaga chettu, *Tel.*—A large tree, widely diffused in India, yieding a hard strong heavy wood, much used at Vizagapatam in house-building; said to be not very durable. (Wight, No. 107; Mysore, Bangalore.)

70. *Ficus glomerata.* Rulla kith-mara, *Can.* (Mysore.)

71. *Ficus Indica.* Banyan tree. Ala-maram, *Tam.* Alada-mara, *Canarese.* (Mysore, Bangalore; Hort. Gard.)

72. *Ficus infectoria.* Bassari-mara. (Mysore.)

73. *Ficus nitida.* (Hort Gard. 5.)

74. *Ficus racemosa.* Atti-mara. (Mysore, Tinnevelly, Travancore.)

75. *Ficus religiosa.* The pippul tree. Arasa-maram, *Tam.* Rangi-mara, *Can.* Rávi-chettu, *Tel.*—A very poor wood. (Mysore, Bangalore.)

76. *Ficus virens.* Guvi manu, *Tel.* (Masulipatam.)

These various species of Ficus are well known, and differ little from each other in their properties. The trees are large, and of rapid growth; but the timber is of little value, being light, open, and soft. The large drops of the banyan, after being well soaked in water, to get rid of the viscid juice, are used for tent poles, and such purposes. Bird-lime is prepared from the fresh juice.

77. *Gmelina arborea.* Cummy-maram, *Tam.* Gumudu-chettu, *Tel.*—A large timber tree, growing in mountainous districts. The wood is light, of a pale yellow colour, easily worked, and does not shrink or warp; used for picture-frames, decking small boats, for making venetian blinds, sounding boards, palankeen pannels, gram measures, &c. This tree deserves notice; it is very commonly used in the Vizagapatam district for the foundation of wells and other purposes which require it to be submerged in water, where it is remarkably durable. (Wight, 13; Masulipatam, Godavari.)

78. *Gossypium acuminatum.* The Peruvian Cotton Plant, a biennial shrub, useless as timber. (Hort. Gard. 8.)

79. *Grewia tiliæfolia.* Chadachey-maram, *Tam.*—A considerable tree, wood soft, not known at Madras. (Wight, 86; Palghat.)

80. *Grewia Sp.*—Makes good walking-sticks. The wood of

Grewia salvifolia is also used for the same purpose; and the bark of many species yields good fibres. (Hort. Gard. 44.)

81. *Guaiacum officinale.* Lignum vitæ.—This shrub has been introduced from Jamaica, and is found to thrive well, flowering and fruiting readily. Its chief value is for medicinal purposes; but the wood, about 4 inches in diameter, is very hard and close-grained, suited for turning. In time, a supply may be available. (Hort. Gard. 9.)

82. *Guatteria longifolia.* Deodaru, Asoka chettu, *Tel.*—A very handsome, erect growing tree, planted in avenues, at Triplicane and Pondicherry; wood soft and useless. (Bangalore.)

83. *Guazuma tomentosa.*—A tree common about Madras, evidently planted; the fruit is tubercled, about the size of a cherry; introduced by Dr Anderson about 70 years ago. (Hort. Gard. 85.)

83*. *Hardwickia binata.*—Is the *yepi* of Nellore, Guntur, and Masulipatam.

83½. *Hibiscus lampas.* (Hort. Gard. 42.)

84. *Hæmatoxylon campechianum.* Logwood.—This tree has been introduced; the largest as yet much resemble a fine hawthorn tree in habit and size. It grows readily, and seeds abundantly; but it remains to be seen whether it will attain a large size in this country. It is used as a dye, and the bark is astringent. This promising tree deserves attention. (Hort. Gard. 71.)

85. *Hura crepitans.* Sand box-tree.—A middle-sized tree of rapid growth; the trunk is strongly armed, the wood light and useless. The seeds are poisonous. (Hort. Gard. 80.)

86. *Hydnocarpus inebrians.* Mara-vattî, *Tam.*—A large tree; little is known of the wood; the fruit is used for poisoning fish. (Wight, 51; Tinnevelly, Travancore, 37.)

88. *Inga dulcis.* Sweet Inga or Manilla Tamarind. Sima chinta, *Tel.* Kurkapuli-maram, *Tam.*—A most valuable hedge plant (p. 206), used along the line of railway; the wood is hard. Isolated trees of 12 to 18 inches diameter are occasionally found; these resemble the hawthorn in general appearance. It is the *Pithecolobium dulce*, Benth. The pulp of the fruit is eatable; the seed was brought from Manilla to Samulcottah; hence the name "Manilla tamarind." The Spaniards introduced the tree to the E. Indies from Mexico. (Masulipatam.)

89. *Inga xylocarpa.* Tangedu-manu, *Tel.* Jambé, *Hind.*—This tree grows to a large size, and is much valued for house building, on account of its strength and toughness. It is remarkable for its thick woody legume, and is the *Xylia dolabriformis* of Benth.

90. *Jatropha multifida.* Coral-plant.—A garden shrub. (Hort. Gard. 79.)

91. *Jonesia asoca.*—A highly ornamental tree; timber not available. (Hort. Gard. 3.)

92. *Kleinhovia hospita.*—A garden shrub. (Hort. Gard. 70.)

93. *Kydia calycina.*—A middle-sized tree, pretty common along the W. Ghats. (Hort. Gard. 69.)

94. *Lagerströmia microcarpa.* Ben-teak. Ventaku, *Can.* Cutcha catta-maram, *Tam.*—A tree of large size, with a long straight stem; the timber is of ordinary character, easily worked, and suited for purposes where strength and beauty are not required. (Wight 20, and 118, Cannanore; Tinnevelly, Coorg, Travancore, Palghat.)

95. *Lawsonia inermis.* Henna plant. Mendi, *Hind.*—A hedge plant, resembling the English privet; the wood strong, and suited for tool handles, tent pegs, &c.; the leaves yield the dye used by the natives. (Hort. Gard. 33.)

96. *Malpighia punicifolia.* Barbadoes cherry.—An ornamental shrub introduced from the W. Indies. (Hort. Gard. 25.)

97. *Mangifera indica.* Mango tree. Maa-maram, *Tam.* Mamidi chettu, *Tel.* Mavena, *Can.*—A tree of large growth, and generally diffused. The mature wood is dull grey, open, yet durable, if not exposed to wet, of the effect of which it is very sensitive. It is the cheapest wood procurable in Madras; used for packing-cases, boarding, and rough work in general. Mr Rohde says it holds a nail faster than any other wood known to him. (Wight, 39; Mysore, Bangalore, Hort. Gard. 57.)

98. *Melia azadirach.* Margosa. Malai vembu, *Tam.* Turaka vepa, *Tel.*—A tree of moderate size, and in some localities of large size. The mature wood is hard, durable, and handsomely marked. A valuable oil is made from the seed. (Wight, 41; Bangalore, Palamcotta.)

99. *Mimusops Elengi.* Magidam, *Tam.* Pogada manu, *Tel.* Mugali-mara, *Can.*—A tree of moderate size, cultivated for the oil obtained from its fragrant flowers. The wood is little known. (Wight, 40; Mysore, Nellore, Travancore, Rajamandri, Hort. Gard. 54.)

100. *Mimusops hexandra.* Pala-maram, *Tam.*—Frith.

101. *Michelia Champaca.* Sampagi-maram, *Tam.*—A large tree, the wood close grained, and very handsomely marked in a mottled manner. It is, the Jury understand, being tried in Bombay for ship-building purposes. A remarkably large specimen is exhibited by Captain Cunningham; its dimensions are 11½ feet in length, 4½ feet in breadth, and 3 inches in thickness, and it is apparently derived from a tree of very great age. The ornamental character of the wood is well shown in a small tablet (38), contributed by Dr Cleghorn. (Mysore, Coorg, Travancore, 2.)

102. *Morinda citrifolia.* Nona-maram, or Munja pavetti, *Tam.* Maddichettu, *Tel.*—A small tree of common occurrence, the wood and root much used for dyeing red; the wood is deep yellow, easily worked, and used for common purposes. (Wight, 50 and 58; Travancore, Hyderabad.)

103. *Nauclea cadamba.* Caddam, *Hind.* Vella cadamba, *Tam.* Rudraksha-kamba, *Tel.*—A noble tree, wood yellow, used for furniture. (Travancore, Bengal.)

104. *Nauclea cordifolia.* Munja cadamba, *Tam.* Daduga, *Tel.* Heddé, *Can.*—A large tree growing abundantly in the mountainous districts of the peninsula; wood yellow, rather close grained. It is used for common purposes, and easily worked; but is best suited for work which is sheltered, bedsteads, &c., being much affected by alternation of dry and wet weather. *N. parviflora* (nir cadamba) is also frequent on the W. Coast, and is valued for yielding flooring planks, packing-boxes, &c. (Wight, 49; Travancore, Palamkotta, Bangalore.)

105. *Parkia biglobosa.*—A very elegant tree of large size, introduced from Africa; the legumes are filled with a farinaceous pulp; the wood is hard and promising, surrounded by an astringent bark. A watery extract has been prepared, but the value of which, for tanning purposes, has yet to be tested. A supply of timber is not yet procurable. (Hort. Gard. 24.)

106. *Odina Wodier.* Udé-maram, *Tam.* Gumpina, *Tel.*—A large tree, native of mountainous districts, it is grown from cuttings, and planted in avenues, but it yields no shade in the hot weather, being without leaves till June. The wood is difficult to season, but when well seasoned, the central reddish portion is useful for many purposes. (Wight, 5.)

107. *Oegle* marmelos.* Bœl, *Hind.* Vilva-maram, *Tam.* Marêdu, *Tel.*—A thorny tree with ternate leaves; the astringent pulp of the fruit is a valuable remedy in diarrhœa; the wood is hard, but from the great medicinal value of the tree, the timber is not at present available. (Wight, 119; Mysore, Bangalore, Canara, Hort. Gard.)

108. *Pavetta indica.* Pavetti-maram, *Tam.*—An ornamental shrub 4 or 5 feet high, with white flowers; timber very small. (Hort. Gard.)

109. *Pimenta vulgaris.*—The "Allspice" tree, introduced from the W. Indies. Several large trees are at Madras, but the climate of the Carnatic does not seem to suit them. (Hort. Gard. 46.)

110. *Poinciana regia.*—A large tree with showy-coloured flowers. Introduced from Madagascar, still confined to gardens and avenues. The wood seems good. (Hort. Gard. 21.)

111. *Pongamia glabra.* Punga-maram, *Tam.*—This large tree, attaining a height of 40 feet, is very common in S. India, flourishing equally well in the arid plains of the Carnatic and on the subalpine tracts of Mysore. Oil is made from the seeds. Roxburgh says the wood is light, white, and fit for a variety of purposes; here it is used chiefly for fuel. The boughs and leaves are extensively used as manure. (Wight, 78; Travancore, 3; Bangalore.)

112. *Premna tomentosa.* Kolkatté teak, *Tam.*—A small tree. Wood hard and close grained, of a brownish yellow colour, well fitted for ornamental purposes. (Wight, 35; Travancore.)

113. *Prosopis spicigera.* Parambê, *Tam.*—A thorny tree, not uncommon in the black cotton soils, attaining a large size in Mysore. Wood strong, hard, straight grained, and easily worked.

* The correct name is *Ægle.* For properties of fruit, see papers by Drs Grant and Cleghorn in Indian Annals of Medical Science, II., pp. 222–234.

The foliage of the tree and the character of the wood closely resemble those of its congener *Acacia sundra.* (Wight, 84.)

114. *Psidium pyriferum.* Guava tree. Coaya-maram, *Tam.* Sebe-mara, *Can.*—The common guava found everywhere in gardens, which probably found its way to India from S. America through the Portuguese. Wood small, but very hard, used by Dr Hunter for wood engraving, and commonly for pegs, mallets, handles of tools, &c. (Hort. Gard. 29; Mysore, Bangalore, Masulipatam.)

115. *Pterocarpus indicus*, Wall. Padouk, *Burm.*—The "padouk" is a handsome tree, with long waving branches and clusters of yellow flowers, which scent the air. It produces very fine timber, and may be considered one of our most valuable forest trees. This species also yields Gum Kino. (Hort. Gard. 55; Frith.)

116. *Pterocarpus marsupium.* Kino tree.* Vengé-maram, *Tam.* Honi, *Can.* Yegisa, *Tel.*—A large handsome tree, widely diffused, yielding one of the most abundant and useful timbers of S. India; when wet, it gives a yellow stain. Mr Rohde states, that it is better suited for weather boards, exposed venetians, &c., than any other wood he has tried. It is heavier than teak, and more difficult to work. This tree yields the gum kino of commerce which is exported from Malabar. The timber is now being tried for sleepers on the railway. (Wight, 117; Canara, Tinnevelly, Coorg, Palghat, Coimbatore.)

117. *Pterocarpus santalinus.* Red sanders. Rakta sandanam, *Hind.* Sevapu sandanam, *Tam.*—This tree, which grows abundantly in the Naggary Hills, yields the "Red Sandal-wood" of commerce. It is sold by weight as a dyewood, and forms a regular article of export. It takes a beautiful polish; but the high price of the wood for dyeing purposes precludes its use as a timber. (Wight, 88; Travancore, Canara, Naggary Hills, Mysore.)

118. *Pterospermum indicum.* Kyabuka.—This wood is obtained from the knotty excrescences or burrs of *Pterospermum indicum.* It is sawn in slabs 2 to 4 feet long and 2 to 8 inches

* The origin of E. I. Kino was long unknown: the history of the discovery will be found in an interesting paper by Dr Royle. (See Pharm. Jour., IV. 510, and V. 498.

thick. It resembles the hue of the yew, is very hard and full of curls; the colour being reddish-brown, varying to orange. It is very ornamental, and much esteemed in China, India, and England, where it is used for making small boxes, writing desks, and other fancy work. The wood is brought to Singapore by Eastern traders, and is sold by weight. (Singapore.)

119. *Rottlera tinctoria.* Kapela, *Hind.* Sarnakasari-mara, *Tam.* Chendurapu chettu, *Tel.*—A large tree common in the Dekhan and the N. Circars. The red mealy powder which covers the capsules is used in Mysore to dye silk. Wood soft and inferior.

120. *Salmalia malabarica.* Red Cotton tree. Pula-maram, *Tam.* Mullu-elavu, *Can.* Buruga, *Tel.*—A large common tree, flowers of a beautiful red colour; the wood light and spongy, used by muchis in their work, but very inferior. (Wight, 76; Bangalore, Tinnevelly, Travancore, Masulipatam, Hort. Gard.)

121. *Santalum album.* Sandal-wood. Sandanam, *Tam.* Gandaga-mara, *Can.*—This very valuable tree, yielding the sandalwood of commerce, is found in abundance in Coorg and Mysore, and sparingly in Canara. It is usually cut into billets, which are classed according to size, and disposed of by weight. The uses are well known. The scent is believed to be much modified by peculiarities of soil and elevation. (Wight, 94; Travancore, Mysore, Coorg, Masulipatam, Madras, Hort. Gard. 75.) *

122. *Sapindus emarginatus.* Soap-nut tree. Puchi-kottay, *Tam.*—A tree met with about villages all over the country. The fruit used as indicated by the native name, and sold in all bazaars. Wood white, only used for fuel. In many situations, this tree yields a more profitable return than any other fruit tree. (Wight, 75; Hort. Gard.)

123. *Schmidelia serrata.*—A straggling shrub with ternate leaves. Timber very small. (Hort. Gard. 43.)

124. *Semicarpus anacardium.* Marking-nut tree. Shĕng cottē, *Tam.* Bēla, *Hind.* Jidi chettu, *Tel.*—This common tree is of no value as timber. A considerable quantity of the nuts are exported from the Dekhan and Mysore as a mordant. The juice

* For the growth and management of the sandal-wood tree, see Buchanan's Jour. *passim.* It flourishes in a belt between the *Mulnád* (rain country), and *Maidan* (open plain).

is so acrid, that woodcutters are unwilling to cut the tree. (Wight, 95; Mysore, Bangalore, Tinnevelly, and Travancore.)

125. *Sethia indica.* Devadaru, *Tam.*—When fully grown, it is still a small tree. The fruit yields an oil, and the wood is esteemed as a substitute for sandal-wood. (Wight, 92; Travancore, Tinnevelly.)

127. *Soymida febrifuga,* Red wood, or Bastard cedar. Semmaram, or Choar kalli-maram, *Tam.* Somida, *Tel.*—A large tree; tolerably abundant; timber most durable and strong, yet light and easily worked; deserving of attention. (Wight, 12, 96; Travancore, Palamcotta, Penang, Kadapa, Mergui, Moulmein.)

128. *Spathodea adenophylla.*—A small introduced tree. (Hort. Gard. 53.)

129. *Spathodea Sp.* (Hort. Gard. 52.)

130. *Sterculia fœtida.* Pinari-maram, *Tam.* Gurrapu badam chettu, *Tel.*—A large tree, chiefly found on the W. coast and in Mysore, where it is applied to a number of useful purposes. This is one of the trees which are believed to furnish the smaller "Poon spars," much valued for masts of ships (see p. 11). (Hort. Gard. 19.)

131. *Sterculia guttata.* A large tree. (Hort. Gard. 20.)

132. *Stereospermum suaveolens.* Padri-maram, *Tam.* Ulunanthri-mara, *Can.*—A middle-sized tree with pinnate leaves and panicled inflorescence; very fragrant wood (according to Wight), strong and elastic, said to be fitted for making bows. (Wight, 63; Mysore 38.)

133. *Strychnos nux vomica.* Nux vomica tree. Yetti-maram, *Tam.* Musidi, *Tel.*—This well-known tree is small; wood white and very hard, used for ploughshares. The poisonous fruits are the favourite food of the *Buceros malabaricus* or hornbill. (Wight, 128; Travancore, Bangalore.)

134. *Strychnos potatorum.* Clearing Nut tree. Taita-maram, *Tam.* Indupu chettu, *Tel.*—A larger tree than the above; the fruit is well known as possessing the property of clearing water; wood hard and serviceable though of small size. (Wight, 98; Bangalore.)

135. *Syzygium jambolanum.* Jamún, *Hind.* Nawel-maram, *Tam.* Nerala-mara, *Can.* Nerédu, *Tel.*—A fine large tree of common occurrence, suited for avenues; the fruit small and

somewhat astringent; sold in the bazaars. The wood is much used for ordinary purposes, but is of little value. (Travancore, Mysore, Masulipatam, Palamkotta, Bangalore, Hort. Gard.)

136. *Tamarindus indica*, Tamarind tree. Pulia-maram, *Tam.* Chinta chettu, *Tel.* Unara-mara, *Can.*—A large and very handsome tree, of slow growth; the wood hard, durable, and fine-veined, but apt to be faulty in the centre. The ornamental character of the wood is well shown in the handsome specimen contributed by Mr Rohde. It is used in the manufacture of oil and sugar mills, and is largely planted around villages for its fruit and shade. (Wight, 77; Mysore, Bangalore, Guntur, Masulipatam, Palamkotta, Hort. Gard. 50.)

137. *Tecoma stans.*—An ornamental garden shrub. (Hort. Gard. 6.)

138. *Tectona grandis.* Teak, *Eng.* Ték-maram, *Tam.* Ték chettu, *Tel.*—A native of the mountainous parts of Malabar and the country bordering the Godavari, the Moulmein and Rangoon forests. This well-known and far-famed tree grows straight and lofty, with cross-armed panicles of showy white flowers. It seems to require eighty years to attain perfection. The wood is very hard, but easily worked; it is soon seasoned, and, being oily, does not injure iron, and shrinks little. It is probably the most durable timber known; hence its value in ship-building. The Malabar teak is considered the *best*, and is always most valued in our Government dockyards. A valuable report by Dr Falconer on the teak forests of the Tenasserim coast was published in the selection of Records of the Bengal Government (No. ix. 1852). The present price of teak wood of long scantling is Rs. 3 per cubic foot, double the ordinary rate. It is matter of regret, considering the vast importance of teak timber to England as a maritime nation, that the preservation of the teak forests was so long disregarded. (Wight, 100; Mysore, Tinnevelly, Coorg, Rajahmandri, Palghat, Bangalore, Mangalore, Travancore, Penang, Canara.*)

* "Teak timbers are not now procurable at Gwalior, the whole of the teak trees in the forests of Kichiwâra having been cut down by the Mahratta soldiery. Numbers of young trees are now springing up, but many years must elapse before they are mature. The only teak timbers now

139. *Terminalia alata.* Maradam maram, *Tam.* Kara-matti mara, *Can.*—A very large tree, used on the W. coast for house-building and making canoes. (Wight, No. 43; Bangalore, Palamkotta, Mysore, Tinnevelly, Palghat, Travancore.)

140. *Terminalia belerica.* Tanikoi, or tandi maram, katelupa, *Tam.* Tadi chettu, *Tel.*—A very large tree, with a straight trunk and spreading head; wood white and soft, but not much used. The flowers have an offensive smell. The kernel of the fruit is eaten by the natives. (Wight, 11–99; Mysore, Tinnevelly, Travancore.)

141. *Terminalia Berryi.* Vella marda, *Tam.*—This tree attains a large size, especially at the foot of the W. Ghats, where it is used for canoes, &c. (Wight, 111; Travancore, Hort. Gard. 64.)

142. *Terminalia catappa.* Natvadam cotte, *Tam.* Badam, *Tel.*—A beautiful large tree, found in gardens, &c.; the kernels are eaten and are palatable, the "Indian almond;" the wood is also useful. (Wight, 54; Hort. Gard. 63.)

143. *Terminalia chebula.* Pilla marda or Kadukai, *Tam.* Alali mara, *Can.* Hirda, *Duk.* Karaka chettu, *Tel.*—A very large tree; fruit used by harness-makers. The leaves are punctured by an insect, and hollow galls are developed, which are powerfully astringent, and answer well for making ink. They also yield chintz-painters and carpet-weavers their best and most durable yellow. (Wight, 72; Mysore, Travancore, Bangalore.)

144. *Terminalia glabra.* Kara marda, *Tam.*—A large tree, wood dark coloured, very hard, heavy, and strong. Dr Wight speaks highly of this wood, and states that large beams are readily procurable at Coimbatore for house-building purposes. It is very hard, heavy, and durable under water. (Wight, 16; Travancore, Mysore, Palghat.)

procurable are found in the Bâgri Forest, near Indore. The tree does not reach any great size, the largest timbers not being more than 16 feet long by about 9 inches square. Shorter planks, 12 inches in breadth, can also be obtained, but the quantity is limited. Vindhyan teak is much superior to that of Pegu, both in strength and in beauty. The specific gravity is about the same, but the deeply marked and wavy irregular veins of the Vindhyan tree afford a much handsomer cabinet wood than the straight-grained and faintly-marked timber of Pegu."—*Major A. Cunningham.*

145. *Thespesia populnea.* Purasa, *Tam.* Ganga-ravi, *Tel.*—A tree much used for avenues, of quick growth, and yielding good shade. This generally grows from the cuttings; and although the timber is strong, hard, and durable, it is rarely met with good, owing to the trees rotting at the heart. It is procurable, fit for chairs, &c. The tree abounds in old gardens, and about all European stations, thriving best near the sea. (Wight, 79; Mysore, Palamkotta, Hort. Gard. 30.)

146. *Thevetia nerüfolia.*—A garden shrub called the "Exile." The wood is worthless. (Hort. Gard. 17.)

147. *Vachellia farnesiana.* Jali mara, *Can.* Veda vully, *Tam.*—An armed shrub, very common in Mysore and Dekkan, exuding much gum like the babool, which it greatly resembles in its timber; the size is very small. (Wight, 109; Mysore.)

148. *Vatica robusta.* Sál, *Hind.* Gugilam, *Tel.*—A wood in great repute, belonging to the *Dipterocarpeæ.* It is most valuable for house and ship-building, vats for liquids, door frames, and the rails and battens of doors; it is not suited for planks; it twists, shrinks, and warps, whenever the surface is removed, even after many years' seasoning. This wood is in general use for building purposes in the Ganjam and Vizagapatam districts. "From Colonel Baker's excellent experiments, it appears that, compared with teak, its strength is about 1121 to 869. From Major H. Campbell's valuable experiments, unseasoned sál broke with a weight of 1308 lbs., seasoned sál with 1319 lbs., and teak wood with 1091 lbs. It is unquestionably the most useful known Indian timber for engineering purposes." (*Jury Reports, Great Exhibition*, 1851.)

149. *Visenia umbellata.*—A considerable tree of great beauty, with rose-coloured flowers and velvety leaves; introduced from Sumatra, the seeds having been sent to the Hort. Soc.'s Garden by Dr Wallich. (Hort. Garden 36.)

150. *Vitex alata.*—A small tree found in the Naggary Hills; leaves ternate, petioles winged. (Hort. Gard. 32.)

151. *Vitex altissima.*—A large tree, of great beauty when in flower; frequent on the slopes of the W. Ghats; fit for cabinet purposes and for turning. (Wight, 131; Travancore.)

152. *Wrightia antidysenterica.* Veppala, *Tam.* Pála chettu,

Tel.—A small tree, of common occurrence in Mysore and the hilly parts. Its medicinal virtues are worthy of attention, but the wood is of little value. The bark was formerly in request under the name of *Conessi*,* and is still esteemed a valuable drug by the natives. It appears to have lost its value in commerce, from not being distinguished from the bark of *Wrightia tinctoria*, which grows in the same places. (Travancore.)

153. *Wrightia mollissima.*—Introduced from the Naggary Hills. The yellow juice might be turned to account, but the timber is of no value. (Hort. Gard. 68.)

154. *Wrightia tinctoria.* Pala maram, *Tam.*—A small tree, the leaves of which yield an inferior kind of indigo. Wood white and close-grained; said to be suited for turnery. (Wight, 66; Travancore, Bangalore, Palamkota, Penang.)

155. *Zizyphus jujuba.* Yellande maram, *Tam.* Elanji mara, *Mal.* Guti mara, *Can.* Bèr, *Hind.* Regu, *Tel.*—The wild *bèr* tree, common almost everywhere; wood hard and useful, but of small size. It is used for making sandals and saddle trees: occasionally for sleepers. (Wight, 127; Mysore.)

MADRAS EXHIBITION—1857.

Timber and Ornamental Woods.

Jury.—Hon. W. Elliot—*Chairman;* Lieut.-Col. T. T. Pears, C.B.—*Reporter*, Mr W. B. Wright; Mr Williams; Major Maitland.

Associates.—Lieut. Hawkes; Lieut. Beddome.

The observations contained in the report of the jury in this department, in 1855, have not been without their effect on the present exhibition. The general collection of woods exhibited is remarkably interesting, and the contributions from some of the districts very complete. The most important contributions are from Malabar, Palghat, Coimbatore, Madura, Bangalore, Hyder-

* Milburn's Oriental Commerce, i. p. 278.

abad, and Pondicherry. There are also smaller collections from Utakamand, Bellary, Burma, and Masulipatam.

Malabar.—The collection of specimens from Malabar, exhibited by the collector of that district, merits special notice for the care with which the specimens have been prepared, and for the extent and importance of the contribution. It consists of specimens of 60 varieties of timber, two samples of each kind, the one being a piece of about 2½ feet in length, with a section of 3 inches square, as suggested by the jury of the last exhibition; the other being a complete slab, 4 or 5 inches thick, cut across the trunk, and including the bark. By far the greater part of this collection was represented in the Exhibition of 1855, and the woods then described seem not to require notice here. The following woods, of which specimens are found in this collection, appear, however, to be worthy of attention:—

1. Ven (or ben) teak, *Lagerströmia microcarpa.*—This wood is abundant in the district of Malabar. It is not generally considered durable when exposed to the vicissitudes of temperature and climate. It has however been used to a considerable extent of late in ship-building at Cochin, and on the railway. (Malabar, Palghat.)

2. Puvu, *Schleichera trijuga.*—This wood is described by Wight, "List of Timber Trees" (80), as a strong, hard, red wood, generally rather small, used to make pestles, spokes for bandy wheels, and such purposes,* where much strength in small space is required. (Palghat, Malabar.)

3. Agilla, supposed by some to be the Indian cedar-wood,† *Aquilaria agallocha?*—This is a light-coloured wood, with a fine even grain; appears admirably adapted for furniture, and many domestic purposes. It is said to be abundant in Malabar, and has been used for a variety of purposes by the railway engineers. The jury recommend further inquiry regarding this tree, the extent to which it is found in Malabar, and whether known in other parts of the country. (Madura, Malabar, Mysore.)

* Screw rollers for sugar mills, cotton presses, &c. ("Gibson's Handbook," p. 34.) Kusum, *Dak.* Shaguda, *Can.*—H. C.

† This is probably *Chickrassia tabularis.*—H. C.

4. *Vitex altissima*, named by the exhibitor, "Magellu," *Mal.* "Kat milla," *Tam.*—It is thus described by Wight: "This is a large tree frequent on the lower slopes of the ghat mountains; but I am not acquainted with the timber, except in so far as can be learned from a small outside specimen, which seems close-grained. It is reported fit for cabinet purposes." It would be desirable to learn more of this tree. A specimen formerly grew in Dr. Anderson's garden near the College Bridge, in Madras. Roxburgh describes the wood of one of its congeners, *Vitex arborea*, common in the N. Circars, as of a chocolate colour; when old, exceedingly hard and durable. (Palghat, Malabar.)*

5. *Eugenia caryophyllifolia.* Nawal, *Mal.*—This wood is stated by Wight to be the *Calyptranthes caryophyllifolia* (Ainslie; who speaks of it as a large tree, with spreading branches). It is very common, growing in all parts of the country, well known by its Tamil name "Naga-maram," and by Mohammedans as the "Jamun" tree, the fruit of which, a kind of blue plum, is sold in every bazaar. Roxburgh says the wood is hard, close-grained and durable, and of course is used for a variety of purposes. The wood appears, from the specimen before the jury, to be a close-grained, strong wood, probably useful for building and other common purposes.

The jury cannot better conclude their brief notice of the Malabar collection, than by appending a valuable Memo. upon eight different woods of that district, drawn up by Mr Sinclair, supt. of carriage and waggon building under the Railway Coy., which has been placed at their disposal by Mr Wright, the locomotive supt. of the Madras Railway:—"I have examined thirteen different kinds of timber, which are easily procurable at Beypur, and have selected eight kinds of the best description, of which I recommend purchases to be made, in the proportion of one thousand candies: thus,

Sample.	Tam.	Botanical.	Candy.			Rs.	A.	P.
No. 1.	Karamarda.	*Terminalia glabra.*	100	Price about,		4	0	0
2.	Erul.	*Inga xylocarpa.*	200	...	...	4	0	0
3.	White Cedar.	?	200	...	...	4	0	0
4.	Agilla.	*Chickrassia tabularis?*	150	...	...	6	0	0

* Dr Gibson reports well of this tree.—"Handbook," p. 42.

Sample.	Tam.	Botanical.	Candy.		Rs.	A.	P.
No. 5.	Red Cedar.	*Soymida febrifuga?*	50	Price about,	3	8	0
6.	Pillamarda.	*Terminalia chebula.*	50	... ...	3	0	0
7.	Vellamarda.	*Terminalia alata.*	50	... ...	0	0	0
8.	Ben-teak.	*Lagerströmia microcarpa.*	200	... ...	3	0	0

"1. *Karamarda*, Rs. 4 per candy.—This wood grows large, generally sound and plentiful; is very suitable for strong framings, and very durable in works. It is, however, rather coarse in fibre, curly grained, and difficult of planing, or dressing off clean for painting or varnishing. In seasoning, it also appears to open in grain, and shows a few weather shakes of a small kind. In consequence of this propensity, the shrinkage appears very small per foot of surface. Its density is 5 lbs. 12 oz. per superficial foot. It is procurable 25 to 30 in feet length, and about 15 inches diameter, middle girth. It seasons in twelve to fifteen months in planks, and is not touched by white ants.

"2. *Inga xylocarpa*, Erul, price Rs. 4 per candy.—This wood is similar to No. 1. It is, however, more straight-grained, and more easily planed, or cleaned off for painting. It shrinks in seasoning about $\frac{1}{8}$ inch per foot of surface, the density is 5 lbs. 10 oz. per foot superficial. It is procurable in 25 or 30 feet lengths, and about 15 inches diameter; it seasons when cut into planks in twelve months, and is very lasting either under or above ground; takes paint or varnish very well, and is not affected by white ants.

"3. White cedar ———, price Rs. 4 per candy; grows plentifully and large, but is not generally sound at heart, if exceeding 24 inches in diameter at middle of 35 or 40 feet log. This is a very useful wood for general purposes, and, in consequence of its large dimensions, converts economically into scantling of all sizes. It is easily planed and worked; the shrinking properties are great in seasoning, being about $\frac{1}{2}$ inch in 12 inches, the density is 4 lbs. per foot superficial, is durable above ground, and very lasting, if kept free from moisture.

"4. Agilla, Rs. 6 per candy.—This wood grows similar in size to the Erul (2). It is rather curly and cross-grained in its fibre, and is difficult of planing clean for painting, on account of the grain rising on the surface after being cleaned off; it shrinks

¼ inch per foot; the density is 3¼ lbs. per foot superficial; it is a bright-coloured wood, and looks well varnished; it is also of a tough nature, though not so heavy per foot cube as the others.

"5. *Cedrelacea*, Red cedar-wood, Rs. 3.8.0 per candy.—This wood grows large, is of a middling quality, easily planed and worked; seasons with a shrinking of ⅜ inch per foot superficial; it also keeps close and sound; the density is 2 lbs. ¾ oz. per foot superficial; it is straight-grained, and very useful in many kinds of work. The supply is, however, rather limited.

"6. *Terminalia chebula*, Pilla-marda, Rs. 3 per candy.—This wood is similar in all respects to the sample No. 1, Karamarda, except colour, which is yellowish brown, its density 4½ lbs. per foot, and the supply plentiful.

"7. *Terminalia alata*, Vella-marda, per candy.—This wood is similar to 6, but of a whiter colour; it shrinks ⅜ inch per foot superficial; its density is 4¼ lbs. per foot.

8. *Lagerströmia microcarpa*, Ben-teak, Rs. 3 per candy.—This wood grows of a good size and straight-grained; is of a lasting quality above ground; if kept free from moisture, it is easily planed and worked; its density is 4 lbs. 8 oz. per foot superficial, its shrinking properties are ¼ inch per foot; it is rather strong in nature, and will cast in seasoning, if not properly stored. It is useful for heavy framings, and such like works.

"Some of the sample logs had been seasoned by steeping in water, and others had not been long felled; the density, therefore, must only be considered as approximating to the various differences in the woods, and not as their actual weight when dry and seasoned."

MADURA.—The next contribution to be noticed is that from Madura, exhibited by Mr Parker, the collector. It consists of 32 specimens, of various forms and dimensions. The collection is interesting, but contains few woods not already known and reported on at the former exhibition. Among the woods not then displayed, the jury observe the following:—

1. *Guettarda speciosa*. Punkai wood. Madura, Mysore.—This is a large-sized handsome tree, common in gardens, but not supposed to abound in the forests. The specimen is small, but

exhibits a closeness of grain and other characteristics rendering it deserving of further inquiry.

2. *Mimusops elengi.* Magadam-maram. Pondicherry, Madura.—This wood is said to be employed in cabinet-making, and appears, from the specimens here presented, to be well suited to that purpose, being light, with a tolerably close and even grain. Dr Wight speaks of it as a cultivated plant, not much used, and little known: this merits further inquiry.

3. *Sethia indica.* Devadarum, Sembulinga. Madura, Bangalore, Guntur, Hyderabad.—This wood is described and mentioned by Wight, who considers it identical with *Erythroxylon areolatum.* Ainslie (*Mat. Med.* 4to ed., pp. 187, 213) was informed that a kind of wood oil was obtained from this tree in the Tinnevelly district. He adds that the wood is small, of a reddish brown colour, and very fragrant, so that the people of Mysore use it instead of sandal-wood.

The rest of the woods found in the Madura Collection were noticed in the jury's report at the Exhibition of 1855.

Palghat.—The collection from Palghat is exhibited by Kistna Chettyar. The specimens, 102 in number, are small, but have been arranged with great care, the native and botanical names being given with each specimen. The jury notice in this collection *Conocarpus latifolius,* which will be subsequently referred to in the Coimbatore collection. They observe also a specimen of *Dichrostachys cinerea.* Vadatata-maram, *Tam.* Veluturu chettu, *Tel.*—This is described in Wight's List, No. 105, as a small tree, or rather large shrub; wood very hard and strong, but too small for any except common purposes.

Coimbatore.—The collection from Coimbatore, Kistna, Maramut supt. exhibitor, consists of 34 specimens, about 13 inches long, with a cross section of 3 inches square. Great pains appear to have been taken in the preparation of these samples, and in the determination of the names. Almost all the trees best known and most highly valued in this part of India are represented in this collection. Among those which deserve notice here, are,—

Briedelia spinosa. Mullu-vengé. Coimbatore.—This is described by Wight as a wood not known, though the tree is not uncommon, and attains a considerable size among the Alpine jungles.

Conocarpus latifolius. Vella-naga or Vekali, *Tam.* Coimbatore, Palghat.—The wood is heavy, light-coloured, and close-grained. The tree is tall and handsome, furnishing an excellent and very strong timber. The ashes of this tree are in demand, as an article of diet, among certain wild tribes, inhabiting the forests about the Nilgiri Hills. The demand for it has been attributed to the large proportion of pure carbonate of potash which it yields—the diet of the same people including a large quantity of tamarinds. A handsome specimen is to be seen near the gate in front of the house known as Muneapillay's Garden, at Sydapet.* It is found abundantly in the N. Circars, where Roxburgh describes it as universally esteemed for every economical purpose; towards the centre it is of a chocolate colour, and is exceedingly durable. For house and ship-building the natives reckon it superior to every other sort except *Pentaptera tomentosa* and teak ("Flora Indica," vol. ii. p. 444); merits further inquiry.

Nerium (Wrightia) antidysentericum. Veppala-maram. Coimbatore, Palghat, Madura, Mysore.—This wood is said by Wight to be excellent for cabinet-making purposes. It is found also to answer for wood-engraving in the School of Arts. Ainslie, after describing the medicinal properties of the bark, speaks of the tree as being prized in Cochin China for its beautiful white wood, which is of a fine grain, and fit for making furniture. The specimen before the jury seems to be taken from a young tree, and does not therefore well represent the timber.

Pondicherry.—The jury have to notice a very full and carefully prepared collection of specimens of wood from Pondicherry. These are all small pieces well adapted for exhibiting the grain, colour, and specific gravity of the several woods, but not furnishing pieces of sufficient dimensions for experiments on their strength. The exhibitor, M. H. de Querret, engineer, has enhanced the value of his collection by a brief account of each tree, the purposes to which it is applied, the medicinal proper-

* *C. acuminatus* (Roxb.)

ties, and the local as well as the botanical name. It is remarkable that this interesting collection of woods, in which many of the finest and most valuable trees of S. India are represented, is made entirely within the settlement of Pondicherry.

Eugenia racemosa is a tree represented in this collection only, and was not produced in the former exhibition. It is described as a wild tree, attaining to a large size. This tree is noticed by Ainslie, who gives an account of its medicinal properties. (*Mat. Ind.*, vol. ii. p. 56.) It is *Barringtonia racemosa*, (Roxb.)

Strychnos nux-vomica.—A small specimen is found in this collection. The jury learn on good authority that white ants will not touch this wood, which is characterised by a remarkably bitter taste. It is used extensively for building in the N. Circars, found to grow to a large size in hill districts, though commonly small and stunted on the plains.

Dalbergia sissoo.—A deep purple, rather heavy wood. The specimen exhibited under this name appears to be the true *Dalbergia latifolia*, or rosewood. It is stated on the authority of Major Lawford, that the true Sissu, *Dalbergia sissoo*, is found in great abundance in Wainad. The wood used under this name in the Bombay Gun-carriage Manufactory is supplied from the forests on the W. Coast. The subject deserves further inquiry.

UTAKAMAND.—Mr M'Ivor, supt. of the Horticultural Garden of Utakamand, exhibits a small collection, consisting of 28 specimens, for the most part of woods generally known as being of value and importance. The jury observe the following as being especially deserving of notice: *Sarcococca trinervis*, or Nilgiri boxwood, reputed to be very common on the hills. Wood hard and durable; might be used in the arts as a substitute for the real box.

Dodonæa viscosa, common on the Nilgiris; wood elastic, and useful for tool handles.

Sapota elengoides, a large tree, common on the Nilgiris; wood strong and elastic, and, like the hawthorn, burns well when green.

Grewia tiliæfolia.—This wood is well known in central India, and much used in public works, and also in the Jabbulpùr factory. Dr Wight speaks upon report disparagingly of this wood, but it is valued in some parts of the country as a strong and durable timber, and one that grows to a large size.

Artocarpus echinata is represented by Mr M'Ivor as a large tree, yielding a good wood, though apparently not much used. Little appears to be known of this wood, which deserves further inquiry.

Stereospermum (sp.) Padri-maram.—There appear to be three useful species of this genus—viz., *Stereospermum chelonoides*, yielding wood of a reddish colour, said by Wight (*List*, No. 110), to be the strongest of the two noticed by him. *Stereospermum suaveolens* is described by him as a considerable tree, frequent in the Walliar jungles, wood strong and elastic, said to be fitted for making bows. (*List*, No. 63.) The third species has recently been discovered in the valley of the Godavari, and is of smaller size than the others, but appears to possess useful properties.

Cochin.—This collection consists of specimens of wood found in the district of Malabar. The samples are well prepared, but the value of the collection is unfortunately much reduced in consequence of no botanical names being affixed to them.

The jury cannot close their report on the woods exhibited, without calling attention to the number and variety of useful and valuable trees existing in the forests of this Presidency. Independent of the many reported to be useful in medicine and the arts, the large number of handsome and ornamental trees, and others, yielding valuable timber, cannot but strike one in looking through the lists. The districts which abound in useful woods are Canara, Malabar, Salem, Kadapa, Coimbatore, Tinnevelly, Guntur, Vizagapatam, and Ganjam.

Of the many useful woods standing in the forests, a very few only are in common use for domestic and agricultural purposes among the native population. It is singular that up to a very late period—it may almost be said that up to the present time—the servants of Government in the P. W. D. have taken little interest in any but the teak, palmyra, and mango woods. All others were classed under the general denomination of *jungle-woods*, and some of the finest timber of the world, thus named, has been applied in the construction of buildings which, having been considered temporary, were not thought deserving of teak-wood roofing.

There can be no doubt but that up to the present time the waste of timber in every part of the country has been very great.* The attention of Government has been lately directed to the preservation of forests, chiefly and prominently to teak, sandal, and other woods of known value; and it may be hoped that one result of these interesting exhibitions may be to convince Government and society at large of the immense value of property standing in our forests in the shape of trees, of great variety and less useful qualities, perhaps, than teak, but in some cases and for some purposes even superior to that wood—many of these timbers being not only heavier but stronger, and possessed of higher elasticity than teak.

The first serious inquiries into our forest resources that seem to have been made, originated in the demand for railway sleepers. Some difficulty was experienced at first in getting agents to contract for supplies. The jungles were unknown to all but a few native woodcutters, who alone appeared capable of resisting the fever; the demand for these durable woods among the native population was too limited for any man of capital to think of entering upon the business. The sub-collector of Vellore appears to have taken a lively interest in the matter, and to have organised a system for working the jungles of Salem and S. Arcot bordering upon his own district. He supplied the Railway Co. with about 54,600 sleepers, most of them woods of the best quality. The price of these, varying from $2\frac{3}{4}$ to $3\frac{1}{2}$ cub. ft. in contents, has been, on an average, Rs. 3–2. A list was given (p. 61) of the woods sanctioned for use on the railway. A report from the resident engineer, of a portion of the line open, shows the extreme importance, and the great difficulty attending the selection, and even the recognition, of the several varieties of woods. "You will observe that out of 1507 sleepers, the number actually removed, I have only been able to get the names of 487. I have already mentioned the very great difficulty experienced in getting an accurate account of the description of sleepers re-

* The appointment of Conservator of Forests was made in Dec. 1856.

moved, owing to the fact that no two of the village carpenters give the same name for a sleeper."

"Of the 487 sleepers examined, as many as 458 are reported to be of unauthorised woods. This is, of course, owing to the ignorance of the only persons the engineers could procure to name the woods, or possibly to their being bought over by the contractor. To my personal knowledge, the sleeper-contractors tried every expedient to pass bad woods upon us; and I have myself been more than once deceived by sleepers which were brought to me carefully sawn of the exact dimensions, of great weight, and apparent hardness. The carpenter gave names which were authorised, and I passed them; these I afterwards found were of Táni wood,* and had for a long time been steeped in water to make them heavy and solid looking. After a short exposure in the road, they dried, and began almost immediately to decay. Of the authorised woods removed, there are only 29 out of 487; and of these 29 only 2 were rotten, the remainder being split." The jury cannot doubt but that much good will be effected by the attention given to this subject in the general and local exhibitions of this Presidency.

A list, prepared with much care by Lieut. Beddome, exhibits several new kinds of wood found in the Godavari forests, and is appended to this Report, the jury being of opinion that its publication is calculated to be extremely useful.

T. T. Pears, *Reporter.*

TELUGU CATALOGUE OF TREES †

Indigenous in the Godavari Forests and the Circars between Bhadrachellum and Condapilly. By Lieut. R. H. Beddome, Asst. Conservator of Forests.

Ari (*Bauhinia racemosa*). Wood not used—slow matches are made from the fibre.

* *Terminalia Belerica.*

† "Flora Andhrica; a Vernacular and Botanical List of Plants in the Telugu Districts of the N. Circars," printed at Madras in 1859. By Walter Elliot, Esq., M.C.S.; contains much valuable information.

Anduga (*Boswellia glabra*). Wood soft and useless.

Alli (*Memecylon tinctorium*). Wood only used for fuel.

Anasandra (*Acacia ferruginea*). Wood very hard and useful: this tree is very like *Prosopis spicigera* when in leaf.

Aravi nim (*Sclerostylis atalantioides*). This tree I found in the Circars only. Wood yellow, and very hard, might be used as a substitute for box; it is always small.

Balusu (*Canthium parviflorum*). A dark coloured, hard, and pretty wood—good for turning.

Barranki (*Trophis aspera*). On the mountains it grows to a large size; wood only used for fuel.

Buruga (*Salmalia malabarica*). A soft useless wood.

Barë kälä goru (*Spathodea Roxburghii*). Wood is said to be useless. Roxburgh, however, says that it is used for various purposes. Buffaloes are very fond of the leaves.

Boja, Godavari Forests; Konda Tangedu [Circars], (*Inga xylocarpa*). A valuable timber; grows very large on the mountains.

Bilugu (*Chloroxylon Swietenia*). The satin-wood.

Bhutànkhusam (*Croton oblongifolium*, R.). Wood reddish; said to crack soon.

Botta karami (*Nauclea parviflora*). Wood close grained, hard.

Buda darmi (*Careya arborea?*). Wood soft and useless. Slow matches are made from the fibre.

Badama (*Terminalia Catappa*). Wood very strong.

Boma-mari (*Ficus asperrima*). Wood useless.

Botku, *Cordia* (*new species*).* A very beautiful wood. It would answer as a substitute for maple, for picture-frames, &c. This tree is abundant in the Godavari forests near Mahadeopur; but does not extend to the Circars. It is found near Warungul. It is also indigenous to the Jubbulpur forests, where it is called "Deyngan." It is, I feel certain, the tree described by Mr Griffiths as *Hemigymnia Macleodii*. He described it from dried specimens, and thought that the leaves were opposite (instead of alternate); otherwise his description and native name agree.

Bandaru (see *paspu karami*). *Nauclea cordifolia*.

* Specimens were forwarded to Dr Hooker, and named by him *Cordia Macleodii*.

Chinta (*Tamarindus indica*). The tamarind tree, a beautifully grained wood.

Chilla (*Strychnos potatorum*). A very hard and close grained wood.

Chitta matta (*Gardenia gummifera*). A small tree. The wood is hard. The natives eat the fruit.

Chandan (*Pterocarpus santalinus*). A hard red wood (Red Saunders of commerce), not found on the right bank of the Godavari.*

Chilaka duduga (*Guatteria cerasoides*). Appears to be a tolerably hard wood, and does not seem to warp. The natives, however, do not use it, and say that it is soft.

Chinangi (*Lagerströmia parviflora*). Wood said to be good.

Chinna morali (*Buchanania latifolia*). Wood considered useless. The fruit is prized for its oily kernel.

Chinna nare (*Eugenia salicifolia*). Wood not used except for fuel.

Chinna gumudu, Chinna gumar (*Gmelina asiatica*). A small tree. Wood only used for fuel.

Chinna kâlinga (*Dillenia pentagyna*). A very strong, hard wood, abundant on the Indrawatti and in jungles on the left bank of Godavari; not known on the right bank.

Chillanki (*Inga umbellata*). Found only in the Circars. I did not examine this wood.

Chinna botku (*Cordia angustifolia*). Wood used for posts and in house-building. This tree is common about villages in the Circars, but I never saw it in the jungles.

Chinna navuli (*Niebuhria linearis*). Wood useless; only found in the Circars.

Dampara, Godavari forests; Gumpini [Circars]. (*Odina Wodier*). Wood said to be soft and useless by the natives; that of old trees is tolerably strong.

Duria maddi, also Kora maddi and Koraman (*Briedelia spinosa*). Wood appears to be very strong and good. Cattle eat the leaves voraciously.

Dundillam (*Calosanthes indica*). Wood soft and useless.

Dulchirram (*Acacia Kalkora*). An enormous tree. Wood hard and reddish.

* Red Saunders or Ruby-wood is much shipped from Madras in short billets or root pieces, very heavy.

Dudippa, Godavari forests; Chetippa, Circars (*Hymenodyction*). A large tree. Wood not used in the Godavari forests.

(*H. excelsum?*). The stipules are gland tipped, not serrate. If it be *H. thyrsiflorum* (Roxb.), it is probably not distinct from *H. excelsum.* In the Circars, all native gun stocks are made from the timber of this tree. The bark, which is intensely bitter when fresh, is used near Bhadrachellum as a febrifuge.

Devadaru (*Sethia indica*). Wood reddish; hard. It is little more than a shrub.

Gadda nelli (*Celtis orientalis*). A worthless wood. Indian nettle tree.

Gugal (*Shorea robusta*). Abundant on the banks of the Indrawatti; a valuable timber. This tree yields the dammer. See *Vatica.*

Gara (*Balanites œgyptiaca*). Wood only used for fuel.

Guaku (*Randia uliginosa*). Wood said by the natives to be useless.

Garugu (*Garuga pinnata*). Wood soft and useless.

Gumar tek (*Gmelina arborea*). The large trees yield a very hard durable wood. The yoke for bullocks is made from it.

Goti (*Zizyphus xylopyrus*). Wood said to be soft, except from the large trees.

Ippi (*Bassia latifolia*). A strong wood, but never felled by the natives. The flowers yield a toddy, and an oil is extracted from the seeds.

Iriki (Godavari) }
Peda-botku (Circars) } (*Cordia Myxa*). Wood never used by the natives in the Godavari forests. In the Circars, ploughs are made from it.

Juvi (*Ficus tsiela*). Wood useless and soft.

Jana palaseru (*Antidesma paniculata*). Wood never used; it seems tolerably hard.

Jitegi [Godavari Forests], }
Irugudu chettu [Circars], } (*Dalbergia latifolia*). A valuable mottled black timber.

Jidi mamidi (*Anacardium occidentale*). Only about villages and rare.

Jiri (*Semicarpus Anacardium*). A soft useless wood.

Jana (*Grewia Rothii?*). Wood very hard, and much used in the Circars. The name is applied to several sp. of *Grewia.*

Jammi (*Prosopis spicigera*). The natives say that this wood is very inferior. This is very different from Dr Wight's account. May his specimens not have belonged to *Acacia ferruginea ?*

Kanregu (*Flacourtia sapida*). A hard close-grained wood which does not warp; worthy of attention.

Káringá (Godavari forests), Tella manga, (Circars), (*Gardenia lucida*). Wood not used on the Godavari, but it is in the Cir cars. It seems to be very hard, close-grained, and adapted for turning.

Kori (Godavari forests) [Korivipal, Circars] (*Ixora parviflora*). A hard wood.

Karpà (*Barringtonia acutangula*). Wood useless.

Kursia—Kursi (*Cluytia collina*). Wood very hard, reddish.

Kàlà goru (Godavari forests); also Chinna kala goru Mokká Yàpà (Circars). (*Bignonia sp.*, *Sterospermum sp.*) A useful wood, abundant in the Mahadeopur forests, rare in the Circars. This appears to be new. Leaflets 4 or 5 pair, with an odd one, perfectly glabrous, entire or serrulate; ramifications of the panicle not decussate; glabrous large ensiform bracts at the ramifications; flowers inodorous; stigma long, slender.

Kàlà goru (*Bignonia chelonoides*). A good fancy wood, abundant on the right bank of Godavari. I did not meet with this or *B. suaveolens* in the Circars.

Kàlà goru (*Bignonia suaveolens*). Wood very similar to *B. chelonoides*, but of a redder hue.

Kondà bodagâ (   ). Wood softish; a large tree with lanceolate leaves, not observed in flower. The bark of this tree is very glutinous when peeled off; it is bound on wounds and said to be very healing.

Kumkumà (*Rottlera tinctoria*). Wood said to be useless.

Karchià (*Nyctanthes arbor tristis*). A hard useful wood, does not attain much size.

Kala mesara (*Casearia tomentosa*). Wood said to be of no value; it soon splits.

Karakà (*Terminalia Chebula*). A very hard valuable timber.

Kaniga (*Pongamia glabra*). Wood said to be strong; it does not appear to be used.

Kondà gogu (*Cochlospermum Gossypium*). Wood useless.

Komi (*Stylocoryne Webera*). Wood prettily marked and hard, much esteemed by the natives; however, it is very small.

Kankadu (*Sapindus emarginatus*). A yellowish prettily-grained wood; it is tolerably hard.

Konda mámidi [Circars only] (*Protium Roxburghiana*). Wood not used. The leaves and every part of the tree possess a strong smell like mangoes.

Kola mukki [Circars and lower Godavari jungles (*Wrightia tomentosa*). Wood not used; it appears close-grained. The juice is a permanent yellow dye. Bark given internally for scorpion bites.

Loluga (*Pterospermum Heyneanum*). Wood pinkish and hard; it is generally hollow in the centre.

Manchi jamudu (*Euphorbia tirucalli*). Grows to a large tree. Wood seems hard, but is not used.

Mamidi (*Mangifera indica*). The mango tree.

Mushtee or Musidi (*Strychnos Nux-vomica*). Wood very hard and strong; white ants will not touch it.

Mulaka (*Hyperanthera Moringa*). Horse-radish tree; only about villages; wood useless.

Maredu (*Ægle Marmelos*). Wood very strong. The native dhol is made often from this wood.

Mare (*Caryota urens*). Abundant on the banks of the Indrawatti. It yields a wine, and also a meal-like sago.

Makkam (*Schrebera Swietenioides*). A very hard, valuable wood; it never warps.

Muni Motku (*Erythrina suberosa*). Wood soft and useless.

Motku or Modagu (*Butea frondosa*). Wood said to be useless; it yields a bright red gum, known as Butea Kino, and sold in the bazaars.

Morilli [see pedda and chinna morali].

Mandai (*Randia dumetorum*). Only used for fuel.

Marri (*Ficus indica*). The drops of this tree yield a heavy, hard timber, used for tent poles, &c.

Muchi tanki, Godavari forests, Warungul (*Diospyros, sp.*). *Female* flowers with 4 anthers; the filaments inserted on a receptacle below the germ, berries 8-celled. *Male* flowers, stamens

16–18; filaments 2–3 cleft, each division with its anther. A very hard light-coloured wood.

Neral (*Syzygium jambolanum*). Wood said to be strong.

Nar yepa, Godavari (*Hardwickia binata*). Wood red, very hard and heavy, often hollow in the centre.

Nella maddi (*Terminalia tomentosa*, also *T. coriacea*). Valuable well known timbers.

Nara botku (*Eriochlœna Hookeriana*). A strong hard wood—(something like the Botku, a new species of Cordia.)

Navuru also Nagul (*Premna tomentosa*). A pretty looking wood—worthy of attention as a fancy wood.

Nella sandra (*Acacia sundra*). A very hard wood—on the Godavari, the musal is always made from this wood.

Navilli [Godavari]
Navili [Circars] } (*Ulmus integrifolia*). The natives say that the timber is useless—it appears, however, to be hard.

Nella kaka mushti [Circars only.] (*Diospyros sylvatica*). Wood whitish, and very hard.

Nilla manga [Circars only] (*Randia sp.*) Wood very hard and close grained—suitable for turning—(a good sized tree, armed).

Nella balasu [Circars] (*Canthium didymum.*) Wood said to be hard. I did not examine it.

Nella regu [Godavari forests]
Narlingi [Circars] } (*Acacia amara*). Centre wood mottled, and of a dark colour, like old seasoned oak.

Nakira (*Ximenia americana*). Wood only used for fuel.

Nevali eragu (*Vitex arborea*). Wood hard, of a yellowish brown colour.

Nella maddi (*Maba buxifolia*). Very small—but a hard pretty wood.

Pachi, also Paunchi (*Anogeissus acuminatus*). A very strong hard timber. *Conocarpus acuminatus*, W. & A.

Pedda sopara [Godavari forests]
Yerra pachiaru [Circars] } (*Dalbergia frondosa*). A strong useful timber.

Porilla sopara [Godavari]
Tella patsaru [Circars] } (*Dalbergia paniculata*). Wood useless—it is arranged in rings, with softer substance between the layers.*

* The specimens here reported on had probably been attacked by insects.

Pal dautam [Godavari] } (*Ehretia lævis*). A hard valuable
Pedda pul mera [Circars] } wood, though not of great size.

Pedda Karinga (*Gardenia latifolia*). Wood close grained; promises well for turning.

Papirri also Papatta (*Pavetta tomentosa*). Wood hard, but very small.

Pedda man (*Ailanthus excelsa*). Wood soft, never used by the natives.

Paspu Karami [also Bundaru] (*Nauclea cordifolia*). A yellowish valuable wood; that of the very large tree is superior—from smaller trees it seems rather soft.

Pul-i-shinta (*Bauhinia malabarica*. Said to be a good hard wood.

Pala, also pedda pala (*Mimusops hexandra*). Wood very hard.

Pusku (*Schleichera trijuga*). Most abundant in Godavari forests. Wood hard, heavy, and strong. The large musal for pressing the Sesamum Oil is always made of it—also ploughs.

Pedda kalinga (*Dillenia speciosa*). A very hard wood. In jungles N. of Godavari.

Pedda dulchirram [Godavari], Dirasana [Circars], (*Acacia speciosa*). A valuable timber.

Pedda chitta duduga (*Uvaria tomentosa*). A very strong yellow wood, much similar but superior to *Nauclea cordifolia*. Cowars are made from it—also used in house building—it does not warp.

Pedda ari (*Bauhinia purpurea*). Wood softish.

Pedda morali (*Buchanania angustifolia*.) Wood not used, seems rather hard.

Pala, also chinna pala (*Holarrhena antidysenterica*). Wood worthless.

Pedda kal mesura (*Casearia ovata*, R.)? Wood light yellow, hard, does not warp—worthy of attention. A large tree—leaves ovate, oblong, glabrous, serrulate flowers; 8-androus; capsule

I have since seen good specimens of this wood, which seems worthy of attention. Col. Maitland wished to try it in the Gun-carriage Manufactory, but I could not procure logs of sufficient size in the Anamalai Forests. —R. H. B.

3-valved with 3 ridges on the outside of fruit. Fruit used to poison fish.

Pasgar gince (same as Nella sandra; which see).

Pautengi (*Briedelia montana*). Wood hard, dark coloured—small tree.

Patcha botku [Circars only] (*Cordia polygama*). Strong close-grained wood (small and crooked).

Punki (*Gyrocarpus Jacquini*). Wood soft and light, much used for making cowrie boxes and toys, takes paint and varnish well. Tella Punki (*Givotia rottleriformis*) is used for the same purposes.

Rella (*Cathartocarpus Fistula*). Wood said to be strong.

Reygutti (*Capparis grandis*). Wood very hard and good.

Renga (*Zizyphus Jujuba*). Wood strong, and much used by the natives.

Ravi (*Ficus religiosa*). Wood useless.

Sitapul (*Anona squamosa*). The custard apple. Covers miles of country in the Dekkan.

Sunari (*Ochna squarrosa*). Wood reddish and pretty, but it warps and splits. The juice of the tree applied to sores.

Siriman (*Anogeissus latifolius*). Wood said to be one of the hardest in the forests. It grows to an enormous size. Axles of carts are generally made of this, the *Conocarpus latifolius*, W. & A.

Somi (*Soymida febrifuga*). Wood very hard and valuable—never rots under ground—very much used in building—of a reddish colour.

Sopara (see pedda and porilla sopara).

Tek (*Tectona grandis*). The teak tree.

Tella maddi (*Terminalia glabra*). A well known timber.

Torelaga (*Limonia acidissima*). Wood very hard—worthy of attention.

Telega (Godavari forests and Dekkan (*Gardenia sp*). Bark whitish mealy swollen. Leaves with mealy down underneath. Fruit globose, size of a cricket ball, not crowned with any portion of the calyx. Wood very hard, and seems good for turning.

Thandi (*Terminalia Belerica*). Wood useless.

Tharra (*Grewia tiliæfolia*). Grows very large on the mountains—a valuable timber—much used for handles of axes, pellet bows, cowars, walking sticks.

Tunki [Godavari], teak [Circars], (*Diospyros melanoxylon*). The centre wood black, and very heavy. The Godavari ebony.

Tella motku (*Dalbergia Ujenensis*). Wood valuable; it is rather rare.

Tabasu (*Sterculia urens*). Wood soft and useless.

Tella sopara [Godavari forests only] (*Acacia elata*). Wood strong, and much valued.

Telsu [Godavari], Shinduga [Circars], (*Acacia odoratissima*). A valuable well known timber.

Togari mogali [Godavari], Mogali [Circars], (*Morinda exserta*). Wood hard and useful, does not warp.

Tella sundra (*Acacia sundra*). Wood very good and strong—abundant in the Ankisáh jungles.

Togur Motku, or Moduga (*Butea superba*). Wood fibrous and useless.

Tella tuma (*Acacia leucophlœa*). Wood hard; it is used for various purposes by the natives.

Tuma (*Acacia arabica*). Wood valuable and well known.

Tella manga (*Gardenia lucida.*) A close-grained wood. I think it well adapted for the lathe.

Tella pal (*Wrightia tinctoria*). A beautiful wood, hard, and like ivory—most valuable for turning.

Tella kaka mushti, [Circars only] (*Sponia ?*). Probably *Celtis Wightii*, Wight's Icones, t. 1971. One of the hardest woods I have ever met with—light-coloured, well worthy of attention.

Tella punki [Circar hills only] (*Givotia rottleriformis*). A very light soft wood. See remarks under Punki.

Usirika (*Emblica officinalis*). A hard valuable wood.

Ulinda also Yelinda (*Diospyros chloroxylon*). Armed leaves lanceolate oblong downy. *Male*, 16 anthers, one above the other, on generally 16 filaments. *Female*, 9 anthers (sterile?), stigmas 4-5, germ 8-10 celled. Berries 3-seeded. A very hard useful wood, grows to a large tree on Circar mountains; it is generally a shrub about the Godavari forests.

Usiki manu [Godavari], Uri-widdi [Circars], (*Cratæva Rox-*

burghii). Wood very hard. The native dhol is often made of this wood.

Udugu (*Alangium decapetalum*). An ornamental, beautiful wood—attains a fair size in the forests.

Wodi (*Spathodea Rheedii*, *Bignonia spathacea*, Roxb.) Wood strong, whitish.

Wanza [Godavari], same as Gadda nelli [of Circars]; which see.

Yegisa (*Pterocarpus marsupium*). A well known timber. The native dhol is often made of this.

Yepa also Yapa (*Azadirachta indica*). A valuable timber.

Native names unknown: *Sterculia colorata*. Godavari forests. Wood useless.—*Bignonia xylocarpa*. Wood very hard, tree rare in Godavari forests.—*Putranjiva Roxburghii*. A close-grained, very hard valuable wood. The tree is anything but common.—*Trewia nudiflora*. Wood said to be only used for fuel.

NOTE.—This list was drawn up by Lieut. Beddome, Asst. Conservator of Forests, principally in the upper valley of the Godavari, and admits of being enlarged. The names should be compared with Mr Elliot's *Flora Andhrica* already referred to.—H. C.

DOCKYARD TIMBER.*

The growing importance of Indian forests to the British Government gives practical value to all efforts made to ascertain the quantity and quality of the timber which they yield. In the preceding list of woods, p. 225, reference is made to Angili (*Artocarpus hirsuta*), and also an allusion to the circumstance that the supply of this wood for ship-building purposes to H. M. Dockyards has formed a subject of correspondence. On 19th April 1860, the following Memorandum was furnished to Government by me :—

"1. When travelling on the western coast, I took every means of ascertaining the quantity of angili timber procurable. With a view to obtain the fullest information, I addressed the Resident of Travancore, the Collector of Malabar, and the Assist. Conservator of Forests in N. Canara. Their replies having now come to hand, I beg to submit a summary of them. The communication of Mr Maltby and its enclosures I annex entire, being full of interest.

"2. *Tree—Localities where procurable.*—The tree *Artocarpus hirsuta* of botanists is of great size. It is confined to the W. coast, and is particularly abundant at an elevation of 3000 ft. in Malabar, Cochin, and Travancore, where it is much used for canoes, ferry-boats, and house-building. In habit, it resembles the jak tree, to which it is allied. The Dutch governor of Cochin, *Henricus von Rheede*, figured the tree in his *Hortus Malabaricus* (1686), and praised† the timber. In Canara, the tree

* Under SHIPBUILDING, STRENGTH OF MATERIALS, and TIMBER, much information will be found—(*Ency. Brit.*, 1861.)

† Vol. iii., t. 32.

is now scarce, and of insufficient size. This year, great difficulty was experienced along the coast in obtaining a sufficient number of logs for the preparation of 103 Government ferry-boats. In Malabar and Wainâd, the tree (there called *ayni*) is abundant, and is largely felled by European settlers when clearing land for coffee cultivation. There is no trade, however, to enable me to judge of the quantity procurable; and the localities are almost inaccessible.

"3. *Price.*—The market price at Quilon was Rs.3 to 4, but now it is Rs.6 to 8 per candy. The present price at Allepi is Rs.8 to 10 per candy; of large size, Rs.12. The quantity annually available of the stated size at Allepi and Cochin will seldom exceed 230 loads.

"4. *Quality and Quantity.*—Angili stands next to teak in the estimation of ship-builders; and the demand for this wood is increasing. The present annual supply in the territories of Cochin and Travancore averages from 6000 to 7000 candies, but not more than one-tenth part would square to the required dimensions. This appears to arise chiefly from the difficulties of transport, as the trees are of great size. No difficulty is anticipated in providing annually 3000 tons along the Travancore coast. Mr Crawford suggests a contract at Rs.14 per candy; while Mr Kohlhoff proposes an agent to give advances to contractors, and to arrange for shipment.

"5. It will be observed that the estimates vary considerably. However, there is one opinion as to the abundance of the tree in the S. Provinces; and the opening up of two new roads which have been for some time under the consideration of Government—I refer to the Karkúr Ghat in Malabar, and the proposed road from the Anamalai Hills to the Cochin backwater*—would facilitate the delivery of the wood. These great lines (the latter especially), would open up dense forests, and throw much angili timber into the market. On the whole, I think that, if considered desirable, 3000 loads of the dimensions stated might be exported annually, at a cost not exceeding Rs.14 per candy,†

* The importance of this road is recognised by Sir C. Wood, in a despatch, dated 23d March 1861, and its construction urged.

† Equal to 13¼ cub. feet.

—probably less on an average; but as all kinds of labour are rising, I take Mr Crawford's valuation. The greater portion would be obtained in Cochin and Travancore, and a smaller quantity in Malabar.

"6. If the dockyard authorities require planking as well as beams, and specify the size, in all probability it would facilitate the supply; as defective wood would be left behind, and the planks would be more portable, the carriage of large timber being almost impracticable in many parts of the country.

"7. If a steady trade in angili was established, it might be advisable to form plantations on the banks of navigable rivers.

"8. It is worthy of remark, that the wood referred to by Dr Gibson,* Conservator of Forests, Bombay, is not the same as that to which I allude. The ayni (*Terminalia coriacea*) is common in N. Canara, and a useful wood it is, but not to be compared to the angili of Travancore for ship-building purposes."

The Resident of Travancore, in forwarding to me the opinions of Messrs Kohlhoff and others on this subject, says:—"You will observe that they vary a good deal in the estimates. As far as I can learn, this timber is very abundant in these provinces; but, as is so commonly the case, all the forests which are most accessible have been denuded by the common timber-dealers of all trees of a large size. But there are forests both in Cochin and Travancore which the timber-dealers cannot work with profit, but which, if worked on a proper system, by opening out roads, would yield a large supply. Mr Kohlhoff describes one large tract of this kind in the Cochin territory, and there are many others. I believe that if the British Government should be able to ensure a market for timber, of such size as is described in your letter, at the rate of Rs.12 or 14 per candy, to the extent of say 1000 loads per annum for the next five years, the jungles might be worked in a systematic manner, to the great advantage of these territories."

Mr H. Crawford, Commercial-Agent, Allepi, writing to the Resident, says:—"I have the honour to acknowledge your letter, with enclosure from Dr C. The quantity of angili yearly exported

* 1st Dec. 1859.

from this is not under 4000 candies, which is only a moiety of what is cut down in these forests yearly; the principal portion goes to Cochin. The price is now Rs. 8 to 10 per candy. The wood is well suited for the floors and bottom planking of ships, as high as the bends; but the fastenings, where not trenailed, must be of copper, as, unlike teak, it corrodes iron rapidly. There will be no difficulty in providing 3000 tons along the coast yearly. The price in planks, from 25 to 30 feet long by 12 to 14 inches broad, and 2½ to 3 inches thick, is from Rs. 120 to 170 per corge. I beg also to state, that if H. M. Govt. would enter into a contract with the sirkar for the regular purchase of say 3000 tons of angili yearly, it might be worth while our undertaking the supply at, Rs. 14 per candy unsquared.

Mr J. S. A. Kohlhoff, Conservator of Cochin Forests, writes :— "I have the honour to acknowledge the receipt of your letter, enclosing a letter from Dr Cleghorn, calling for information regarding the probable quantity of angili wood obtainable annually in the Cochin forests, and beg to state in reply, that, owing to the high rate that angili wood sells at in the market, and it being considered more durable than teak for building boats, &c., such great quantities of it have been annually taken away by timber-merchants, that the greater portion of these forests are almost exhausted of timber of this description. There is, however, a tract of magnificent virgin forest, at an elevation of nearly 3000 feet, about 40 miles S.E. of Trichur, extending to the S. and W. of the chain of hills marked *Nocoon bund* on the Survey Map, No. 62, which have never been penetrated by timber-merchants, where I have observed the angili growing in abundance, many trees of the largest dimensions, and have been informed by the kaders (or hill men), that the tree is very numerous in all the sholas (or dense jungles) on those hills. I have reason to believe, therefore, that this tract of forest is fully capable of yielding at least 2000 candies of angili timber annually, of superior quality and dimensions; as also a good supply of poon spars for ships' masts. As the rivers that traverse these forests are intersected by numerous cataracts, and other natural obstacles to the floating down of rafts; and as it will not only be very expensive, but also difficult, to procure a sufficient number of elephants to work this forest on a large scale, the best mode for ensuring the regular transmission of a fixed quantity of timber to the coast annually would undoubtedly be to open a good cart road to it from these forests, which would not only be advantageous for the transmission of teak, blackwood, poon spars, and angili for the sirkar; but, as many timber-merchants would also avail themselves of it for the removal of common jungle-wood, the fee for these, and the toll they may be called upon to pay for the use of the road, would in a very short time pay the cost of its construction. And should this road be carried northwards to the British frontier, it would open out a traffic between Cochin and Coimbatore direct, which would add another item of revenue to the sirkar in the duties which might be levied on articles exported from and imported into the country."

Mr J. Munro, Cottayam, writes:—"With reference to the annual supply of angili from the forests of Travancore and Cochin, of the size mentioned by Dr C., I beg to state, that though the annual supply of this wood averages from 6000 to 7000 candies, yet I doubt whether, on selection, a tenth of this quantity would be found of sufficient dimensions to yield the minimum size required, viz. 35 feet by 16 inches square. Angili logs of this size, as first class timbers, find a ready sale in the Allepi and Cochin markets, at Rs. 12 per candy; but the quantity annually available will seldom exceed 230 loads. Logs of smaller size vary in price from Rs. 5 to 12 per candy in the above markets."

Mr C. F. Kohlhoff, Conservator of Forests, Travancore, writes:— "I have the honour to acknowledge the receipt of your letter, and in reply beg to state, that the angili wood trade in Travancore is an open trade, wherein the sirkar have no dealings whatsoever. Merchants entering on this trade have to obtain a permit for felling trees in the forest, and pay the sirkar a fee, or rather a nominal price of 12 chuckrams (As. 6 pice 8) per candy, and a year's time is allowed for taking away the wood paid for; the logs they bring down vary in dimensions from 14 in. to 2½ ft. in diameter, and from 20 to 35 ft. in length, with merely the sapwood clipped off. Larger timbers are obtainable; but as the expenses and labour attending their transit are great, they are converted into canoes, and floated down the rivers. The angili stands in estimation next to the teak, and the demand for this wood for ship-building purposes has of late years increased. The market price of the wood a few years ago was only from Rs.3 to 4 per candy. It has since risen from R.6 to 8; and if I may venture an opinion, will still further rise. If, however, the timber required by H. M. Govt. is expected to be free of the heart of the tree, comparatively little wood will be secured, since in that case the wood will have to be taken from between the heart and the sapwood; and to admit of such selection, the trees must be upwards of 44 in. in diameter. Only a small number of such sized trees will be found, and the attendant expenses and labour will be proportionately increased. But if no objection to the core exist, and the Government are willing to take such timber as is generally considered merchantable in the markets of this country, doubtless, on an average, about 2000 logs might be procured annually of the specified dimensions, by entering into contracts with merchants, and making the necessary advances; and to effect this the Government should appoint an agent. But as it is presumed that all the wood for H. M. navy will not be required in thickness of 16 in., I beg to observe, that timber-merchants are in the habit of bringing down planks from 25 to 35 ft. long, 15 to 20 in. wide, and 2½ in. thick; and they might be got to supply planks of greater thickness, as may be agreed upon."

The Collector of Malabar writes :—" The price of ayni or angili at present is about Rs.7 per candy; but what quantity of the timber could be supplied at this rate must, I conceive, be learnt from experience, once a demand in the export trade has been created."

POON SPARS.

In the last Report of Dr Gibson, Conservator of Forests, Bombay, attention was directed to the subject of Poon Spars, and and their value for naval purposes. These are supplied entirely from Canara and Coorg, but with no system for regulating the supply. The matter engaged the attention of the Bombay Government, who applied to the Commissioner of Mysore for information as to Poon Spars, and Teak Timber growing in the Coorg forests. These communications were submitted for my opinion, the substance of which is contained in the following paragraph.

The poon trees ought to be strictly conserved as a royalty, as was the system under the native Government, and in cases where the extension of coffee cultivation approaches the poon trees, clumps or belts should be spared, particularly on the western slope of the ghats, with sufficient jungle round them to draw up the bole, as the value of the tree depends upon the spar being without knot or flaw. In cases of solitary poons suited for masts, the spar should be dragged to the edge of the coffee clearing, beyond the reach of conflagration, as was recommended in my First Report, par. 34, for Teak and Blackwood (p. 16).

The remarks of Capt. Martin as to the working of the Coorg forests, under the small establishment recently formed, are judicious. It seems inexpedient that Government should undertake, under ordinary circumstances, the carriage of poon spars and teak logs. This work can be effected at a lower rate by contract; as the country improves in prosperity, the number of contractors will increase; and in the present instance a large establishment must be formed specially for the purpose, which would entail great expense for superintendence. Contractors for the supply of poon spars and telegraph posts usually bring a letter to the superintendent; and every assistance should be afforded in marking and pointing out the timber best suited for their purposes, in the localities most accessible to the trunk road or the river.

Abstract of Experiments on the Strength of Woods tried at Guntur in 1840, *and at Singapore in* 1843.
Furnished by Captain S. Best.

No.	Names.	Length.	Breadth.	Depth.	Cubic inches.	Weight.	Specific gravity.	Length between supports.	Weight sustained before breaking.	Corresponding deflection in the middle.	Deflection corresponding to	Weight sustained.	Remarks.
		Inches.	Inches.	Inches.		Oz.		Inches.	Lbs. oz.	Inches.	Inches.	Lbs. oz.	
1.	*Mimosa arabica*, Babul (*Hind.*), Tummakurra (*Tel.*),	62·625	1·375	2	172	96	964	59·156	539·2	1·8125	0·5 1·094	155 12 346 0	The weights were removed, and the wood became again perfectly straight.
2.	*Borassus flabelliformis*, Palmyra, Tār (*Hind.*),	62·625	1·375	2	172	96	964	59·156	255·14	1·1875	0·5 1·0	104 0 217 4	This specimen was cut partly across the fibres.
3.	Do. Do.	62·625	1·375	2	172	96	964	59·156	474·1	1·71875	0·5 1·0 1·5625	117 2 230 2 423 4	Cut parallel to the fibres, but ⅜ths were of the pithy internal wood.
4.	*Bambusa arundinacea*, common hollow bamboo, Bāns (*Hind.*), Mungil (*Tam.*),	62·625	D. 1·625 to 1·875	Δ 1	136·5	49	of the solid part 620	59·156	423·4	3·375	0·531 1·0625 1·5 2·0625	88 8 168 10 255 14 320 4	D. exterior diameter. Δ inner diameter.

5.	Dābu Dāgu (*Mal.*)	73	2·	1·469	214·0	130	1050	66	...	...	0·6	141	8	The weights were removed, and the wood became again perfectly straight.
6.	Do. do. do.	73	1·469	2·	214·0	130	1050	66	953·8	3·40	1·2	497	0	
											0·51	240	8	
7.	Murubbu / Marbow (*Mal.*),	73	1·42	2·	207·5	114	949	66	728·8	3·02	0·78	228	8	
											1·52	478	8	
8.	Krānji (*Mal.*),	73	1·45	1·8	190·5	152	1379	66	1103·8	3·95	1·8	978	8	
											1·28	803	8	
											0·6	403	8	
9.	Dāmalāut (*Mal.*),	73	1·3	1·9	180·33	124	1188	66	753·8	3·2	0·8	228	8	
											1·7	478	8	
10.	Sirāya / Poon (*Mal.*),	73	1·35	1·95	192·0	84	756	66	503·0	2·67	0·4	103	0	
											1·2	303	0	
11.	Do. (two pieces, one on the other),	73	1·23	1· / 1·	179·5	78	756	66	278·8	6·10	2·48	153	8	
											3·40	208	8	
12.	Do. (eight pieces, one on the other),	73	1·5	0·277 / 0·277 / 0·277 / 0·277 / 0·277 / 0·277 / 0·277 / 0·277	243·0	80	568	66	...	...	3·12	16	13	
											5·58	33	8	
											8·16	50	3	
											10·64	64	1½	
											12·02	70	10	
13.	Do. one piece,	73	1·45	1·95	206	85·33	709	66	547·0	3·33	1·0	155	0	
											1·5 / 1·75	322	0	The deflection, originally 1·5, increased in 24 hours to 1·75.
											1·25	220	0	This was borne 4 days without further deflection.
											2·0	372	0	

The four first experiments were tried by J. Goldingham, Esq., and myself. Having no other convenient weights, and the Public Treasury being close to the spot where we were trying them, we made use of bags containing each Rs. 500, and weighing with their contents each 12 lbs. 4 oz. The pieces of wood were laid on the supports *not fixed.* The deflections were measured in the middle after each bag was added, but it would not serve any useful purpose to show them all in detail. The remaining experiments were tried at Singapore by Lieut. C. M. Elliot, of the Engineers, and myself, and with great care. We used as weights on this occasion bricks, of which 9 weighed 25 lbs. The 11th and 12th experiments were tried in order to test the formula $W = \frac{b\,d^2}{l}$.

The general results of these experiments are shown in the subjoined table, in which, for the sake of comparison, are entered (Nos. 14, 15, 16, 17) experiments by Professor Barlow, and (Nos. 18 and 19) by Lieut. Brown, U. S. Engineers, quoted in Mahon's "Elementary Course of Civil Engineering," pp. 47 and 48.

No.	NAMES.	l	b	d	W″	f	$\frac{W'' l^3}{4bd^3 f}$ or E	W	$\frac{3lw}{2bd^2}$ or R
1.	Tumakarra, .	58·15	1·375	2·0	350	1·125	1390312	539	8548
2.	Palmyra, No. 1,	58·15	1·375	2·0	170	·875	868236	...	...
3.	Do. No. 2,	58·15	1·375	2·0	...	...	...	474	7517
4.	Bamboo, . . .	58·15	D = 1·75	Δ = 1·	270	1·625	1030406	423	7706
5.	Dabu Dagu, .	66·0	2·00	1·41	141½	0·6	3023361	...	...
6.	Do. do. .	66·0	1·41	2·00	378	0·78	3087872	953	16728
7.	Marbow, . . .	66·0	1·42	2·00	303	1·0	1917066	728	12688
8.	Kranji, . . .	66·0	1·45	1·80	803½	1·28	5335333	1103	23243
9.	Damalaut, . .	66·0	1·30	1.90	303	1·12	2180683	753	15885
10.	Poon, ...	66·0	1·35	1.95	228	0·87	1881695	503	9700
11.	Do. 2 pieces, .	66·0	1·23	1·00	139	6·10	1331535	139	11187
12.	Do. 8 pieces, .	66·0	1·50	0·277	8¾	12·02	1641136	...	...
13.	Do. 1 piece, .	66·0	1·45	1·95	322	1·75	1230034	547	9821
14.	English Oak, .	84·0	2·0	2·0	200	1·28	1447026	637	10032
15.	Pine, ...	84·0	2·0	2·0	150	0·931	1492099	...	...
16.	Cast Iron (soft gray),	78·0	1·5	3·0	440	·075	17185533	...	...
17.	Forged Iron (English),	36·0	1·0	1·0	560	·025	261274700	...	...
18.	Pine, ...	85·2	2·75	5·55	...	...	...	5189	7829
19.	Cast Iron, . .	36·0	1·0	1·0	...	...	...	800	43200

In the above Table l is the length between the supports, b the breadth, d the depth, W the breaking weight, $R = W\frac{3\,l}{2\,b\,d^2}$, W'' is the weight answering to f the deflection, and $E = W''\frac{L^3}{4\,b\,d^3\,f}$.—$\Delta$ is the interior diameter of the bamboo, and D the exterior. For it, $R = W\frac{3\,l\;D}{2\,D^4 - 2\,\Delta^4}$ and $E = \left(\frac{W''\;l^3\;D}{3.\,6f \times D^5 - \Delta^5}\right)$.

$\frac{E}{5} = E$ and $\frac{R}{6} = S$ in the table of data, page 150, in the edition of Professor Barlow's work, published in 1837.

The following particulars I obtained from an intelligent Chinese carpenter at Singapore, named Ah-See-Ah.

Dābu, Dāgu, or Dāwu, is used for beams in houses, piles, &c. It is a strong durable wood, and grows to a large size.

Marbow is used for furniture, windlasses, handspikes, ship gun-carriages. It is a very fine wood, but does not grow so large as the preceding.

Krānji.—The strength of this wood is very remarkable, being more than double that of oak. The Chinese use it for the stern-posts of their junks and for anchors, and they export it from Singapore. A log 24 feet long and 1½ foot square is worth ten dollars.

Dāmālāut and Tampeenus are used for beams and posts in houses, and for joists. Dāmālāut cracks and shrinks, lasts long, except in water, where worms destroy it. It grows to 90 feet in length by 2½ feet square. Piles 24 feet long and 1 foot square cost at Singapore four dollars each. The Chinese exchange the masts they bring from China for Singapore Dāmālāut. A mast worth one hundred dollars at Singapore will sell for five hundred in China.

Tampeenus is very difficult to saw, but is a good wood, lasting long, not injured by exposure, and not so liable to crack as Dāmālāut.

The Sirāya or poon is the most abundant wood in Singapore. Small spars are called Bintāngo. The best sort of poon is grown on the hills, and called Bātū Sirāya. It is distinguished by white fibres running lengthwise. The Sirāya grows to 100 and

130 feet long, squaring 3 feet at the butt. It is easy to saw and work up, used for all building purposes, but not capable of enduring exposure or moisture for a long period. Planks 20 feet by 1 foot by 4 inches are worth a dollar—16 feet by 11 inches by $1\frac{1}{4}$ inch about a quarter of a dollar each at Singapore. Masts 90 feet long and $2\frac{1}{2}$ feet in diameter may be procured for forty dollars.

DISTRIBUTION OF FOREST TREES.

The subject of geographical botany is now exciting much attention, and very deservedly; for independently of its interest in itself, it is capable of throwing much light on the vexed questions of the nature and origin of species, and on the changes of climate which the earth has experienced in past periods. The Smithsonian Institution has just issued an interesting pamphlet on this subject relating to the Trees of North America, from which we make the following extract,* which refers to the mode of collecting specimens for purposes of *accurate comparison,* strongly insisted upon in the Jury Report, p. 221.

"Collections of the leaves, fruits, bark, and wood of our native trees are particularly desirable, and from as many localities as possible, in order to determine both their range and abundance, and also to decide those knotty points, as to true specific distinctions, which still perplex the most skilful botanists. The specimens from each tree should be kept carefully together, and the name of the locality and collector given in full. Without such collections no information as to the large genera of oaks, hickories, magnolias, and, in fact, most others, can be at all depended on or made use of. A good way of preserving a complete set from each species of tree is to obtain two pieces of the thick bark of the trunk about a foot square, *taking care not to rub off the mosses or lichens,* which are often very characteristic of the tree. Other specimens of bark from the branches, sufficient to show all its changes in appearance, and twigs with leaves, flowers, and fruits, may be pressed between the trunk bark, with sufficient paper of any kind intervening, to absorb all moisture. One change of this paper will usually be sufficient (especially if the

* Canadian Naturalist and Geologist, vol. vi. p. 223.

bark is dry); and fruits, if large and hard, may be so fixed as to hang outside, wrapped in paper. *Particular care is necessary to prevent mixture of specimens.* Blocks of wood from the trunk and branches at various seasons are also desirable for experimenting upon.

"Observations as to the relative abundance of each tree at the various stations may be expressed numerically, thus: very rare, 1; occasionally met with, 2; not uncommon, 3; common, 4; very common, 5; abundant, 6, &c.; using numbers up to 10, and explaining them. Frequently several trees will be found so nearly alike in abundance as to require the same number. Notice should also be made of the nature of the country and soil—whether mountainous, rocky, gravelly, sandy, or swampy,—which will help to determine the limits of the natural regions."

EXTRACT FROM JURY REPORT. CLASS XXVI, 1855.

The following Tabular View of the woods used for furniture in Madras is contributed by Dr Cleghorn:—

Common Furniture.—1. Chittagong-wood; 2. Teak-wood; 3. Tun-wood; 4. Jak-wood.

Carved and Ornamental Furniture.—1. Ebony; 2. Blackwood, or East Indian Rosewood; 3. Satin-wood; 5. Kiabuca wood.

1. Chittagong wood (*Chickrassia tabularis*) is more used at Madras in the making of furniture than any other wood. It is light, cheap, and durable.

2. Teak-wood (*Tectona grandis*) is probably the most durable of all timbers; it is very hard, and very heavy. It is extensively used for bullock trunks, and for house and camp furniture, for which it is well adapted, as it does not split. (The increasing price has diminished its use for ordinary purposes.)

3. Tun-wood (*Cedrela Tuna*) resembles its congeners, chittagong wood and mahogany, and is very much used for chairs and other furniture all over the Peninsula.

4. Jak-wood (*Artocarpus integrifolia*) is an excellent timber, at first yellow, but afterwards brown; when made into tables and well kept, it attains a polish little inferior to mahogany. In England, it is used as well as satin-wood for making backs of hair-brushes, &c.

1. Black Ebony (*Diospyros melanoxylon*), and other species. This well known and much admired wood (*lignum nigrum non variegatum?*) is very hard, heavy, and susceptible of a high polish. It is seldom obtained of great size.

2. E. Indian Blackwood or Rosewood (*Dalbergia latifolia*) is an excellent heavy wood, suited for the best furniture. It can be procured in large quantities, and of immense size, especially in Wainad; the wood contains much oil, which is exhibited in Cl. IV. (by the Gangam Local Committee.) In large pannels it is liable to split.

3. Satin-wood (*Swietenia Chloroxylon*) is hard in its character, and, when polished, it is very beautiful, and has a satiny lustre; it is much used for picture frames, rivalling the birds-eye maple of America. It is occasionally used by cabinetmakers for general furniture, but it is liable to split.

4. Sandal-wood (*Santalum album*) is found in abundance in Mysore and Canara; it is chiefly remarkable for its agreeable fragrance, which is a preservative against insects. It is much used in making work-boxes, walking-sticks, pen-holders, and other small articles of fine ornament, but cannot be procured of a large size.

5. Kiabuca-wood, or Amboyna-wood (*Petrospermum indicum*). A handsome specimen of this ornamental wood is exhibited by Dr Sanderson. It is imported from Singapore. It is beautifully mottled, of different tints, evidently produced by excrescences from the tree. The wood is chiefly used for inlaying, or for making desks, snuff-boxes, puzzles, &c. These are exhibited by the Madras Local Committee.

In accordance with the suggestion thrown out by the Jury (p. 218), rewards were offered at the School of Arts for woods adapted for wood engraving. Specimens were consequently sent to Dr Hunter, and experiments made by him, the results of which are furnished in the following communication which appeared in the *Edinburgh New Phil. Journal, July,* 1860.

The Guava (*Psidium pyriferum*) was found to be close-grained and moderately hard, with a thin bark and pretty uniform texture of both the outer and inner parts of the wood when cut across the grain. It cut easily and cleanly like firm cheese, and gave delicate lines; but being softer than boxwood, it did not stand the pressure of printing, though it yielded very good impressions with a burnisher. The art of printing from woodcuts, for illustrating literature in India, being in its infancy, many of the early impressions were spoilt from too heavy pressure. For four or five years the guava was used, and answered well for bold engraving, and for cutting blocks of large letters; attempts to cut small letters upon it for a Tamil alphabet proved a failure, though the large Tamil and English alphabets succeeded well, and were useful for several purposes, as printing large school and diagram letters, stamping on cloth and clay to get letters or numbers for use in schools. The guava-wood was found to vary much in texture, the large trees yielding a soft, coarse wood, while the small wood from hilly districts was hard and fine in the grain. Samples sent to England, and tried for engraving, were pronounced to be too soft, and inferior to English boxwood.

The Satin-wood (*Chloroxylon Swietenia*) proved to be hard, but uneven in the grain, coarse in the pores, and, like many woods of a large size, harder and denser in the centre than near the bark. Under the graver it was found to splinter. This wood was condemned, as unsuited for wood-engraving, both in Madras and England.

The Palay (*Wrightia tinctoria*). The native name is vague, being applied to a number of woods that have a milky juice. The wood, however, is better known to the public as one from which native toys are frequently turned. It is a pale, nearly white wood, close and uniform in the grain, but too soft to stand printing. It cuts smoothly, but does not bear delicate cross-hatching. It was pronounced unfit for wood-engraving in England, though well suited for turning, carving, and inlaying with darker woods.

Veppalcy (*Wrightia antidysenterica*) was found to be very hard in the centre, but soft in the outer portions, and liable to the attacks of insects. On examining this wood under the microscope it gave promise of being suitable for the purpose, from the closeness of texture and the polish left by the chisel in cutting it across the grain, but the uneven quality, and the softness of the outer parts, showed that it was not fit for engraving. Its chief use is for posts and rice-beaters.

Sandal-wood (*Santalum album*) proved to be the nearest approach to the boxwood in working quality, hardness, and durability under pressure. This is a moderately-sized wood, with thin bark, which is usually a criterion of fine even grain. It cuts smoothly, the chips curl well under the graver, and the oily nature of the wood seems to preserve it from splitting when wet. There are considerable differences in sandal-wood, according to the locality from which it is procured, the small, dark-coloured wood of 5 inches diameter, grown on dry rocky soil, being the best. Many hundred engravings have been executed upon this wood, and it has been found occasionally to equal boxwood, though not quite so hard. It is an elastic wood that hardens on exposure to the air, and stands a good deal of rough usage in the press; some blocks have yielded upwards of 20,000 impressions without being worn out. The large pale sandal-wood is not so good as the small dark kinds. This wood was not tried in England, its price being too dear; but on comparing it with boxwood, which sells in England for one penny the square inch, it was found to be cheaper in India than boxwood in England.

The Ber-fruit tree (*Zizyphus Jujuba*) gave good promise under the microscope, but proved to be a soft, spongy, light wood, that did not stand cross-hatching or pressure. It is used for native sandals.

The wood of the wild orange (*Citrus Aurantium*) bears a strong resemblance in appearance to box in working qualities, and is often as hard, but, like the sandal-wood, the small old trees from the hilly districts yield the best wood for engraving. It has a thin bark, a bright yellow colour, and a uniform and close texture. The cultivated or garden orange has a coarse wood with an uneven texture.

The small tree (common in the gardens of Madras) known as

the China Box (*Murraya exotica*) has also been submitted for examination. On trial it proved to be like the wood of many of the Aurantiaceæ or orange family, hard and close in the grain near the centre, but softer near the bark. The cross section of this tree is very irregular.

The wood of the coffee-tree (*Coffea arabica*) disappointed the expectations that had been formed of it. The first piece of this sent to the School of Arts was very hard, unform and close in the grain, but small. Some pieces of old trees, 6 inches in diameter, were afterwards procured, but they proved to be soft, uneven in grain, and not fit for engraving, though the wood is well adapted for ornamental carving or inlaying. The specimens sent us were badly selected. This wood works beautifully on the turner's lathe, and cuts very sharply under the chisel, gouge, or graver; it is deserving of more attention for ornamental carving and inlaying. It harmonises well in colour with the wood of orange and that of the *Inga dulcis* or Kurukapulli. It approaches in colour and grain to walnut, but is too coarse for engraving, though fit for gunstocks and cabinet work.

The only other woods tried were—(1.) A very close-grained fine and uniform wood (*Dodonœa viscosa*), sent from the Nilgiris under the name of iron-wood, used for turning and for making walking-sticks. It worked well under the graver and on the turning-lathe, but the piece sent was too small to print from; and (2.) A piece of Fustic (*Maclura tinctoria*), grown in the Horticultural Garden at Madras, but this proved to be too soft and coarse for engraving, though a rich-coloured bright yellow wood, suited for inlaying.

About two years ago, it was reported that true boxwood was discovered in the N. W. Provinces, and a log was procured for the School of Arts by Captain Maclagan, of the Rurkee College, and forwarded to Calcutta for despatch to Madras; but had not appeared at the time of this Report.

CHARCOAL MANUFACTURE.

The best-sized wood for this purpose is of the form generally understood as Billets. An ordinary-sized kiln requires about 25,000 billets, cut as nearly as possible of the same length. Procure a pole about 25 feet long and 6 to 8 inches thick, straight, and of uniform thickness. Provide yourself with four forked sticks of the shape of fig. 10. Erect the pole perpendicularly on the spot where the kiln is to be made, and place the four forked sticks round it, arranging pieces of wood from fork to fork, and across, to make a hollow space in the centre of the kiln for containing combustible matter, this forming a space of about 18 square inches, as fig. 11. Provide the person stacking the billets with a yard measure, and let him proceed to place the end of the measure against the pole, sitting at the other end of the measure; the billets are then to be placed in an almost perpendicular position against the cross pieces, and as close together as possible, each cooly stacking right and left to join his neighbour's work on either side. Thus he goes on stacking until he has come to the end of his measure; all having done the same, a perfect circle will be the result. After having filled up all interstices that may have occurred from crooked or large billets, each cooly pulls out his measure to another yard in length, and proceeds as he did before. Having done this the third time, the kiln will measure 18 feet in diameter, and will contain 25,000 billets. The coolies then mount the first layer of billets, and commence stacking from the pole, until

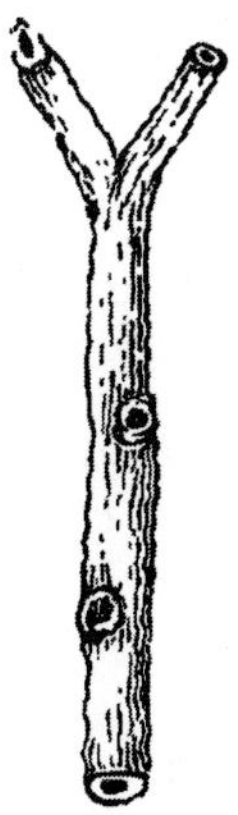

Fig. 10.

they come to the end of the first layer, and so on a second, third

Fig. 11.

and fourth layer, until the kiln is completed (as shown in fig. 12). Cover in the whole kiln with turf, turning the grass side in-

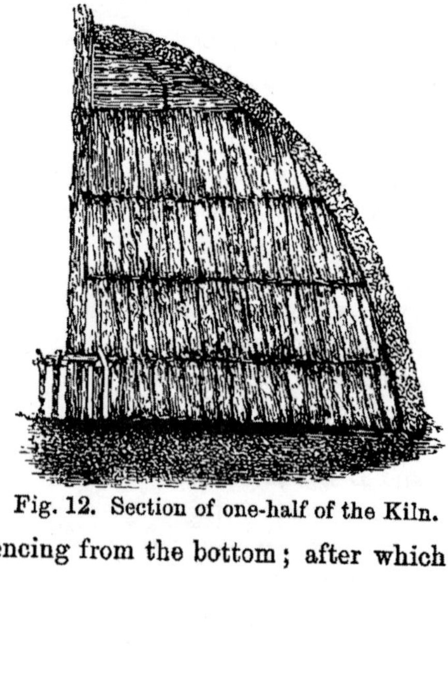

Fig. 12. Section of one-half of the Kiln.

wards, commencing from the bottom; after which throw a small quantity of loose earth over the turf, beating it down with the back of a spade.

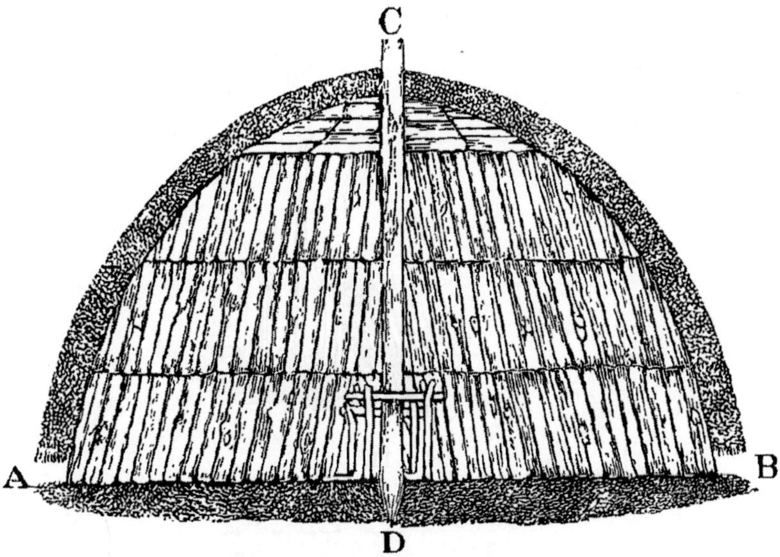

Fig. 13. Vertical Section of Kiln.

After the whole kiln has been covered in, let one or two men ascend the kiln and pull out the pole, leaving an empty space from top to bottom of kiln. From the top, drop in a ladleful of ignited charcoal; and immediately this is done, open out one turf at the bottom of the kiln, say at A. (fig. 13.) This will cause a draft of air in the direction of A D C, and in a few minutes, flames will be seen ascending at C. Let this continue for 5 or 10 minutes; till you have satisfied yourself the billets in the centre of the kiln are on fire, when one man must be sent up with a large turf to close the opening at C, over which he should sprinkle earth to keep in all flame. *From this moment no flame must be allowed to escape from any part of the kiln.* When the opening at C has been closed, one at B should be made. The billets in the direction of D A and D B will then ignite faster than any other, and when smoke is seen escaping between every turf in the direction of A C and B C, the openings at A and B must be closed and fresh ones made, say at E and F (fig. 14); these will be closed in their turn, and others made at G, H, I and J. Shortly after this is done, it will be perceived that smoke is proceeding uniformly from every crevice, when all air-holes at the

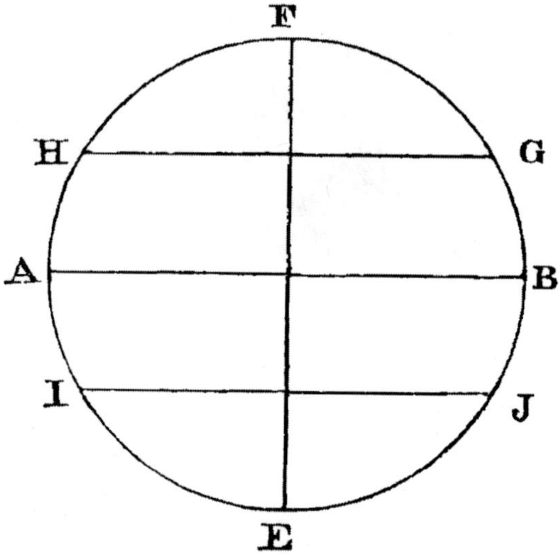

Fig. 14. Horizontal Section of Kiln.

bottom must be closed. The whole kiln will then fall in, and assume something of the following appearance (fig. 15) at the end of 36 hours.

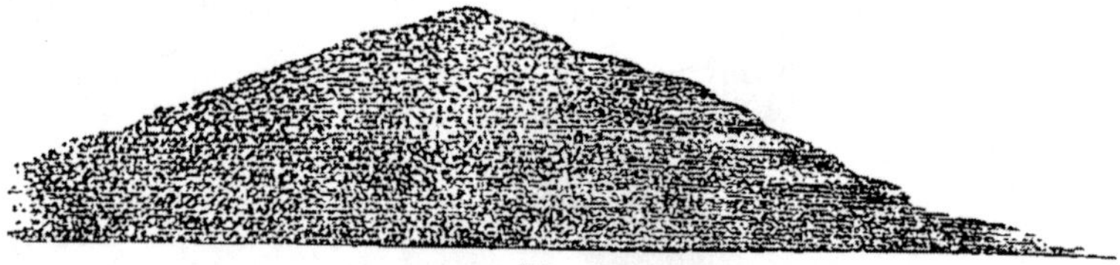

Fig. 15.

Earth enough must then be thrown on with shovels to *extinguish all smoke.* At the end of 36 hours more, the charcoal may be raked out. A few buckets of water should be in readiness, if required, to put out the sparks of fire which may remain.

Great care must be taken to stop every fissure in the casing; and if, from bad management, the heap settles, and the casing falls in at any part, the cavity must be filled up with green wood

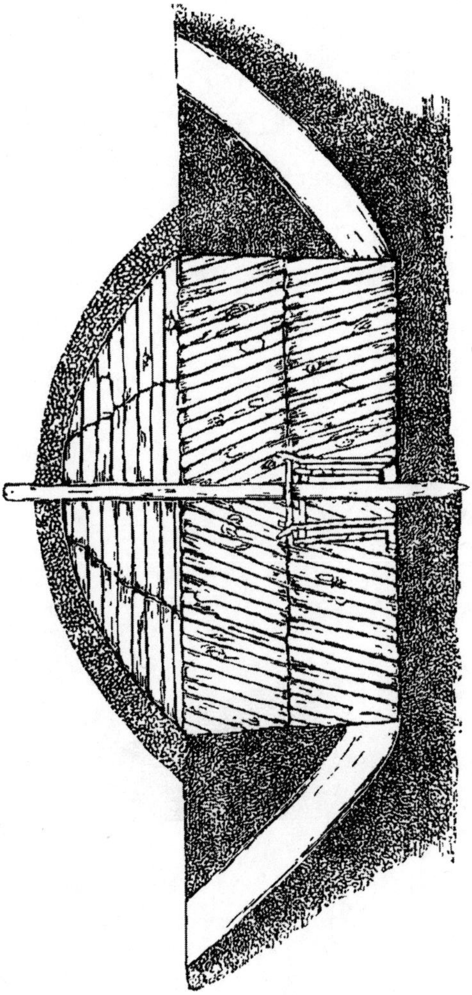

Fig. 16.
Vertical Section of a Charcoal Pit, with Vent-holes and covering of Sods.

kept ready for the purpose, more sods thrown on, and covered with earth. As soon as the dense smoke ceases, and the wood burns with a light transparent smoke, the whole is closed in and watched, lest any fissure should open.

When burning in pits, the system is the same, but vent-holes are formed in the sides; and the covering of sods, &c., being more accessible, is more easily formed and kept.

In pits, the wood is more conveniently packed, as shown above, (fig. 16); and the logs in the middle of the lower course should be dry, and have a few chips and refuse charcoal from former kilns among them; in other respects, the practice is the same as with the piled kiln.

In some places, it may be convenient to form a kiln by digging out the side of a hill, as fig. 17; but in all cases the system is the same. If the process is properly conducted, the bulk is little reduced.

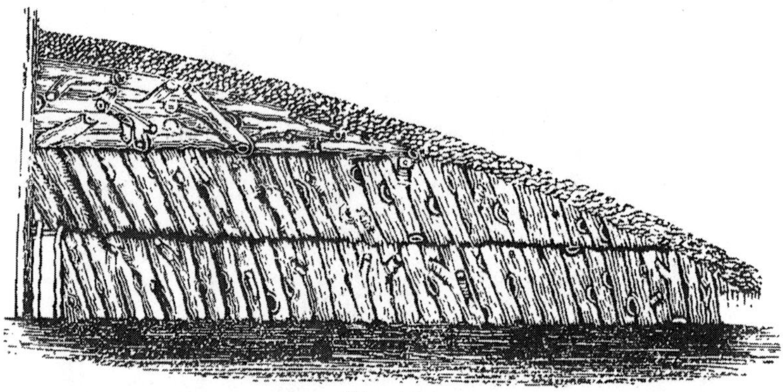

Fig. 17.

In this tropical climate, where vegetation is so rapid, it is not necessary to cut down trees for charcoal, but merely to lop off lower branches. On dry forest land, a crop of wood sufficient for charcoal can be obtained every fifth or sixth year; and on alluvial land, every third year.*

H. CLEGHORN,
Conservator of Forests.

* These remarks were drawn up and circulated mainly for the benefit of the Public Works Department, Madras.—H. C.

W. H. McFarlane, Lithr. Edinr. D. Hamilton delt.

EXPEDITION TO THE HIGHER RANGES OF THE ANAMALAI HILLS, COIMBATORE, IN 1858.*

The excursion described in the following pages was planned by Dr Macpherson, Inspector-General of Hospitals, and myself, with a view to explore the Southern Range of the Anamalai (*i.e.*, Elephant Hills), in the district of Coimbatore, which are sparingly laid down in the Great Trigonometrical Survey Map, while the peculiarities of their Fauna and Flora had not been recorded.

The project was approved by the Right Honourable Lord Harris, then Governor of the Madras Presidency, and the services of Major D. Hamilton were sanctioned by his Excellency Sir Patrick Grant, Commander-in-chief, to accompany us as artist, to delineate the characteristic features of the country.

According to previous agreement, the village, ten miles from Pulachy and six from Anamalai,† was the place of rendezvous. The party consisted of J. W. Cherry, Esq., acting-collector of Coimbatore, Drs Macpherson and Cornish, Major D. Hamilton, 21st N. I., Capt. Fane, Lieut. R. H. Beddome, 42d N. I., T. B. French, S. L. Koe, W. Fraser, civil engineer, and O. B. Irvine, Esq., assistant-collector, accompanied with seven elephants. We started at 4 A.M., and arrived at the Anamalai River at 20 minutes past 5; the distance six miles, and the road much trodden by sheep and cattle. By the light of early dawn we distinguished the candelabrum-like stems of *Euphorbia antiquorum*, and the drooping foliage of *Salvadora indica*, which in habit resembles the weeping willow, and here attains a large size, the trunk being 10 inches in diameter.

After crossing the river, which was deep and rapid, in leaky basket-boats, we traversed a number of paddy fields, and entered

* Read to the Royal Society of Edinburgh, 29th April 1861, and printed in their Transactions, vol. xxii.

† "North Latitude 10″ 27. East Longitude 77." Plate viii. Panorama of mountain range from this village, showing the eastern aspect.

the bamboo and tree jungle which lies in the hollow between the river and the ascent to Punachi, and which becomes exceedingly thick and wet along the water-courses. After proceeding about a mile, we ascended, by a winding bullock path, and reached Punachi at 9.30; the ghat we calculated to be at least three miles long. It is very steep, but easy enough for coolies. In one or two places we dismounted; the ponies scrambled over the boulders easily, but the elephants, though lightly laden, followed slowly and with difficulty, not reaching the huts till near dusk. The most trying work for laden elephants is crossing the bed of mountain streams (*vide* Plate IX.), as the sloping boulders offer a precarious footing for these heavy animals. From the top of the ghat to Punachi is above three miles of ascent and descent. About two miles from the top may be seen a magnificent precipice (about 200 feet high). The bluff rock overhanging the Torakudu river is reddish porphorite. The hills, like the Nilgiris and the Coimbatore district generally, consist of gneiss, and belong to the metamorphic rocks. Veins of felspar and quartz were common, some of them very large, crossing the foliated gneiss at right angles. The gneiss was generally of a grey colour, but in some places it was reddish. No crystalline limestone, such as is found associated with the gneiss in Coimbatore, was observed.

According to instructions given by Mr Cherry, the Kaders had prepared three huts and stabling for us, in an open space, about 50 yards east of the coffee plantation belonging to Ramasamy Mudelliar. These huts were admirably constructed, much superior to their own dwellings, and quite water-tight. The uprights were made of jungle trees tied together by strips of bark, the cots of bamboo, and the thatch of the glabrous leaves of a species of *Saccharum*. The coffee plantation was commenced twelve years ago; the soil is rich; the trees are at least 14 feet in height, left entirely to nature; a beautiful stream, however, is taken advantage of to irrigate the garden. The produce is much smaller than it might be under systematic management. There are some good teak trees standing in the middle of the plantation.

In the neighbourhood of Punachi, three or four large cattle

D. Hamilton

W. H. McFarlane, Lith^{r}, Edin^{r}

W. H. MFarlane, Lith. Edin.

FOOT OF PUNACHI PASS, CROSSING THE TORAKUDU RIVER.

kraals were seen, each containing from 50 to 80 head of cattle. Behind our hut was a waterfall, which is distinctly seen from Anamalai. The Punachi river tumbles over a precipice, which seems to be the edge of a considerable tract of table-land; this we regretted we had no opportunity to explore. Near to it are several dense sholas; and above the cascade some bison pasture-ground and ibex rocks.

Teak occurred for the first time on some undulating knolls, two or three miles before reaching the village, and on the slopes of the basin leading to the river. The teak tree here is not of superior dimensions, but is widely diffused, forming nearly half of the forest at this place. Many of the trees would yield second-class logs; and they improved in size as we descended the gorge. Being in flower, the white cross-armed panicles formed a striking feature in the landscape. There is much fallen and decaying teak within three miles of the huts. I inspected the jungle, both in going and returning, and walked across in different directions, to estimate approximatively the number and size of the trees. The value of standing wood is about Rs. 50,000, and of fallen timber at least Rs. 5000. I counted fifty trees on the ground well worth removal if there was easy transport. We saw further up the valley much Véngé (*Pterocarpus marsupium*) and blackwood (*Dalbergia latifolia*), which became more abundant as the elevation increased. These trees seem to prefer an altitude somewhat greater than teak, whilst the Vella nagá (*Conocarpus latifolius*), of great size, occurs with the teak, or prefers a lower range. The sholas near Punachi, between 3000 and 4000 feet above the sea, are very dense and rich in their flora. The following are a few remarkable forms observed:—A new species of *Jenkinsia* (Wallich); *Chondrospermum; Agrostistachys indica* (Dalzell); *Solenocarpus indicus*, a tree called by the Kaders "Palle-ille," the leaves of which are eaten; *Elæocarpus, Monocera*, a new species of *Cookia* (Mur Kuringi), with a delicious fruit; *Glycosmis pentaphylla, Pierardia macrostachys*, with an edible fruit; *Cleidion javanicum* ("Walle"); *Mesua*, with very large fruit; *Calophyllum*,* a species with narrow lanceolate leaves;

* *C. angustifolium*, R.? the poon spar tree.

Orophea, two new species; *Unona pannosa*, *Guatteria coffeoides*, *Cyathocalyx zeylanicus*, *Garcinia*, *Pterospermum obtusifolium*, *Sterculia guttata*, *Machilus*, *Casearia*, a new species; *Euonymus*, two apparently new forms, one with downy leaves, and the other much like a lime tree; *Agrostemma*, two species; *Ophioxylon*, a new species, with falcate bracts; *Pothomorphe subpeltata*, *Acranthera zeylanica*, *Nephelium erectum*, a very gorgeous species of *Pachycentria*; and two rare Euphorbiaceous trees, *Dimorphocalyx glabellus* and *Desmostemon zeylanicum*, lately described by Mr Thwaites.

Many of the trees in the dark sholas are covered with beautiful epiphytes, especially the *Hoya pauciflora*, *Æschynanthus zeylanicus*, and *Sarcanthus filiformis*. The dripping rocks with *Klugia*, two species, *Epithema*, &c.; cardamoms with rich aroma, and the true ginger plant, abound in these sholas. The rocks in the beds of all the rivers, from 3000 to 4500 feet, are covered with a showy orange-coloured balsam (*Impatiens verticillata*). It often forms a fringe at the line of watermark, or appears in patches between the forks of a cascade. At a higher elevation, other species take its place, especially one figured in the "Madras Journal of Science, 1859"—*Impatiens Tangachi*, (Beddome). A truly aquatic fern, a new species of *Pleopeltis*, grows in great abundance on rocks at the bottom of the Torakudu river.

16*th*. Started at 8 A.M., having left five elephants and our heavy baggage; after two miles we came to a river. There is a large body of water 100 feet wide, 1½ to 2 feet deep. Immediately below the ford is a village of low-caste people. Much time was lost in crossing on elephants and afterwards in cutting a road through tangled brushwood, each man being furnished with a billhook or shikaree knife. In the bed of the river we observed *Entada Pursœtha* and *Adelia neriifolia*. At 4 P.M. we agreed to bivouac, and erected temporary huts. Plate XI. presents the view up the valley from our camp, and gives a good outline of the Tangachi and Akka Mountains. About two miles after crossing the river, we made a detour to avoid a mass of rocks which descends to the water edge. We could ride as far as the waterfall at the foot of the Tangachi. In this place, as there are few bamboos and no *Saccharum*, we employed other

D. Hamilton, del[t]

ANCIENT CROMLECH.

hutting materials. Some gigantic *Crotolaria* and *Indigofera* stems were used for the walls, the stems being interwoven between the uprights, and the thatch was made of *Andropogon Schœnanthus*, L. (Ginger grass); fortunately no rain fell during the night. In the short march to-day, the teak gradually became smaller and less frequent, and disappeared altogether two miles before reaching the Torakudu waterfall.

Opposite our bivouac was a remarkable rock called Cundita-malai, apparently 200 feet in height, on the precipitous scarp of which was a rattan cable 80 feet long, securely fixed above. This chain was formed of large rings of the *Calamus* stem, connected by another straight rattan which passed down through the centre of the loops; by means of this the Kaders descend the face of the rock to collect honey, &c. (*vide* Plate XII.) The river during this day's march tumbles over huge boulders of broken rock, and takes a south-east direction.

17*th.* Started at a quarter to 8, and reached the huts near the Torakudu waterfalls at half-past 9, which are picturesque and very beautiful. About two miles below these falls, Major Hamilton discovered an ancient cairn or cromlech (*vide* Plate X.), a quarter-mile to the left of the path, similar to those found in other parts of Coimbatore, and consisting of four immense stones, the upright slabs about 5½ feet high, and the covering stone 11 feet by 5 feet. On the south of the valley, where the cromlech was found, is the ridge from the end of which Major Hamilton's sketch was taken, showing the general course of the river, which is here north-west. The site of the huts was not well chosen, being in the bed of a stream below the falls, while there was no lack of good encamping ground around. There are here three waterfalls,—a true fall of about 50 feet; another of about 100 feet; and a rapid cascade of 120 feet; which could not easily be approached.

Opposite the encampment is an Irular village of eight or ten houses, with a patch of ragi (*Eleusine coracana*, Gartn.) cultivation; and near this was another village of Muduvars. The day was fine, sometimes rather hot at night. Blankets were necessary, as it became cold towards morning. Very little dew fell, and at 6 A.M. there was none.

18*th*, 9 A.M.—As the two remaining elephants could not proceed further, the beds were carried by coolies, and each of the party took his own provisions for the day. We now ascended a steep rugged hill, impassable for horses on account of the immense masses of detached rocks; one in particular, resembling a haystack, about 40 feet high, from the summit of which a rattan chain similar to that described was suspended (*vide* Plate XII.) We proceeded through dense sholas for three miles, in the middle of which we crossed the river by a temporary bridge formed of a large tree felled by the Kaders for the purpose. *Rubus lasiocarpus* (bramble) was first seen here.

After walking six miles round the base of the Tangachi, we emerged from the woods, in which were traces of wild elephants, upon a steep open grass hill. At this point the view across the valley of the Torakudu was very grand, extensive dense sholas skirting the rocky and precipitous hills, the summits being shrouded in mist. The *Rhododendron arboreum* first occurred here—the elevation ascertained by Mr Fraser to be about 5000 feet. We continued to ascend the steep side of the hill till we arrived at the huts, which were situated on a lower spur of the Akka, near the edge of a large shola. Thick mist and violent rain came on soon afterwards. A herd of twenty-five bison were seen grazing on the opposite hill, and there were fresh traces of others near the hut.

19*th*, *Sunday*.—Nothing seen. Thermometer, minimum 54°, maximum 60°. Elevation calculated to be 5600 feet. Cold wind whistled freely through the grass huts, the stakes were loosened, and the temporary erection nearly came down.

20*th*, *Monday*.—It rained all morning. The Kader guides were unwilling to proceed. However, we started at 10 A.M. in search of the great valley alluded to in Captain Michael's Report,* and in an hour reached a beautiful ridge shooting out from the base of Akka-malai; there was short, sweet pasture, and numerous indications of bison. The weather continued unfavourable, and so misty, that except during a few gleams of sunshine, we saw little of the country.

* Captain J. Michael, 39th N.I., visited these ranges in 1851; his MS. Report was of great use to us.

PLATE 12.

From this ridge (Bison Ridge) we skirted the base of the Akka-malai, keeping above the sholas, and ascended the western side of the high range, which is clothed with remarkably short grass, to the right of the Akka. The previous afternoon some of the party ascended the shoulder of the Akka, which is considerably higher. Unfortunately, owing to the dense mist, they were not rewarded by a good view of the surrounding country. Mr Beddome has favoured me with the following note of his ascent:—"The rocky Akka mountain, which is probably upwards of 8000 feet high, is quite covered near its summit with several undescribed species of *Impatiens*. The only other new form I observed on this mountain was a curious crassulaceous plant with fleshy peltate leaves, growing in sheltered moist nooks of the rock.

"Balsams are very abundant on these hills. *Impatiens balsamina*, *Dasysperma*, *albida*, *maculata*, *campanula*, *chinansis*, *tomentosa*, *verticellata*, *oppositifolia*, *Kleinii*, *tenella*, *rivalis*, *acaulis*, *modesta*, *latifolia*, *lucida rufescens*, *Goughii*, *cordata*, and several undescribed species."

Having proceeded several miles along this range, the summit of which was hidden in mist, we turned to the south-east. The mist suddenly cleared, and we got a glimpse of numerous ibex on the rocks above, and saw a valley which appeared to be five miles long and two broad, with large sholas on the other side. The wind and rain increased as we proceeded. We came to the junction of the streams, near which is a beautiful waterfall about 350 feet high. The general character of the valley struck several as being like Pykara on the Nilgiris. The weather continuing very unfavourable, our attendants fatigued, and our provisions exhausted, it was necessary to retrace our steps.

Some of the herbaceous plants observed adorning the higher hillside pastures are:—*Flemingia procumbens*, *Phaseolus pulniensis*, *Anemone Wightiana*, *Lysimachia Leschenaultii* and *deltoidea*, *Utricularia*, *Ranunculus reniformis*, *Gentiana pedicellata*, with many others. But these examples are sufficient to show the similarity of the Flora to that around Utakamand. Two curious and new species of *Podostemaceæ* cover the rocks in the beds of rivers.

21*st*. We left early, and much regretted our inability to remain another day. In looking back, we could see the highest range distant about 12 miles, north-east. The outline of this is well represented in Major Hamilton's sketch.

22*d*. Major Hamilton and Messrs Koe and Fraser descended into the gorge to examine the entrance to the hills by the valley of the Torakudu river, when the Major took the sketch given in Plate XIII. If a path can be constructed in this direction, the ghat near Punachi would be avoided, and the distance shortened by several miles. The rest of the party explored the forest, and descended the ghat by which we ascended. The day of our departure was fine and bright, and we obtained a clear view of the higher ranges from the lower valley of the Torakudu.

About a month after our visit (8th November), Lieut. Beddome rode up in one day to the higher ranges, and had a fine view of the summit.

He writes—"The part that we traversed forms only a small portion of the valley, and is shut out from the rest by a sloping ridge covered with dense shola, which rises out on the opposite bank of the river. The greater part of the valley lies beyond this ridge; another meandering river runs through the larger portion of the valley; and towards the further extremity there is a large swamp, which could probably be converted into a fine lake. The valley extends two or three miles beyond the succession of waterfalls which we visited. It is widest just beyond these falls, where it must be four miles across; and the whole of the centre is comprised of undulating hillocks, very fine sites for building. From the Akka mountain, which I ascended, there run two high ridges, almost of the same height as the mountain itself; between these is a narrow valley, through which a river runs, eventually reaching Michael's Valley by the series of falls we visited. The mountains on the opposite side of the valley seem very high, and from the top of the Akka there appeared to be a good extent of table-land there. My time was very limited, or I should have explored the higher unknown portion of these mountains. I ascended the Tangachi Peak, which is very different in character from the Akka; the ascent lies through

PLATE 13.

dense sholas till within half a mile of the summit; thence the mountain is covered with almost impenetrable brushwood 6 to 10 feet in height, consisting chiefly of *Myrtus*, *Dodonœa*, *Rubus*, *Litsœa*, and *Atylosïa*. The mountain has a great many rocky caverns and crags towards the summit."

Again, under date 25th February 1859, Lieut. Beddome writes, "that he and Mr Bryce went to that high land beyond Michael's Valley, where there is a good extent of undulating table-land. The highest peak of the Anamalais, below which there appears to be table-land, is at least 25 miles beyond the valley, and seems to be very difficult of access. We had white frost in the valley."

I now append Dr Macpherson's views on the eligibility of this range for a sanatarium and for future colonisation. The general appearance and character of these high lands resemble the Nilgiris. Here are the same rounded eminences and dense sholas, extending continuously for miles, their edges fringed with *Strobilanthes*, and ceasing abruptly. The hills are conical, and the slopes covered with short rich grass, abounding with medicinal plants, as the *Exacum bicolor* and *Ophelia elegans* (Gentians); the woods contain *Hymenodyction excelsum* and other species of the Cinchona family. Heavy rains, evidently the breaking up of the south-west monsoon, fell continuously during the period of our stay on these upper regions. The want of shelter, and the difficulty of procuring supplies, prevented us from proceeding to the highest parts of the range, which appeared to be about 12 miles in a south-east direction from the extreme point the party reached. We therefore reluctantly returned to the low country without fully attaining our object, having been absent eight days. Three distinct tribes inhabit the Anamalai Hills; they are denominated Kaders, Paliars, and Malsars. The Kaders perform no menial labour. As their name implies, they are the lords of the hills; they carry a gun, and loads also as a favour; they are expert at stalking game, but are deeply offended if called coolies. They are a truthful, trustworthy, and obliging tribe, and exercise some influence over the Paliars and Malsars. Small in stature, their features resemble the African (Plate VII.); they have curly hair, tied in a knot behind, and file the four front teeth of the upper jaw to a point, as a marriage ceremony. "The Paliars are chiefly herdsmen and merchants, while the Malsars are cultivators of the soil. None of these tribes reside at a higher elevation than 4000 to 5000 feet above the sea. All deal in the rich produce of these hills, and barter with the people in the plains their cardamoms, turmeric, ginger, honey, wax, resins, millets, soap-nuts, gall-nuts, &c., for rice, tobacco, &c. They are very expert in climbing trees, and the precipitous face of rocks, in search of honey. To accomplish the former, where there are no boughs, they drive short bamboo spikes into the tree, and thus form a ladder, by means of which they ascend the highest forest trees; and they reach the latter by means of chains formed by rings made with rattan, which being secured to a point above, drops down the face of the rock. We observed some of these chains full 50 and 80 feet in length. The upper ranges are in undisturbed possession of wild beasts; we saw a large herd of bison, with deer and ibex in numbers, and also traces of wild elephants.

"The best period to prosecute inquiry into the upper ranges of the Anamalai mountains would be after October, or in the hot season. From their position, they are considerably under the influence of the south-west monsoon, but less so than the Kundahs at Sissipara; and I think it is worthy of inquiry to ascertain whether here, also, may not be found a climate as bracing and welcome to the enervated constitution of the European invalid as exists on our better known hill stations. The soil on the summit of these fine mountains is deep, and covered with rich pasture. Streams of water are numerous, and appear as if they flowed throughout the year. From the extent of forest, the resemblance of the flora to that of Ceylon, and the corresponding altitude of these hills, I believe they are suitable for the cultivation of coffee on a large scale, and for colonisation of small communities of Englishmen; a measure which would be attended with the happiest results, as it adds at once to our military strength, and, in course of time, would give us the means, to a certain extent, of recruiting our army."

It will thus be seen that the result of our excursion was not without interest. Some curious botanical novelties were found;

the timber resources of the district were ascertained, and a large tract of country, suitable for coffee culture, was traversed, which will doubtless be the scene of future colonization.

H. CLEGHORN,
Conservator of Forests.

The following extracts from reports by Capt. Michael and Lieut. Beddome contain additional information regarding the supplies of water and the timber resources of the district. It will be seen that to the former officer the credit is due of having first explored this interesting hill tract. "On the 22d October, 1851," he writes, "we ascended the hill, on the face of which the hut stood, which is connected with the Akka and Tangachi malai, and about the same height, but suited our purpose better, as it ran further into the interior, and gave us a better view of the surrounding country; we found the height at the top to be 7000 feet; and observed a fine open valley about five miles in length, extending along the base of this hill, running from north to south, and watered by two small streams which unite at the north extremity, and fall over a rock forming the Torakudu river. At the south extremity is a conical hill covered with grass and small sholas on its sides, which appears to be the watershed of the whole range, the streams in the valleys falling off in every direction from the base of it; though there are many higher peaks, we were confirmed in this opinion by the fact that the sholas are smaller and less frequent in this spot than elsewhere: both to the north and south, heavy sholas extend continuously for miles, while here they were in small patches of a few acres. This watershed point we concluded to be the hill marked "Paducalumudy" in the Trigonometrical Survey Map (Sheet No. 62). From this we could see what is evidently the highest mountain point in the range. It is a rounded eminence, lying some 12 miles off in a south-easterly direction, and apparently not within the Travancore boundary; but as our time was limited, we could not visit it.

"On the 23d, we went about five or six miles over very difficult ground on the steep side of a hill to the long valley above mentioned; and crossing the two small streams just above their confluence, found an old hut which had been built some time before by the Paliars of Dhulli, on one of their excursions in search of hill produce. In this hut we remained three days, exploring the vicinity, and ascertained that the whole of this beautiful valley is about 6000 feet above the level of the sea. It is covered with slopes of short grass, full of flowers of the same description as are usually found on the Nilgiris, or rather at Kunur. The stream ran through small swamps, and was fringed with the Rhododendrons, Ferns, &c. The *Anemone*, *Pedicularis*, *Exacum*, *Salep Misree*, and the large white lilies, were in great abundance; the sharp edges of the sholas were very marked, as they are about Utakamand and the Kundas. The thermometer stood at 56° in the morning, and at night the cold was very intense.

"We did not see many wild animals; but the tracks of elephants, bison, deer, &c., covered the valley in every direction. It is probable that, when the forest is burned in the lower parts of the hills, the wild animals come up here in great numbers. I was in hopes that we should have fallen in with some 'Muduvars,' who had been described to me as inhabiting these mountains. It appears they do not frequent these higher ranges, but, like the 'Kurumbars' and 'Irulars' of the Nilgiris, only cultivate and live on the slopes of the hills at a lesser elevation.

"I regret very much that my time would not admit of our reaching the highest point and ascertaining the height; for, as far as we could judge from such a distance, it must be upwards of 8000 feet above the sea level, and near it was a considerable extent of table-land much higher than the valley we were in.

"It took us two days to reach Anamalai; but even in the present rugged state of the paths, I think the journey might easily be done in one day. J. MICHAEL."

Lieut. R. H. Beddome, Assist. Conserv. of Forests, described the last excursion on 17th April 1860 :—"I have made a trip to the higher ranges of the Anamalai Hills, and explored the country lying south of Michael's Valley, and also the Anjinad Valley (in the Survey map marked 'Kujeenad'), between the Anamalais and Pulnies. I was accompanied by Mr E. C. G. Thomas, Assist. Collector of Malabar. Proceeding round the ridge of hills which form the south side of Michael's Valley, we came upon a track which led over a beautiful undulating country to the southern ridges of the Anamalais, which overlook the Anjinad Valley. We found a well-beaten path leading down to Anjinad. The head of the ghat is six or eight miles to the south of Michael's Valley. We here found a beautiful piece of table-land, situated to the right of the pass down to Anjinad, well watered, sheltered by high hills to the south, and lying about 6000 or 6500 feet above the sea-level. I encamped here for several days, and explored the surrounding country. Mr Thomas proceeded down the Anjinad Ghat, crossed the valley, and ascended the Pulnies by Munjapatti. To the east of the pass down to Anjinad there is much higher table-land, probably 7000 feet above the sea, copiously watered by several springs and streams. This spot, and the table-land on which I was encamped, would form an admirable site for a station. They are separated from each other by a valley, which is the head of the pass down to Anjinad. The ghat down into the Anjinad Valley is nowhere precipitous; and a good road might easily be made from Anjinad. The scenery here is magnificent. The view north towards the Akka and Tangachi Peaks is very grand; and to the south lies the Anjinad Valley, thousands of feet below, with the Pulnies towering beyond. I explored for ten miles the country to the west of my encamping ground. These southern ridges of the Anamalais are the chief water sources of the whole range. In four or five different places I found regular channels which conduct much of the water which would otherwise flow towards Michael's Valley down into the Anjinad Valley. These channels have been dug by the Muduwars and Puliars, who inhabit this valley and the slopes down to it. To the west of my encamping ground there are several other beautiful spots of table-land, and also another fine valley, similar to Michael's Valley, but with the slopes less precipitous.

Hitherto I have only known three tribes inhabiting the Anamalai Hills—viz., Kaders, Puliars, and Malsars. There is, however, a fourth tribe, "the Muduwars." Ten of this tribe joined us when first we ascended the mountains, and told us that they lived in a small village on the high land to the north of the

Akka and Tangachi Peaks. They carried our baggage for one march, but all decamped in the night, and we saw no more of them. We were afterwards joined by a dozen Puliars, who remained the whole time. From the southern ridges of the Anamalais, another Muduwar village was pointed out to me. It was below my encamping ground, on the slope towards the Anjinad Valley. This village was known by the name of Kodakárá. There appeared to be an extensive clearance of the shóla near the village. I one day met three Muduwars from this village, not far from my encampment; they were armed with powerful bows and arrows, and were in search of ibex and samber. They had a large dog with them.

The shólas on these higher ranges are composed of very large trees, and are generally open, there being little or no underwood. Amongst the trees the following orders are chiefly represented: *Myrtaceæ*, *Lauraceæ*, *Olacaceæ*, *Araliaceæ*, *Oleaceæ*, *Ternströemiaceæ*, and *Magnoliaceæ*. I found a few new plants; but two attacks of fever whilst upon the hills prevented my exploring as much as I could have wished. In many of the streams and rivers there were beds of most lovely balsams, in full flower, even at this season of the year. Two gorgeous flowers are characteristic of these hill streams, *Sonerila grandiflora*, with a new and very large species of *Exacum* or Hill Gentian. There is apparently no trace of either the Rose or Strawberry on these mountains, which is curious, as both are so abundant on the Pulnies and Nilgiris. The three species of *Rubus* are, however, very common. The Anjinad Valley is about 1500 feet above the plains. I proceeded to this valley, and from different parts of the slopes obtained a complete view of it. I was much disappointed, there being no forest worth mentioning in any part of the valley. About the village of Anjinad (or Maraur, as it is sometimes called), and in fact all over the valley, there is a great deal of rice cultivation, with some bamboo jungle. Where there is forest it is very open, and the trees much stunted; with the exception of a few scraggy trees, there is no teak. Between the higher ranges of the Anamalais and the valley of the Ambravati there are some very fine plateaus of superb shóla forest, admirably adapted for the cultivation of coffee.

TEAK PLANTATIONS.

In several parts of this work, reference is made to the experiments made (in the Madras Presidency) to propagate teak. Of these the most important and most prosperous were the efforts made by Mr Conolly, the late collector of Malabar. His object was to establish nurseries, in order to replenish the teak forests, which were rapidly becoming thinned; the demand for the timber being so great, and so steadily on the increase, as to indicate, at no distant period, a scarcity of large-sized logs much to be deprecated. This scarcity is being realized, especially now that so much is required to meet the purposes of the Railway Department. Besides, from the fact that teak, and, *par excellence*, Malabar teak, is acknowledged to be the most valuable timber for ship-building purposes yet known, and consequently always preferred at our Government dockyards, it is evident that all efforts tending to preserve and propagate trees so important to the State, and so valuable in commerce, cannot be over-estimated. Mr C.'s first experiments were made nearly twenty years ago; these, however, were on a very limited scale, and attended with very partial success. Subsequently a large tract of land, in the neighbourhood of the Beypur River (25 square miles in extent), was selected by that gentleman for the purpose of converting it into teak plantations. Large quantities of seeds were sown, and thousands of saplings were planted; but the former failed to germinate, and the latter did not present a thriving appearance. This state of things was ascribed to a variety of causes, and led to a series of changes both of men and expedients. At this stage of matters, and while Mr Conolly was feeling the want and advocating the necessity of a trained arboriculturist, the nurseries were visited by M. Perrottet, a French botanist, who, after making a thorough inquiry, stated his opinions fully, in the form of a report. Dr Wight's opinion was similarly obtained; and as it also is on record, it seems desirable to quote, to some extent, the correspondence, based on the variety of opinions expressed at that time on this subject:—

MR CONOLLY'S EXPERIMENTS.

The tahsildar, who advised Mr Conolly to prepare the seed, had come to the conclusion, that the seeds which germinated in the forests without any cultivation were prepared for growth, or, in other words, lost their outer coating by the great heat caused by the fires which annually consume the brushwood, and that therefore this process should be imitated as closely as possible in artificial sowing. Mr Conolly accordingly caused a large quantity of seeds to be spread on the ground in a bed, and covered with a light coating of hay. The hay was then gradually burnt, so as only to singe the rind without injuring the kernels of the seeds. They were sown in beds previously prepared for the purpose, and covered over lightly with hay to keep them cool, and to prevent the heat of the sun injuring them. This process also proved unsuccessful, though a few of the seeds vegetated. Mr Graham, the sub-conservator, then made some other experiments. He says,—

"Not being satisfied with the above process of preparing seeds for sowing, I applied fire to a few of them, and found, from the trial, that the coating covering the shell acted like turf, which convinced me that in this process the seed inside the shell must be destroyed, or in a manner roasted, and therefore be rendered unfit for vegetation. I then threw a few of the seeds into water, to see what effect the water had on them. I found on this trial that the coating acted something like a sponge, and contained as much water as convinced me that the shell and seed must rot before the time usual for the seed's vegetation, which is mentioned in the tahsildar's letter to be forty days.

"Being unable to get any useful information on the subject from any of the proprietors of forests in this part of the country, and being convinced that the shell ought to be cleared of the spongy coating before being put into the ground," Mr Graham had six thousand so cleared with the knife, and had them sown, on the 4th of January 1843, "in beds of about sixteen yards long, and one and a quarter broad, along with fourteen thousand prepared by fire, the whole covered over with a light coating of hay; and in sixteen days after they had been put into the ground, on removing the old hay to replace it with fresh, I discovered that five of the seeds cleared with the knife, and one of those prepared by fire, had vegetated."

Shortly after the above experiments, Mr Graham discovered that the white ants could be usefully employed in clearing the seeds; he therefore intended trying some seeds from which these insects had taken off the spongy coating, and reporting the result.*

M. PERROTTET'S REPORT.

M. Perrottet, in his report, first notices the necessity of preserving the teak trees from injury by the natives. He says:—

"Everywhere I remarked that the trees which constitute these forests were mutilated by the people living in the neighbourhood. Whenever these men are in want of a piece of wood for the handle of a work-tool, or any other purpose, they go and procure it for themselves in the woods, cutting at random, and without any precaution; from whence it follows that the trunk thus mutilated shoots again with difficulty, and the shoots produced are crooked and stunted."

M. Perrottet accordingly recommended the fencing of these forests, "to show that it is forbidden to enter them," and to hold the tahsildar responsible for injury done to the trees. The nurseries which were formed on "separate ground, for the purpose of raising teak plants, M. Perrottet entirely condemned, as being, in his opinion, "a ruinous system, and one which will never

* Dr Brandis lays great stress upon strewing the seeds on the surface. Mr Gordon of Moulmein states that the dry and ripe seeds brought in from the villages are strewed on the ground, and readily germinate in eight, ten, or twenty days; but many do not sprout, and many are lost during transplantation.—H. C.

fulfil the end proposed." He suggested the sowing of seeds in the forests, with the precautions necessary to their germination, as well as the replanting of shoots from the roots of old trees. In order to prepare the seed before sowing, M. Perrottet recommended their being stratified, either in boxes, or in a damp warm soil, sheltered from the rays of the sun. The process to be observed, if a box was used, was to place in it successive layers of earth, composed of vegetable manure and seeds, till the box was filled, taking care, however, that the box was not so deep as to cause the seeds at the bottom to rot. This mass was to be frequently watered for forty days, by which time it was expected the seeds would germinate, when they should be carried to suitable spots in the forests, and placed in couplets or triplets, or in twos and threes, in holes of about two inches at the deepest, and slightly covered with a small portion of earth. These holes should be at the distance of about six feet from each other. The trees, when they grow, being thus near one another, shoot more perpendicularly, without throwing out lateral branches. All lateral branches should be cut, from the ground to the summit of the tree; but up to the height of twenty feet they should be cut smoothly. When the young plants from the seed have attained a height of between one and two feet, all trees and brambles, which at first were necessary to shade them, should be removed, to give the teak air and light, "elements thenceforth indispensable to the progressive development of these trees." M. Perrottet, however, was more in favour of the system of propagation by replanting the shoots from the roots of old trees, which he thought an easier and a shorter one for multiplying teak trees.* He said,—

"I have remarked, wherever I have seen teak trees, that from their roots, and especially from those that were cut close to the ground, young trees were produced; that is to say, from some parts of their roots straight and vigorous shoots sprung forth. We should profit then by those means which Nature points out, by going into the forests, slightly uncovering some of the roots, and cutting them in some places, in order to cause the develop-

* This will not succeed; occasionally stump shoots become useful trees, but they are generally much inferior to seedlings.—H. C.

ment of more shoots; we should thus, in a short time, have trees of handsome growth. Another precaution which I wish to see taken in this country for the preservation of forests, especially those of teak, relates to the proper cutting of trees. Instead of barking, mutilating and hacking the base of the tree, as is now done, I would wish, on the contrary, that they should be cut with care, and as close to the ground as possible. As the teak tree shoots very willingly from its roots, by cutting it smoothly, and with a good hatchet, you would, as a first result, see springing from the circumference of the cut (which should be made slanting, or, like the mouth of a flute, to facilitate the running off of the rain) several suckers, of which you would only suffer the strongest and straightest to grow, and, as a second, you would have fine trees and abundance of them." (Papers on the Teak Forests of India, 1852, p. 231, *et seq.*)

M. Perrottet recommended, in conclusion, that his suggestions should be submitted "to a man instructed in vegetable physiology and arboriculture;" and Mr Conolly cites this suggestion as confirming his opinion of the necessity of having a properly qualified sub-conservator.

DR WIGHT'S OPINION.

Dr Wight, referring to the practice of Mr Graham, wrote that he did not see the "necessity for the laborious operation of removing the pips from the pulp" previous to sowing the teak seed, but, on the contrary, was of opinion that Nature gave the seed the covering for the purpose of promoting its fertility. In support of this opinion, he mentions the cinnamon seed as being covered with a similar coat, which at first would appear to be a serious impediment to germination, whereas this coat is really essential to its vegetating. The manner in which vegetation is promoted, is by gathering the seeds together in a heap, and covering them lightly with straw or fern, when in a few days fermentation begins, heat is generated, and with the heat vegetation commences. The seeds thus prepared are immediately sown, and a sufficiently large proportion are found to vegetate. Judging, therefore, from analogy, Dr Wight thought, that instead of the teak seed rotting, as Mr Graham supposed, when the spongy coating became full of water, the contrary would be the result; and for that purpose not only must the sponge be filled with water, but it must be kept constantly moist until vegetation begins, which is indicated by the bursting of the shell, and the protrusion of the young plant. This process, owing to the thickness and density of the shell, as compared with the size of the seed, takes some time to accomplish. Dr Wight, assuming then, that, as in the case of the cinnamon seed, heat would more speedily excite vegetative action, advised Mr Conolly to try to promote it in two ways: *first*, by making a heap of the seeds (which must be previously soaked for an hour in water), and leaving them to ferment in the same manner as the cinnamon seed. They might then be sown in shaded beds of very light, sandy, well-moistened soil, and covered over with a quantity of fallen leaves, which could be kept in their places by sprinkling a little earth over them. These arrangements should be completed before the rains, till which time the beds are to be kept moist by occasionally watering them. The *second* plan was, to throw the seeds into nearly boiling water, 180° to 200° Fahr., and leaving them there until the water cooled; to proceed then as in the former case. These plans, however, Dr Wight said, were merely theoretical, and might prove as unsuccessful as the others which had been tried; but, he added, "Of one thing I am quite sure, that much moisture is required, and, I strongly suspect, the heat of fermentation, which is naturally produced at the beginning of the rains, where heaps of decaying vegetation happen to be accumulated, and that it is in such situations the seeds sprout."

MR GRAHAM'S REMARKS.

Mr Conolly referred the reports of M. Perrottet and Dr Wight to Mr Graham, the sub-conservator, who made his remarks thereon, and gave some further details regarding the germination of the teak seed, which may be noticed, as being the fruits of experience and observation. The first point which Mr Graham takes up in his remarks, is the stratifying or heating of the seed previously to sowing it. This, he maintains, will not answer, although the process does not injure the kernel; for, he says,—

"When vegetation takes place, the seed bursts a piece out of the side of the shell, and comes clear out of it; it is therefore necessary that earth be in contact with the young root, so that it is able to lay hold on it for nourishment. In the event of its not being able to do this, and bring itself out of the shell, it in the course of an incredibly short space of time turns of a bluish colour, and perishes; and therefore, if raised in a box, or in heaps, it would perish as soon as germination had taken place." Moreover, seeds in this state do not bear removal, for they quickly perish on being accidentally exposed by carelessness in watering the beds in which they have been sown, although immediately covered again with proper care. Another objection to the plan of stratifying arose from uncertainty as to the time the seed took to vegetate. The tahsildar and M. Perrottet allowed forty days for vegetation to be completed, but Mr Graham had known seeds to vegetate from the eleventh day after sowing. On the question whether the outer coating of the teak seed was essential or not to its germination, Mr Graham was of opinion that nature had provided it to absorb moisture, and by engendering damp (not heat, as Dr Wight said), it destroys the vitality of the seed; otherwise, argued Mr Graham, nearly every seed in the forest should germinate, whereas only a very small number did vegetate, and these, he asserted, were seeds which had been cleared by the white ants, and not by the annual burning of the grass. Of the six thousand seeds which he had cleared with the knife, not less than four thousand had vegetated up to the date of his writing; thus proving that the outer coating of the seed must be removed before sowing, to ensure vegetation. Mr Graham further remarked, that M. Perrottet erred in stating that the natives cut teak for their tools and other implements, as they preferred for such purposes the tough junglewood, which was very plentiful; and that he was mistaken also in his scheme of planting the forest from old roots, as, out of eighteen thousand planted by Mr Smith, there were then scarcely thirty in existence. M. Perrottet's recommendation, that the lateral branches of the teak trees should be cut off smoothly with the trunk, was likewise injudicious; for by so doing the part cut will always shrink into the trunk, leave holes, and thus aggravate the very defects which were to be avoided. A better plan would be, to leave on the trunk a small projection of the branch cut, so as to allow of its shrinking without injuring the trunk. Mr Graham concluded, by recommending nurseries at a distance from water, and on the clearest ground that could be procured, in order to avoid the swarms of insects which, he said, devoured anything newly sprung from the ground. He also informed Mr Conolly that the simplest mode of ascertaining whether teak seeds were good, was to throw them into a vessel of water, when the good seeds would sink, and the bad ones float.

Shortly after writing the above, Mr Graham resigned the office of sub-conservator. Mr Conolly, upon this (with a view to further experiments in sowing teak seed), urged anew the necessity for an arboriculturist being procured from England. The Board of Revenue supported this proposition, the Government favourably recommended it to the Court of Directors, and, pending their decision, authorised Mr Conolly to appoint a native sub-conservator, on a salary of Rs.50 a month.

The experience from subsequent trials near Calicut of the various plans suggested by Dr Wight and M. Perrottet for insuring the germination of the teak seed, enabled Mr Conolly "to discern, with considerable accuracy, the best means of arriving at this wished-for result;" and though the discovery took place too late to enable him to profit that year by the proper season for sowing, he was able to put into the ground, in a favourable locality, a few miles below Nelambur, 10,000 young plants, of which 7000 were in a healthy and prosperous condition. The sub-conservator had also put down in the same spot, and elsewhere, 3000 saplings, which he transplanted from the surrounding forests. A few of these were reported to be looking well; but the remainder, owing probably to the injury to which plants are liable on removal to new situations, had drooped, and were likely to perish. Under these circumstances, Mr Conolly did not advise Government to obtain more land, except on very favourable terms. He however wrote,—"It was absolutely necessary that Government should come forward and take the initiative in the formation of new forests to replace those which have vanished from private carelessness and rapacity—a work too new, too extensive, and too barren of early return, to be ever taken up by the native proprietor. But to do this effectually, to ensure the Government resources from being frittered away with no good result, it is essential, as I have shown in my report of 12th June 1840, that the duty and responsibility of the planting be entrusted to some person who is thoroughly qualified to undertake it." The Board of Revenue at Madras, in again advocating this measure, wrote,—"To ensure these noble forests being turned to the best advantage, they should be placed under the especial charge of some person sent from England for the purpose, and who, from his practical acquaintance with the system of planting and with the science of arboriculture generally, may be best qualified for that peculiar duty."

The Government of Madras having again urged the necessity of obtaining the services of a properly qualified person from England, the Government of India, on the 22d June 1844, forwarded the whole of the correspondence to the Court of Directors, with a recommendation that an experienced arboriculturist be appointed.

In Jan. 1845, the Government of India, on the recommendation of the Government of Madras, authorised an increase to the teak plantation establishment of the collector of Malabar, which raised its aggregate cost from Rs. 221 to Rs. 314–8 per month, including Rs. 50, the salary of the native sub-conservator. This increased establishment was represented as necessary in consequence of the extended scale on which planting and sowing were being carried on by Mr Conolly, whose report calls for some notice. In the report of October 1844, he says, that from November 1843 to May 1844 he employed the conservancy establishment in clearing and preparing a considerable quantity of ground in four different sites, named Manasherry, Ariacode, Yedacode, and Iravelly Cow. The second and third sites were on the Nelambur or Beypur River, the first on a tributary stream, and the fourth close to Nelambur itself, so that the soils and circumstances of each were more or less different. Here Mr Conolly caused to be put down in the course of May, June, and July 1844, 50,000 young plants, which had been raised in adjacent nurseries; and he said of them, "The generality of these plants look healthy, but there is a marked difference in favour of those raised at Yedacode and Iravelly Cow, which have a very promising appearance. I have every confidence that this promise will be fulfilled, and that they will become fine saplings. My confidence is founded on the excellent condition of a few hundred plants which I had put down last year so soon as the difficulty with regard to the seed had been mastered. Nothing can surpass the beauty of these plants. In from 12 to 16 months they have shot up to 8 feet or more, with a healthy and strong stem. In fact, I consider the *experiment* of raising healthy saplings to be at an end, and I have no hesitation in recommending to the Government that the important object of replanting wastes with teak be carried on with vigour in the sites which have been proved to be so well suited for it." With this view Mr Conolly intended confining himself, at Manasherry and Ariacode, to the care of the plants raised there, and to planting on an extensive scale at Yedacode and Iravelly Cow, which seemed to be the sites best adapted for the purpose, and where there was abundance of available space. There was, however, yet another difficulty to be overcome before the plans pursued by Mr Conolly could be perfected: this was the pruning and tending the young plantations. On this point Mr Conolly was endeavouring to afford all the assistance he could to the sub-conservator, who was a native of the district, by instructing him from books which had been sent out for the purpose by the Court of Directors instead of the arboriculturist, for whose services so many applications had been made.

The progress of Mr Conolly's operations may be gathered from the following Minute of the Marquis of Tweeddale, the Governor of Madras, dated 8th December 1846:—

MINUTE BY THE MARQUIS OF TWEEDDALE.

8th December 1846.

"I have carefully examined the teak plantations which have

been planted under the direction of Mr Conolly, collector of Malabar, and under the immediate superintendence of a native of that district, trained by himself. The Government had not provided that officer with the assistance of a European educated as a forester, or with any agent who understood practically the rearing of young plants, the management of young trees, the selection of soils adapted to the growth of particular plants, the transplanting of seedlings from the seed-bed, the appropriate distance at which the plants should be placed from one another, the thinning and pruning of young trees, and the causes which require it, and who possessed such other practical information as is necessary for the successful management of plantations, and for bringing them to maturity. Mr Conolly, however, felt it to be his duty to make the attempt, with the assistance of books and a small 'Forester's Guide' sent to him by the Court of Directors.

"These plantations are now one, two, three and four years old, and Mr Conolly has himself told me that the more he reads, and the older his plantations become, the greater difficulties he has to contend with, from not possessing practical knowledge himself, either as a nurseryman or forester; nor does he feel assured that his endeavours to forward the Court's views will be fully successful, unless he can procure the assistance of a forester who has had experience in planting and pruning trees, and felling timber, and who can impart his knowledge to the natives. There is on their part no want of inclination to learn—on the contrary, there is every desire and great aptitude; but they must be convinced that the person who superintends is master of his business. A district of many square miles in extent was purchased on account of Government, affording a wide field of operations. The oldest plantation on it which I examined was rising four years. The plan pursued by Mr Conolly appears to have been very judiciously conceived and executed. The spot selected for the first essay was situated on the banks of the Nelambur or Beypur river, stretching over an extent of five miles. The first operation was to clear the banks, extending to a certain distance into the interior, of all jungle trees, in the most economical manner. The difficulty of getting the seeds to germinate in their hard shell was, after much delay and frequent failures, at length overcome by steeping them in boiling water, so as to produce the same effect by the heat so generated as the constant fires in the jungle do on the seeds which there germinate. By this process the plants spring rapidly from the seed-bed, and when three months old they are transplanted, holes are dug in the ground, and the soil is trenched 12 inches deep, at intervals of 8 feet, so as to give air to the plants, and little opposition to their tap-roots (in their delicate state after transplanting) in their downward search for food. I may observe, that the future prosperity of the teak plantations depends upon the soil selected being of that quality and in that situation in which nature has ordained that the tree shall thrive, so as to provide it with sufficient nourishment and with a suitable exposure. On these circumstances will chiefly depend the close grain of the timber and its durability when exposed to varieties of climate: these will also prevent the canker of the heart of the tree, which is sure to follow if the tap-root penetrates soil not suited to its wants.

"After minute inspection of the plants of different ages in the plantations, and of all the arrangements connected with them, I was so much struck with the efficiency and ability which marked all the operations, that it appeared to me that the director of the undertaking must either have had practical experience as a nurseryman, or that he possessed a mind so constituted that he could select from the mass of information written on the planting and management of forests from time to time, such as was necessary to carry on the work in a practical and satisfactory manner. The latter I found to be the case; and I can assure the Honourable Court, that their expression of confidence in Mr Conolly's exertions for establishing a good system of management in the teak forests, as far as the plantations are now advanced, is well merited. I have had much experience in plantations and woods on my own account at home, as well as in those of other proprietors, but I never saw a better commencement than in the Government teak plantations of Malabar.

"The proximity to water-carriage, the gradual clearing of jungle towards the interior for security to health, and to prepare for extending the plantations into the interior; the education of so many workmen and *maistries*, both for working the plantations, and for the management of the natural woods (making good roads of communication as the plantations advance), are all objects of essential consequence to future success in a new undertaking, and have all been carefully attended to. I have thus far expressed an opinion upon what I have seen. I do not pretend to offer any opinion upon the result, as I am unacquainted with the quality of the soil or subsoil generally throughout Malabar; but I have been able to assist Mr C., by informing him that the best mode of ascertaining the suitability of the soil to the tree is to dig pits near fine-grown teak trees, as deep as the end of the tap-roots penetrate, and experience will afterwards teach him, from the appearance of the surface-soil, what kinds of subsoil he may expect to meet, and how far the situation selected is adapted for bringing the teak timber to maturity; I believe I may give the above opinion as an axiom not to be controverted. In Great Britain, this labour is not required, as the stratification of the soil is generally known from means not possessed in this country. I may remark, from all I have heard and observed, that teak requires the same soil as oak, viz., a strong pure clay; and from the peculiar localities in which the teak forests of Malabar and Canara are found, dotted as they are over the immense tracts of jungle and forests of other woods, there is sufficient evidence of their partiality for particular soils and situations, and it may be found that there is an imperative necessity for teak being planted in the quality of soil it naturally prefers—at all events, a due consideration should be early given to this vital point by Mr C., as a tree in the latter years of its growth may become defective, from not giving timely attention to these circumstances.

"In thinning and pruning the plantations, great practical experience is required; and I should say from my observations, that in Malabar more than in any other country in which I have travelled, this arises from the great rapidity of vegetation. In the four year old plantation, an experienced planter could tell the age of the trees from the marked difference of the bark on each year's growth, which is beyond any former experience of mine in other countries. From the great weight of leaves on the upper stem in plantations of the last year's growth, if they were saturated with rain, and a squall of wind followed, they would, I think, run much risk of injury by the tops of the plants being broken off: both experience and careful superintendence on the spot would at such times be necessary.*

"The plants generally averaged twenty feet high at four years old; it is at this period (or, perhaps, during the previous year) of the growth of a plant that a knowledge of the proper means of counteracting its rapid growth in height is necessary. Thinning the plants, and allowing the air to circulate around them, gives encouragement to the lateral branches to shoot out, and by the sap flowing into them the inclination of the plant to spire up is checked; great care is necessary that this process should be gradual, and carried out cautiously as required. When the lateral shoots are well pronounced, all having a tendency to grow upwards should be cut off, a judicious selection of the main branches to be left should then be made, and the smaller branches pruned. On selecting the height on the boll of the plant, at which the first lateral branch should be allowed to stand, consideration must be given to the natural height to which a teak tree grows, and the branches should be left on the four sides, so as to counterpoise one another, and to stop the upward growth of the tree until its roots take a firm hold of the ground, and are able to supply a sufficient quantity of sap for its nourishment, so that the plant may gradually increase in substance in proportion to its height. In the use of instruments, a sharp knife is necessary for pruning plantations; in all such cases a clean cut must be given, so as to prevent the tree from being wounded. The rude instruments I saw in use will never answer in a well-conducted forest or plantation, where clean sound timber is to be produced. In the case of pruning natural-grown forest trees, a saw may be necessary for amputating a large limb, but the wound should be dressed over by the clean cut of a knife, or small axe, or some sharp instrument, to

* During a gale of wind, two years ago, several hundred trees were broken or blown over in this plantation. Much mischief is also caused by troops of monkeys springing upon the topmost branches, often breaking the leading shoot.—H. C.

prevent dampness or rain affecting it, or causing decay to follow the base of the branch into the centre (or green-wood) of the tree; great care must be taken to prevent forking in the branches, as decayed vegetable matter soon lodges in the clefts, moisture is then attracted, or wet from the rain is retained, and a rot is generally conveyed to the centre of the tree. It would appear to me, where so great an interest in the successful preservation and increase of teak plantations and forests is taken by the Hon. Co., that a competent person should be employed, whose whole time and attention should be devoted to that duty. I know that it would be satisfactory to Mr C. if he had an intelligent forester under him; and, from the conversations I held with that gentleman, I am assured that, unless he has a person possessing these qualifications, he does not see how he can do justice to a charge so purely practical; nor will his other duties allow him more time than occasionally to superintend such an establishment as will be necessary for doing the work required in the plantations or teak forests. In my own opinion, also, it appears impossible for Mr Conolly to give sufficient attention to so large a concern, and I do not see how either the plantations or the forests can have justice done to them without the constant supervision of an experienced European eye. I would not remove the duty from his charge, but I would allow him a practical forester, whose time and attention should be given, under Mr C.'s direction, to the management of the plantations and forests, and, if found practicable and advisable, his attention might likewise be directed to the growth of cardamoms, cinnamon, and other spice and valuable timber trees.

"The more I conversed with competent judges, and examined the defects of the plank timber sent down to Capt. Williams (inspector of teak timber for the dockyards of Bombay at Calicut and Cochin), the greater necessity appeared to exist that my recommendation should be followed out. The same defects in the planks occur here as at home, proceeding generally from the same causes.

"If my recommendation should be complied with, nearly all difficulties would be overcome on this head, and this most valuable produce of Malabar, so abundant a source of wealth, and so important to the State, would probably be raised to an extent and brought to a perfection hitherto unknown; but if competent practical skill and undivided attention is not given to the teak, I see no ground of hope that the supply will be greatly, if at all increased, or a field of supply created to any extent. I cannot, therefore, too strongly express my opinion of the great importance I attach to fostering the plans and supporting the exertions of Mr Conolly."

DR CLEGHORN'S REPORT TO COLLECTOR OF MALABAR.

"I this week (Aug. 1857) visited all of the extensive teak plantations on the banks of the Nelambur river, and it gives me great pleasure to bear testimony to their flourishing and satisfactory state, which promises apparently certain ultimate success, and reflects great credit both upon the judgment of the zealous originator (Mr Conolly), and upon the perseverance of Chatu Menon, the sub-conservator, who has, almost from the very beginning, tended the nurseries, and watched the young plants.

As regards the system of *planting*, I have no special improvements to suggest. The seedlings are in a most healthy and thriving condition. The rows grow with singular regularity and mathematical exactness. The latter sowings are the finest, partly because the site of Nelambur is preferable to that of Arriacode, and partly because the distance of six to eight feet between the seedlings has been found to answer much better than one yard, which was tried at first.

There seems to be only one essential to the entire success of this great experiment, viz., the careful systematic thinning and pruning of the plantation. The good effects of Mr M'Ivor's visits to Nelambur are manifest in the present state of the portions planted in 1843, 1844, and 1845, which had the benefit of his skilled treatment in 1853, 1854, and 1855.

It appears to me that a smaller piece of land should be cleared for planting next season, and that the time and labour of the establishment should be chiefly directed to prosecuting the necessary pruning and thinning, which has not been fully carried out for the last two or three years.

I was happy to find that the three daffadars, as well as the sub-conservator, were fully acquainted with the details of the system of planting, and any one of them is capable of carrying it out in other localities if required. The important point of rearing teak plantations being now fully established, it is my hope that the Conolly system of planting may be extended to the Anamalai Hills and to N. Canara.

Considering the age of Chatu Menon (58), and the serious loss which would be occasioned if he found it necessary to retire from service, it seems desirable that an assistant should be appointed to share the duties of the charge, which have increased much, as the plantation has yearly been added to, and is now too much for one individual.

The blackwood (biti) *Dalbergia latifolia* being at present almost equal in value to teak, and the available supply being also much exhausted, I would propose that an experimental sowing of this should take place. The seeds might be sown in the same manner; and at the same season as the teak. It appears to be very hardy, and grows freely in almost every soil and situation on both aspects of the Western Ghats.

I have requested the sub-conservator to draw up and forward a statement of the work usually done in each month of the year, and I shall feel much obliged by your forwarding to me a translation of the document. I do not intend to make any alteration in the system of management; and propose that the sub-conservator and his establishment remain under the collector or his assistants, trusting that the same supervision will be exercised as heretofore.* I would feel much obliged by the favour of your supplying me with an outline sketch of the Beypur River, showing the patches of land along its banks which which have been planted, thereby serving as a forest chart."

These plantations were visited by Lord Dalhousie, and afterwards inspected by Lord Harris, who expressed, in a minute,

* Subsequently the charge of these plantations was transferred to the Forest Department. An annual visit is paid by Mr M'Ivor and Mr Hall to carry out thinning and pruning to the required extent—in accordance with the wishes expressed by Lord Tweeddale and Lord Harris in their respective Minutes.

dated Nov. 1858, the high gratification he experienced in observing the result of Mr Conolly's experiment (*vide ante*, p. 41). The following information is the last on record regarding these plantations :—

EXTRACT LETTER from H. CLEGHORN, Esq., M.D., to the SECRETARY to GOVERNMENT.

27th September 1860.

Sir,—I have the honour to acknowledge the receipt of the order of Government, dated 25th inst., calling for information regarding the supply of teak-timber of large dimensions from the W. Coast for Admiralty purposes. The old forests of Malabar do not now contain much timber of frigate* scantling. In N. Canara there is abundance of teak, but a small proportion only of the first class—probably not more than one log in eight of those brought to Sedashigur. In Travancore and Cochin there is much more teak of large size. We could supply from Malabar and Canara several thousand logs annually, varying from 18 inches square and 20 feet long, to 10 inches square and 12 feet long. We have also a large number of first-rate butts 24 inches square, and not exceeding 6 or 8 feet in length. For any demand of larger sizes, I am sure Travancore and Cochin offer better prospects, and Burmah the best, as regards size and cheapness.

Inches.		Feet.	Per 50 cub. ft.
18^2	×	20	£8 0 0
15^2	×	20 .	7 10 0
12^2	×	20	7 0 0
10^2	×	20 .	6 10 0
Butts 24^2	×	6 to 8 .	5 0 0

On our coast the price of timber has very largely increased, and fluctuates greatly; at present, prices would probably run as entered above for timber brought to the water's edge. If a large and continuous supply is required for H. M. Navy, it would be advisable to establish an agency on the W. coast. The

* 18 inches square × 38 to 32 feet long, is so called on the W. Coast.

Bombay Government has now an agent, whose head-quarters are at Calicut. If this officer could not undertake the duty, a separate agent, on say Rs. 400 per mensem, with an establishment of 100 more (in round numbers), would be required. This officer would receive from our depôts, or buy from private owners, and ship the timber procured.

Looking at the increasing scarcity, and the greatly augmenting demands for timber, I think Government should begin at once to plant freely. The Conolly plantations are now beginning to pay and promise well. I would urge the doubling of the grant for this. We now plant nearly 70,000 trees annually for about Rs. 3000, which include the care of those already planted; with Rs. 6000, or only £50 per mensem, we could almost double the rate of progress, and I am confident it would prove a good investment. I have explained my views to Lieut. Beddome, who will arrange satisfactorily for this extension of operations, if Government sanction it.

Order of Government.

12th October 1860.

1. A copy of this letter will be forwarded to the Secretary of State, in reply to par. 5 of his Despatch of the 21st August, No. 60.

2. Dr Cleghorn states, that about 70,000 trees are annually planted in the Conolly plantations at a cost of about Rs. 3000, and he is confident that nearly twice as much could be done were the allowance raised to Rs. 6000. The Governor in Council considers this proposal to be one which ought certainly to be adopted. The proposed outlay is trifling, while the advantage, independently of the ultimate money profit, will be incalculable a few years hence.

1 Native Sub-Conservator,	Rs. 50
1 Assistant,	10
2 Overseers at Rs. 8,	16
1 Do.	5
Carry forward,	Rs. 81

	Brought forward,	Rs. 81
1 Daffadar,		5
7 Kolkars @ Rs. 5,		35
4 " @ Rs. 4,		16
50 Coolies @ Rs. 3½,		175
Adikar,		2½
	Total,	314½
	For twelve months,	Rs. 3774

3. Before applying for sanction, however, to the Government of India, Lieut. Beddome, to whom, it is observed, Dr C. has explained his views, will be requested to submit a detailed statement of the establishment proposed to be entertained. The annual cost of the existing establishment is found to be Rs. 3774.

4. He will also be desired to lay before Government a concise statement of the present condition of the plantations, and of the money returned received from them in the official year 1859–60.

5. This information should be submitted with as little delay as possible.

J. D. Bourdillon,
Sec. to Govt.

From Capt. H. R. Morgan, Officiating Conservator of Forests, to Secretary to Government.

27th December 1860.

1. Sir,—With reference to G. O. dated 12th Oct. 1860, I have the honour to submit a detailed statement of the increased establishment proposed for the Nelambur teak plantations.

2. The collector is of opinion that the supervision is in too great a proportion to the labour, and I agree with him, but this can be adjusted hereafter.

3. The money return for 1859–60 was as follows :—Receipts, Rs. 4715-0-0; Disbursements, Rs. 3011-0-1; Balance in favour of Government, Rs. 1703-15-11.

4. The former grant was Rs. 3000, the proposed grant amounts

to Rs. 6000, and I would strongly recommend that it be sanctioned.

5. The collector of Malabar is of opinion that the returns will equal the proposed grant; further, that 120,000 trees can be planted for the above sum.

6. Of late years, the planting of new ground has not been carried on to the extent it formerly was, consequent upon the establishment being occupied in thinning the already existing plantations (even these have not been sufficiently thinned), and the demand for an increased establishment is most urgent.

Order of Government.

15th January 1861.

The acting-conservator should at once revise the proposed establishment, so as to make the supervising duly proportionate to the working agency. The Government meanwhile sanctions that now proposed.

J. D. BOURDILLON,
Sec. to Govt.

Before leaving this subject, it ought to be stated that in 1854 Dr Falconer, in a Report to the Bengal Government, investigated the causes of the failure of teak plantations in that Presidency.* These may be briefly summed up under the following:—

"I am of opinion, that the over-crowding of the trees, by close planting, was at the root of all the failures that have followed the attempts at growing teak in plantations in Bengal." . . . . "The tenacious compact nature of the alluvial soil is unfavourable to the descent of tap-roots; and the consequence is, that the trees early acquire a tendency to throw out horizontal roots close to the surface. These very frequently form buttresses which rise up on the trunk, giving rise to what are called 'fluted boles,' which lead to great waste in converting the timber into squared logs." . . . . "Another fact of great import, as regards the diminished vigour of the teak grown in Bengal, was

* Records of Bengal Government, No. xxv.

noticed by me in a previous Report,* namely, the inferior size of the fruit or nut, which I found to be about 50 per cent. inferior in size and weight to that of the natural forests of the Tenasserim provinces. Latitude, and mere temperature, within a few degrees, would seem to be of less importance, for it is well known that excellent teak timber is grown in the valley of Nerbudda."† . . . . "But there was a grave error in the early planting arrangements, which was fatal to success. The trees were planted at intervals of 10 feet apart, and as they grew up, it never appears to have been thought necessary to thin them. The consequence was, that the trees choked and starved each other, and the plantations were irreparably injured. In these plantations, the trees, after many years' growth, were allowed to stand at 10 feet apart, whereas it has been stated in a previous communication to Government,‡ that 'first-class teak cannot be grown at a less distance apart than 40 feet, or 27-2 trees to the acre, or for useful timber of smaller scantling, 30 feet interval, giving 45-4, or in round numbers 50 trees to the acre.'

"Planting operations on a large scale have been commenced on the Madras side since 1843, with the same laudable design that led the Government of Bengal to attempt the same thing here in 1800 and 1812. The young trees have been planted to the number of 450,000, at 8 feet apart. It is to be hoped, that the failure on this side will be before them, as a beacon to warn them from committing the errors which were fallen into here, and which proved so ruinous in the end.

"H. FALCONER, M.D."

FOREST RULES IN PEGU.

1. The forests of the province of Pegu being the property of Government, the following rules are published for their conservation, and in order to ensure success for the measures taken for their future extension.

* Report on the Tenasserim Teak Forests, par. 70.

† The northern limit of teak is in Bandalkhand. *Vide* Hooker and Thomson's Flora Indica, p. 147.

‡ Report on the Tenasserim Forests, par. 88.

2. The officers appointed for the administration of the forests are—

(1.) The Superintendent.
(2.) The Assistants in Districts.
(3.) Goungs and Goung-gwais in Forest Tracts.

3. No person is permitted to girdle or to fell any teak tree, large or small, except by the express orders of the superintendent or his assistants.

4. No person is permitted to cut or break off the branches of teak trees, or otherwise injure them.

5. Other trees besides teak, which may have been girdled by order of the superintendent, are likewise neither to be felled nor removed, except by orders from the same officer.

6. The felling, or dragging of trees, which any person may be permitted to remove from the forest, must always be done in such a manner as not to break or injure any teak trees.

7. No person shall remove, or cut in pieces, or otherwise deface any teak log lying within the boundaries of any forest, except by order of the superintendent.

8. No person is permitted to set fire to any teak timber, standing or felled.

9. Should, therefore, natthat or seasoned timber, or logs, be found in a place selected for a toungya or hill-plantation, the men who intend working the toungya, before doing so must fell and remove the same to such distance that the fire of the toungya cannot reach them.

10. In the case above mentioned (No. 9.), no special permission is required for the felling or removing of teak timber to form toungyas; but information must be given of this having been done to the nearest goung-gwai, who is ordered to visit every village in his district soon after the rains.

11. No toungya is to be formed on any spot of ground on which stand any number of teak trees exceeding fifty (large or small), seedlings included. In special cases, the superintendent or his assistants may grant permission for toungyas to be formed in such spots where it appears to them that the teak cannot be made available for the use of the forest department.

12. Nurseries or plantations formed by order of the Superintendent of Forests are not to be injured in any way.

13. Whenever the superintendent or his assistants may think it fit to reserve any tract in the forest, no tree, shrub, or dead timber in the said tract is to be injured, felled, or removed, except by the servants of the forest department. No tract of a size exceeding ten acres is to be thus reserved without the special sanction of the Commissioner.

14. Whenever the Superintendent of Forests, or his assistants, may find it necessary to mark trees of any kind with the Government mark, such trees are neither to be cut or injured in any way.

15. Poles or other signs put up to mark the boundary of a reserved tract, or for other purposes; likewise sheds, bridges, fences, or buildings of any kind, together with roads, and ditches, erected or made by orders of the superintendent, are not to be removed or injured in any way.

16. It will be the duty of the forest goungs and goung-gwais to see that these rules are not violated; and should they in any case be infringed, to report the same to the superintendent or his assistants.

17. Private parties in the districts near the forests, and at a distance from the principal rivers, who may be desirous of purchasing teak timber for their own use in the district, may obtain the same by applying to the superintendent. If the application can be granted, orders will be given to the forest goung-gwais to point out the trees or logs available for the purpose. The purchasers will have to fell and to remove the timber within a fixed time. The price to be paid for the same will be settled by the superintendent, and one-fourth of it is to be paid before any timber is felled. If the timber be not removed within the time specified, it will be liable to be confiscated, and the amount paid in advance forfeited.

18. Permission to bring away branches of felled trees or other small pieces of timber, such as slabs cut off from squared logs, or the stumps remaining after the tree has been felled, will be given to parties applying for the same on their depositing a certain sum as a security, and on payment of a fixed price for one year's

grant, in one forest district. The grant, however, as well as the deposit, will be forfeited in case the parties bring away or destroy any timber besides that stipulated for.

19. Parties residing in the districts near the forest, and at a distance from the principal rivers, who may be desirous of obtaining teak timber for the erection of buildings for religious purposes, or the common benefit of the public, as Christian churches or chapels, schools, kyoungs, zayats, bridges, &c., may apply for the same through the local authorities to the deputy or assistant commissioner of the province. The latter, in case he finds it advisable to recommend the application, will forward the same to the Superintendent of Forests, who will decide whether any or the whole of the timber required can be given out of the Government forests. The applicants, to whom the timber available will be pointed out by the forest goung-gwais, will be required to fell and remove the same to the place where it is to be used, within a fixed time. Timber for these purposes will be given gratuitously; but on the expiration of a year from the time of the timber being made over to the parties, an account will be called for by the Superintendent of Forests, showing how it has been used. Should it not have been applied for the purposes specified in the application, he will be at liberty either to take possession of the timber, or to impose a fine on the parties concerned, equal to twice the average market value of the timber.

20. Any person who infringes any provision of the forest rules, or any subordinate of the forest department who wilfully neglects his duty, will be liable to a fine not exceeding two hundred rupees, and on default of payment, to imprisonment for a term not exceeding six months, without labour. In cases where the infringement involves theft of timber, the offender will be liable to be proceeded against in the criminal court.

21. All cases of violation of the forest rules may be tried and decided by the Superintendent of Forests, either by personal inquiry into the facts, or on the record of inquiry made by a forest assistant. In any case the decision, and the grounds for it, shall be recorded, and the same will be open to appeal to the Commissioner.

22. Whenever a person is sentenced to fine, and in default to

imprisonment, by the Superintendent of Forests, the person so sentenced shall be forwarded without delay to the officer in charge of the district within which the offence was committed, together with a copy of the sentence, and the said officer shall forthwith proceed to execute it.

By order of the Commissioner,

D. BRANDIS,
Supt. of Forests in Pegu.

RANGOON, 1st *Jan.* 1857.

FOREST RULES IN SIND.*

1. None of the Sind forests are rented out on contract. Timber is felled under the immediate supervision of the forest kárkún. The parties requiring timber make a written application to the forest ranger, stating the name of the forest, and the sizes and kind of timber required; an order to the forest kárkún to cut the timber is endorsed on the application. The receipt, along with actual measurements, is forwarded to the forest ranger's office, where the bill is made out and forwarded to the forest tuppedar for the recovery of the sum due. No timber is allowed to be cut without a written order from the forest ranger; and at the time of its being cut, either the kárkún or a jamâdár is present. As one or two peons are attached to the forest, valuable timber cannot easily be carried off clandestinely; at least such cases are extremely rare.

2. Fuel and timber are sold in the same manner as any other commodity. Fuel is sold by retail only at one place, leading from the forest to the town of Sukkur; it is there weighed, and the money paid to the kárkún stationed there; this kárkún is under the supervision of the forest kárkún. Fuel sold to public departments, the railway, the Indus Flotilla, &c., is paid to the forest ranger direct, the bills being made out according to the receipts forwarded by the forest kárkún to the ranger's office.

* From a Report by N. A. Dalzell, Esq., Forest Ranger, containing replies to queries forwarded by the Collector of Coimbatore.

Weekly statements of the balance of fuel are made to the forest ranger.

3. The establishment of the forest department consists of 1 forest ranger, 2 deputies, 1 inspector, 1 accountant, 1 head munshi, 1 second munshi, 2 writers, 12 forest kárkúns, 2 daroghas, 13 jamâdárs, 98 peons. The forest ranger has the general management and control over the whole department; he personally inspects the forests during six months of the year. The deputies are stationed at distant points, and assist in the inspection of the forests, sending in weekly reports of their doings. The inspector also aids in the same duties, and examines carefully the account-books of the forest kárkúns.

Each forest kárkún or tuppedar has charge of four or eight forests situated within a distance, from one end of his charge to the other, of from 15 to 50 miles. He travels almost constantly from one end of his charge to the other, transacting business, such as issuing pass-notes for grazing, looking to the preparation of fuel, paying labourers, superintending the cutting of timber, measuring the same, writing his accounts, making advances of money to woodcutters, watching the river banks, and many more things of this kind. Under each forest kárkún there is one jamâdár, who also travels about through the forests, seeing that the peons do their duty, and making reports to his immediate superior. One or two peons are attached to each forest; there they remain constantly; they seize any cattle grazing without a pass; they look after the preservation of the forest, and are in general held answerable for any damage which may be done. The total cost of the establishment is Rs. 2199 per month.

The total extent of forest under supervision is 700 square miles on the lowest computation, and thus the cost of supervision is on an average Rs. 3 per square mile per mensem. The total receipts last year, 1858–59, were Rs. 72,150, and the net profits Rs. 28,994; this year, 1859–60, the receipts are calculated at Rs. 90,000, and the net profits at Rs. 40,000. The net profits have always been a little more than the cost of establishment. It is calculated that this year, 1859–60, for every rupee expended in establishment Government will receive back Rs. 2–9–7.

BANGALORE GARDEN.

REPORT TO THE MADRAS GOVERNMENT.

Sir,—I have the honour to report the result of my recent visit to Bangalore, to confer with the Commissioner of Mysore regarding the establishment of a Horticultural Garden at that station. I left Madras on the 28th ult., arrived on the 29th, and found Mr Jaffray, the Supt. of the Madras Gardens, awaiting my arrival. The Commissioner (Sir Mark Cubbon), received me with much cordiality, entered warmly into the project, and promised his cheerful co-operation.

The first step was necessarily to determine on a suitable site. With this view, several localities were examined; and it was ultimately agreed that the Lal Bagh (formerly selected by Hyder for a garden) was, on the whole, the most eligible spot for the purpose.

The Lal Bagh comprises an area of rather more than forty acres, well situated, and sloping gently towards the north. The soil, judging from a crop of sugar-cane now on the ground, and from various other products, is generally good. The supply of water in ordinary seasons is abundant; and the tank at its upper extremity admits of easy enlargement, if this be found necessary. Water was moreover found near the surface at several places; and there are great facilities for irrigating the ground, without incurring the heavy expense of erecting and working picottahs. There is a good gateway, seed-house, and (in part) a wall, all needing repair to a trifling extent, but still in such preservation and condition as materially to lessen the preliminary outlay at starting. The only objection to this site is its distance. The road can be considerably shortened by avoiding some curves which occur in its course. Admitting this objection fully, I still do not think it of such importance as to outweigh the other advantages of the locality. It would, of course, be desirable to have the garden in the middle of the cantonment, if that were possible, for the convenience of the residents; but I do not think those persons really interested in horticulture, and therefore likely to further the object in view (and these are many), would lay much stress on this, especially when the climate of Bangalore—admitting of comfortable and healthy exercise to a late hour, and often all day—is considered. I certainly saw no other site so well adapted as the Lal Bagh in all other respects.

Some years since (1839), an Agri-Horticultural Society was established at Bangalore, under the auspices of the Commissioner, who made the Lal Bagh over to them, and afforded other assistance in the way of convict labour, &c. In all other respects, the Society was supported by private contributions; but the constantly fluctuating number of subscribers, the frequent departure of valued supporters, and other similar causes, led to the dissolution of the Society in 1842; and the garden was then restored to the Commissioner. Since that period little has, of course, been done to it beyond keeping the walks clean, &c. There are, however, some fine trees, such as West India tamarinds, Moreton Bay chestnuts, olives from the Levant, two Spanish oaks, *Calysaccion longifolium*, &c., which an able superintendent may turn to good account for ornamental purposes. The question of site having thus been disposed of, the next point is the establishment requisite.

From my experience in connection with the Madras gardens, and the results on the Nilgiris, which have followed Mr M'Ivor's employment, I have no hesitation in declaring, that the entertainment of a skilful and practical European superintendent is indispensable. The object in view is not merely to improve the culture of indigenous productions, but at the same time to naturalize exotics, and prepare both for introduction in the plains. For such purposes, European skill and ability, both theoretical and practical, are essentially necessary. I would therefore propose that a superintendent should be entertained on a salary of Rs. 150 per mensem, with a suitable residence in the gardens, or their immediate neighbourhood. An excellent house might be built for Rs.2000, or one might be rented for Rs.30 or 40 per mensem; but I should advise building in the garden in preference to renting at a distance, as the constant presence of the superintendent is a matter of great importance.

The superintendent should have a writer acquainted with English and the vernaculars, who might be engaged probably for Rs.25 per mensem. For the permanent establishment of maistries and gardeners, I should propose an allowance of Rs.125 per mensem. Extra aid might be required at particular seasons; but this cannot be estimated, and must be charged as a contingency, in common with manure, tools, &c. The fixed expenditure would thus be Rs.300 per mensem; and I am confident that it would be better economy to incur this outlay, than to attempt to carry out the project with insufficient means. For the repair of existing buildings, clearing the ground, gravelling the walks, and other preliminary work, a sum of Rs.2000 would probably suffice, with such assistance in the way of convict labour as the commissioner might find it expedient or convenient to afford at first, though such assistance must not be expected afterwards, there being objections to the permanent employment of prisoners in such a place. The expense, then, proposed would be a monthly grant of Rs. 300, and a single grant of Rs. 2000, exclusive of the sum required for the provision of a house for the superintendent.

As to management,—the garden, the superintendent, and every person connected with it, should be under the immediate and exclusive control of the Commissioner, whose decision and orders must in all cases be final. Any other course would only be attended with embarrassment; and no other is likely to ensure the success of that undertaking.

The commissioner will probably find it convenient to place the immediate superintendence of the garden under the charge of some of his subordinates, either singly or as a committee. The superintendent of the Bangalore Division, the secretary, and the surgeon for the time being, would be willing and able to relieve him of details; but this, of course, is a matter for the consideration of the Commissioner.

I am decidedly opposed to the plan of a subscription garden. It has been tried, and failed financially, and the system is attended with some serious defects. There is no single head to control operations, and carry them out systematically and continuously; and the tastes and objects of the committee of management are various. One committee considers a vegetable garden the most important—the next may incline to floriculture; and among these desultory plans and changing views of successive bodies the superintendent can do little progressive good, and is too frequently in collision with one or other of his superiors.

I propose, therefore, that the Bangalore garden should be a Government establishment, solely under the Commissioner, who will have no difficulty in framing a few simple rules for the guidance of the superintendent.

The superintendent will of course require a reasonable degree of freedom in which to exercise his talents, and experimentalise; but he must distinctly understand his position of entire subordination to the Commissioner.

As regards the course to be followed, I would recommend that while efforts be made to render the garden self-supporting, it should be borne in mind that it is not designed as a commercial speculation,—that far higher objects are in view,—and that injury instead of advantage will ultimately but certainly accrue if the gardens be suffered to enter into competition with the market-gardener, and drive him out of the field.

The great objects are the improvement of indigenous products, the introduction of exotics, the supply of these to the hills and plains when acclimatised, and the exhibition to the people of an improved system of cultivation in practical and successful operation. Seeds and plants should invariably be sold at a fair price to all applicants; but none should be given gratuitously, except for public purposes, and then only with the Commissioner's approval. By public purposes, I mean not merely for those of Government, as plantations, avenues, &c., but for distribution to scientific persons for experiment; to public institutions, &c. After providing for the Bangalore garden, those at Madras and Utakamand should be considered entitled to the preference (which of course will be mutual), and exchanges should be arranged with the Calcutta and other gardens.

As above stated, the Mysore Agri-Horticultural Society was dissolved in 1842, owing to the constantly fluctuating state of society in the station; but it is universally admitted, that much good was effected during the four years of its existence. Most of the approved European vegetables were brought into general cultivation, and several exotic fruit trees were successfully introduced, and the finer varieties propagated. Gardening among the Mysoreans received a considerable impulse, as shown by the increased quantity and improved quality of European fruits and vegetables procurable in the bazaars.

In conclusion, it appears to me, that the advantages to Southern India generally, arising from the garden in contemplation, promise to be very great, if the scheme be carried out under the superintendence of a competent person, permanently appointed to the charge.

There can be no doubt that the climate is highly favourable, and the soil capable of producing the best description of many vegetable products. Bangalore is much better suited for agricultural and horticultural experiments than either Utakamand or Madras; and, from its central position and intermediate elevation, the finer kinds of vegetables and better sorts of graft trees may be disseminated with great success to the neighbouring ranges of hills, such as the Bababuden, Ramanmalai, Shevarai, and Pulnis.

H. C.

30th August 1856.

REPORT TO COMMISSIONER OF MYSORE, 1858–59.

BANGALORE, *20th November* 1859.

SIR,—Two years having elapsed since the operations at the Lal Bagh commenced, I now submit the following account of the garden operations for the Consideration of the Commissioner, with the superintendent's summary of work, abstract of expenditure, and abstract of distribution:—

In the early part of 1856, Sir William Hooker, Director of the Royal Gardens, Kew, and the late Dr Royle, of the East India House, were solicited to assist in procuring the services of a skilled superintendent for the proposed garden. An agreement was also forwarded, specifying the terms upon which the superintendent was to be selected.

To avoid delay, a maistry gardener (Heera Lal) was engaged on a salary of Rs. 25 per mensem; and the gentlemen forming the committee (Superintendent Bangalore Division, Secretary to the Commissioner and Dr Kirkpatrick), adopted preliminary measures, with a view to preserve all the more interesting botanical specimens, and to make the grounds generally as attractive as possible. An elegant cottage, to serve as the dwelling and office of the superintendent, was completed at a cost of Rs. 2000. The garden wall has been built at a cost of Rs. 540; the walks have been gravelled and increased to 24 feet in width; and two large manure pits have been prepared.

After a delay of six months, and the interchange of several communications, one gardener of great merit having thrown up the appointment on account of the state of India, Mr New, who had been in charge of certain portions of the Royal Gardens, Kew, and who possessed high testimonials from the Committee of Management of the Belfast Garden, was selected by Sir William Hooker. Mr New reached Madras on the 4th, and Bangalore on the 10th April 1858. He brought two valuable cases of plants from the Royal Gardens at Kew, containing novelties from Australia, &c. About the same time two Wardian cases were received from the Botanical Garden, Calcutta, and one from Sydney; for the latter the garden is indebted to Mrs Pearse. A large collection of fruit trees has been received from the Government garden at Utakamand, including China limes, Malta oranges, &c.

In 1858-59 the disbursements were Rs. 6512-0-2, of which, however, Rs. 1980 were expended on buildings, and for other similar purposes, which will not recur. In this, the second year only of the garden, the large sum of Rs. 801-11-8 has been realised by sales of produce at low rates. The rest of the expenditure being met by grants from the Treasury. In future years the sanctioned amount of Rs. 300 per mensem will prove sufficient for all ordinary purposes. The general distribution of plants is increasing, as the abstract (see p. 94, *ante*) will show; and from the central position of Bangalore, I entertain no doubt that the Lal Bagh Garden will be a centre from which great benefit will radiate to the district, both by road and by rail. Measures are being taken for forming a select library of horticultural books in the superintendent's office, which will be extremely useful, and is a necessary appendage of a public garden.

H. CLEGHORN.

SUMMARY OF OPERATIONS AT THE LAL-BAGH DURING 1858–59.

During the past year much work has been done of a preliminary character. On my arrival I found the water in the tank sufficient only for a few days' supply: the early sinking of wells became a necessary step. One was commenced and sunk to the proper depth, and afterwards stoned up by contract; three others have been dug, and stones laid down in readiness for building when a sufficient depth is attained. Near the entrance a circular reservoir has been built for supplying water to the surrounding garden plants; in addition to its usefulness in this respect, it has been rendered ornamental by the introduction of select aquatic plants. Channels of brickwork are being constructed on the eastern side, for conveying water from the tank to the lower parts of the garden. They will effect a considerable saving, as heretofore much was absorbed in passing along the open ditch.

The broad carriage-drive encircling the garden has been completed, as well as the walk round the central lawn, and leading up to the tank bund; a rustic octagon for creepers has been erected, which being nearly covered with plants, has a good effect. A walk has been made on the top of the bund for its entire length, which is very much resorted to—the high position ensuring a cool breeze at any hour of the day. The bund has also been sloped and planted. Much useless and decayed timber has likewise been removed.

A small house in the central part of the garden has been repaired, and conveniently fitted up for a seed-room; on each side of it a greenhouse is being erected for the growth of such plants as require shelter in their early stages, but which eventually may be transferred with safety to the open compartments.

The outhouses erected for bullocks, tools, and garden produce are well adapted for the purpose. They are built of durable stone, found in the vicinity of the garden, and, from their tasteful design, add considerably to the beauty of this portion of the grounds.

Many of the best kinds of fruit-trees, such as apples, pears, peaches, nectarines, apricots, plums, oranges, strawberries, grapes, figs, and limes, have been obtained, and an adjoining piece of ground, which is well fenced and watered, has been set apart for their cultivation. The nursery ground is being walled, and a small pit, required for propagating purposes, has been constructed.

A set of the spice plants has been presented by E. B. Thomas, Esq., C.S., Coimbatore, who has given much useful information regarding their cultivation. The sandal and sappan trees have been raised largely from seeds and planted out, as well as the teak tree, the latter in smaller quantity, as it requires longer time to vegetate.

Of a collection of seeds and two cases of plants, presented by Sir W. Hooker, many have succeeded, and appear to suit this climate, especially those from N. Africa, Teneriffe, Madeira, and the Azores. Cape plants also do well. Australian plants are making most rapid growth. *Grevillea robusta*, received from J. Rohde, Esq., although scarcely a year planted, and then only 9 inches high, is now more than 10 feet. Some Himalayan trees, raised from seeds presented by Dr T. Thomson of Calcutta, amongst which are *Dalbergia sp.*, *Benthamia fragifera*, *Cornus macrophylla*, *Cotoneaster affinis*, &c., are thriving well. A packet of Himalayan seeds has also been received from Dr Jameson of Saharunpore.

The cultivated portion of the garden has been enlarged, the

borders round the lawn widened and rearranged, beds of choice flowers have been made on each side of the central walk, the lawn has also been carefully levelled, much of the spurious grass eradicated and replanted with a good kind.

Six young boys have been taken on trial; they have been instructed in reading, geography, &c. They appear to be tolerably intelligent.

A few plants of economic value are already contained in our collection, amongst them *Dioscorea Batatas* or Chinese yam, West India arrow-root, the Kaurie pine from New Zealand, &c. The conspicuous specimens have been legibly labelled by means of wooden tallies, giving the botanical and vernacular names.

In addition to the donations above mentioned, the following have been contributed:—Sir Mark Cubbon, seeds of coniferæ; General Beresford, various ornamental plants; Capt. Cunningham, orchids and flower seeds; Capt. Wilkinson, engineer, orchids and Cape bulbs; Capt. Puckle, numerous orchids, ferns, coffee seeds, and other plants; Capt. Mayne, engineer, garden seats; Capt. Tripe, garden seats and select creeping plants; Capt. Pearse, Australian seeds and European flower seeds; Rev. J. A. Rodgers, English vegetable seeds; Dr Paterson, hyacinth bulbs, English vegetable and flower seeds. Mr M'Ivor, Supt. of the Government garden, Utakamand, has sent fruit trees and seeds; many valuable plants and seeds have also been received from the Agri-Horticultural Society of Madras.

W. New, *Supt.*

REPORT TO THE COMMISSIONER OF MYSORE, 1859-60.

Sir,—I have the honour to forward a summary of operations in the *Lal Bagh* for the past year 1859-60. Mr New gives a truthful and modest description of what has been done; and I can aver, he has made every effort to improve the beauty of the garden, to introduce plants of value, and to distribute them as generally as possible.

Roads and Walks.—These are all in good order, gravelled, and kept free from weeds. The long metalled drive remains available for the use of carriages; and the garden is frequented by a considerable number of visitors from all classes of the community. The walk on the tank bund will be extended.

Buildings.—Mr New's cottage, the seed-house, bullock-sheds, and forcing-house, are in excellent condition; and the wall completed on the eastern boundary is a great improvement. The only work at present in contemplation is the stoning up of several wells in the fruit-garden, which are in a dilapidated condition.

Water Supply.—The construction of channels and reservoirs has been a great improvement,—economising labour, and facilitating the irrigation of distant parts of the garden.

Australian Plants.—Some of the plants received from the Government garden at Sydney have thriven beyond our expectation, particularly *Castanospermum australe*, some *Eucalypti*, and *Acacia lophantha.* The seeds received through Brigadier C. A. Browne from Melbourne have germinated well, and several species new to S. India have thus been introduced. These are planted together in the upper part of the garden, and form a group characteristic of the Flora of their native country. The temperature of Mysore is too high for some of the species received, unless they are transported to the higher ranges, as Nundidrug and the Bababuden Hills.

Tea.—A number of plants were raised from seed, and a portion of them transmitted to Nundidrug. The climate of Bangalore does not seem suitable, the seedlings not being so healthy as those at Mercara and Bababudens, where there is a higher elevation, and more moisture.

Medicinal Plants.—I have always felt that it is of great importance to introduce and extend the cultivation both of officinal and of indigenous plants reputed to possess curative properties. At present Jalap, Hyoscyamus, and Guaiac, of the former class are being cultivated,—Bæl (*Ægle Marmelos*), and *Tylophora vomitoria*, of the latter. It is hoped that the number of medicinal plants will be increased from year to year.

Cinchona.—The great experiment of introducing the Quiniferous Cinchonas of S. America will shortly be made, under the superintendence of Mr Markham. It seems desirable to concentrate our efforts at first on one or two localities in the Nilgiri Hills : and afterwards we hope to propagate this invaluable plant by seeds and cuttings in other favourable localities, as the Bababuden Hills. Meanwhile, however, I have suggested that a packet of seeds, and a number of living plants, should be entrusted to the care of Mr New.

Cultivated Plants.—It has always appeared to me, that the useful influence of these gardens over the surrounding country would be increased, by showing to the mass of the people the best mode of cultivating the indigenous crops of the district; and for this, Mr New's practical knowledge of "agriculture" fits him. During the past year, grain, potatoes, and sweet potatoes, have been grown with great success. The effects of manure, deep trenching, and clean weeding, were demonstrated to the market-gardeners and the public.

Fruit-Garden—I look for much ultimate benefit from this department. The trees are as yet too young to bear; but efforts have been made to put down the best varieties of grapes, oranges, figs, and apples.

Firewood Experiment.—In the difficulty which at present prevails in so many districts with regard to the supply of fuel, any data as to the comparative value of quick-growing trees are important. Our experience leads us to believe that *Guazuma tomentosa*, from its rapid growth, deserves special attention. *Cassia tomentosa* and *Acacia lophantha* are likewise under experiment for the same reason, and give good promise.

A catalogue has been made of interesting plants introduced during the year, exclusive of the medicinal plants before-mentioned. The coniferæ, *P. longifolia*, cypresses, and deodar, appear to thrive well.

The Commissioner will be glad to observe that 2000 seedlings have been prepared for the railway department; and I believe 500 trees have been supplied for planting the neighbourhood of the dragoon barracks.

From a comparison of the receipts and expenditure of the past two years, it will be seen that, while in 1858–59, the sales realized Rs. 801-11-8 ; in 1859-60 the receipts rose to Rs. 2904-11-0 being an increase of Rs.2102-15-8. This result must be considered *highly satisfactory*.

One interesting feature ought to be noticed, viz., that native gentlemen and market-gardeners visit the garden, and make purchases, especially of grafted fruit-trees.

An interchange of plants has been arranged with the Calcutta, Madras, and Utakamand Gardens, with the Royal Garden, Peradenia, Ceylon, and also with those at Sydney and Melbourne.

SUMMARY OF OPERATIONS AT THE LAL BAGH DURING 1859–60.

Greenhouses.—Since the date of my last summary, the greenhouses on each side of the seed-room have been completed. The glass and wood-work having been done by contract, at a cost of Rs.671-9-9, these structures have been already of great value in forwarding specimens for out-door planting. In them the bread-fruit trees were reared, which have been planted out in the garden, as well as distributed to the four divisions of Mysore.

Terrace and Brickpit.—A terrace, surrounding the above, with three flights of stone steps, has been nearly completed. The large amount of material necessary to fill the brickpit in the rear has been a source of heavy labour.

Water Channels and Reservoirs.—The formation of channels for conducting water over the garden has been vigorously proceeded with during the hot months; 2094 yards of brick and chunam drains have been constructed, and 42 reservoirs, each 2 feet square, have been built in the most convenient sites for economising labour.

New Ground on East Side.—The eastern boundary fence has been removed for a distance of fifty yards.

Australian Eucalypti.—The low ground near the bund has been considerably raised, by the addition of new earth, and a row of Australian *Eucalypti* planted in it, by the side of the carriage road. The situation seems to be well adapted for these plants, many of them being now fifteen feet high.

Tea Plants.—Some tea plants, raised from seeds sent by Dr Cleghorn from Kunur, have been planted upon the slope of the bund; a few have also been forwarded to Nundidrug for trial, where the climate may be more suitable for their growth.

Walks.—Suitable walks have been constructed, leading from the large reservoir near the gate to the carriage road on both sides of the garden. Plants of *Michelia*, *Benthamia*, *Latania*, *Kniphofia*, &c., have been put down in the adjoining borders.

Jalap Plants.—Some plants of the true jalap (*Exogonium Purga*), raised from seed sent by Dr Cleghorn, have grown, and flowered so freely, that a considerable quantity of seeds have been obtained from them. Preparations are being made for putting down a large quantity of this useful drug.

Plants added to Collection.—A number of valuable and interesting plants have been added to the collection during the year. The names are given in the Catalogue of Garden Plants which follows.

Crops.—Crops of various kinds have been grown on the cultivatable parts of the garden, chiefly with the view of clearing the ground of noxious weeds, and preparing it for the reception of permanent plants; and also to show the natives a careful and neat system of agriculture.

Timber Trees for Railway.—Two thousand timber trees have been reared for the Railway Company, and are now in baskets, ready for removal during the rains.

Firewood Experiment.—Seeds of two Australian species of Acacia, considered valuable on the Nilgiri hills for firewood, have been furnished by Dr C. for trial here; one of them (*A. lophantha*), is a most rapid grower, and appears to suit this climate well.

Fruit-Garden.—In the fruit-garden walks have been constructed, and many additional trees planted; a large well is being stoned up; two structures for grapes have been erected on the adjoining high ground.

Donations.—The gift by Abdoolah Sahib of the large specimen (15 feet high) of *Araucaria excelsa*, which adorns the lawn, deserves special acknowledgment. The following contributions have also been received:—General Cullen, tubers of *Cyrtopera Cullenii*;

Brigadier Pole, English flower seeds; Captain G. M. Martin, two plants of *Amherstia nobilis;* Dr Cleghorn, a constant supply of indigenous and other seeds; J. Rohde, Esq., bulbs and other plants; Dr Thomson, valuable Himalayan seeds, also a collection of American vegetable seeds; Mr Moore, Sydney, a Wardian case of valuable plants, and a package of seeds.

Interchanges.—Plants have been interchanged with the Agri-Horticultural Society's Garden, Madras, and with the Government garden, Utakamand. Seeds have also been furnished to the Botanic Garden, Bombay.

William New.

1*st May* 1860.

Note.—The catalogue of the plants in the Bangalore Garden is appended. This being the first organised effort to introduce exotics into Mysore, the result will be full of interest, though a sufficient length of time has not elapsed to ascertain to what extent they may be cultivated successfully.

H. C.

CATALOGUE OF PLANTS

IN THE

PUBLIC GARDEN, BANGALORE, June 1861.*

I. PHANEROGAMS.

a. Dicotyledons.

1. *Ranunculaceæ.*
Naravelia zeylanica, *Dec.*
Clematis Gouriana, *Roxb.*
coriacea, *Dec.*
Adonis autumnalis, *L.*
Nigella damascena, *L.*
Aquilegia vulgaris, *L.*
Delphinium Consolida, *L.*
Ajacis, *L.*

2. *Dilleniaceæ.*
Dillenia speciosa, *Thunb.*

3. *Magnoliaceæ.*
Michelia Champaca, *L.*
Nilagirica, *Zenker.*

4. *Anonaceæ.*
Uvaria sp. (*Anamalais.*)
Anona squamosa, *L.*
reticulata, *L.*
muricata, *L.*
Artabotrys odoratissimus, *Br.*
Guatteria longifolia, *Wall.*

5. *Berberaceæ.*
Berberis aristata, *Dec.*

6. *Nymphæaceæ.*
Nymphæa Lotus, *L.*
Nelumbium speciosum, *Willd.*

7. *Papaveraceæ.*
Papaver Rhœas, *L.*
somniferum, *L.*
dubium, *L.*
Argemone mexicana, *L.*
Chryseis californica, *Lindl.*
tenuifolia, *Lindl.*
Glaucium luteum, *Sm.*

8. *Fumariaceæ.*
Fumaria parviflora, *Lam.*, var. Vaillantii.

9. *Cruciferæ.*
Matthiola annua, *R. Br.*
Cheiranthus Cheiri, *L.*
Nasturtium officinale, *L.*
Capsella Bursa-pastoris, *L.*
Iberis umbellata, *L.*
odorata, *L.*
Malcomia maritima, *L.*
var. alba.
Erysimum Peroffskianum, *F.* et *M.*
Lepidium sativum, *L.*
Brassica oleracea, *L.*
Raphanus sativus, *L.*
Heliophila araboides, *Sims.*
Schizopetalon Walkeri, *Sims.*

10. *Resedaceæ.*
Reseda odorata, *L.*

* Drawn up at Dr Cleghorn's request by Mr William New, superintendent, and communicated to the Botanical Society of Edinburgh 11th July 1861.

11. *Capparidaceæ.*
Gynandropsis pentaphylla, *Dec.*
Cleome purpurea, *L.*

12. *Bixaceæ.*
Bixa Orellana, *L.*

13. *Cistaceæ.*
Cistus purpureus, *Lam.*
Helianthemum vulgare, *Gært.*

14. *Violaceæ.*
Viola odorata, *L.*
tricolor, *L.*
Walkeri, *Wight.*
Ionidium suffruticosum, *Ging.*

15. *Droseraceæ.*
Drosera intermedia, *Hayn.*

16. *Polygalaceæ.*
Polygala speciosa, *Dec.*
arvensis, *Willd.*

17. *Pittosporaceæ.*
Pittosporum flavum, *Hook.*
undulatum, *Vent.*
coriaceum, *Ait.*
salicinum, *Lindl.*

18. *Caryophyllaceæ.*
Gypsophila elegans, *Bieb.*
Stellaria media, *L.*
Cerastium vulgatum, *L.*
Dianthus barbatus, *L.*
deltoides, *L.*
Caryophyllus, *L.*
var. plena.
plumarius, *L.*
sinensis, *L.*
var. plena.
Saponaria calabrica, *Bieb.*
Silene Armeria, *L.*
quinquevulnera, *L.*
pendula, *L.*
Viscaria oculata, *Lindl.*
Lychnis Chalcedonica, *L.*

19. *Linaeæ.*
Linum usitatissimum, *L.*
var. alba.
grandiflorum, *Desf.*
trigynum, *L.*

20. *Malvaceæ.*
Malope trifida, *Cav.*
Malva sylvestris, *L.*
Althæa rosea, *Cav.* vars.
Urena lobata, *L.*
Pavonia odorata, *Willd.*
Lavatera Thuringiaca, *L.*
Hibiscus tricuspis, *Cav.*
Lindleyi, *Wall.*
vitifolius, *L.*
cannabinus, *L.*
Rosa-sinensis, *L.*
rubro-plenus.
flavo-plenus.
carneo-plenus.
grandiflorus.
radiatus, *Cav.*
mutabilis, *L.*
var. plena.
Sabdariffa, *L.*
syriacus, *L.*
var. plena.
liliiflorus, *Cav.*
Lampas, *Cav.*
esculentus, *L.*
vesicarius, *Cav.*
Thespesia populnea, *Corr.*
Gossypium herbaceum, *L.*
Barbadense, *L.*
acuminatum, *L.*
Abutilon striatum, *Dicks.*

21. *Bombaceæ.*
Adansonia digitata, *L.*
Eriodendron anfractuosum, *Dec.*
Ochroma Lagopus, *L.*
Bombax malabaricum, *Dec.*
Helicteres Isora, *L.*
Kleinhovia hospita, *L.*
Guazuma tomentosa, *H. B. K.*
Dombeya palmata, *Cav.*
Brachychiton acerifolium, *Schott.*
Visenia velutina, *Voigt.*

22. *Tiliaceæ.*
Corchorus acutangulus, *Lam.*
Triumfetta angulata, *Lam.*
Grewia asiatica, *L.*
Berrya Ammonilla, *Roxb.*
Elæocarpus serratus, *L.*

23. *Ternströemiaceæ.*
Cochlospermum Gossypium, *Dec.*
Thea viridis, *L.*
Camellia japonica, *L.*

24. *Aurantiaceæ.*
Atalantia monophylla, *Dec.*
Triphasia trifoliata, *Dec.*
Glycosmis pentaphylla, *Corr.*
Bergera Kœnigii, *L.*
Murraya exotica, *L.*
Feronia Elephantum, *Corr.*
Ægle Marmelos, *Corr.*
Citrus decumana, *L.*
Aurantium, *Risso.*
Bergamia, *Risso.*
Limonum, *Risso.*
medica, *Risso.*

25. *Hyperiaceæ.*
Hypericum mysurense.

26. *Guttiferæ.*
Calophyllum inophyllum, *L.*
Calysaccion longifolium, *Wight.*
Garcinia coniocarpa, *Wight.*

27. *Erythroxylaceæ.*
Sethia indica, *Dec.*

28. *Malpighiaceæ.*
Malpighia punicifolia, *Dec.*
heteranthera, *Wight.*
Banisteria laurifolia, *L.*
Stigmaphyllon aristatum, *A. de J.*
Hiptage Madablota, *Gært.*

29. *Sapindaceæ*
Cardiospermum Helicacabum, *L.*
Sapindus emarginatus, *Vahl.*
Sapindus fruticosus, *Roxb.*
Nephelium Litchi, *W.* et *A.*

30. *Meliaceæ.*
Melia Azidarach, *L.*
Azidarachta indica, *Juss.*
Munronia Nilagirica, *Wight.*

31. *Cedrelaceæ.*
Cedrela Toona, *Roxb.*
Chloroxylon Swietenia, *Dec.*

32. *Ampelidaceæ.*
Vitis quadrangularis, *Wall.*
vinifera, *L.*
Ampelopsis Roylii, *Hort.*

33. *Geraniaceæ.*
Pelargonium inquinans, *Ait.*
Radula, *L'Herit.*
zonale, *Willd.*

34. *Tropæolaceæ.*
Tropæolum majus, *L.*
minus, *L.*
canariense, *L.*
Lobbianum, *Hook.*

35. *Balsaminaceæ.*
Balsamina hortensis, *Dec.*
var. plena.

36. *Oxalidaceæ.*
Averrhoa Bilimbi, *L.*
Oxalis corniculata, *L.*
variabilis, *Jacq.*
sensitiva, *L.*

37. *Zygophyllaceæ.*
Guaiacum officinale, *L.*

38. *Rutaceæ.*
Diosma virgata, *Thunb.*
Ruta graveolens, *L.*

39. *Ochnaceæ.*
Ochna squarrosa, *L.*

40. *Coriaceæ.*
Coriaria nepalensis, *L.*

41. *Celastraceæ.*
Celastrus emarginata, *Willd.*
Ilex cornuta, *Lindl.*

42. *Rhamnaceæ.*
Zizyphus Jujuba, *Lam.*
Ceanothus triquetrus, *Dec.*

43. *Homaliaceæ.*
Aristotelia Macqui, *L.*

44. *Terebinthaceæ.*
Odina Wodier, *Roxb.*
Rhus lanceolata, *L.*
Mangifera indica, *L.*
Anacardium occidentale, *L.*
Semicarpus Anacardium, *L.*
Spondias Mangifera, *Pers.*

45. *Moringaceæ.*
Moringa pterygosperma, *Gært.*

46. *Leguminosæ.*
Piptanthus nepalensis, *Don.*
Podalyria sericea, *Lam.*
Lupinus Hartwegii, *Benth.*
mutabilis, *Sweet.*
luteus, *L.*
pubescens, *Benth.*
polyphyllus, *L.*
Crotalaria juncea, *L.*
retusa, *L*
bifaria, *L.*
verrucosa, *L.*
laburnifolia, *L.*
mysorensis, *Roxb.*
Rothia trifoliata, *Pers.*
Ulex nanus, *Willd.*
Spartium junceum, *L.*
Cytisus albus, *L.*
Laburnum, *L.*
intermedium, *Marnock.*
Lotus jacobæus, *L.*
Trifolium pratense, *L.*, var.
Trigonella Fœnum-græcum, *L.*
Medicago sativa, *L.*
Indigofera enneaphylla, *L.*
hirsuta, *L.*
pulcherrima, *L.*
atropurpurea, *Ham.*
violacea, *Roxb.*
Tephrosia candida, *Dec.*
Wistaria sinensis, *Dec.*
Robinia Pseud-acacia, *L.*
Sesbania ægyptiaca, *Pers.*
Agati grandiflorum, *Desv.*
var. alba.
Clianthus puniceus, *Sol.*
Sutherlandia frutescens, *Br.*
Swainsonia galegifolia, *Salisb.*
Cicer arietinum, *L.*
Pisum sativum, *L.*
Vicia Faba, *L.*
Lathyrus grandiflorus, *L.*
odoratus, *L.*
Arachis hypogæa, *L.*
Æschynomene aspera, *L.*
Desmodium triflorum, *L.*
Hedysarum coronarium, *L.*
Onobrychis sativa, *L.*
Clitoria ternatea, *L.*
Kennedya rubicunda, *Ven.*
monophylla, *Ven.*
Canavalia gladiata, *Dec.*
Mucuna prurita, *Hook.*
Erythrina indica, *L.*
var. alba.
ovalifolia, *Roxb.*
Blakii, *B. N.*
secundiflora, *Brot.*
suberosa, *Roxb.*
laurifolia, *Jacq.*
Butea frondosa, *Roxb.*
Dolichos uniflorus, *Lam.*
Lablab vulgare, *Savi.*
Psophocarpus tetragonolobus, *Dec.*
Cajanus indicus, *Spreng.*
Cantharospermum pauciflorum, *W. et A.*
Abrus precatorius, *L.*
Pterocarpus marsupium, *Roxb.*
Brachypterum scandens, *Bth.*

Pongamia glabra, *Vent.*
Dalbergia latifolia, *Roxb.*
Sissoo, *Roxb.*
Edwardsia grandiflora, *Salisb.*
Sophora tomentosa, *L.*
Virgilia capensis, *L.*
Castanospermum australe, *A. Cunn.*
Hæmatoxylon campechianum, *L.*
Parkinsonia aculeata, *L.*
Poinciana pulcherrima, *L.*
var. lutea.
regia, *Bojer.*
elata, *L.*
Cæsalpinia Sappan, *L.*
sepiaria, *Roxb.*
Coriaria, *Willd.*
digyna, *Rottl.*
Cathartocarpus Fistula, *Pers.*
Roxburghii, *Dec.*
Cassia alata, *L.*
florida, *Vahl.*
aurata, *Roxb.*
glauca, *Lam.*
Amherstia nobilis, *Wall.*
Jonesia Asoca, *Roxb.*
Tamarindus indica, *L.*
var. in occ.
Bauhinia purpurea, *L.*
var. alba.
acuminata, *L.*
variegata, *L.*
tomentosa. *L.*
Adenanthera pavonina, *L.*
Prosopis spicigera, *L.*
Mimosa rubricaulis, *L.*
Acacia robusta, *Burch.*
lophantha, *Willd.*
mucronata, *Willd.*
verticillata, *Willd.*
speciosa, *Willd.*
suaveolens, *Willd.*
longifolia, *Willd.*
stricta, *Willd.*
Albizzia Julibrissin, *Durazz.*
Inga Hæmatoxylon, *Willd.*
Houstoni, *Willd.*
dulcis, *Willd.*

47. *Rosaceæ.*

Amygdalus persica, *L.*
Armeniaca vulgaris, *Lam.*
Prunus domestica, *L.*
Kerria japonica, *Dec.*, var. plena.
Geum coccineum, *L.*
Rubus biflorus, *Ham.*
rosæfolius, *Sm.*, var. plena.
Fragaria virginiana, *Mill*, var.
Rosa Damascena, *Mill.*
rubiginosa, *L.*
indica, *L.*
multiflora, *Thunb.*
moschata, *Mill.*
centifolia, *L.*
Lawrenciana, *Sweet.*
pomponia, *Dec.*, var. De Meaux.
Eriobotrya japonica, *Lindl.*
Cotoneaster affinis, *Lindl.*
buxifolia.
microphylla.
Pyrus communis, *L.*
Malus, *L.*

48. *Granateæ.*

Punica Granatum, *L.*

49. *Combretaceæ.*

Terminalia Catappa, *L.*
Bellerica, *Roxb.*
Poivrea purpurea, *Commers.*
Combretum densiflorum.
grandiflorum, *G. Don.*
comosum, *G. Don.*
Quisqualis indica, *L.*

50. *Onagraceæ.*

Fuchsia serratifolia, *Hook.*
corymbiflora, *Lindl.*
(many vars.)
Gaura Lindheimerii, *Spach.*
Eucharidium concinnum, *F.* et *M.*
Clarkia pulchella, *Pursh.*
Godetia Lindleyana, *Spach.*
Œnothera suaveolens, *L.*

51. *Haloragaceæ.*
Myriophyllum intermedium, *Dec.*

52. *Lythraceæ.*
Ameletia indica, *Dec.*
Cuphea platycentra, *Benth.*
Lawsonia inermis, *L.*
Lafoensia Vandelliana, *Dec.*
Lagerströemia indica, L.
var. alba.
Reginæ, *Roxb.*

53. *Myrtaceæ.*
Psidium pyriferum, *L.*
var. variegata.
pomiferum, *L.*
Cattleyanum, *Sabine.*
Acklandæ.
Eucalyptus robusta, *Sm.*
concinna.
globulus, *Lab.*
perfoliata, *Desf.*
virgata, *Sieb.*
Myrtus communis, *L.*
Rhodomyrtus tomentosus, *Dec.*
Jambosa vulgaris, *Dec.*
malaccensis, *Dec.*
Barringtonia speciosa, *Forst.*
racemosa, *Blum.*
Careya arborea, *Roxb.*

54. *Cucurbitaceæ.*
Zanonia indica, *L.*
Bryonia scabrella, *L.*
Momordica Charantia, *L.*
Benincasa cerifera, *Savi.*
Lagenaria vulgaris, *Ser.*
Cucumis Melo, *L.*
sativus, *L.*
Trichosanthes anguina, *L.*
palmata, *Roxb.*
Cucurbita maxima, *Duch.*
Citrullus, *L.*
ovifera, *L.*

55. *Papayaceæ.*
Carica Papaya, *L.*
Modecca palmata, *L.*

56. *Passifloraceæ.*
Passiflora alata, *Ait.*
minima, *Jacq.*
Leschenaultii, *Dec.*
quadrangularis, *L.*
laurifolia, *L.*
serratifolia, *L.*
cuneifolia, *Cav.*
cærulea, *L.*
kermesina, *Sk.* et *Otto.*
var. purpurea.
fœtida, *Cav.*
Middletoniana, *Paxt.*
Murucuja ocellata, *Pers.*

57. *Turneraceæ.*
Turnera ulmifolia, *L.*
var. angustifolia.

58. *Loasaceæ.*
Bartonia aurea, *Sims.*
Blumenbachia insignis, *Schr.*
Cajphora lateritia, *Hook.*

59. *Portulaceæ.*
Portulaca quadrifida, *L.*
Thellusonii, *Dec.*
grandiflora, *Hook.*
oleracea, *L.*
Calandrinia Lindleyana, *Dec.*

60. *Crassulaceæ.*
Kalanchoe crenata, *Haw.*
Bryophyllum calycinum, *Sal.*
pinnatum, *Hook.*
Sempervivum tabulæforme, *Haw.*

61. *Ficoideæ.*
Mesembryanthemum tricolor, *L.*
crystallinum, *L.*
pomeridianum, *L.*
Glinus trianthemoides, *Heyne.*
Tetragonia expansa, *L.*

62. *Cactaceæ.*
Opuntia Dillenii, *Haw.*
spinosissima, *Haw.*
cochinellifera, *Haw.*
Cereus erectus, *Haw.*

Cereus crenatus, *Hook.*
Epiphyllum truncatum, *Pfeiffer.*
Pereskia Bleo, *H. B. Kth.*

63. *Saxifragaceæ.*

Hydrangea hortensis, *L.*
japonica, *L.*

64. *Umbelliferæ.*

Hydrocotyle asiatica, *L.*
Didiscus cæruleus, *Dec.*
Apium graveolens, *L.*
Petroselinum sativum, *Hoffm.*
Carum Carui, *L.*
Fœniculum vulgare, *Adans.*
Pastinaca sativa, *L.*
Daucus Carota, *L.*
Coriandrum sativum, *L.*

65. *Araliaceæ.*

Panax fruticosum, *L.*
cochleatum, *L.*
Hedera Helix, *L.*

66. *Caprifoliaceæ.*

Cornus macrophylla, *Wall.*
Benthamia fragifera, *Lindl.*
Lonicera Leschenaultii, *Wall.*

67. *Loranthaceæ.*

Loranthus loniceroides, *L.*

68. *Rubiaceæ.*

Spermacoce hispida, *L.*
Chasalia thyrsiflora, *Thwaites.*
Coffea arabica, *L.*
Pavetta indica, *L.*
Ixora coccinea, *L.*
parviflora, *Vahl.*
Bandhuca, *Roxb.*
undulata, *Roxb.*
Chiococca racemosa, *Jacq.*
Hamelia patens, *Jacq.*
Pentas carnea, *Benth.*
Rondeletia speciosa, *Todd.*
Bouvardia triphylla, *L.*
Manettia glabra, *L.*
Cinchona Calisaya, *L.*, vars.
Nauclea parviflora, *Roxb.*
Randia dumetorum, *L.*
Gardenia florida, *L.*
var. plena.
Mussænda frondosa, *L.*

69. *Valerianaceæ.*

Centranthus ruber, *Dec.*
macrosiphon, *Dec.*

70. *Dipsacaceæ.*

Scabiosa atropurpurea, *L.*
Knautia orientalis, *L.*

71. *Compositæ.*

Ageratum mexicanum, *L.*
Aster amelloides, *L.*
Callistephus chinensis, *Dec.*
Vittadenia triloba, *Dec.*
Bellis perennis, *L.*
Brachycome iberidifolia, *Benth.*
Centauridium Drummondii, *Tor.* et *Gray.*
Pluchea indica, *L.*
Eclipta prostrata, *L.*
Dahlia variabilis, *Desf.*
Siegesbeckia orientalis, *L.*
Melampodium macranthum.
Xanthium orientale, *L.*
Zinnia elegans, *L.*
var. plena.
Guizotia oleifera, *Dec.*
Rudbeckia digitata, *Ait.*
Dracopis amplexicaulis, *Cass.*
Gymnopsis uniserialis, *Hook.*
Calliopsis bicolor, *Rchb.*
Drummondii, *Hook.*
coronata, *Hook.*
Coreopsis lanceolata, *L.*
Helianthus tuberosus, *L.*
annuus, *L.*
Bidens chilensis, *L.*
Spilanthes oleracea, *L.*
Ximenesia encelioides, *Cass.*
Sanvitalia procumbens, *Juss.*
Tagetes patula, *L.*
erecta, *L.*
Gaillardia picta, *Hook.*

Gutierrezia gymnospermoides, *Tor.* et *Gray.*
Helenium tenuifolium, *Nutt.*
Galinsoga brachystephana, *R.* et *Pav.*
Sogalgina triloba, *Dec.*
Sphenogyne speciosa, *R. Br.*
Madia viscosa, *Dec.*
Madaria elegans, *Dec.*
Cladanthus proliferus, *Dec.*
Achillea Millefolium, *L.*
Leucanthemum vulgare, *Dec.*
Pyrethrum Parthenium, *L.*
Chrysanthemum indicum, *L.*
tricolor, *L.*
Argyranthemum frutescens, *Webb.*
Dimorphotheca pluvialis, *Dec.*
Cotula australis, *Hook. fil.*
Cenia turbinata, *Commers.*
Artemisia indica, *Willd.*
Abrotanum, *L.*
Ammobium alatum, *R. Br.*
Humea elegans, *Sm.*
Rhodanthe Manglesii, *Lindl.*
Acroclinium roseum, *Hook.*
Helichrysum bracteatum, *Don.*
var. alba.
Cacalia sempervirens, *Vahl.*
Cineraria lanata, *Willd.*, var.
Senecio Cineraria, *Dec.*
Jacobæa, *L.*
Calendula arvensis, *L.*
Osteospermum spinosum, *L.*
Echinops echinatus, *Roxb.*
Xeranthemum cylindraceum, *Dec.*
Centaurea Cyanus, *L.*
Amberboa moschata, *Dec.*
Carthamus tinctorius, *L.*
Onopordum Acanthium, *L.*
Cynara Scolymus, *L.*
Cichorium Intybus, *L.*
Tragopogon porrifolius, *L.*
Lactuca sativa, *L.*

72. *Lobeliaceæ.*

Lobelia Erinus, *L.*
heterophylla, *Cav.*
syphilitica, *L.*
Pratia angulata, *Hook. fil.*

73. *Campanulaceæ.*

Campanula Vidalii, *H. C. Wat.*
rapunculoides, *L.*
Specularia Speculum, *Dec.*
Trachelium cæruleum, *L.*

74. *Gesneraceæ.*

Gesneria tubiflora, *L.*
Achimenes longiflora, *Hook.*
pedunculata, *Benth.*
Gloxinia speciosa, *Bot. Reg.*

75. *Myrsinaceæ.*

Ardisia crenulata, *Ven.*
polycephala, *Wall.*
Jacquinia ruscifolia, *L.*
Corynocarpus lævigatus, *Forst.*

76. *Sapotaceæ.*

Achras Sapota, *L.*
Mimusops Elengi, *L.*
Bassia latifolia, *Roxb.*
longifolia, *L.*

77. *Ebenaceæ.*

Diospyros Sapota, *Roxb.*

78. *Oleaceæ.*

Noronhia emarginata, *Poir.*
Ligustrum sinense, *Hort.*

79. *Jasminaceæ.*

Jasminum Sambac, *Ait.*
var. plena.
latifolium, *Roxb.*
auriculatum, *Vahl.*
ligustrifolium, *Wall.*
trinerve, *Vahl.*
heterophyllum, *Roxb.*
revolutum, *Sims.*
officinale, *L.*
Nyctanthes arbor tristis, *L.*

80. *Asclepiadaceæ.*

Cryptostegia grandiflora, *R. Br.*
Hemidesmus indicus, *R. Br.*

Calatropis gigantea, *R. Br.*
Sarcostemma brevistigma, *W.* et *A.*
Oxystelma esculentum, *R. Br.*
Gomphocarpus fruticosus, *R. Br.*
Asclepias curassavica, *L.*
Tylophora asthmatica, *R. Br.*
Pergularia odoratissima, *L.*
Stephanotis floribunda, *Thouars.*
Hoya carnosa, *Browne.*
imperialis, *Hook.*
ovata.
Ceropegia ensifolia.
Jacquemontiana.
fimbriata, *E. Mey.*
juncea, *Roxb.*
Boucerosia umbellata, *W.* et *A.*
Stapelia revoluta, *Mass.*

81. *Apocynaceæ.*
Allamanda cathartica, *L.*
Schottii, *Pohl.*
Thevetia neriifolia, *Juss.*
Cerbera Odollam, *Gærtn.*
Tabernæmontana coronaria, *R. Br.*
Vinca rosea, *L.*
var. alba.
Plumieria acuminata, *Ait.*
alba, *Jacq.*
Vallaris dichotoma, *Wall.*
Beaumontia grandiflora, *Wall.*
Wrightia mollissima, *Wall.*
antidysenterica, *R. Br.*
Nerium odorum, *Ait.*
var. plena.
Echites suberecta, *Willd.*
picta.
paniculata, *Roxb.*

82. *Strychneæ.*
Strychnos Nux-vomica, *L.*
potatorum, *L.*

83. *Pedaliaceæ.*
Sesamum indicum, *L.*
Pedalium Murex, *L.*
Martynia fragrans, *L.*
craniolaria, *Swz.*

84. *Bignoniaceæ.*
Bignonia suberosa, *Roxb.*
venusta, *Ker.*
gracilis, *B. Cav.*
xylocarpa, *Roxb.*
Amphilophium Mutisii, *H. Birk.*
Spathodea adenophylla, *Wall.*
crispa, *Wall.*
campanulatā.
Stereospermum suaveolens, *Dec.*
chelonoides, *Dec.*
Tecoma capensis, *Lindl.*
jasminoides, *G. Don.*
Stans, *Juss.*
Eccremocarpus scaber, *Ruiz* et *Pav.*

85. *Cobæaceæ.*
Cobæa scandens, *Cav.*

86. *Polemoniaceæ.*
Phlox Drummondii, *Hook.*
Collomia linearis, *Nutt.*
Gilia tricolor, *Benth.*
Leptosiphon densiflorus, *Bth.*
aureus, *Benth.*
Ipomopsis elegans, *Rich.*

87. *Convolvulaceæ.*
Evolvulus alsinoides, *L.*
Porana volubilis, *Burm.*
Convolvulus parviflorus, *Vahl.*
tricolor, *L.*
var. alba.
Jacquemontia violacea, *Chois.*
Exogonium Purga, *Chois.*
Calonyction Roxburghii, *Chois.*
Ipomœa sinuata, *Ort.*
Pes-capræ, *Sweet.*
sessiliflora, *Roth.*
coccinea, *L.*
Nil, *L.*
Quamoclit phœniceum, *Choisy.*
var. alba.
Batatas edulis, *Choisy.*
betacea, *Choisy.*
Pharbitis hispida, *Choisy.*
cærulea, *Choisy.*

Argyreia speciosa, *Swt.*
cuneata, *Ker.*

88. *Cuscutaceæ.*

Cuscuta reflexa, *Roxb.*

89. *Boraginaceæ.*

Cerinthe major, *L.*
Echium vulgare, *L.*
Nonea lutea, *Dec.*
Myosotis arvensis, L.
palustris, *L.*
Borago officinalis, *L.*
Trichodesma indicum, *R. Br.*
Tiaridium indicum, *Lehm.*
Heliotropium peruvianum, *L.*
Omphalodes linifolia, *Lehm.*

90. *Cordiaceæ.*

Cordia Myxa, *L.*
Sebestena, *L.*

91. *Hydrophyllaceæ.*

Nemophila insignis, *Dougl.*
maculata, *Benth.*
atomaria, *Fisch.*
discoidalis, *Fisch.*
Eutoca viscida, *R. Br.*
Whitlavia grandiflora, *Harv.*
Phacelia congesta, *Hook.*

92. *Solanaceæ.*

Habrothamnus elegans, *Endl.*
Petunia nyctaginiflora, *Juss.* var.
Nicotiana Tabacum, *L.*
Datura Stramonium, *L.*
fastuosa, *L.*
chlorantha, var. plena.
Nicandra physaloides, *Gærtn.*
Capsicum annuum, *L.*
frutescens, *L.*
Physalis peruviana, *L.*
flexuosa, *L.*
Solanum arboreum, *H.* et *B.*
Balbisii, *Duval.*
tuberosum, *L.*
nigrum, *L.*
giganteum, *Jacq.*
Lycopersicum esculentum, *Mill.*
Brugmansia suaveolens, *Wen.*

93. *Scrophulariaceæ.*

Browallia elata, *L.*
demissa, *L.*
Brunsfelsia americana, *L.*
Salpiglossis sinuata, *R.* et *P.*
Schizanthus pinnatus, *R.* et *P.*
Calceolaria hybrida, *Hort.*
Verbascum Thapsus, *L.*
Alonosa Warcewitzii.
Angelonia salicariæfolia, *Kth.*
Linaria bipartita, *Desf.*
Antirrhinum majus, *L.*
Maurandia Barclayana, *Ldl.*
Lophospermum scandens, *Hook.*
Phygelius capensis, *Mey.*
Collinsia bicolor, *Bth.*
grandiflora, *Bth.*
Pentstemon Hartwegii, *Bth.*
campanulatus, *Willd.*
Russelia juncea, *Zucc.*
multiflora, *H. B. K.*
Mimulus moschatus, *L.*
Torenia asiatica, *L.*
var.
cordifolia, *Roxb.*
Digitalis purpurea, *L.*
Veronica spicata, *L.*
Franciscea eximia, *Scheidw.*
uniflora, *Pohl.*
Crescentia alata, *H. B. K.*

94. *Labiatæ.*

Ocimum canum, *Sims.*
basilicum, *L.*
sanctum, *L.*
Plectranthus tuberosus, *Roxb.*
Coleus barbatus, *Bth.*
aromaticus, *Bth.*
Lavandula vera, *Dec.*
Salvia argentea, *L.*
sclarea, *L.*
coccinea, *L.*
officinalis, *L.*
splendens, *Sello.*
patens, *L.*

Salvia bicolor, *Lam.*
Horminum, *L.*
Monarda didyma, *L.*
Origanum Majorana, *L.*
Thymus vulgaris, *L.*
citriodorus, *Pers.*
Hyssopus officinalis, *L.*
Leonurus tataricus, *Burm.*
Holmskioldia sanguinea, *Retz.*
Mentha Piperita, *L.*
Melissa officinalis, *L.*

95. *Verbenaceæ.*

Aloysia citriodora, *Ort.*
Verbena venosa, *Hook. et Gill.*
urticifolia, *L.*
melindres, *Hook*, var.
officinalis, *L.*
Stachytarpheta mutabilis, *Vahl.*
jamaicensis, *Vahl.*
Lantana indica, *Roxb.*
melissæfolia, *Ait.*
aculeata, *L.*
mixta, *Spreng.*
Vitex trifolia, *L.*
Premna latifolia, *Roxb.*
Tectona grandis, *L.*
Gmelina asiatica, *L.*
Volkameria Kæmpferii, *Willd.*
Clerodendron fragrans, *Ait.*
var. plena.
siphonanthus, *R. Br.*
sp.? (Mauritius).
roseum, *Wall.*
Duranta Ellisia, *L.*
Plumieri, *L.*
Petræa volubilis, *L.*
Callicarpa Reevesii, *Wall.*

96. *Acanthaceæ.*

Thunbergia grandiflora, *Roxb.*
alata, *Hook.*
laurifolia, *Hook.*
Meyenia erecta, *Nees.*
Hawtayneana, *Nees.*
Hexacentris coccinea *Nees.*
mysorensis, *Hook.*
Ruellia formosa, *Andr.*
Goldfussia isophylla, *Nees.*
Asteracantha longifolia, *Nees.*
Barleria Gibsoni.
cristata, *L.*
acuminata, *Wight.*
nov. sp? (Anamalais).
Crossandra axillaris, *Nees.*
infundibuliformis, *Ait.*
Aphelandra cristata, *Ait.*
aurantiaca, *Lindl.*
Graptophyllum hortense, *Nees.*
var. picta.
var. atropurpurea.
Gendarussa vulgaris, *Nees.*
Eranthemum pulchellum, *Andr.*
Rhinacanthus communis, *Nees.*
Dicliptera spinosa, *Nees.*
Peristrophe lanceolaria, *Nees.*

97. *Primulaceæ.*

Anagallis indica, *L.*

98. *Plumbaginaceæ.*

Plumbago zeylanica, *L.*
rosea, *L.*
capensis, *Thunb.*

99. *Nyctaginaceæ.*

Boerhaavia erecta, *L.*
Abronia umbellata, *Juss.*
Mirabilis Jalapa, *L.*
Bugainvillea spectabilis, *Commers.*
Pisonia aculeata, *L.*
morindifolia, *R. Br.*

100. *Plantaginaceæ.*

Plantago asiatica, *L.*

101. *Amarantaceæ.*

Gomphrena globosa, *L.*
Achyranthes aspera, *L.*
Pupalia orbiculata, *Wight.*
Amaranthus polygamus, *L.*
spinosus, *L.*
caudatus, *L.*
hypochondriacus, *L.*
Celosia argentea, *L.*
cristata, *L.*

102. *Chenopodiaceæ.*
Atriplex hortensis, *L.*
Spinacia oleracea, *L.*
Beta vulgaris, *L.*
Chenopodium ambrosioides, *L.*

103. *Basellaceæ.*
Basella alba, *L.*
Boussingaultia baselloides, *H. B.*

104. *Begoniaceæ.*
Begonia fuschioides, *Hook.*
dipetala, *Graham.*
nitida, *Ait.*
discolor, *Ait.*
ulmifolia, *Haw.*
palmata, *Don.*
tomentosa, *Schott.*
ricinifolia.

105. *Polygonaceæ.*
Rheum rhaponticum, *L.*
Polygonum orientale, *L.*
Fagopyrum, *L.*
rivulare, *Rott.*
Rumex sanguineus, *Sm.*
vesicarius, *L.*
Acetosa, *L.*

106. *Lauraceæ.*
Cinnamomum Cassia, *L.*
Persea gratissima, *Gært.*
Tetranthera monopetala, *Roxb.*
ferruginea, *R. Br.*

107. *Proteaceæ.*
Leucadendron argenteum, *R. Br.*
Grevillea robusta, *A. Cunn.*
linearis, *R. Br.*
Telopea speciosissima, *R. Br.*
Stenocarpus Cunninghamii, *R. Br.*

108. *Santalaceæ.*
Santalum album, *L.*

109. *Aristolochiaceæ.*
Aristolochia labiosa, *Ker.*
bracteata, *Retz.*
indica, *L.*

110. *Euphorbiaceæ.*
Pedilanthus tithymaloides, *Neck*
Euphorbia neriifolia, *L.*
Tirucalli, *L.*
Bojeri, *Hook.*
antiquorum, *L.*
pilulifera, *L.*
Poinsettia pulcherrima, *Grah.*
var. alba.
Hura crepitans, *L.*
Stillingia sebifera, *Willd.*
Sapium indicum, *Willd.*
Acalypha indica, *L.*
Aleuritis triloba, *Forst.*
Jatropha panduræfolia, *Roxb.*
multifida, *L.*
glandulifera, *Roxb.*
Curcas purgans, *Adans.*
Janipha Manihot, *Kth.*
Ricinus communis, *L.*
Codiæum variegatum, *L.*
var. longifolia.
Rottlera tinctoria, *Roxb.*
Trewia nudiflora, *L.*
Croton Tiglium, *L.*
Phyllanthus Niruri, *L.*
Emblica officinalis, *Gært.*
Cicca disticha, *L.*
Securinega nitida, *Commers.*
Buxus sempervirens, *L.*
Reidia floribunda, *Wight.*

111. *Urticaceæ.*
Urtica scabrella, *Roxb.*
Boehmeria sp. (Sikkim.
Cannabis sativa, *L.*
Humulus Lupulus, *L.*

112. *Moraceæ.*
Morus indica, *L.*
Ficus elastica, *Roxb.*
repens, *L.*
Carica, *L.*
religiosa, *L.*
indica, *L.*

113. *Artocarpaceæ.*
Artocarpus integrifolia, *L.*
incisa, *L.*

114. *Piperaceæ.*
Chavica Betle, *Miq.*

115. *Amentiferæ.*
Salix indica, *L.*
Corylus Avellana, *L.*
Quercus Robur, *L.*

116. *Casuarinaceæ.*
Casuarina muricata, *Roxb.*
equisetifolia, *Forst.*

117. *Coniferæ.*
Pinus longifolia, *Roxb.*
Pseudo-strobus, *Lindl.*
sylvestris, *L.*
Araucaria excelsa, *R. Br.*
Cunninghami, *Ait.*
Bidwilli, *Hook.*
Cookii, *R. Br.*
Dammara orientalis, *Lam.*
robusta.
Juniperus recurva, *Ham.*
Thuja orientalis, *L.*
var. Warcana.
Cryptomeria japonica, *Hook.*
Cupressus torulosa, *Don.*
cashmeriana.
funebris, *Endl.*
lusitanica, *Thunb.*
Lawsoniana, *Muer.*
sempervirens, *L.*
Callitris quadrivalvis, *Vent.*
Podocarpus longifolia, *Hort.*
Frenula Gunnii, *Hook. fil.*
sp? (Sydney.)

118. *Cycadaceæ.*
Cycas revoluta, *Thunb.*
Macrozamia sp.?

---

b. Monocotyledons.

119. *Dioscoreaceæ.*
Dioscorea sativa, *L.*
alata, *L.*
bulbifera, *L.*
Batatas, *Thunb.*

120. *Smilaceæ.*
Smilax ovalifolia, *Roxb.*
deltoidea.

121. *Roxburghiaceæ.*
Roxburghia gloriosioides, *Dryander.*

122. *Orchidaceæ.*
Dendrobium chrysanthum, *Walt.*
Eria densiflora, *Wall.*
Bletia hyacinthina, *Lindl.*
Vanda spathulata, *Spreng.*
Roxburghii, *R. Br.*
teres, *Lindl.*
Aerides odoratum, *Lour.*
Cymbidium ensifolium, *Sw.*
Satyrium sp? (Nilgiris.)
Cœlogyne media, *Wall.*
Vanilla aromatica, *Swz.*

123. *Zingiberaceæ.*
Alpinia calcarata, *Roscoe.*
nutans, *Roscoe.*
Zingiber Zerumbet, *Roscoe.*
officinalis, *Roscoe.*
Kæmpferia ovalifolia, *Roxb.*
Amomum angustifolium, *Son.*
Curcuma longa, *Roxb.*
Costus speciosus, *Sm.*

124. *Marantaceæ.*
Canna indica, *L.*
lutea, *Roscoe.*
edulis, *Ker.*

125. *Musaceæ.*
Musa sapientum, *Roxb.*, var. superba.
Strelitzia regina, *Banks.*

126. *Iridaceæ.*
Iris germanica, *L.*
florentina, *L.*
Pardanthus sinensis, *Ker.*
Tigridia Pavonia, *Juss.*
Antholyza æthiopica, *L.*
Tritonia crocata, *Ker.*
Crocus speciosus, *L.*

127. *Hæmadoraceæ.*
Anigozanthus rufus, *R. Br.*

128. *Hypoxidaceæ.*
Curculigo orchioides, *Roxb.*

129. *Amaryllidaceæ.*
Amaryllis formosissima, *L.*
psittacina, *Ker.*
Zephyranthus candida, *Herb.*
Nerine sarniensis, *Herb.*
Crinum asiaticum, *Herb.*
Hæmanthus coccineus, *L.*
Cyrtanthus obliquus, *Ait.*
Pancratium zeylanicum, *L.*
Narcissus Tazetta, *L.*
Alströemeria aurea, *L.*
Bomarea salsilla, *Mirb.*
Doryanthus excelsa, *R. Br.*
Agave americana, *L.*
var. variegata.
vivipara, *L.*

130. *Liliaceæ.*
Tulipa suaveolens, *L.*
Lilium longiflorum, *Wall.*
Gloriosa superba, *L.*
Agapanthus umbellatus, *L'Herit.*
Polianthes tuberosa, *L.*
var. plena.
Kniphofia Uvaria, *Hook.*
Phormium tenax, *Forst.*
Sanseviera zeylanica, *Ros.*
cylindrica.
Aloe indica, *Royle.*
Yucca gloriosa, *L.*
angustifolia, *Pursh.*
Allium fragrans, *L.*
Cepa, *L.*
Allium sativum, *L.*
Porrum, *L.*
Ornithogalum elatum, *B. Rep.*
Hyacinthus orientalis, *L.*
Asphodelus fistulosus, *L.*
Asparagus sarmentosus, *L.*
officinalis, *L.*
Dracæna ferrea, *L.*
terminalis, *Willd.*

131. *Bromeliaceæ.*
Ananas sativus, *Schult.*

132. *Pontederaceæ.*
Pontederia dilatata, *Haw.*

133. *Commelynaceæ.*
Tradescantia discolor, *L.*
Commelyna cœlestis, *L.*
bengalensis, *L.*
Cyanotis fasciculata, *Rom.* e

134. *Palmæ.*
Areca oleracea, *L.*
Seaforthia elegans, *R. Br.*
Caryota urens, *L.*
Borassus flabelliformis, *L.*
Corypha umbraculifera, *L.*
australis, *R. Br.*
Livistona mauritiana, *Wall.*
Chamærops humilis, *L.*
Phœnix sylvestris, *Roxb.*
Cocos nucifera, *L.*
Arenga saccharifera, *Lab.*

135. *Pandanaceæ.*
Pandanus odoratissimus, *L. fil.*

136. *Araceæ.*
Colocasia odora, *Roxb.*
Amorphophallus campanulatus, *Roxb.*
Caladium bicolor.
Dracontium polyphyllum, *L.*

137. *Orontiaceæ.*
Calla æthiopica, *L.*
Acorus Calamus, *L.*

138. *Pistiaceæ.*
Pistia Stratiotes, *L.*

139. *Gramineæ.*
Oryza sativa, *L.*
Zea Mays, *L.*
Coix Lachryma, *L.*
Panicum miliaceum, *Willd.*
jumentorum, *Pers.*
Spinifex squarrosus, *L.*
Cynodon Dactylon, *L.*
Eleusine coracana, *Gært.*
Lagurus ovatus, *L.*
Avena sativa, *L.*
Poa annua, *L.*
Briza maxima, *L.*
Dactylis glomerata, *L.*
Lamarckia aurea, *Mönch.*
Festuca duriuscula, *L.*
Bambusa arundinacea, *L.*
Lolium italicum, *Braun.*
Triticum hybernum, *L.*
Saccharum officinarum, *L.*
Andropogon Schœnanthus, *L.*
Sorghum saccharatum, *Pers.*
vulgare, *Pers.*

II. CRYPTOGAMS.

140. *Filices.*
Drynaria quercifolia, *Bory.*
Hemionitis cordata, *Roxb.*
Platycerium alcicorne, *Gaud.*
Cheilanthes farinosa, *Kaulf.*
Pellæa geraniifolia, *Fee.*
Adiantum caudatum, *L.*
Capillus-Veneris, *L.*
Onychium auratum, *Kaulf.*
Pteris longifolia, *L.*
arguta, *Vahl.*
serrulata, *L.*
Blechnum orientale, *L.*
Asplenium præmorsum, *Sw.*
Nidus, *L.*
Nephrodium molle, *R. Br.*
Nephrolepis hirsutula, *Presl.*
Gleichenia dichotoma, *Hook.*
Lygodium scandens, *Sw.*

141. *Ophioglossaceæ.*
Ophioglossum vulgatum, *L.*

142. *Marsileaceæ.*
Marsilea quadrifolia, *L.*

UTAKAMAND GARDEN.

6th August 1857.

1. For some years, I have read the Reports of this Government Institution with much pleasure, although I had not seen Mr M'Ivor or his garden; but this year, my forest duties necessitating my proceeding to the Nilgiri Hills, I delayed forwarding the remarks called for, until I had an opportunity of ascertaining by inspection, and noting in some detail, "the present condition, resources, and prospects of the institution."

2. Ten years have elapsed since the Marquis of Tweeddale originated the scheme of this garden; and the Court of Directors selected (on the recommendation, I believe, of Dr Royle and Sir William Hooker), the present superintendent, who is eminently qualified by early training at the Royal Gardens, Kew, for carrying out the objects of the institution.

3. The earlier stages of the garden's existence have passed; and I need not perhaps allude to the great difficulties to be overcome in commencing a garden on these mountains with a scanty income of Rs.100 per mensem, and the experience to be gained before exotics from various lands could be successfully introduced. I will, however, observe, that the present condition of the garden is very creditable to Mr M'Ivor, who has laboured by himself from the beginning without the aid of professional advice; and although much remains to be done, yet, on making inquiry, I find it generally admitted by visitors that great progress has been made during the past year.

4. In the upper part, the borders and beds have been well planned and arranged, and have a neat and trim appearance. The view from the higher terraces is romantic; and from them only can the general plan be well seen and understood. On the

grassy banks, along the sides of the main walk, are clumps of showy flowers; and scattered through the ground are fine standard *Acacias*, *Eucalypti*, *Coniferæ*, *Psoralea*, *Swainsonia*, *Pultenæa*, *Humea*, *Hakea*, &c. Excepting a few specimens of *Mahonia Leschenaultii*, *Rhododendron arboreum*, *Sapota elengoides*, *Myrtus tomentosa*, *Ilex Wightiana* and *Viburnum acuminatum*; all the rest of the trees in the garden seem to be introduced.

5. The lower part of the garden is not in good order. It was originally a swamp, and suffers from frost in clear winter nights; the cold air formed on the slopes of the mountains rolls down into the valley and envelopes the herbage, blighting many tender plants. It is now protected from the high winds by rows of Australian trees, and there is a prospect of Mr M'Ivor devoting his energies to it as sóon as the conservatory is finished. As dahlias and many other plants which are not hurt on the upper slopes are killed by the frosts below, and as this evil cannot be entirely averted, it is proposed to make this part a grassy lawn for exhibitions of native produce, with an avenue of 50 feet in breadth leading from the gate to the conservatory.

6. *General Results.*—I have great pleasure in observing that the introduction of the seeds obtained through Government from Saharunpore, Darjiling, China, Australia, and the Cape, has been most satisfactory. A very considerable number of timber and forest trees, shrubs and herbaceous plants, have been secured to the country, and thrive remarkably well. This of itself renders the efforts of Mr M'Ivor of great importance, especially as the seeds are sufficient for abundant distribution.

7. *Timber Trees.*—Amongst the timber trees are the blue gum tree, the deodar, and the Patagonian pine, perhaps I may add the Turkey oak, Turkey box, and the Irish yew, these latter are still of small size. The European pines (*Larix* and *Abies*) have not answered well. On the other hand, the *Acacia robusta* of Australia is in such abundance as to stamp a peculiar feature in the scenery, which is entirely wanting in the drawings of Utakamand (Colonel M'Kurdy's) printed fifteen years ago.

8. *Fruit-Trees.*—The best varieties of English apples and pears are cultivated. Figs and vines grow well; also oranges and lemons—these latter succeed remarkably at the branch garden

"Kalhatti," which I visited and found the following trees bearing fruit:—Natal plum (*Arduina bispinosa*), Newton pippin, Malta orange, St Michael's orange, Spanish citron, and Ischia figs. Numerous grafts and seedlings have been sent to various parts of the country, as to Ramandrug in Bellary, Kudramuka, South Canara, and the Bababuden Hills, Mysore. A complete set of fruit trees is about to be supplied to the Bangalore garden, from which, by reason of its central position and the cheaper carriage, I expect there will be a most abundant distribution of valuable productions radiating over the country.

9. *Medicinal Products.*—The *Digitalis purpurea* (foxglove) is grown for the supply of the medical stores on annual indent; the spearmint and peppermint thrive remarkably in the upper garden, and could be supplied in large quantity. Two large and healthy jalap plants are in great luxuriance; these Mr M'Ivor proposes to remove to the subsidiary garden at Kalhatti, with the hope of being able to propagate them extensively. This would be a great result. Two cinchonaceous plants from Patagonia, received from Mr Lobb under the name of *Cinchona micrantha*, and a small specimen of the *Cephäelis Ipecacuanha* are in the garden, but they appear to suffer from the misty atmosphere. It is of the utmost consequence that the introduction of the true Cinchonas should be fairly tried on the Nilgiris, and Mr M'Ivor is well able to conduct the experiment. The drugs have been hitherto delivered free of charge; it seems to me that the cost of production should be charged to the Medical Department, as this Institution has always been hampered for want of funds.

10. *Buildings.*—The conservatory, sanctioned at an estimated cost of Rs. 4300, is far advanced towards completion, and will unquestionably be a great acquisition to the garden. The structure was designed by Capt. Francis, Engineers, and approved by Mr M'Ivor. The delay in its erection has been unavoidable, as reported by the Committee.

11. The seed-house lately suffered serious damage from fire, and requires to be rebuilt. The site selected by Mr M'Ivor is close to his bungalow, in a dry and convenient situation. This is a most important department of the garden, from which seeds, ripe and correctly named, can be at all times distributed to

various parts of the country. An alteration of this old seed-house, so as to admit four or even six apprentices' sleeping quarters, would be highly advantageous. A plan and estimate, amounting to Rs. 1650, has been forwarded,* I understand, by the Committee for sanction. This provides, I believe, for flues and close-fitting drawers, dryness being essential for the preservation of seeds.

12. *Seeds.*—Mr M'Ivor has made some important attempts at growing European vegetable seeds in India. Experimental samples of many kinds have been sent by him to Dr Wight, and these are now under trial in the garden of the Horticultural Society, London. If a favourable opinion be given, Southern India will no longer be dependent for kitchen-garden seeds upon England, France, or the Cape. So far as the seeds have been tested in this country the result has been favourable, especially the lettuce, carrots, &c. It has occurred to me that the soldiers' gardens of this Presidency should be supplied with Nilgiri and English seed in equal quantity; and from the reports received, a few deductions may be drawn as to their comparative value.

* * * * *

14. *Abstract of Distribution.*—This table shows the parties to whom plants, &c. have been sent gratis, or sold at the published rates, and gives a highly satisfactory return of "Sales to the Public." I believe that the distribution of seeds and propagation of plants still admits of great extension, and I trust the amount of despatches under all heads may year by year increase.

15. *Finances.*—The statement in future years may be improved by entering more into detail, and showing clearly the various items of receipt and expenditure, as, for instance, the expenses of the Kalhatti nursery and the horse allowance for visiting it, and the monthly outlay for labour. These appear at present under the head of "Working expenditure." The accounts should be audited by one or more of the Garden Committee.

16. In the previous report of the garden, it was stated that the total outlay was about Rs. 200 per mensem, but this year I am happy to observe that the income has risen to nearly Rs. 400 per mensem, being Rs. 100 of Government allowance, and about Rs. 300 by sales. This shows an encouraging state of progress in

* 6th July 1857.

a financial point of view, and has allowed Mr M'Ivor to carry out considerable improvements in the upper garden.

17. *Prices.*—The extreme facility with which many trees and plants may be propagated, and the comparative mildness of the winter, during which season many exotics continue to grow from cuttings (if planted out of the reach of frost) would warrant their sale at a reduced rate.

18. It is the object of Government to introduce as many species as possible at the lowest cost, consistent with the repayment to the garden of the actual expenses of introduction and propagation, with a sufficient surplus to meet the repairs of buildings, &c., and to admit of the extension of operations.

19. A strong feeling generally prevails that the prices named in the catalogue are high, and I cannot doubt but that advantage would arise from lowering them (as formerly urged by me). I have discussed this point with Mr M'Ivor, who naturally adduces the fact, that the income of the garden depends largely upon sales; I am disposed to meet his objection, by recommending that Government should sanction the debit of the actual cost of drugs supplied to the Medical Board, and of trees to the Department of Public Works. Certain trees, for instance, might be supplied to the roads at A. 1 each, or Rs. 5 per hundred, and the coolie hire for collecting and preparing the drugs should, I think, be charged to the Medical Department; this, Mr M'Ivor states, would allow of a reduction of 25 per cent.

20. The *Acacia robusta*, weeping willow, cypress, ivy, &c., are of very easy culture, and could certainly be sold at a reduced rate. Fuchsias, chrysanthemums, geraniums, &c., would be dear at English prices; but with fruit trees especially, a low price is to be desired. Vines and figs propagate readily from cuttings; apples and pears can be grafted during great part of the year, and a cheaper rate would repay their cost. Plums, peaches, and cherries are more difficult of propagation, and their price might reasonably be higher. On the whole, it appears to me that a continuance of the present rates will cause a partial failure of the object of the Institution, and induce residents to procure plants and seeds from England instead of availing themselves of the local establishment, where the same plants are procurable.

21. *Apprentices.*—Apprentice D. Hopkins, aged seventeen years, has been three years in the garden; for the two first years he received Rs. 10, and this year Rs. 15 per mensem. He writes the garden accounts, and has been trained to practise grafting, budding, &c. It is proposed that he receive Rs. 20 a month during the fourth and last year of his apprenticeship. Another lad, aged thirteen, has been instructed for six months, but was found to be deficient in preliminary training.

22. The system of instituting a class of apprentices is a good one, of special importance to young lads of European parentage, and I hope it may be followed out. Mr M'Ivor could now take the supervision of two or three more, say from the Male Asylum. Lads of robust health and moral conduct should be sent.

23. *Rules.*—With reference to the restrictions considered necessary by the Committee and Mr M'Ivor, I think the following rules, which have been found to answer well in the Calcutta and other Government gardens, will be suitable :—

RULES.

1. To keep on the walks, especially near the shrubberies and flower beds.
2. Not to break flowers, leaves, or branches, or cut names or the like on trees.
3. Not to disturb the gardeners.
4. Not to offer them money or presents of any sort.
5. No shooting allowed. Horses and dogs are also prohibited.
6. The hours of admittance are from 6 o'clock A.M. to 6 P.M.

There is an outside road belonging to the garden, by which visitors may ride to the higher part; but the admission of horses and conveyances within the gate seems objectionable, and does not obtain in other institutions. The road above mentioned would give visitors a complete command of the whole garden, and many of the invalids could walk down through any part of the grounds, to whom the ascent would be difficult.

24. In the weekly market at Utakamand, there is an increasing display of fine specimens of garden produce. The proposal of establishing an annual exhibition of vegetables, fruits, and flowers, is a good one. Government might contribute

Rs. 100 towards the expenses of this, on the condition that the committee raise an equal sum from among the residents.

25. *Kunúr Nursery.*—Before leaving the Nilgiri hills, I visited the Kunúr subsidiary garden in company with Mr M'Ivor. It is well sheltered and well watered, situated 1½ mile from Kunúr. Nine gardeners are employed, including the maistry, at the cost sanctioned of Rs. 50 per mensem. The orange appears to grow here in as great perfection as at Malta or Canton, and when the garden is in full operation, will probably do away with the necessity of keeping up the Kulhutty nursery, which might be then sold with advantage. There would be three gardens, forming a graduated series in one line of road—alpine, subalpine, and tropical; viz., Utakamand, Kunúr, and Burliar. The latter, indeed, is the private property of E. B. Thomas, Esq., collector of Coimbatore; but from his zeal in arboriculture, and great liberality to all applicants, its usefulness for disseminating tropical products is almost as great as if it were public property. In the note is given a list of the fruit trees, aromatic shrubs, &c., now cultivated in this rich but confined nook, in which the chocolate tree, nutmeg, allspice, &c., have succeeded admirably, and from which it is the hope of Mr Thomas that they may be extensively spread over congenial climates, such as the Wainád and other parts of Malabar.*

26. Before closing, I venture to suggest that Mr M'Ivor having now served the Government for nearly ten years without any increase of salary sought or proposed, might reasonably be allowed an increase, so as to raise his allowance to Rs. 200 per mensem, on the express condition that he devotes his whole time *unreservedly* to Government service. In addition to the garden superintendence, he might be required to undertake the management of certain tree plantations in the immediate vicinity of Utakamand, to which I shall allude in a separate communication.

27. In conclusion, it occurs to me that S. N. Ward, Esq., Civil and Session Judge of Coimbatore, having occasion to visit

* Jak trees, nutmeg trees, clove, allspice, cinnamon, chocolate, vanilla, peach, orange, lime, pumplemoos, Granadilla, mangosteen, rose-apple, loquat, pine-apple.

Utakamand on duty from time to time, would be a valuable addition to the garden committee, from his special attainments as a scientific naturalist, and the great interest which he takes in the progress and prospects of this institution.

28. The list of plants offered for sale might next year be printed separately from the report, on thin paper, and extensively circulated to horticulturists and other supporters of the institution.

H. CLEGHORN.

Extract Report 1858.

As I entered fully into the past history of this Institution in a Memorandum 6th August 1857, I confine my remarks at present to the alterations effected during the past year, which I have myself witnessed.

The lower part of the garden as well as the approach to the gateway have undergone very considerable improvement. The residents and visitors with whom I have spoken have generally expressed their approval of the changes which have taken place in the laying out of the garden within the last two years. The broad walk near the entrance, with coniferous trees, &c., on either side, is well planned; and it is evident that Mr M'Ivor has taken great pains to arrange the garden with a view to ornament.

Conservatory.—The conservatory sanctioned in 1855, and alluded to in last report as being erected, has been completed, with the exception of inside fittings and outside painting, and is being filled with orchids and other interesting plants, which will not only be a great source of attraction, but be of material aid to naturalists visiting the hills. Though the structure is not so picturesque as could be desired, I trust that this adjunct will prove of great value to the garden. The defects of construction alluded to by Mr M'Ivor certainly exist; but it must be remembered, 1*st*, that the building was proceeded with after an interval, owing to the suspension of public works; 2*d*, that buildings of this description form a separate branch of business in England, and the details of construction require an experience not often found in this country.

Sketch Plan of Garden.—The plan of the arrangements in the garden will, it is expected, prove useful. I beg to suggest that it be lithographed, and that the descriptive letterpress accompanying it should form a small pamphlet, to be had at the garden gate. Strangers wishing to see the collection would find it convenient to study the position of the respective plots, ponds, &c.

Labelling of Plants.—It would be advisable to attach labels to the plants in the garden, most of which are new to the majority of visitors; and in this climate, where air and exercise are taken all the day long, permanent plant-labels, to designate the different species, would be a useful means of instruction and attraction, and tend to correct errors of nomenclature.

Systematic Catalogue.—The garden having been now ten years in existence, a classified catalogue of the plants *actually growing in it* would certainly be a useful contribution both to casual visitors and to men of science. This *Hortus Nilgirensis* should be arranged according to the natural system, and indigenous plants should be distinguished from those which are cultivated or naturalized.

Medicinal Plants.—The dried leaves of the English foxglove (*Digitalis purpurea*), which grows freely, are supplied to the medical stores. The dandelion (*Leontodon Taraxacum*) threatens to become a weed in the garden. The true peppermint (*Mentha Piperita*) fringes several of the ponds, and the Indian hemp (*Cannabis indica*) luxuriates at Kalhatti. Pharmaceutic preparations of these and other officinal plants, as belladonna, might be made at Utakamand; but this duty does not properly belong to the superintendent of a Government botanical garden.

Hill Berberry.—I may here mention, that Dr Maitland has recently prepared a considerable quantity of the extract of Hill berberry (*Berberis tinctoria*, W. and A.), which is coming into repute.

Jalap.—The tubers of the jalap plant received a few years ago from S. America, through Messrs Veitch and Son, are now increasing in size and giving shoots at Kalhatti, and Mr M'Ivor hopes soon to raise a number of young plants for distribution to Mysore, &c.

Cinchona.—The experiment of introducing the quinine-yielding Cinchona plants is well worthy of trial, especially in the Nilgiris. If possible, it should be conducted on a large scale, and with several species of the genus to be planted in various parts of the hills. It is well known that the most valuable species (*Cinchona Calisaya*) has been successfully introduced into the Dutch Netherlands; and it is certainly most desirable that the British Government should make the attempt to obtain the cinchona either from Java or from its native habitat in the Andes.*

Seeds.—Some time ago, the report of the seeds transmitted to the Horticultural Society, London, for experimental growth, was unfavourable; but a note received by Dr Wight from Professor Lindley, enclosing a memorandum of the garden Supt. at Chiswick, and forwarded to Mr M'Ivor for his information, places matters in a different light. Mr Henderson's report is very satisfactory, showing that only three of the assortment of vegetable seeds sent on trial did not germinate, viz., the orange-horn carrot, the Brussels sprout, and Swede turnip.

Utakamand Nursery.—The position of the garden seems to have been selected solely with reference to ornamental capability, and the nurseries are at present widely dispersed, wherever small available spots can be found, and none are situated so that carts can be brought near for the removal of plants. There is in fact a deficiency of suitable ground for the purpose of a nursery. The lower garden, where the ground is tolerably level, is within the influence of the frost, and the upper garden is difficult of access and deficient in soil; the latter is a serious inconvenience when the plants for sale are in baskets of earth. It is difficult to suggest a remedy for this defect. If the nursery were at a distance it would be removed from supervision, and every site within limits of the garden is open to the objections stated. If it were possible to purchase some adjoining ground, the difficulty might be obviated, and then the nursery and its expenses might be kept distinct from those of the garden. This would be a good arrangement for Mr M'Ivor, while the facilities for intending purchasers would be so much increased, that the expenses attending the change would be speedily repaid. If this be feasible, it is probable that such a stock might be kept up as would

* Since my return to England, this experiment has been made on a large scale. I fully anticipate a successful result.—H. C.

enable the Supt. to supply plants to applicants engaged in laying out grounds at reduced prices in accordance with the system adopted in England, where large quantities of other than choice plants are sold at very reduced rates.

Kalhatti Nursery.—This nursery, situated half way down the Sigur Ghat, lies convenient for purchasers in Mysore and Wainád. There is a large stock of fruit trees and of seed vegetables. Two gardeners only are employed, and these are not sufficient to keep the garden clean of weeds.

Kunúr Nursery.—The subsidiary garden here has been considerably enlarged since my last inspection (1857), and consists of five terraces in a sheltered situation, with a south-east aspect. The stock of fruit trees, figs, vines, peaches, apples, and oranges, were looking well. I observed also Guinea grass and seed balsams, and I have no doubt that there will be a considerable demand in the increasing stations of Kunúr and Jackatalla, where a European sanatarium is established; perhaps also at Kotagiri.

When the Kunúr nursery is in full vigour, and when the organisation of the garden lately established by the Commissioner of Mysore is complete, it may be desirable to dispose of the Kalhatti nursery, and to establish in lieu of it a subsidiary garden in the Wainád, for the diffusion of chocolate and spice plants, cloves, nutmeg, and vanilla.

I would gladly see private gardeners undertake the work of propagating and retailing plants after their first introduction, as I do not consider their subsequent diffusion to belong properly to a Govt. establishment. There are numerous market-gardeners in and around Utakamand, some of whom have been employed in the Govt. garden, yet they do not seem to have found it to their advantage to establish nurseries.

Proposed Auction.—Mr M'Ivor has been compelled to keep up a much larger stock of plants to meet casual demands than is needed for the requirements of the garden, and he has personally proposed to me to dispose of the surplus stock by auction every year, which seems to be a good suggestion, calculated to promote the diffusion of many useful trees and plants.

Mr M'Ivor appears to have underrated the results of the early efforts of residents on the hills, who, as I am credibly informed, introduced many varieties of fruit and other trees under greater difficulties than are at present encountered, steam communication and Wardian cases not having been then available. The correspondence between Mr Sullivan and Dr Wight, published in the Madras Agri-Hort. Soc. Proc., relates to some of these first attempts at introduction on the Nilgiri hills. Several varieties of fruit trees are still found in the Billicul garden and elsewhere. In the older gardens, many specimens of well grown coniferous trees (different spec.) are seen, particularly Kaity, Cluny, Kempstow, Dimhutty; and several private individuals are now in the habit of getting large consignments of valuable plants from England and the colonies.

In addition to the donors, Dr Royle, India House, Mr Veitch of Exeter, and Dr Jameson, Saharunpore, are specially mentioned by Mr M'Ivor. I have to express special obligation to Dr T. Thomson, the Supt. of the Botanical Garden, Calcutta, who forwarded several valuable packets of seeds and four Wardian cases containing rare plants, many of which were collected by himself in the neighbourhood of Darjiling; these were distributed to the Madras, Bangalore, and Utakamand Gardens.

Extract Report 1859.

I have lately carefully inspected the garden on numerous occasions, and I am happy to say that great progress has been made in it. It is exceedingly well laid out, and advantage has been skilfully taken of the picturesque site. A number of very fine plants have been introduced,* and in the course of a few years, the garden, for its extent and standing, will not suffer by comparison with any out of England. It is satisfactory also to find that many valuable plants are being gradually disseminated through the country; but we cannot expect to derive the full benefit of the garden in this respect until the system of railways and canals is completed. At present, the expense, difficulty, and risk of transport, materially retard the dissemination of plants.

* *Wellingtonia gigantea*, *Dioscorea Batatas* (Chinese yam), *Cupressus Lawsoniana*, *Tacsonia longiflora*, *Meconopsis simplicifolia*, *Edwardsia*.

I will now proceed to remark briefly on such parts of Mr M'Ivor's report as seem to me to need special notice.

Conservatory.—The present conservatory is certainly an unsightly building, but it was erected under difficult circumstances. I have requested the district engineer to include the estimate for its external improvement, and for the necessary fittings and repairs in the interior (which will not cost more than about Rs. 1000), in his next budget; and I would recommend that, under that officer's general superintendence, the work should be entrusted to Mr M'Ivor, who, from having been brought up at Kew Gardens, is well acquainted with such edifices, and will, I am sure, do the work well.

I hope hereafter to remedy the great loss in transit from Madras, but, in common with other departments, we are very much at the mercy of the cart and transit owners. The completion of the railway will be of the greatest importance in this respect; and it will be desirable hereafter, as far as the season may permit, to make Beypur the place of shipment for plants to and from Europe.

Kunúr Nursery.—I trust that the inferiority of Kunúr seeds is only owing to the garden being of recent formation (this is only its second year), and to the difficulty hitherto experienced in procuring good manure. Kunúr has great advantages in position and climate; and when the railways are open, I look to it as the nursery for Southern India. I hope that manure will be obtained before long from the rapidly increasing settlement.

Kalhatti Nursery.—My objections to this nursery are, that it is situated in a somewhat inaccessible position, and that being on the road to Mysore, the tract of country under it will be ultimately very fairly supplied from the Bangalore garden. It is obviously undesirable to multiply nurseries and gardens unnecessarily, especially in such a limited tract as the Nilgiri range. They distract the attention of the superintendent, and involve additional expense. Moreover, there are few plants, likely to be extensively propagated, which *will* grow at Kalhatti and will *not* grow at Kunúr; and for these few I doubt the expediency of maintaining an additional garden at the former place. For these reasons I still think the Kalhatti nursery may be given up in two or three years, by which time the Kunúr garden will be in a condition to supersede it. Mr M'Ivor is mistaken in supposing that I advocated its *immediate* abolition, as that would involve the sacrifice of the plants in it before others could be supplied from Kunúr.

Utakamand.—Mr M'Ivor's application of moss is most important, and he deserves great credit for it. It will prove a great advantage to Government in economising space and soil in the nurseries, and to purchasers in saving expense of transport. This discovery will render it unnecessary to purchase additional land, as proposed last year. As regards the supervision of all the woods and plantations on the Nilgiris, I have already stated my opinion in my report of last year (dated 13th November 1858), that such an extensive charge would be beyond the powers of any *one* man. I think Mr M'Ivor's energy and zeal are already sufficiently taxed with the charge of the gardens and two distant nurseries, the planting of the Jackatalla road, and his voluntary assistance in laying out the soldiers' gardens. As regards the future, we have the prospect of endeavouring to introduce the Cinchona next year; and, in fact, each year will bring with it similar important duties requiring his skill and experience.

Distribution of Plants.—Mr M'Ivor's tabular statement shows that plants, &c., to the value of about Rs. 200 monthly have been distributed, exclusive of exchange. On looking over his list of applications I find that supplies have been sent to Ahmednuggur, Saugor, Trevandrum, and other stations.

Progress of the Garden.—The gardens, in common with other Departmental works, have suffered from the great and sudden rise in the rate of wages at Jackatalla, which has cost us 15 per cent. extra, and, indeed, we have retained our labourers only by the expedient of agreeing to employ their wives and boys in the gardens, and to give them some increase of pay themselves. As the Government grant for labour is only Rs. 100 per mensem, this is a serious matter to us.

Cinchona.—The introduction of the Cinchona is a most important subject. A moderate grant will be required to prepare a suitable site for the plants at the upper end of the gardens, the nurseries, and perhaps in other localities. As regards the *manufacture* of drugs, I think this should be left to private enterprise, the gardens merely supplying the plants freely at the cheapest practicable rates.* So far as the wants of Government are concerned, supplies of the materials could be sent to the stores for preparation.

Collecting Indigenous Plants.—Within reasonable limits, I have no objection to occasional trips for this purpose. I think, however, that a report of important discoveries should be submitted for the information of Government and the public; and that specimens of every new plant should at once be forwarded to the Royal Gardens at Kew, surplus specimens being sent, at Mr M'Ivor's discretion, to such private nurserymen as will give him plants in exchange.

Extract Minute by Sir Charles Trevelyan.

I have visited the garden, and entirely agree with Dr Cleghorn, that Mr M'Ivor deserves great credit for the manner in which he has laid it out. The garden is both a beautiful pleasure ground and a valuable public institution for the improvement of indigenous and the naturalisation of foreign plants; and it has been formed from the commencement by Mr M'Ivor, with great industry and artistic skill, out of a rude ravine. The facilities for utilising the varied resources of this beautiful climate will be greatly increased after the opening of the railway from Madras to Beypur.

The sum required for the completion of the conservatory is Rs. 1000; and as it is desirable that the substantial portion of the work should be executed before the rains, I authorised this to be done out of funds at the disposal of the district engineer, at an estimated cost of Rs. 500.

C. E. TREVELYAN.

UTAKAMAND, 24*th February* 1860.

* Medicinal plants available:—*Atropa Belladona*—Belladonna; *Hyosciamus niger*—Henbane; *Leontodon Taraxacum*—Dandelion; *Mentha Piperita*—Peppermint; *Cannabis indica*—Indian Hemp; *Diosma crenata*—Bucku.

SUGGESTIONS RELATIVE TO THE ESTABLISHMENT OF SOLDIERS' GARDENS IN INDIA.

1. If the object in the establishment of these gardens be merely to provide the soldiers with a source of rational amusement in their leisure hours, it is obvious that any degree of rigid superintendence or control would be out of place, and might make the project unpalatable to the men. The interference of the officers should be in the way of advice and encouragement rather than of control. So long as the men turn their gardens to account in the way most congenial to their individual tastes, interference should be avoided, and, generally speaking, the only occasion for its exercise will be in the rare case of an individual applying his garden to a purpose offensive or prejudicial to his neighbours.

2. If, on the other hand, the object be to raise vegetables for the use of the men, without reference to their recreation, superintendence will of course be required; and the more skilled it is, the more profitable and productive will the garden be.

3. Assuming, however, that the first is the chief object to be attained, I shall proceed to make a few suggestions bearing on that point.

4. The extent of the ground, its position, and its capabilities, are the first considerations.

5. These will often present defects which it is difficult to modify. The ground should, if possible, be sufficiently extensive to meet all requirements, prospective as well as present, and it should be of a good quality, of a light soil, with abundance of good water, and as *near the barracks* as may be practicable.

6. The first step should be to lay out good gravel walks, as tastefully as possible. The main walks should be 12 or 18 feet wide, the secondary walks not less than 6 or 8; and they should be planned so as to take full advantage of the ground, its prospects, &c. Convenient arbours should be erected here and there; trees for shade planted in suitable spots; and, generally, such improvements effected as will make the place an agreeable resort to the men and their families. This will not involve any great expense, for the labour of the men will be available, and, either

among themselves or their officers, some one will probably be found competent to plan and to carry out the work. In this part of the project, general effect is to be regarded, and not the wishes of individuals.

7. The grounds having been laid out as a whole, the next step will be to allot plots to individuals.

8. Generally speaking, a space of 50 feet long by 50 feet broad, of good, culturable ground, will suffice for each man; minor paths should be led off from the secondary walks at suitable points, and from these each man will draw off a small path for his own plot. The plots can be separated from each other by edging, gravel walks, or such fences as the men fancy; a space of 2 or 3 feet should be allowed as the boundary of each plot. Within his plot each man should be free to do as he pleases, provided he does nothing to offend his neighbours or to injure their gardens. No one should be allowed to enter another's plot without his permission, or in any way to molest or interfere with him. The ground should be made over to him in fair condition, and he should be allowed to cultivate it as he likes: one man will raise vegetables; another flowers; a third will train vines; and so on as individual tastes incline. The main object will be attained: the men will be drawn away from the canteen, and will have an agreeable and a healthy occupation, while, under other circumstances, they would be idle, drinking, or getting into trouble.

9. The garden, as I propose it, would be open to all the regiment, and would be a pleasant place of resort for them. The men, their wives, children and friends, would be free to walk about the place as much as they pleased, and to roam over the whole, except the appropriated plots, to which the owners alone could give them access. Thus the garden would be a benefit to all: those who have no taste for gardening would have an agreeable lounge; those who like that pursuit would not only be able to indulge their taste, but would have the additional gratification of seeing their friends going about admiring and enjoying the results of their industry, and this would have the best effect in stimulating them to greater exertions. A good extent of ground is the great desideratum to secure both these objects; and it should be remembered that all the ground not actually required

for plots might be laid down in grass, or planted with useful trees, and the produce thus help to pay expenses.

10. It will be necessary for Government, in the first instance, to dig wells here and there, and to construct channels to convey water to small reservoirs, placed so as to supply several contiguous gardens. Generally, it will be preferable to let the men draw water from these, instead of cutting up the paths by channels leading into their plots. The wells may be fitted with pumps like one recently erected at the Horticultural Society's Gardens by Mr Jaffrey, which raises 40 gallons per minute. These are inexpensive, and can easily be worked by two men.

11. It will further be necessary for Government to provide tools and seeds. The more expensive tools, such as garden rollers, shears, pickaxes, wheelbarrows, &c., should form a general stock, and be lent to the men as required. There should also be a certain proportion of the cheaper and more frequently used implements, six-pronged forks, spades, hoes, &c., for the gratuitous use of the men; but every inducement should be held out to them to purchase tools; they might be given at reduced prices, and the men might be allowed to pay for them by instalments. A suitable lock-up place will be required for the tools, where they should be collected *clean* every night. Some provision might also be beneficially made for the repair, and even the manufacture, of the commoner tools, on the spot, by the men themselves, as the ranks of a European regiment frequently include artificers trained to different branches of industry before they entered the army. A large open shed will be required in the garden for various purposes, and in this a forge should be erected with benches, &c. Working implements might be furnished in certain proportions, or lent as required from the Arsenals, and the gardening tools might here be repaired by the owners, or by others conversant with carpentry, blacksmith's work, &c., and new tools might also be made for sale. At first, of course, liberality must be exercised in lending tools; but, after a while, the artificers of the regiment should be required to provide all the cheaper description for themselves, Government furnishing the larger and more expensive, as forges, saws, sledge-hammers, &c., &c. Iron and wood should be supplied from the

stores on payment, if the men desire it. By these means, another section of men would have an interest in the garden, and be furnished with useful and profitable means of employment. Other branches of industry might of course be added, if desired.

12. Seeds might be given gratuitously, or at nominal prices. They cannot well be raised by the men, and the best plan will be to procure them through the agency of the Horticultural Society, which would probably undertake to supply them at cost prices, or at a fixed charge. It is very essential to procure the best seeds, and at the proper times; and in these respects, as well as in selecting suitable kinds, the Society possess great advantages. The Society could also furnish plants; and opportunities of forwarding them with public stores or return carts might be taken advantage of. Many seeds might be procured from the gardens at Utakamand and Bangalore, probably without charge, as Government in a great measure supports these gardens.

13. Each station garden should also be provided with a few books on gardening for the use of the men. A small sum of money, £15 or £20, would suffice for this purpose; and a few periodicals, such as the Gardeners' Chronicle, should be added as published. In Nagpore and Saugor, Speeds' Handbook would prove very useful; in Hyderabad, Riddel's Manual of Gardening; in Madras, Wight's Calendar and Jaffrey's Hints; and on the Nilgiri Hills, M'Ivor's Reports.

14. In many cantonments, the scourings of the streets, &c., are removed at Government expense. These might be given to the men, who would otherwise find a difficulty in procuring manure. Besides, at all these stations there will be commissariat cattle, and the manure derived from these will be available for the garden, and will probably be sufficient for it.

15. Animals should not be admitted on any account, or quarrels will be frequent. If disputes occur among the men, the best plan to arrange differences, not amounting to offences, will probably be by arbitration. The punishment for continued quarrelling, or for any serious offence, should be exclusion from the garden for a certain period.

16. Some arrangements will be necessary for the protection of the gardens at night, and during the absence of the men; a good

hedge of the aloe Mysore thorn, or some such plant, will be required to prevent cattle from entering.

17. The means of the men being limited, care should be taken to avoid putting them to much expense, but the other extreme of doing everything for them should be equally avoided. Their labour at least should be required, Government defraying the general expenses, as wells, laying out, &c., which occur only at the outset.

18. In the above suggestions, my object has been to make the proposed gardens a source of gratification to the entire regiment, as well as to the small section of it which may be fond of gardening; and to avoid meddling with the men as much as possible, so as to render it a place of ease and enjoyment for them after the labours and restraints of their profession. It is difficult, in so small a compass as a memorandum, to say much on the mode of cultivation to be followed; but the works I have referred to in par. 13 will supply the necessary directions on this point.

H. Cleghorn.

17th Sept. 1855.

BOTANICAL INQUIRENDA.

Extracted from the Admiralty Manual of Scientific Inquiry.

India, Siam, Indian Archipelago, China, &c.

Catechu.—Observe the processes by which the various kinds of catechu, cutch, *Terra japonica*, and gambir are obtained; and if from trees, whether from others besides *Acacia Catechu*, *Areca Catechu*, and *Uncaria Gambir*. We wish to identify the trees with the respective extracts.

Grass Oils.—The grasses used in India for affording the fragrant essential oils, known as lemon-grass oil or essence of verbena, ginger-grass oil, citronelle, &c., require investigation. What, for instance, is the source of the essential oil imported from Ceylon as oil of lemon-grass? It is considered quite distinct from citronelle, which is also a production of the island.

Benzoin or Gum Benjamin.—Obtain complete specimens of the tree which affords this drug in Siam.

Cardamoms.—The so-called wild or bastard cardamom of Siam is produced by *Amomum xanthioides*, Wallich, a plant of which *complete* and *well-preserved* specimens are requested, in order that it may be described and figured.

The seeds *per se* have been imported into England, while the empty capsules are found in the drug-shops of China. Are the latter exported from Siam to China?

What is the origin of the cardamom called by the Chinese *Yang-chun-sha*, the Hairy China Cardamom of pharmacologists? It is said to be produced in the province of Kwang-tung, and it may be a native of Cochin China.

Nothing is known of the origin of the Scitamineous fruit, to which the name large round China cardamom has been given, and which is known to the Chinese as *Tsaou-kow.* The same remark applies to the bitter-seeded cardamom, *Yĭh-che-tsze*, and ovoid China cardamom, *Taou-kwo* or *Quâ-leu.* It is probable that all of them are productions of the south of China, or of Cochin China.

Cassia Bark.—Specimens are much desired of the tree which affords this bark in Java, on the Malabar coast, in the south of China, and in Cochin China. Botanical specimens should, in all instances, include good samples of the bark, young and old, obtained from the same tree.

Cassia Buds.—These are the immature fruits of a *Cinnamomum*, native of Cochin China, specimens of which are requested. An inferior kind of cassia buds, known as *Lavunga-pu*, is found in Malabar. What is the species that affords it?

Aromatic barks of other *Laurineæ*, as *Culitlawang*, *Massoy*, *Sintoc*, are objects of commerce in the Indian Archipelago, and are but imperfectly known in Europe. The traveller should embrace the opportunity, when it occurs, of seeing the bark collected, and of obtaining authentic specimens of it, and of the tree yielding it.

Galangal Root.—Endeavour to procure the plant affording this drug, which is imported from the south of China.

Elemi.—This resin is abundantly produced in the forests of the Philippines, where it often assists in giving a cheerful blaze to the fire of the traveller. It is also exported from Manilla as a drug. The tree that affords it is probably a *Canarium;* but it is desirable to have complete specimens, in order to ascertain the species with exactness.

There are other resins, of whose origin little is known, which have been imported as *Elemi*.

The Botanical Student will find other subjects of inquiry alluded to in the Jury Reports of the Great Exhibition, London, 1851, and of Paris, 1855; also in the publications relating to the various exhibitions of produce held within the last few years at Madras, and in the provinces.

BIBLIOGRAPHY.

I. GENERAL.

1. SYSTEMATIC WORKS USEFUL TO BOTANICAL INQUIRERS.

Asiatic Researches. Calcutta, 23 vols. They contain many valuable papers by Sir W. Jones, Colebrooke, Roxburgh, and others.

Anderson, T.—Florula Adenensis: a systematic Account, with Descriptions, of the Flowering Plants hitherto found at Aden. By Thomas Anderson, Esq., M.D., F.L.S., H.M.'s Bengal Medical Service. With Six Plates. Published in the Jour. Lin. Soc., vol. v. 1860.

——— A Monograph of the Acanthaceæ.

Arnott, Dr G. A. Walker—Descriptions of Some New or Rare Indian Plants. Ann. Nat. Hist., vol. iii. pp. 20, 85, 150.

——— Pugillus Plantarum Indiæ Orientalis, 4to. Vratislaviæ, 1836.

——— *Vide* Wight.

Bentham, George—Synopsis of Dalbergieæ, a tribe of Leguminosæ. 8vo. London, 1860.

——— Monograph of the Scrophulariaceæ, in De Candolle's Prodromus, vol x.

——— Monograph of the Labiatæ, in De Candolle's Prodromus, vol. xii.

——— Flora Hong Kongensis. 8vo. London, 1861.

Blume, C. L.—Bijdragen tot de Flora von Nederlandsch Indie. Batavia, 1825–26.

——— and Fischer, J. B.—Flora Javæ. Brussels, 1828–36.

——— Rumphia, 4 vols., fol. Lugd.-Bat., 1836–48.

Boissier, E.—Diagnosis Plantarum Orientalium. In Ann. des Sci. Nat. Paris.

Bontius, J.—Historia Naturalis et Medica Indiæ Orientalis.

Brongniart, Ad.—Sur la Famille des Rhamnees. Plates, 1826.

Burmann, N. L.—Flora Indica, cui accedit series Zoophytorum Indicorum, necnon Prodromus Floræ Capensis. Plates. 4to. Ludg.-Bat., 1768.

——— Index Horti Malabarici.

Cambassédes, J.—*Vide* Jacquemont.

——— Monograph of Sapindaceæ, in Mem. du Musee. Paris.

Clusius, C.—Exoticorum libri decem, quibus Plantarum, Aromatum, aliorumque Fructuum, historia describuntur; item Pet. Belonii Observationes, &c. Folio. Antv., 1605.

——— Rariorum Plantarum Historia, &c. Folio. Antv., 1601.

Colebrooke, H. T.—Memoirs in Asiatic Researches, and Transactions Linnean Society.

Commelinus, C.—Flora Malabarica. Ludg.-Bat., 1696.

——— Icones Plantarum, præsertim ex Indiis collectarum, &c. 4to, plates. Ludg.-Bat., 1716.

De Candolle, A.—Géographie Botanique raisonnée, ou Exposition des faits principaux et des lois concernant la distribution géographique des plantes, &c. 2 col. maps. 8vo. 1856.

——— Prodromus Systematis Naturalis Regni Vegetabilis, sive Enumeratio contracta ordinum, generum, specierumque plantarum huc usque cognitarum. 14 vols. 8vo. Paris, 1824–56.

——— *Vide* Walpers' Repertorium.

Dillwyn, L. W.—Review of the References to the Hortus Malabaricus of Rheede, royal 8vo. Swansea, 1839.

Drury—The Useful Plants of India, with Botanical Descriptions, Vernacular Synonyms, and Notices of their Economical Value in Commerce, Medicine, and the Arts. By Major Heber Drury, Madras Army. One volume, 8vo. Madras, 1858.

Endlicher, S.—Genera Plantarum sec. ordin. natur. dispos. 1 vol. 8vo and 4 Supplements. Vind., 1840–50.

——— Enchiridion Botanicum, 8vo. Leipz., 1841.

Forskal, P.—Flora Ægypta-Arabica ed. Niebuhr. Hauniæ, 1775.

Gaertner, J.—De Fructibus et Seminibus Plantarum. 3 Tom. (3° T. supplementum Carpologiæ, C. F. Gaertneri), c. 225 tabb. Lips. et Stuttg., 1788–1805.

Gray, Asa—Manual of the Botany of the Northern United States, arranged according to the Natural System, with Introduction, Outlines, Glossary, &c. One volume. Boston (Mass.), 1848.

——— Flora of the North American States.

——— Illustrations of the Genera of North American Plants.

GRIFFITH, W.—Posthumous Papers, published by J. M'Clelland, comprising—Notulæ Botanicæ, 4 vols. 8vo; Calcutta, 1848–54. Icones Plantarum Asiaticarum, 4 vols. 4to; Calcutta, 1847–54. Palms of British India, 139 plates, fol. Calcutta.

HAMILTON, F. Buchanan—A Commentary upon Rheede's Hortus Malabaricus, published in the Linnean Transactions.

HOOKER, Sir W. J.—Icones Plantarum, 10 vols. London, 1854.

——— J. D., and T. THOMSON—Flora Indica, vol. i. Lond., 8vo, 1855.

——— and T. THOMSON—Præcursores ad Floram Indicam. Cruciferæ. By J. D. Hooker, Esq., M.D., F.R.S. & L.S., and T. Thomson, Esq., M.D., F.R.S. & L.S. Jour. Proc. Lin. Soc., vol. v. 1861.

——— Botanical Mission to India, in the Kew Miscellany, 2d vol.

JACQUEMONT, V.—Fragm. de l'ouvr. intit. Voyage dans l'Inde. Cambessedes—Plantæ rar. quas in India Orient coll. V. J. Texte: Pag. 1–176. Planches 143–180. Paris, 1844.

LAMARCK, J. B. Monet de, Encyclopedie Methodique. Paris, 1793.

LINDLEY, JOHN—The Vegetable Kingdom, 1 vol. 8vo. 5th Edition. London.

LOUDON, J. C.—Cyclopædia of Plants, 1 vol. 8vo.

LOUREIRO, Jo. DE—Flora Cochin-Chinensis. 1 vol. 1790.

MARTIUS, C. F. P. DE—Genera et Species Palmarum. 1823–50.

NEES AB ESENBECK, C. G.—Systema Laurinearum. Berol, 1836.

——— Monograph of Acanthaceæ, &c., &c., in De Candolle's Prodromus.

OLIVER, D.—The Natural Order Aurantiaceæ, with a Synopsis of the Indian Species. By Daniel Oliver, Esq., F.L.S., Professor of Botany in University College, London. Jour. Lin. Soc., vol. v. 1861.

PLUKENET, L.—Opera, viz., Phytographia, Almagestum, Amaltheum, &c., 4 vols. 4to. London, 1691–1720.

PRITZEL—Iconum Botanicarum Index. An Alphabetical Register of upwards of 86,000 representations of Phanerogamic Plants and Ferns, compiled from Botanical publications of the 18th and 19th centuries. 1200 pp. 4to. Berlin, 1855.

——— Thesaurus Literaturæ Botanicæ omnium gentium inde a rerum Botanicarum initiis ad nostra usque tempora, xv. millia opera recensens, 4to. Lips., 1851.

RETZ, A. J.—Observationes Botanicæ. Plates. 1 vol. Lips., 1791.

He published many of the plants discovered by Kœnig and Klein.

RHEEDE, A. H. VON—Hortus Indicus Malabaricus, continens Regni Malabarici apud Indos celeberrimi omnis Generis Plantas rariores adornatus per H. van Rheede et J. Caserum cum notis, &c. 12 vols. Amst. 1678–1703.

Roth, A. W.—Novæ Plantarum Species, præsertim Indiæ Orientalis. Halberst., 1821.

He published most of Heyne's plants.

Royle, J. F.—Illustrations of the Botany and other branches of Natural History of the Himalayan Mountains, and the Flora of Cashmere. 100 plates, 2 vols. royal 4to. 1839.

Roxburgh, Dr W.—Flora Indica, or Descriptions of Indian Plants, with Additions by Carey and Wallich, 2 vols. 8vo. Serampore, 1820–24.

——— Flora Indica, or Description of Indian Plants, by Dr Roxburgh, 3 vols 8vo. Serampore, 1832.

——— Plants of Coromandel, 3 vols. folio. London, 1795–1816.

——— Hortus Bengalensis, a Catalogue of Plants in the Calcutta Botanical Garden.

Ruiz, H. et J. Pavon—Flora Peruviana et Chilensis sive Novorum Generum Plantarum Peruvianarum et Chiliensium Descriptiones et Icones, 3 vols. Madrid, 1794–1802.

——— Prodromus Floræ Peruvianæ et Chilensis. Madrid, 1794.

*** The above rare work is illustrated with 362 engravings, the 3 vols. containing 325, and the Prodromus 37.

Steudel, G. G.—Synopsis Plantarum Glumacearum, 2 vols. imp. 8vo. Stuttg. 1856.

——— Nomenclator Botanicus, seu Synonymia Plantarum Universalis, 2 vols. royal 8vo. Stuttg. 1824–41.

Wallich, N.—Plantæ Asiaticæ Rariores; or, Descriptions and Figures of a Select Number of unpublished East Indian Plants, 3 vols. imperial folio, containing 300 beautifully coloured plates. 1829.

Wallich's Catalogue. A Numerical List of Dried Specimens of Plants in the East India Company's Museum, collected under the superintendence of Dr Nathaniel Wallich, of the Company's Botanic Garden at Calcutta. One folio volume. London, 1828.

——— Description of some Rare Indian Plants. 14 Plates, 4to.

Walpers, Dr G. W.—Repertorium Botanices Systematicæ, 6 vols. 1842–48. This work forms a Supplement to De Candolle's Prodromus.

——— Annales Botanices Systematicæ, tom. i.–iv. 1848–57.

Willdenow, C. L.—Linnæi Species Plantarum. He describes many of Klein's and Rottler's plants.

Wight, R., and Arnott, G. A. Walker—Prodromus Floræ Peninsulæ Indiæ Orientalis, vol. 1, 8vo. London, 1834.

——— Illustrations of Indian Botany, 2 vols. 1838–53.

——— Icones Plantarum Indiæ Orientalis, 6 vols. 1838–53.

——— Contributions to Indian Botany. London, 1834.

2. ARBORICULTURE.

Abercrombie—Propagation and Botanical Arrangement of Plants and Trees, Useful and Ornamental, 2 vols., 12mo. 1784.

Arboretums, Formation of, Horticultural Magazine, Part V.

Aldrovandi, U.—Dendrologia Naturalis, scilicet Arborum Historiæ. Cuts. Francof., 1671.

Aubert du Petit Thouars, A.—Sur la Vegetation, Melanges Botaniques, et Memoires sur la Culture des Arbres Fruitiers. Plates. 3 vols. Paris, 1809–15.

Austen, Ralph—Treatise of Fruit Trees. Second Edition. Oxford, 1643.

Beaunier, S.—Le Guide des Propriétaires et des Jardiniers, pour le Choix et la Culture des Arbres. 1821. 8vo.

Bonard, Dr—Forets de la France. Par M. Bonard. 8vo, avec supplément. 1827.

Boutcher—Treatise on Forest Trees. 8vo. Plates. 1776.

Brown, James—The Forester: A Practical Treatise on the Formation of Plantations, the Planting, Rearing, and Management of Forest Trees. By James Brown, Wood Manager to the Earl of Seafield. Third Edition, with numerous Engravings. Royal 8vo. 1861.

Countryman's Recreation, or the Art of Planting, Graffing, and Gardening, in three Books: the first Book declaring divers ways of Planting and Graffing, &c.; the second Book treateth of the Hop Garden, and hath to name "A perfect Platforme of a Hoppe Garden, &c.;" the third Book is the Expert Gardener, &c. In 1 vol. small 4to. Curious woodcuts. Are to be sold at Michael Young his Shop, Coven-Garden. London, 1640.

Cook, M.—Manner of Raising, &c., Forest Trees. 12mo. Figures. Third Edition. Lond., 1724.

Cotton, C.—Planter's Manual, &c. 12mo. 1675.

Cree, Gavin—Outline of System of Pruning Forest Trees. 8vo.

Desfontaines—Histoire des Arbres et Arbisseaux, 2 vols. Paris, 1809.

DUBREUIL, A.—Cours Élémentaire, Théorique et Pratique, d'Arboriculture. Fourth édition. 850 figures. 12mo. Paris, 1857.

——— Sur les Arbres Fruitiers. 120 engravings. 12mo. 1854.

——— Instruction Élémentaire sur la Conduite des Arbres Fruitiers. Greffe,—taille,—restauration des arbres mal taillés ou épuisés par la vieillesse,—culture,—récolte et conservation des fruits; deuxième édition. Paris, 1857. 1 vol. grand in-18, avec 120 figures.

DUHAMEL—Traité des Arbres et Arbustes, 4 vols. fol., containing 260 plates by Redouté, beautifully coloured. 1800–9.

——— Traité des Arbres et Arbustes qui se cultivent en France en pleine terres, 4to, 2 vols., numerous plates and cuts. Paris, 1755.

EVELYN, J.—Silva, or a Discourse of Forest Trees, and the Propagation of Timber, with an Historical Account of Standing Groves. Numerous plates, 4to. 1776. Best edition by Hunter, 2 vols. 4to, 1812.

Gardener's Chronicle, a Newspaper of Rural Economy, &c., edited by Professor Lindley, from its commencement, in 20 vols. 1841–61.

GORRIE, A.—On the Pruning of Forest Trees—Prize Essay of Highland and Agricultural Society: Transactions, vol. xii. p. 141.

HOTTON—Manuel de l'Elagueur, ou De la conduite des Arbres Forestiers. Par M. Hotton. Paris, 1829, in-12.

JAFFREY, A.—Hints to Amateur Gardeners in Southern India. Madras, Pharaoh, 1858.

JAMESON, W.—Report on the Government Garden at Saharunpore. 1855.

KASTHOFER—Guide dans les forêts, ouvrage destiné à l'instruction des propriétaires de bois. Par M. Kasthofer; trad. par F.-L. Monney. 1830, 2 vols. in-8, fig.

Library of Entertaining Knowledge—Timber Trees; Fruits; with wood engravings. 1830.

LOUDON, J. C.—Encyclopædia of Trees and Shrubs. 1842.

——— Arboretum et Fruticetum Britannicum, or the Trees and Shrubs of Britain, Native and Foreign, illustrated with nearly 3000 plates of Trees and Shrubs, 8 vols. 8vo. 1844.

LYONNET—Observations sur les Semis et les Plantations de quelques Arbres utiles. Par M. Lyonnet. Paris, 1515. In-8.

M'IVOR, W. G.—Reports of the Government Botanical and Horticultural Garden, Utacamand. 1853–60.

MICHAUX, F. A.—North American Sylva, a Description of the Forest Trees of the United States, Canada, and Nova Scotia. Translated into English by A. L. Hillhouse, 3 vols. 8vo. Paris, 1819.

MICHAUX—Histoire des Chenês de l'Amerique Septentrionale, fol., 36 pl. Paris 1801.

——— Mémoire sur le Zelkoua (*Planera crenata*), Arbre Forestier. Par A. Michaux. 1831, in-8.

NOYER—Forêts Vierges de la Guyane Française. Par M. Noyer. 1827, in-8.

NUTTALL—The North American Sylva. Philadelphia, 1842.

OURCHES, C. D'—Aperçu Général des Forêts. Par C. d'Ourches. 1805, 2 vols. in-8, avec 39 pl.

PHILIP, R.—General Management of Plantations. By Mr Robert Philip, forester, Brechin. Prize Essay Highland Society of Scotland.

PHILLIPS—Sylva Florifera; the Shrubbery Historically and Botanically treated, with Observations on the Formation of Ornamental Plantations and Picturesque Scenery, 2 vols. 8vo. 1823.

Plantations, Des, de leur Nécessité en France, de leur Utilité dans les Départemens du Midi, pour l'Assainissement de l'Air. Par Datty. Arles, 1805. 1 v. in-8.

Planting for Timber ; in part 25 of the Horticultural Magazine.

PLINGUET—Traité sur les Réformations et les Aménagemens des Forêts. Par Plinguet. Orleans, 1789, in-8.

PONTEY—Treatise on the Theory and Practice of Planting Forest Trees. 8vo. 1814.

Pruning Forest Trees. Part 1 of the Horticultural Magazine.

RATZEBURG, J. T. C.—Forst-naturwiss, Reisen in Deutschl. Berlin, 1842. 4 tom. 8vo.

SELBY, J. P.—History of British Forest Trees indigenous and introduced. 1842.

SMITH, ARCHIBALD, M.D.—On the supposed Influence of the Moon on Vegetation in Peru.

ST HILAIRE, JAUME—Traité des Arbres Forestiers, ou Histoire et Description des Arbres dont la tige a de 30 à 120 pieds d'élévation. Par M. Jaume-Saint-Hilaire. 1824. In-4. 90 pl. col.

ST MARTIN—Traité de la Culture du Chêne. Par Juge-de-Sainte-Martin. 1788. In-8, fig.

STRUTT, J. G.—Sylva Britannica, or Portraits of Forest Trees distintinguished for their Antiquity, Magnitude, or Beauty. 40 plates, imp. 8vo. 1830.

TAYLOR—Arbores Mirabiles, or a Description of the most remarkable Trees, Plants, and Shrubs, in all parts of the World. 12mo. 1812.

VARENNES FENILLE—Mémoire sur l'Administration Forestiére, sur les qualités individuelles des bois indigènes. Par Varennes Fenille, 2e edit. Paris, 1807. 2 vols. in-8.

WATSON, P. W.—Dendrologia Britannica, 172 coloured plates. 2 vols. royal 8vo. 1825.

3. ECONOMIC.

BAMBOO.

On the Economical Uses of the Bamboo. By Alexander Hunter, M.D., F.R.C.S.E., Madras School of Industrial Arts. Trans. Bot. Soc. Ed., vol. vi. p. 221.

On the occurrence of Palms and Bamboos, with Pines and other forms considered Northern, at considerable elevations in the Himalaya. By Major Madden, H.E.I.C.S., F.R.S.E. Trans. Bot. Soc. Ed., vol. v. p. 185.

Remarks on the Growth of *Bambusa arundinacea* in the large Conservatory, Chatsworth. By Mr Robert Scott. Trans. Bot. Soc. Ed., vol. iv. p. 25.

On the Growth of the Bamboo Cane in the New Palm-House at the Royal Botanic Garden. Communicated by Mr M'Nab. Trans. Bot. Soc. Ed., vol. vi. p. 220.

BÈL TREE (*Ægle Marmelos*)—its valuable properties. By Lieut. J. F. Pogson. A. H. Soc. Jour., vol. x. p. 157.

On the Indian Bèl (*Ægle Marmelos*). By J. Pereira. Pharm. Jour., vol. x. p. 165.

CASSIA—Wight, R.—On *Cassia obtusa*. Mad. Jour. of Science, 1835.

CÆSALPINIA CORIARIA.

Queries and Replies regarding the profitable culture of the American Sumach (*Cæsalpinia coriaria*) in India. Journal A. H. Soc., vol. v. p. 135.

Value of, for Dyeing and Tanning. Several papers in Jour. Agri. Hort. Soc. Beng., vol. iv.

Or Dividivi, Properties of. Pharm. Jour., vol. v. p. 443.

CINCHONA.

Correspondence regarding the introduction of the Quiniferous Cinchonas of South America into India. A. H. Soc. Jour., x. p. 138.

Gonzalez, de, Aguero F. P.—Descripcion Historial de la Provincia y Archipielago dé Chilóe. 1791.

On the Tree Producing Red Cinchona Bark. By John Eliot Howard. 8vo. 1860.

CINCHONA.

Lambert, A. B.—Description of the Genus Cinchona. 13 plates. 1797.

Mutis, Arcano de la Quina. Madrid, 1828.

Ruiz, H.—Quinologia o' Tratado del Arbol de la Quina o' Cascarilla, Madrid, 1792; with the Supplement, 1801; and other Tracts on the same subject, by Ruiz, with plates. 1 vol. Madrid, 1792–1821.

Histoire Naturelle des Quinquinas, par H. A. Weddell, reviewed in Kew Misc., vol. ii. p. 95.

CINNAMON.

Leschenault de la Tour—Notice sur le cannellier de l'isle de Ceylon, St Denis. 4to. 1821.

Marshall, Henry, F.R.S.E.—Observations on Cinnamon. Edin. N. Phil. Jour., vol. xxviii. p. 27.

Nees ab Esenbeck de Cinnamomo Disputatio. 12 plates, some coloured. 1823–4.

Wight, Dr Robert—On the *Laurus Cassia* of Linnæus, and the Plants producing the Cassia Bark of commerce. Ann. Nat. Hist., vol. iv. p. 179.

CLOVE.—Buce on the manner of Cultivating the Clove Tree in the island of Dominica. London, 1797.

COCO-NUT.—The Palm and its uses. By H. Cleghorn, M.D. Ed. N. Phil. Jour., vol. xiv. 1861.

COFFEE.

Douglas's History of the Coffee Tree, with Supplement. 1727.

Gardner, George—Report on the Brown Scale, or Coccus, of the Coffee-plant. Kew Misc., vol. ii. p. 353.

Guerin-Menneville et Perottet, memoire sur un insecte et un champignon qui ravagent les cafiers aux Antilles. Paris, 1842. 8vo.

DRY ROT.

Balfour, Prof. J. H.—On the Structure and Growth of Timber and Dry Rot in Wood. Edinburgh, 1857.

Remarks on Boucherie's Method of Preserving Timber. By Professor Balfour. Trans. Bot. Soc. Edinburgh, vol. v. p. 170.

Dickson, Robert, M.D.—Dry Rot, and means of preventing it. London, 1837.

Faraday, Professor—On the Prevention of Dry Rot in Timber. London, 1836.

FENCES AND HEDGES.

On the Hedge Plants of India, and the conditions which adapt them for special Purposes and particular Localities. By Hugh Cleghorn, M.D. Trans. Bot. Soc. Ed., vol. iv. p. 83.

Culture of Plants for Fences, in part 48 of the Horticultural Magazine.

GAMBOGE—A new variety of Gamboge from Mysore. By R. Christison, M.D., in Pharm. Jour., 1846.

GUTTA TREE.

Memorandum upon the South Indian Gutta Tree (*Bassia elliptica*). H. Cleghorn, M.D. Madras, 1858.

Culture of, in Hort. Mag., part 38.

Gutta Percha. By T. Oxley, Esq., A.B., Senior Surgeon of the Settlement of Prince of Wales' Island, Singapore and Malacca. Discovery of the Gutta by Europeans, 22—Botanical description, 22, 23—Range, habitat, mode of procuring, 24—Properties, uses, application to the practice of surgery, 26—Great superiority to bandages and splints in cases of fracture, &c., 26–28—Capsules for vaccine virus, 28, 29—Patents in England for cleaning the gutta and removing its acidity; means of procuring it pure where it is produced, 29. Jour. Ind. Archip. vol. i. pp. 22–29.

Gutta Percha. Memorandum by Dr d'Almeida. Jour. Ind. Archip. vol. i. p. 22–78.

Gutta Percha of Surinam. Jour. Bot. Soc., vol. vi. p. 58.

Gutta Percha—Griffith, Mr, on. Jour. A. H. Soc., vol. iii. p. 146.

INSECTS.

On the Effects Produced by some Insects upon Plants. By James Hardy. Trans. Bot. Soc. Ed., vol. iv. p. 75.

Loudon and Westwood's Treatise on Insects Injurious to Gardens, Forests, and Farms, translated from the German of Köllar, illustrated by 60 woodcuts, foolscap 8vo. 1840.

Ratzeburg, J. T. Ch., Die Forst-insekten. Berlin. 3 vols. 4to. 1837.

Vide Coffee, Pines.

KINO.

Of *Butea frondosa*. J. F. Royle. Pharm. Jour., vol. v. p. 500.

Tanning Properties of. Pharm. Jour., vol. viii. p. 24.

East Indian. J. F. Royle. Pharm. Jour., vol. v. p. 495.

Origin of. Pharm. Jour., vol. iv. p. 510.

KINO.

Malabar Tree yielding. Pharm. Jour., vol. v. p. 498.

New Source of. By R. Christison. Pharm. Jour., vol. xii. p. 377.

MAHOGANY TREE.

The Culture of. By T. Chaloner. Liverpool, 1850.

Wood, produce of Botanic Garden, Calcutta. Jour. Ag. Hort. Soc., vol. v. p. 13.

Directions for Culture of. Jour. Ag. Hort. Soc., vol. v. p 15.

MANGO TREE.

Culture of, in Mysore. By —— Ingledew, Esq. A. H. S. Jour., vol. i. p. 263.

Buist, Dr—On Mango-grafting on the branch principle. Trans. A. H. Soc. Bomb., vol. i. pp. 44–49.

Account of the successful Propagation by Seed of a superior variety. Communicated by P. Homfray, Esq. Jour. A. H. S., vol. iv.

Introduction of, from Northern India into Algeria. Trans. A. H. S., vol. vii. p. 186.

Varieties of, cultivated in Southern India. By H. Cleghorn, M.D. Trans. Bot. Soc. Ed., vol. vii. 1861.

MORA TREE.

Schomburgk, R. H., Description of the Mora Tree (*Mora excelsa*, Benth.) Linn. Trans., vol. xviii. p. 207.

MULBERRY.

Perottet, sur le culture du Mûrier. Paris, 1840.

Seringe (N. C.), Description, culture et taille des mûriers, leurs espèces et leurs variétés. Paris, 1855, 1 vol. grand, in-8, avec figures dans le texte, accompagné d'un atlas in-4 de 27 planches.

Tinelli—Hints on the Cultivation of the Mulberry. New York 1837. 8vo.

NUTMEG.

Account of the Cultivation of, Jour. Ag. Hort. Soc., vol. vi. p. 176.

Plantations in Banda. By T. Oxley, A.B., Surgeon. Jour. Ind. Archip. N.S., vol. i. p. 127.

Trees, on Disease of the, in Singapore. By Andrew T. Jaffrey. Tr. Bot. Soc. Ed., vol. vi. p. 368.

OILS—Notes on the Vegetable Oils of the Madras Presidency. By Lieutenant Hawkes. Madras Jour. N.S., vol. iii. p. 150.

OLIVE.

Collection de mémoires sur les oliviers. Paris, 1822, in-8.

OLIVE.

Amoreux—Traité de l'olivier, histoire et culture de cet arbre, extraction de l'huile, etc.; 2e edit., in-8. Paris.

De Candolle—Notice sur le culture de l'olivier. Bibl. Univ. de Geneva, vol. x. 1825.

Notice of the Produce of the Olive Crop in the Island of Corfu during the past Season, in a Letter from Mr Mackenzie, Corfu, to Dr George Lawson, dated January 11, 1858. Trans. Bot. Soc. Ed., vol. vi.

Culture of the, in part 50 of the Horticultural Magazine.

PINES.

On the Economical Uses of the Roots of Coniferous Trees. By Mr M'Nab. Tr. Bot. Soc. Ed., vol. vi. p. 229.

Notes upon Californian Trees. By Andrew Murray, F.R.S.E. Trans. Bot. Soc. Ed., vol. vi. p. 210.

Carriere, E. A.—Traité Général des Coniferes. 1855.

Measurement of certain Coniferous Trees, taken at St Fort, Fife. By George Patton, Esq., Advocate. Communicated by Mr M'Nab. Trans. Bot. Soc. Ed., vol. vi. p. 221.

On the Injurious Effects of *Uroceras gigas* on Fir Trees. By Alexander Thomson, Banchory. Trans. Bot. Sec. Ed., vol. v. p. 159.

Account of the Insect which infests the seeds of *Picea nobilis*. By Andrew Murray, F.R.S.E. Trans. Bot. Soc. Ed., vol. v. p. 187.

Cook, Captain S. E.—On *Pinus* and *Abies*, with remarks on a new species. Ann. Nat. Hist., vol. iii. p. 296.

Traité pratique de la culture des pins à grandes dimensions, des cèdres du Liban, des mélèzes et des sapins; par L. G. Delamarre, 3e édit., avec des notes de MM. Michaux et Vilmorin, 1831, in-8.

Historique de la création d'une richesse millionnaire par la culture des pins; par L. G. Delamarre. 1827, in-8. Fig. col.

Don, Professor David—Descriptions of two new Genera of the natural family of plants called *Coniferæ*. Linn. Trans., vol. xviii. p. 163.

Gordon and Glendinning, the Pinetum; being a Synopsis of all the Coniferous Plants at present known, with descriptions, history and synonymes, comprising nearly one hundred new kinds. 8vo. 1858.

Lambert, A. B.—Description of the Genus Pinus and the

PINES.

Family of Coniferæ. 72 coloured plates. 2 vols. royal 8vo. 1832.

Pinetum Woburnense, or a Catalogue of Coniferous Plants at Woburn Abbey. 67 coloured plates, royal 8vo. 1839.

Richard, L. C.—Commentatio Botanica de Coniferis et Cycadeis. 29 plates. Stutgardiæ, 1826.

Culture of the Araucaria, in part 36 of the Horticultural Magazine.

Culture of the Cedar, in part 34 of the Horticultural Magazine.

Culture of the *Cedrus deodara*, in part 21 of the Horticultural Magazine.

PLANTATIONS.—Des, de leur nécéssite en France; par Datty, 1 vol. in-8.

ROBINIA.

Lettre à M. François de Neufchâteau, sur le robinier; par Médicus, in-12.

Lettre sur le robinier ou faux-acacia; par M. François de Neufchâteau, 1803, in-12., fig.

SAND-BINDING PLANTS—Note on the Sand-binding Plants of the Madras Beach. By Hugh Cleghorn, M.D. (With a Plate, *Spinifex squarrosus.*) Jour. Agr. Hort. Soc., vol. ix. p. 174.

SEA-SIDE PLANTING—In part 16 of the Horticultural Magazine.

SISSOO—(*Dalbergia Sissoo*) successful cultivation of the Sissoo Tree in the Mysore Territory. Journal A. H. Soc., vol. v. p. 123.

Produce of Calcutta Garden. A. H. S. Jour., vol. v. p. 13.

TALLOW TREE—On the Uses of *Stillingia sebifera*, the Tallow Tree of China. By D. J. Macgowan, M.D. Trans. Bot. Soc. Ed., iv. p. 145.

TEA.

Report on the cultivation of the Tea Plant of Upper Assam. By Wm. Griffith. Calcutta 1838.

Report on Tea Cultivation in the North-west Provinces and in the Punjab. By W. Jameson. Calcutta, 1857.

In Java, Cultivation and Manufacture of. Jour. Ag. Hort. Soc., vols. v. vi. and vii.

Plant, Discovery of in Sylhet. Jour. Ag. Hort. Soc., vol. ix. pp. 207, 342.

On the Progress of Tea Cultivation at Darjiling. Communi-

TEA.

cated by Dr A. Campbell, Superintendent. Jour. A. H. Soc., vol. x. p. 229.

On the Progress of Tea Cultivation in Cachar. By Lieut. R. Stewart, Officiating-Superintendent. Jour. A. H. Soc., vol. x. p. 193.

TEAK PLANTATIONS OF BENGAL.

H. Falconer's Report in Records of Bengal Government, No. xxv. of 1857.

Timber Traffic of Tenasserim Provinces. Calc. Rev., Sept. 1853.

Forests in Tenasserim Provinces. Capt. Latter, Maulmain, 1848.

———— Dr Falconer's Report. Calcutta, 1851.

——— of Arracan, A. H. Soc. Jour., vol. iii. p. 218.

——— in Sandoway District, A. H. Soc. Jour., vol. iv. p. 46–50.

——— of Bombay Presidency. Dr Gibson's Handbook, 1857.

——— of Madras Presidency. Dr Cleghorn's Reports, 1856–60.

——— Directions for Cultivating the Teak Tree, (Roxburgh) A. H. S. Trans., vol. ii. p. 50.

Dr Gibson on Teak Plantations in the Southern Conkan—Correspondence on Teak Forests. Trans. A. H. Soc. Bomb., vol. i. p. 49–94.

Falconer and Gibson on the Teak Forests of India. Kew Misc., p. 256. 1853.

TIMBER.

On a mode of Protecting Timber from Fire. By F. A. Abel, Esq. Trans. Bot Soc. Ed., vol. vi. p. 153.

Hill on the construction of Timber, 44 plates. 1774.

On the Timber of Victoria. George Holmes, Esq.

Holtzapffel, Charles.—Descriptive Catalogue of Woods used in Britain, with notes by Dr Royle. London 1852.

On Indian Woods that have been tried for Engraving. By Alexander Hunter, M.D., Madras. Trans. Bot. Soc., Ed., vol. vi. p. 358.

Munro, Capt.—Timber Trees of Bengal. Jour. As. Soc. Beng.

Representations of Inland and Foreign Wood, as well Trees as Shrubs, containing plates of 493 specimens. By J. C. Sepp. 4to. Amsterdam 1778.

Timber and Tonnage. By Robert Murray, Engineer-Surveyor to the Board of Trade. Enc. Brit. 1860.

VEGETATION.
Vegetation of Brazil, in part 39 of the Horticultural Magazine.
Vegetation of New Holland, in part 53 of the Horticultural Magazine.
Vegetation of California, in part 50 of the Horticultural Magazine.
Vegetation of the Antarctic Regions, in part 15 of the Horticultural Magazine.

WASTE LAND.
Waste Land, Planting and Management of, see parts 4 and 5 of the Horticultural Magazine.

WOOD, OIL, a substitute for Copaiba. D. Hanbury, Pharm. Jour., vol. xv. p. 321.

—— RED SANDERS, Colouring Matter of. P. Bolley, Pha. Jour., vol. vii: p. 288.

II. GEOGRAPHICAL AND LOCAL.

1. INDIA GENERALLY.

BALFOUR, E. G.—Cyclopedia of India, Commercial, Industrial, and Scientific. Madras, 1857.

BARTOLOMEO'S, FRA. P. DA SAN—Voyage to the East Indies, with an Account of the Manners, Customs, &c., of the natives. 8vo, half calf. 1800.

FAULKNER'S, ALEX.—Dictionary of Commercial Terms in India. Bombay, 1850.

HAMILTON'S Geographical, Statistical, and Historical Description of Hindostan and adjoining countries. 2 vols. 4to. 1820.

MILBURN'S Oriental Commerce. 2 vols. London, 1813.

ROYLE'S, J. F.—Essay on the Productive Resources of India. Royal 8vo, cloth. 1840.

SONNERAT—Voyages aux Indes Orientales et a la Chine, 4 vols. in 2, with a volume of 140 fine plates in 4to. Together 3 vols. Paris, 1782.

TAVERNIER'S, J. B.—Travels in Turkey, Persia, and the East Indies, with a Description of the Countries adjacent to the Caspian and Euxine Seas. Illustrated. Folio. 1678.

VALENTIA, LORD—Travels in Hindostan. 1803.

VALENTYN—Onden Nieuw Oost Indien, &c. A Collection of Voyages to the East Indies, Japan, &c. 5 vols. fol., with many plates of Nat. Hist. Dordrecht en Amst., 1724–26.

2. MADRAS.

AINSLIE, J. W.—Materia Medica of Hindostan, 1st edition, 4to. Madras, 1813.

ANDERSON, DR JAMES—On the introduction of the Bastard Cedar (*Guazuma tomentosa*). Corresp. 12mo. 1793–94, and 4to, 1795.

——— On the Cultivation of the Mulberry. Corresp., 1790–96. 12mo.

——— On the Introduction of Various Trees. Corresp. 1796–1800. 12mo. Madras, 1800.

——— On the Cultivation of Cotton; on Plants producing Fibres useful for Cordage, &c. *Ibid.*

——— On the Cultivation of the Nopal, &c. Corresp. Madras, 1808.

——— Thirteen Letters to Sir Joseph Banks on the Cochineal Insect, with figures of various species of Opuntia. 4to. Madras, 1787.

BEDDOME, R. H.—On the Vegetable Products of the Pulney Hills. Mad. Jour., vol. xix. (iii. N.S.) p. 85.

CLEGHORN, H.—Notice on Sand-binding Plants of the Madras Beach. Mad. Jour., vol. xviii. (ii. N.S.) p. 85.

——— Hortus Madraspatensis—Catalogue of Plants indigenous and naturalised in the Agri-Horticultural Society's Garden. Madras. 1853.

COTTON, Col. F. C.—On the Teak Forests of the Anamalai Hills. Mad. Jour., vol. xviii. p. 80.

ELLIOT, WALTER—Flora Andhrica, a Botanical List of the Vernacular Names of Plants in the Telugu districts. Madras, 1859.

HAWKES, H. P.—The Oils of South India. Mad. Jour., vol. xix. p. 1.

HEYNE, DR B.—Tracts on South India.

INDIGO, manufacture of. Mad. Jour., vol. viii. p. 197.

TREES.—On the Influence of Trees on Climate. Mad. Jour., vol. xv. p. 400.

WIGHT, ROBERT—On the Nuth Grass of the Ceded Districts. Mad. Jour., vol. ii. p. 38.

——— On Mudar and the Asclepiadæ. Mad. Jour., vol. ii. p. 70.

——— On the Courtallum Flora. Mad. Jour., vol. ii. p. 380; vol. iii. p. 84.

WIGHT, ROBERT—Suggestions for a New System of Grafting. Mad. Jour., vol. iii. p. 26.

——— On the Land Winds of Coromandel. Mad. Jour., vol. iii. p. 32.

——— On the Gamboge Tree. Mad. Jour., vol. iv. p. 300; vol. ix. p. 121.

——— Contributions to Indian Botany. Mad. Jour., vol. v. pp. 1, 15, 300.

——— On the Pulney Mountains. Mad. Jour., vol. v. p. 280.

——— On *Cassia Burmanni* v. *obtusa*. Mad. Jour., vol. vi. p. 7.

——— On the Cultivation of Cotton. Mad. Jour., vol. vi. p. 79.

——— On a New Genus of Asclepiadæ. Mad. Jour., vol. vii. p. 142.

——— On the Fruit of Cucurbitaceæ. Mad. Jour., vol. xii. p. 43.

——— On Separation of the Pomegranate from Myrtaceæ. Mad. Jour., vol. xii. p. 254.

NOTE.—The remaining portion of the Bibliography having been too late for the printer, will appear in the next Forest Report.—H. C.

GLOSSARY.

*For the use of readers unacquainted with Indian words, we annex an explanation of a few vernacular terms, which occur in the following pages:—*P. *indicates Persian;* H. *Hindustání;* A. *Arabic;* T. *Tamil;* B. *Burmese; and* S. *Sanscrit.*

Amani, H., literally in hand.

Bag, P. (prop. *bagh*), a garden.

Bala-ghat. Above ghat.

Bazar, an exchange or market-place.

Bund, P (*band*), a dam or dyke.

Bungalow, H. (prop. *banglá*), a thatched house; any house.

Butcha, P. (*bachchah*), the young of any animal; a child.

Chena. A term used in Ceylon for the rude system of culture called *Kumari*, and *Tungya* in Pegu.

Cherry, T. (prop. *cheri*), a termination meaning village, but often applied to towns, as Pondicherry.

Choultry, T. (*chawadi*), a post-house, resting-hall for travellers. Used only in the Madras Presidency.

Coolie, T. (prop. *kuli*), a porter, carrier, or labourer.

Cote, H. (*kota*), a fort or castle.

Cutcherry, H. (prop. *Kachari*), a court of justice; a civilian's office.

Dak or *dauk*, H. (prop. *dâk*), a post or post-office; also a relay of horses or bearers.

Darkhast, H., an application for so many trees at a fixed rate.

Darogah, P. (*daroghah*), a superintendent, chiefly applied to the head native officer of a police station or custom-house.

Devasthanam, H., a temple.

Dhobee, H. (*dhobi*), a washerman.

Droog, S. (*durga*), a hill fort, as Chittledroog.

Enam, A. (prop. *in'am*), a gift; land granted in free tenure. The holder is *inamdar*.

Fasli, H., a year; a term used in the Revenue Department.

Ghaut, H. (*ghat*), a pass between mountains, the mountains themselves, especially the Eastern and Western ranges, which separate the table land from the narrow strips of low coast that intervene between them and the sea.

Gherry, S. (*giri*), a mountain, as the Neilgherries, prop. *Nilgiris;* also a fort, prop. *gadhi*, as Rutnagherry, prop. *Ratnagadhi.*

Goungs and *Goungwais*, B., are native revenue officers in charge of districts.

Gumasta, A writer who keeps the accounts of the Forest Depôts.

Hackery, S. (*chakra*), a rudely made cart. This word is propably an Anglo-Indian corruption of *chakra*, "a wheel."

Jemadar, A. P., a native officer, corresponding to our ensign or lieutenant.

Jhageerdar, P. (prop. *jágirdár*), the holder of land granted for services.

Kárkún, a native officer in charge of a range of forest. Used in the Bombay Presidency.

Koss, S. (*kos*), a measure of length which varies in different provinces, generally about two miles.

Kotwal, P., the chief officer of police in a city or town.

Kurumbar. A wild forest tribe.

Luzar, B., a log of short length.

Maidan, P. (*maidan*), a plain.

Moonshee, A. (*munshi*), literally, a writer.

Nallah or *Nullah*, H. (prop. *nala*), a brook; a watercourse; the channel of a torrent.

Nathat, B., or seasoned timber.

Nuddee, S. (prop. *nadi*), a river.

Nugger, S. (*Nagar*), a city, as Ahmednugger, prop. Ahmadnaga, city of Ahmad.

Patel, H., the headman of a village, who, in

Canara, superintends the cutting of marked trees.
Patimar. A sort of native vessel on the Malabar Coast.
Payen-ghat. District below ghat.
Peon, P., a messenger; a foot attendant.
Pore or *Poor*, S. (a town; used chiefly in compos., as Berhampur.
Puttun, S. (prop. *pattanam*), a town, chiefly in compos., as Shrí Ranga Pattanam; Seringapatam, and Madras-pattanam.
Ryot (raiyat), a peasant.
Rackanasta. A term applied to stunted Teak, in Canara.
Taluk, H., a district under a Tasildar.
Tirupad, a term applied to the native princes of Malabar, as the Tirupad of Nelambur.
Tungya, B., a clearing in the forest for growing millet, &c., corresponding with the *Kumari* of Canara.
Tuppal, H. (prop. *tappal*), a packet of letters; the post.
Vaida, H. a permit or licence to cut wood.
Zayat, B, a temple, a wooden structure, often containing fine teak timber.
Zumeendar, P. (prop. *zamindar*), landholder; landed proprietor.

ERRATA

Page 44, line 26, for *adapted* read *adopted*.
— 82, foot-note, for *vide ante*, p. 40, read *vide ante*, p. 42.
— 179, foot-note, for *Spagnum*, read *Sphagnum*.
— 348, line 23, for *aurata*, read *auriculata*.
— 353, line 11, for *Alonosa*, *Alonsoa*.

NOTE.—Since the first part of this book was printed, the accounts have undergone examination by the Civil Auditor, and the actual profit of 1859–60 has been ascertained to be Rs. 393,591, instead of Rs. 398,349, as given at page 73.—H. C.

INDEX.

THE END.